Improvisation in Drama, Theatre and Performance: History, Practice, Theory

D1496592

Improvisation in Drama, Theatre and Performance: History, Practice, Theory

Third Edition

Anthony Frost
and
Ralph Yarrow

 palgrave

First edition published 1990

Second edition published 2007

Third edition published 2016 by
PALGRAVE

Palgrave in the UK is an imprint of Macmillan Publishers Limited, registered in England, company number 785998, of 4 Crinan Street, London N1 9XW.

Palgrave Macmillan in the US is a division of St Martin's Press LLC, 175 Fifth Avenue, New York, NY 10010.

Houndmills, Basingstoke, Hampshire RG21 6XS and

175 Fifth Avenue, New York, N.Y. 10010

Companies and representatives throughout the world

Palgrave is a global imprint of the Palgrave Macmillan division of St. Martin's Press, LLC and of Palgrave Macmillan Ltd.

Palgrave® and Macmillan® are registered trademarks in the United States, the United Kingdom, Europe and other countries.

ISBN: 978–1–137–34811–1 hardback

ISBN: 978–1–137–34810–4 paperback

This book is printed on paper suitable for recycling and made from fully managed and sustained forest sources. Logging, pulping and manufacturing processes are expected to conform to the environmental regulations of the country of origin.

A catalogue record for this book is available from the British Library.

A catalog record for this book is available from the Library of Congress.

Library of Congress Cataloging-in-Publication Data
Frost, Anthony.
  [Improvisation in drama]
  Improvisation in drama, theatre and performance : history, practice, theory / Anthony Frost, Ralph Yarrow. — Third edition.
    pages cm
  Includes bibliographical references and index.
  ISBN 978–1–137–34810–4 (paperback) — ISBN 978–1–137–34811–1 (hardback)
  1. Improvisation (Acting)   I. Yarrow, Ralph.   II. Title.
  PN2071.I5F76 2015
  792.02'8—dc23
                                                                        2015027806

Printed in China

To Roddy Maude-Roxby

For Kalila and Zorya Yarrow and
in memoriam Kathleen and William Frost and
for Cathy and Alex Frost

Denn, . . . der Mensch spielt nur, wo er in voller
Bedeutung des Wortes Mensch ist, und er ist nur da ganz Mensch,
wo er spielt.
[For, … man only plays when he is in the fullest sense of the
word a human being, and he is only fully a human being when
he plays.]
(Schiller, *Fifteenth Letter*, 1795: 106)

Contents

Acknowledgements

We owe a considerable debt of gratitude to performers we have talked to and worked with, especially Jacques Lecoq, Roddy Maude-Roxby (*Theatre Machine*), James MacDonald and Malcolm Tulip (*I Gelati*), Simon McBurney and Clive Mendus (*Complicité*), Rena Mirecka (*Teatr Laboratorium*), Shon Dale-Jones (*Hoipolloi*), John Martin (*Pan Intercultural Arts*) and Sanjoy Ganguly (*Jana Sanskriti*); to friends and colleagues who have read and commented on the book at different stages, in particular Julian Hilton, Frances Babbage, David Bradby, Franc Chamberlain and Todd Wronski. Thanks also to many generations of UEA drama students and to those from whom we have learned or continue to learn in other contexts: Clive Barker, Nicholas Brooke, Douglas Brown, Scott Brown, Max Flisher, Birgit Fritz, Amanda Frost, Tony Gash, Tony Hall, David Hirst, Jon Hyde, Val Taylor and Sophie Vaughan. Permission to quote is gratefully acknowledged from Frances Babbage (from her book *Augusto Boal*) and Lucy Smith (from emails).

Introduction and Preface
to the Third Edition

Improvisation is a particular mode of performance activity in which key characteristics of 'performance' can be precisely located. It issues as *performances* (the production of work which is made 'on the spot' or is explicitly open to amendment during performance) and as the culturing in the body of skills and attributes of *performativity* – training for making performance, development of individual and group resources, of the aptitude for renegotiating being and doing in the world.

Now in its third avatar, this book charts a history and a theory of improvisation in theatre work alongside a taxonomy of its practice. It identifies improvisation as a productive and performative mode of behaviour and is concerned to site it particularly within the spectrum of *theatre* practice, identifying how, where and when it operates as a mark of style in production and a mode of training for performers. Much of this territory has been retraversed in terms of performance theory, and a whole raft of publications have appeared, focusing on performance trainers and makers and on the contexts in which they work; many of these books contain explicit examples of exercises and games targeting specific performative purposes.

This edition still traces the origins of impro and its influence in the history of drama and performance-making, both as a social and political phenomenon and as a marker of the position it now occupies in performance training. It retains the historical underpinning (Part 1), which exhibits how improvisatory practices and attitudes have intervened in performance strategies and in the relationship between 'theatre' and society at many times and in many places.[1] We want to underline the function of improvisation as a training methodology (Parts 1 and 2) and to continue to ask, as we began to do in the second edition, if it has paradoxically begun to resemble an orthodoxy. We want to take the remit of the book and of the improvisatory processes it explores a little beyond the conventional proscenium set-up and to ask what's in it for audiences and how this is factored into ways in which performance is developing now. Examples of this work, which include the 'immersive' and the 'site-specific', are included in the more descriptive 'history' section (Part 1); issues arising from it are addressed in Part 3. In particular, we are concerned here to key into understandings of performance as a way of investigating human behavioural process: what we call the improvisatory has a central place in how we conceptualise and enact ourselves and our world.

When we say 'world', that suggests the dimension of how we interact with our environment and how far 'improvisation' is a way of accessing possibilities of extending that. Thus we will open up – again initially as a strand or thread of argument in Part 1 and subsequently in Part 3 – some exploration of the aesthetics of risk and some attempt to construct an ecology of improvisation. These are openings and not complete theses; we also need to find room to offer a glance at improvisation in some other areas the book did not previously mention (stand-up comedy; jazz; poetry; free movement practices); as well as to extend coverage of practice in, for instance, the improv scene in the US, some aspects of impro(v) in Playback Theatre, the territory of LARPing, role-or-game-play and the improvising audience.

Improvisation has always been good at escaping categories and crossing borders, and the moves signalled above confirm and underline that. In addition, its practitioners have been inspired by each other and have produced a rich mix and miscegenation of forms across the globe, which we try to reflect to some extent. So chapter and part divisions are frequently not watertight, historically, geographically and thematically; we do however try in the text and in the Endnotes to signal as many as possible of these cross-currents and provide an extensive Bibliography which may permit or encourage other journeys.

The change of title signals this widening of the brief from the original 'Improvisation in Drama', although we have always contended that theatre, drama and performance form a spectrum; but we are not entering fully into discussion of, for example, dance or Contact Improvisation, because that would be an entirely different book and we have neither the space nor the competence to do that. However, we do take a look at some typical forms of current physical and movement-based work and ask if the principles, taxonomies and processes which they operate can be seen to relate to those we identify as fundamental to the notion of improvisation as exploration of human resource through performance.

The second edition of this book included new material on Lee Strasberg, Michael Chekhov, Sanford Meisner, Eugenio Barba, Sears Eldredge's mask work, Augusto Boal, Improbable Theatre and others, plus extra material on Stanislavsky, Chicago Improv, Dario Fo and Jacques Lecoq; and a substantial section on improvisation beyond the sphere of 'western' theatre and performance. In this third edition we look again at some of this work, add more, rethink and reformulate some of the underlying questions in line

with the issues indicated above and attempt to reconfigure slightly the taxonomy of exercises in Part 2 as well as to add some more examples.

The book retains its original structure and asks the same questions:
What? Why? How? – which often include Where? and When? And, of
course, Who?

What are the kinds of practice which can be described as improvisation (categorisation)? Where and when do they occur (history and distribution)? Why are they significant and why do people want to do them (poetics)? How do they engage with the spectrum of performance production
and training, in particular for the theatre, and with the business of 'making
work' (theory and context)? What can you do and how should you do it
(practice)? Where will you find other detailed guides to this kind of work
(reference)?

We have adjusted the order of chapters and sections in Part 1 so that
the sequence is clear. Essentially, the trajectory of this book broadly follows
a line from the use of improvisation as a component in the rehearsal and
preparation of 'conventional' theatre towards becoming a form in its own
right (including 'improv' and its derivatives) and signals its emergence as
the nub of deconstructive and reconstructive modes of performance, for
individuals, groups and audiences. This schema repeats itself across different geographical and historical zones. Throughout, improvisation and
the improvisatory operate as drives to extend, unpick or relocate form and
relationship and signal an ecology of loss and restitution, of the reordering
of the transaction of who we are and how we engage with what we are not.
The move, which is paralleled by the successive editions the book has gone
through, is thus from improvisation in theatre to improvisation as the dynamic of theatre and performance process.

So we start with an account of improvisation at the basis of European
(mostly Russian, British and French) performer training and rehearsal practice, which leads on to a major application to the writing of plays in the
work of Mike Leigh. Then we move to the US in Chapter 2 and trace the
different strands of 'improv', including their origins and variant strains and
opening up key instances of audience involvement. Chapter 3 examines
how improvisation has taken increasing prominence in work to develop
new forms of performance and kinds of performer, essentially rooted in the
work of major figures in Europe in the 1960s and 1970s and their legacy.
Here, improvisation acquires considerably greater force and begins to function as a determining methodology in the elaboration of physically and
aesthetically eclectic and flexible modes.

We extend the story further in the fourth chapter by addressing the
role of improvisation in work moving 'beyond' the stage: from Grotowski's

'paratheatre' to contemporary moves to include and enhance audience involvement. This chapter discusses a wide spectrum of work which invites various degrees of participation – from the psychodramatic to the somatic – as well as examples of the improvisatory in other genres like poetry, jazz and stand-up. The fifth chapter pushes the geographical boundaries further by considering the place of improvisation in 'non-western' performance, including the Middle East, Asia and Africa.

Part 2 categorises the main stages of impro work as used in performance training in much the same ways as in the first two editions, from ice-breaking through work on individual creativity, to working together and developing a group performance outcome. Although practitioners use different terminologies, the kinds of work are largely similar, and we have tried to suggest a useful way of organising them in sequence. We have somewhat extended the range of examples but retained the same taxonomy, because we think it is still viable and useful as a way of identifying aims and suggesting appropriate exercises. Practical work is also described in Part 1 and indicated in the Notes; the Bibliography specifically identifies books containing practical exercises. We have worked through most of the exercises we describe or refer to, with drama and scriptwriting students, with practitioners in this country and in India, the US and Africa, with groups working to devise or create conventional performances and with those whose aim is to develop group skills, work with particular social groups or engage with political realities. We started out from an experience of the work of Barker, Lecoq and Keith Johnstone and have gone on to explore ways in which their methods have been recontextualised and recombined by Boal, Callery, Chris Johnston and others. The parameters of this journey thus reflect the historical development and extended reach of improvisation during the period between the first and third editions.

The reach and remit of impro work, as we noted in the 2007 edition, overlaps extensively from performance training into the understanding of practice as psychosocial and political intervention: 'remaking the self' is in these terms understood as an embodied activation of the potential for articulation and intervention, and in this edition we extend the discussion of Boalian practice a little further in order to tease out some of the resonances of this. In incorporating investigations of the relationship between improvisation and 'altered states of consciousness' (Drinko 2013) and of the ways in which improvisation-driven work seeks to make offers, both experiential and imaginative, to its audience, we signal further dimensions of the ways in which improvisation continues to be at the heart of attempts to know what we are doing when we perform.

Definitions and attitudes

Improvisation: the skill of using bodies, space, imagination, objects and all human resources to generate or to reformulate a coherent physical expression of an idea, a situation and a character (even, perhaps, a text); to do this spontaneously, in response to the immediate stimuli of one's environment, without preconceptions.

All performance uses the body of the actor, giving space and form to an idea, situation, character, text or event in the moment of creation. It does not matter if the work has been rehearsed for a month, with every move, every nuance of speech learned and practised. In the act of performance the actor becomes an improviser. The audience laughs, and she times the next line differently. She hears the lines of her fellow performers as if for the first time, each time, and responds to them, for the first time. She keeps within the learned framework of the play; she does not make up new lines or alter the play's outcome in any drastic way. Yet the actor improvises; and the relationship between formal 'acting' and 'improvising' is so intricate that we might say that each *includes* the other. Improvisation is a part of the nature of acting, certainly. But, more importantly, acting is only one part of the creative process of improvising.

Impro:

- A way of working with the givens of performance-text
- A way of making you better at being in the moment
- A way of freeing up the physical, structural and conceptual imagination
- A psychophysical training
- and (thanks to Friedrich Schiller for this one) the play drive

Improvisation is immediate and organic articulation, including the verbal, not just response, but a paradigm for the way humans reflect (or create) what happens. Where improvisation is most effective, most spontaneous, least 'blocked' by taboo, habit or shyness, it comes close to a condition of integration with the environment or context and consequently (simultaneously) expresses that context in the most appropriate shape, making it recognisable to others, 'realising' it as act.

Some teachers of juggling begin by giving the pupil three balls and getting the student to throw them up in the air. The tendency is to clutch reflexively, to tighten up, to panic and to try desperately to catch the balls. The teacher will smile, shake his or her head and make the beginner throw the balls again, this time making no effort to catch. The hardest thing to learn is not 'how to juggle', but how to let the balls drop (see Gelb 1981: 103ff.).

It is the same with improvisation. The hardest thing to learn is that failure doesn't matter. It doesn't have to be brilliant every time – it can't be. What happens is what happens; is what you have created; is what you have to work with. What matters is to listen, to watch, to add to what is happening, rather than subtract from it, and to avoid the reflex of trying to make it into something you think it *ought* to be, rather than letting it become what it *can* be.

What happens in a 'theatre' or other 'performance space' is important in the context of the world 'outside'. They exist in a dialectical relationship with each other, rather than in separate compartments. Just as performance may not merely mirror society, but acts as a force within it which changes its shape, so too improvisation of various kinds has often changed the shape and direction of performance. Habit is the great enemy of evolution, as rehearsal (repetition) may be the enemy of innovation. Is the kind of thing that happens in improvisation similar to the processes by which, for instance, a biological structure evolves to new levels of order? It might well be, for improvisation is about order, about adaptation, about truthfully responding to changing circumstances and about generating meaning out of contextual accidents.

In keeping with this spirit, we shall begin as previously with a brief look at what we previously called 'the more liminal or marginal reaches of the subject'.[2] But the margins, as we have come to recognise, can be a place of power too and may actually signal kinds of exploration which are not at all irrelevant.

Early history: shamans, clowns and actors

Improvisation, both within and without drama, is not a new phenomenon. We point to some moments in its history in order to signal the forms it takes and the kinds of effects it incites.

One channel is located in the shadowy figure of the *shaman*: performer, doctor and priest, storyteller and clown. Repository and creator of his people's mythology and cosmology, he is the 'bringer of tales' from that other world. He is a healer, a 'clever-man', a conjuror, in part a charlatan; but also the shape-changer, the agent and site of transformation. He can contact and *make visible* the 'double', the other side of our nature, the spiritual or inner self. It is this shamanistic function of manifesting those forces which are believed to operate on the dark side of human consciousness to which Artaud refers in *The Theatre and its Double* as 'active metaphysics' (Artaud 1938: 33). Whatever means (s)he uses, the shaman says 'yes' to something more than everyday personality and reality, (s)he marks and embodies a threshold state, a capacity for accepting otherness as a source of empowerment.

The ability to set change in motion, to invite a new element into the equation, to change the parameters and the ability to locate the dynamic of that change as a result of 'opening up' to more than what might be thought possible: both are factors of the improvisatory and its implicit investment in a 'more' of being. It may be obvious, but the comment by Indian theatre scholar Ayappa Paniker that you don't go to a performance to get what you could get elsewhere is relevant. Kapila Vatsyayan, writing on traditional Indian performance with its roots in ritual, says that it 'uses the body to transcend the body' (Vatsyayan 1980: 8). It's not that far to multi-role acting (ancient Sanskrit theatre form *Kudiyattam* calls it *pakarnattam*; Balinese *Topeng* celebrates it in the play of many masks).

Shamanistic forms can still be seen around the world. They have relevance to our present study in the way they foreground powerful physical and emotional impulses acted upon without conscious restraint by both performers and onlookers. The dance scholar and ethnographer Eleanor King describes some of the shaman dances of Korea (many of them brought south by refugees from North Korea) as characterised by trance states and feats of perilous balance. King sees these dances in explicitly Dionysian terms: whether it is the unselfconscious expression through dance of *mŏt* and *hŭng* (irrepressible inner joy and beauty-inspired exhilaration: she describes one young participant jumping straight up and down for 236 continuous bars of music – 1888 jumps in all (King 1983: 62)) or the infectious will to dance caught by members of the audience at shamanic *Mugan kŏri* rites; or the comic impersonations and occasionally lewd mimes of young assistant female shamans interspersed with powerful oracular utterances (which recall the origins of ancient Greek mystery religion and the birth of Japanese *kagura* dance), the impulse is ubiquitous despite frequent 'modern' disapproval. The exorcistic form of *salp'uri*, danced by the oldest *mudang* (female shaman), is described by King thus:

It is subtle, full of suspensions, the motion held back, then bursting out with surprising flicks of [her long, white] scarf; teasing, capricious, rapturous, with improvisational impulses, and magnetic command of the body. Here Dionysus himself is captured, subdued, entertained, and sent away, as in no other dance.   (King 1983: 69)

Movement Medicine, a kind of guided freeform dance, seeks to explore and extend participants' capacity to relate to many dimensions of their ecosphere, including the seasons and their own ancestors and descendants; it does so, as we will analyse later, by a movement and exercise taxonomy which closely resembles the one we identify as central to much improvisation process. The current leader of this movement, Ya'Acov Darling Khan, writes that shamanism is 'the oldest human tradition we have through which we as humans can connect to ourselves, each other and the worlds around us in their multitude of forms'.

But the incarnation of the genius of contradiction is not confined to ritual or to trance. The clown:

> represents a vision of the world that both intellectual and so-called primitive cultures have valued highly, a sense of the comic meaningful to children and adults alike, and a dynamic form of acting based on startling technique and inspired improvisation. (Towsen 1976: 4–5)

Clowning often begins within a sacred or religious context, burlesqueing sacred ritual *within* the ritual. Often, too, the clown represents the regressive element, acting out childish or adolescent fantasies of sexuality and scatology which adulthood represses. But the clown soon escapes from the confines of the sacred.[3] His true origin is in the play instinct itself, and the pleasure he provides is too valuable to be restricted to a holy day.

The theatre clown is universal. He appears, for example, in the Sanskrit drama of India, as the apparently slow-witted servant Vidusaka (whose name means 'one given to abuse'). John Towsen makes the important point that the clown's ability to improvise has allowed him to become (for example, in modern Asian drama) a privileged political satirist, outside the confines of the censor (Towsen 1976: 37). That political role has been there throughout the history of clowning: its chief exponent in recent Western drama is, perhaps, Dario Fo.

Clowns were known among the ancient Greeks, too, where they were called, among other things, *planoi* (Nicoll 1931: 253). One history of the actor begins (according to Aristotle, who well understood that the improviser antedates the tragedian; see Aristotle 1965: 34) in the *polis* of Megara, which had a developed tradition of secular drama, known as the Dorian *Mime*. Companies of masked actors popular among the Dorian Greeks specialised in tiny farces on everyday subjects. They were known, most significantly, as *autokabdaloi*, which means 'buffoons' and 'improvisers' (Beare 1950: 149). Their performances probably included obscenities, acrobatics and juggling. At the heart of the performance lay both the burlesqueing – the relativising – of sacred myth and the celebration of the human body.

The parodic impulse coexists with the religious; the profane is intermingled with the sacred. Two thousand years later in Western Europe, the little devils who run amok through the spectators at the Mystery plays, with gunpowder squibs 'in their hands, ears and arses',[4] represent an enduring sense of fun and love of spectacle: the spirit of carnival.

The mime *humanises* the drama. In counterbalance to the demonic he offers the *corporeal*. He is, after all, a physical being; nothing godlike about him! He has a body which likes to stuff its face with food, to shit, to fuck. He is constantly reminding us of our humanity. His costume grotesquely extends his body: a big nose, belly, phallus (Bakhtin 1965: 317).[5] His jokes are crude, even gross. He can reduce Herakles the demi-god to a mere glutton, Dionysos to a drunkard, the sacramental to the excremental. (Bahktin's reading of this behaviour identifies it as a politics of reclaiming the body, and there are some parallels here with the growth of 'physical theatre' – including the vogue for improvisation, happenings and anarchic performance events – in the decades after 1960.)

The mime took many forms in many countries. From the Saxon *scop* and Middle English *gleeman* (and sexy 'glee-maiden' sometimes), to the German *minnesinger*, the French *jongleur* and *trouvère*, the Russian *skomorokhi*, and the Italian *giullare,* their talents ranged from juggling, rope-walking and animal training to minstrelsy and acting. What links them is the way all clowns work with their audiences. The clown has to make contact swiftly. He has to keep our attention in the noise and bustle of a street. That dictates the size and scale of his gestures. Watching good street entertainers is the first step towards understanding the power of *commedia*. It's also a good place to moot the notion of risk, which on one hand is fairly crucial to much improvisation and on the other takes many forms. Street entertainers and stand-ups share at least five forms of it: drying up, losing your audience, getting insulted (or worse), compromising your earning power and losing status. We shall come back to this later, not least via Jacques Lecoq.

Commedia dell'arte means (approximately) the comedy 'of the professional actors' (the *comici dell'arte*), in contrast to the *commedia erudita* (or the *commedia sostenuta*), the 'erudite', written plays created by the courtly amateurs of the theatre in sixteenth- and seventeenth-century Italy.

Sometimes the companies were highly renowned and could afford permanent bases; at the other extreme, the poorer players were attached to, for example, the Venetian *mountebanks,* using their clowning skills to draw crowds in the streets to whom a quack doctor (a shamanistic echo) could peddle his nostrums. Each mountebank employed a *zanni*, a zany clown to pull in and please the crowd by his clever improvisations. The clown would pretend to mock his master, providing a parallel to the master–slave comedies of the ancient world, and a bridge to the farcical master–servant relationship of Pantalone (or Dottore) and Zanni (Arlecchino or Brighella) in the Italian comedy.

Perrucci's description of *commedia all'improvviso*, in his *Dell'arte rappre-sentativa, premeditata, e dall'improvviso* (1699) (Perrucci 1969: 258), provides a very salutary qualification of what professionally improvised drama is really like. Professionals, even professional improvisers, leave very little to chance. *Commedia* is improvisational, but it is rehearsed and practised im-provisation. The actors wear stock masks, each performer as familiar with his mask as with his own skin. It is *commedia a soggetto*, on a subject, or on a scenario (*canovaccio*), known and prepared in advance. As well as the agreed *soggetti*, the performers could fall back on fairly standardised routines called *lazzi*, pieces of rehearsed comic business, accompanied by *battute* (standard-ised repartee) and *concetti* (premeditated rhetorical passages). The *lazzi* and *concetti* would be mastered by all the members of a troupe as part of their training, regardless of which mask they commonly wore. Roberta Carreri notes that for her – and other performers with Eugenio Barba – improvising starts from fixed elements, principles or themes. She considers it princi-pally a training element, whereas Perrucci is talking about the content and structure of a play; but the point is the same.

The *commedia all'improvviso* dominated the European stage for three hun-dred years, spawning local imitations in many countries and influencing many major playwrights – among them Shakespeare, Molière, Marivaux, Gozzi and Goldoni. Nor are its techniques forgotten. They are still with us in, for example, the work of actors from the Lecoq school, and in the plays and more especially the live performances of Dario Fo.

Jon Davison notes that clown (he uses the word without an article) function and behaviour operates similarly to some improvisatory pro-cesses, notably in its ability to contradict expected behaviour, break taboos (Davison 2013: 1-2) and 'free itself from [narrative and] plot mechanics' (29), thus loosening the expected links between 'objects, animals and characters and their normal functions or significance' (ibid) and poten-tially working to rescript/reformulate the world. The disruptive nature of clown is signalled by Grock's 'odd behaviour, accidents, upsets, failures, surprising or unusual use of objects, verbal misunderstandings, misbe-having bodies, bizarre yet logical thinking, and sudden emotional shifts' (15). This erratic or frame-breaking mode has been seen as 'uncivil', sha-manistic or 'a route to spirituality and self-knowledge' (particularly post-1960s); clowns have been described as 'revolutionary', 'immoral', 'chaotic', 'innocent', 'melancholic' – and in many cases the opposite of these as well (1–2). This suggests emotional, psychological and political functions for clown work. Davison also claims that 'the presence of this clown [Launce in Shakespeare's *Two Gentlemen of Verona*] demands a mixed mode of performance' (29), thus implying a polysemantic and polygeneric mode of action and suggesting that 'to clown' might be an important criterion for the performative itself (David E. R. George might concur).

Davison's book describes the fact that much of this activity is delivered through routines, which are meticulously planned, rehearsed and taught. This implies, but doesn't quite foreground, the situation that 'improvisation' here is more a case of what the audience is being offered or surprised into than what the performer does. Improvisation, if it plays a part, does so in the form of an offer, perhaps similar to the involvement of spectators in Chicago improv or spectactors in Boalian Forum. What, however, does the offer actually consist of? Lecoq, Davison notes, thought not much: for him the routines of clown were largely 'mechanical' and thus dead, the offer a bit like the simplistic and predictable multiple choices of a game-show, perhaps. There has indeed at various times been what might be called 'new clown', like Copeau's 'new comedy' (see below); but Davison also notes that the most recent models seem to have become commodified into even more tightly choreographed 'circus' routines as used by, for example, Cirque du Soleil (2013: 117).[6] So the opening is here closed off by the routine and may in other cases be truncated by a fall into cliché.

In terms of the specifics of process, Davison's 'something wrong' list (166) helpfully pinpoints how clown may deliver somewhat more salient opportunities: sequences are deflected by the 'wrong' time, place, object, person, word or action, leading to disruption of norms and expectations: here the 'trigger' is planned but the effect is more open-ended.

'Postmodern' versions of clown, deriving largely from Lecoq, have seen it as a form of personal liberation (finding 'one's own clown', which has become something of a mantra). What we originally wanted to signal (in the first edition of this book) by referring to clowning as 'one of the purest forms of improvisation' (1990: 91) – which Davison implicitly criticises – was its ability to focus surprise and the possibility of a new departure (of action or significance) at the centre of any moment. In that light – and we think that this is what Lecoq is getting at – 'one's own clown' is shorthand for something like 'one's own route (or perhaps, *pace* Barba, 'score') by which to access this quality of being on the edge'. That is very different from a generalised sense of 'being funny' – or worse, hip/cool/hanging out etc.

Clown(ing) is of course more, although also in a way less, than that. Davison signals that it includes techniques, traditions, formulae and conventions which have very little to do with improvisation in the 'pure' sense which we were positing. Nor, often, does improvisation itself. But the outgrowth may depend on the kernel.

Davison comments on Andrei Jigalov's (2009) 'classical' playing of *auguste* to a whiteface (2013: 119) that it 'reproduces the dynamics of a style now out of fashion', but results in 'failure stripped naked ... something akin to tragedy but ridiculously hilarious at the same time'. This perhaps Beckettian achievement picks up an aspect of the clown as understood in the contemporary (postmodern, but also harking back to the Romantic) world. But beyond the potentially glib pathos, this negotiation with 'failure' marks out a space of authentic encounter with the need, or the preparedness, to start from the beginning at each and every moment: in my end is my beginning, as Eliot put it.

Improvisation does not vanish – improvisation is at the heart of all theatre – but the tradition of improvised play-making disappears with the development of the enclosed, plush and decorous theatre space during the eighteenth century. The rise of the function of the director, too, contributes to the disappearance of the tradition. No longer just the stage or company manager, or one of the actors, and no longer just the organiser of rehearsals, the *concertatore*, but an *auteur* in his own right, the director's vision of the performance has often promoted a style of work in which improvised creativity *on stage* is not valued and taught, rather than communally worked-out or improvised moves, gestures and deliveries become the order of the day.

Our own time has seen the resurgence of improvisation. From the last decades of the twentieth century many approaches and practices containing strong elements of what we in this book describe as the *improvisatory* begin to influence performance practice, particularly in the 'West', in significant ways. Drama training and production is now scarcely understandable without reference to many of the people we discuss in this book: Keith Johnstone, Jacques Lecoq, Clive Barker and Michael Chekhov are paramount, but many directors and trainers have garnered attitudes and practices which draw on their work and on that of their forebears like Copeau, or on kinds of mind/body preparation found in Indian or Japanese actor training.

Nick Moseley reports that 'it is generally agreed within the drama school world that there is a need for more practical books which outline and explain the processes of actor training and rehearsal' (Moseley 2005: 3). Nevertheless, there is now a fairly wide selection of books which approach these areas from the angle of improvisation, games and exercises (see Bibliography). Moseley's own *Acting and Reacting* is concerned to promote 'performance as a social and transactional process' (4), which for him is a way of targeting an immediacy and authenticity more rooted in real events occurring between actors than reliance on the more internal focus of some of Stanislavsky or Strasberg's work. In many ways this is the focus too of both Chris Johnston's *House of Games* (1998, reprinted 2005) and Dymphna Callery's *Through the Body* (2001), which draw on the earlier work of Keith Johnstone, Clive Barker, Augusto Boal and Jacques Lecoq among others. This represents a substantial body of work and is a token – as both Callery and Johnston observe – of specific and conscious trends in actor training and performance style in Western theatre over recent decades.

Whereas Johnston's book is targeted towards community and participative theatre practice and therefore chiefly presents strategies for working with groups, Callery is concerned with processes and methodologies for developing individual performative resources. However, both books include a section on devising, in a similar position (towards the end) of their sequence of exercises and tactics. To that extent they both follow the broad trajectory – from freeing up the individual for performance through working together and on to collaborative production – that we trace out in this book. It is significant that books which respond to contemporary felt needs in theatre practice (both authors are practising drama teachers) should signal this path and pass through many of the same stages: working with bodies and working with groups are themselves indicative of the extent to which 'theatre' no longer means only the presentation of a 'finished' product in a purpose-built venue, but has become coextensive as process with understandings of performance and performativity as negotiable sites of political and psychological construction.

As far as the organisation of games and exercises in these books is concerned, Johnston has sections on Initial Focus (Attention, Energy, Imagination and Communication) and Building Group and Teamwork (Supportiveness, Spontaneity, Adaptation and Empowerment); Callery works through Awareness, Articulation, Energy and Neutrality towards Presence, Complicité, Play, Audience, Rhythm, Sound and E-motion. Virtually everyone who has produced this kind of work deals with these aspects, sometimes under slightly different terminologies and with slightly different aims; but there is a general consistency about the ground covered and the kinds of methodologies suggested. The workshop aims suggested by Johnston (recreation, learning, experimentation, debate, confidence-building, research into social conflict and devising a play) are in no sense incompatible with Callery's aim 'to develop understanding of acting as a combination of imagination and technique' (Callery 2001: 4), or indeed the 'actor's need to ... be "in the moment" and to react truly instinctively to the other people on stage' identified on the back cover of Moseley's book. The destined operational contexts are different, but the conception of operational strategies and requirements is remarkably similar. Where Callery for instance echoes Johnston in targeting The Playful Body, The Sentient Body and The Physical Text, Moseley deals with The World of Play, Transactional Improvisation, Learning to Trust your Body and Approaches to Text.

Moseley cites David Mamet's scepticism about the internalised focus of much post-Stanislavskian work, suggesting that dominant twentieth-century acting 'mythology' conditions actors to hide from genuine spontaneity in order to construct a fictional stability to counteract the vulnerability of a 'precarious profession'; however he qualifies Mamet's rejection of actor training as too sweeping and argues for a 'space between' Mamet and Stanislavsky (Moseley 2005: 20), which is charted by a combination of Meisner and Transactional Improvisation. For him, training needs to 'give actors a *craft* and a *process*, while at the same time allowing them to retain total spontaneity'(2005: 21): 'transactional improvisation helps actors to understand their interactions with others and to break out of habitual patterns, while the Meisner-based repetition work trains them to respond to each other without self-censorship'. There are strong echoes of Keith Johnstone here, in the sense that the latter charges conventional ratiocentric models of education with constructing barriers to spontaneity; Moseley's requirements that actors should 'become emotionally open by being physically open' (24), recognise the need to let go of 'defence mechanisms' (25) and 'get into the habit of making big offers' (30) are summarised in the Johnstonian recommendation to adopt a 'yes' attitude (26) to training: do it first and ask questions afterwards, largely in order to play the risk which, according to him, social conditioning tends to minimise. Consequently it is possible to read into Moseley's emphasis on individual openness the seeds of a *politics* of interaction (33, 171), which moves from the need to encounter one's own otherness towards the ability to develop play-skills within a group. Moseley's book, like Callery's and Johnston's, is clearly and directly written and testifies to the experience of working with actors in training in the context of the contemporary worlds and the theatre practice which it requires; it is perhaps more trenchant in places, but persuasively constructs an argument for methodologies which seek to foreground the immediacy of the events which occur for actors as they work. Its clearly articulated premises thus provide a valuable extension to the slightly narrower focus of the other two books discussed here; taken together, they indicate the relevance of many of the central tenets of improvisatory work – presence, play, availability and so on – to contemporary training and practice.

Over recent years more books on improvisation have appeared both in the UK and in the US: for example, two by John Abbott (*The Improvisation Book* and *Improvisation in Rehearsal*) and three books on American short- and long-form improv (Ben Hauck's *Long-Form Improv: The Complete Guide to Creating Characters, Sustaining Scenes and Performing Extraordinary Harolds*; Clayton D. Drinko's *Theatrical Improvisation, Consciousness, and Cognition* and Jeanne Leep's *Theatrical Improvisation: Short Form, Long Form and Sketch-based Improv* (for others see Bibliography)). There are other books on Ensemble theatre making and, as we note later, work on audience participation. There is also of course a lot of work on improvisation in dance. An *Improvisation Studies Reader*, due in 2015, signals that the scope and significance of the field is now extensive.

PART I

Who? Major Practitioners of Improvisation

Introduction

Part 1 offers a survey of major practitioners across time and space, suggesting key areas in the history and range of performance which have been significantly influenced by the principles and processes of improvisation. The book is organised in several ways. The first two chapters look at the work of 'early' (i.e., late nineteenth and early twentieth-century) practitioners in the European and American context in order to establish routes into Academy and Drama School Training; 'traditional' and 'alternative' imply different kinds of performance outcomes and hence different working methods – roughly, those in the tradition of Stanislavsky, and those derived from Johnstone or Lecoq, tending towards different models of identity and role in performance. Geographical and cultural factors (of the UK, USA, Europe, Africa and the Middle East) produce distinct uses and forms of the improvisatory in different contexts and spaces; and applications 'beyond theatre' extend the use of the 'games' model towards psychological, psychokinetic and political encounter. All of these lines of investigation work, on the one hand, towards the definition of the theatrical frame as representational matrix and, on the other, to its exploitation as generic productivity for performers and 'participants'. In not a few cases, these roles and functions overlap. They may also represent or engender different models of the self and its place in society.

I   Improvisation in Training, Rehearsal Practice and Writing (Europe and the UK)

The principle of improvisation

Improvisation is not just a style or an acting technique; it is a dynamic *principle* operating in many different spheres, an independent and transformative way of being, knowing and doing. The twentieth century witnessed an explosion of experiments which have embraced the principle of 'improvisation'. Music, for example, was transformed by the various forms of jazz: technical proficiency allied to improvisation to create a practically inexhaustible synthesis. In modern dance, Isadora Duncan and Martha Graham, in different ways, opened up a wealth of new plastic possibilities for the expressive body. The former immediately and spontaneously danced the truth of what she felt. The latter broke down the rigid formulae of classical ballet and replaced them with a language that responded to the world around as well as within the dancer. The 1960s political philosophy of situationism in Europe and happenings in the United States celebrated the spontaneous and site-specific, most importantly perhaps the conjunction of site, moment, performer and spectator, that is, the place, time and bodies of new event-structures. Many of these forms have been reconfigured in the performance work of the early twenty-first century, so it is worth dwelling on this a little. The examples given above (jazz and twentieth-century modern dance) involve the negotiation of form and freedom, and writing about this often tends to polarise them. In fact, as noted in the discussion of *commedia* in the Introduction, both are involved throughout, in preparation/rehearsal and, sometimes, in performance – arguably more often in site-specific or immersive work of recent times. It has been suggested that most of what passes for 'improvisation' in jazz is anything but that: 'breaks' tend to be repetitive and/or predictable, and they remain strictly within the frame of rhythm and key-signature or depart from it only in 'agreed' ways. So quite a lot of jazz falls back on habit – the habit of the player and the expectation of the listener. But this immersion in pattern is not solely restrictive: as with much Asian performance – and a key criterion adopted by Barba for his own company's work – knowing the 'score' (which may have been developed from a long sequence of experiment, trial and error) is a basis for liberation. Using the term 'improvisation' is a bit sloppy here, because it refers equally to the development process and to potentially unexpected 'leaps' in performance, moments when 'the flower blooms', as *Noh* theatre would have it. But what both time-dimensions trace is a point of change, a happening of something new.

As Martha Graham writes, 'There is a necessity for movement when words are not adequate. The basis of all dancing is something deep within you' (in Roose-Evans 1970: 112). Is improvisation here the honing of a technique or acuity for identifying the moment when things 'change', when something really does 'happen' to the relationship between 'self' (located in the machine of the body-as-agent) and the 'environment' (space, place, time, other performers, audience, score, text, context and so on)?

However, it is true that all theatrical performance ideally strives for a rigorous authenticity: what Stanislavsky called 'artistic truth', perhaps? The lines of development we discuss in this section lead in three principal directions, but each ultimately demands the same degree of commitment and is concerned – though from different angles – with an exploration of 'self' and 'reality' for performers and/or audience.

Improvisation is used in three major contexts. It feeds first into what we might call traditional theatre training, as a preparation for performance and a way of tuning up the performers. We can place this in the (Stanislavskian) tradition of 'character' preparation, or, to put it another way, as a method of schooling the actor to project the 'reality' of the character. It is a process which involves the development of imaginative skills so that the body can experience and express appropriate emotional states: discovering in oneself the self or being of 'another' and presenting it.

We discuss the use of improvisation in actor training below; this line of work initially tends – though not exclusively or rigidly – towards the naturalistic, the documentary and the sociopolitical, with a relatively clearly defined concept of 'character' as the focus of deterministic forces: what D. H. Lawrence called the 'old stable ego of personality' clings to this and inhabits the structure and content of the 'well-made play'. Perhaps the most extreme development occurs in the improvisation-for-performance work of Mike Leigh, where a scripted text arises from improvisation fleshed out by 'sociological' research.

The second tradition (or perhaps anti-tradition) rests on a more radical acknowledgement of the fragmentation of nineteenth-century notions of a consistent personality. The comic and satiric vein, often allied to improvisation, challenges assumptions about stable social personality and 'bourgeois' respectability; taken to extremes, it undercuts political, religious and philosophical myths about the coherence of individual identity and its consonance within a system of stratified order and significance. The work of Jarry, Artaud and Beckett, for instance, extends and foregrounds this destabilisation; it also requires a more radically physical and improvisatory approach to acting, and it is not surprising that alongside this eventually scripted and accepted form of theatre, work on and with improvisation should have continued to develop almost as a form in and for itself. Improvisation of this kind both serves as an exploratory form of theatre and – here we move into the third tradition, 'para-theatrical' context – also locates the issue of self and reality in spheres other than the narrowly theatrical.

The more radical modes of improvisation both accept the consequences of the disintegration of the existential self and attempt to use them positively. Grotowski's actors learn to 'disarm', that is, to arrive at a condition without the protective masks of the familiar or the comfortable escapes of dramatic cliché. The work focuses not on the reality of the character but on that of the *performer*; where it emerges as public theatre, it is the inventiveness and authenticity of the performers in their relationship with the spectators which is foregrounded, as opposed to the presentation of a narrative. Here improvisation and performance are seen as part of a developmental process which can thus extend beyond theatre into, for example, psychotherapy, education and politics.

It is only a step from here, and indeed a step which had already been taken by work like that of Grotowski's para-theatrical period, to the spectrum of concern with location and audience in which they become participants in the event. Yet in another way it is also a step back, towards the *communitas* Victor Turner identified as the dynamic of ritual. In the ongoing exploration of new forms of being, the shaman bites back.

John Martin (2004) notes that improvisation is used in pre-rehearsal, rehearsal and performance, and offers four ways of working with it: solo, in pairs, variations and for groups. He indicates that in addition to Western actor training, improvisation is found in Boalian Forum Theatre (responding to spectator interventions), Japanese *Noh* (gauging the state of the audience), South Indian *Kathakali* (play with audience by popular characters) and West African performance, where dances are 'never the same' (Martin 2004: 102–3). Exercises are organised according to the kinds of energy level they seek to generate and the ways in which they change the nature of the performer's relationship to space. Martin trained at the Lecoq school and has worked extensively with performers from many traditions.[1]

Martin's proposed divisions can be seen to relate both to what we discuss in Part 1 about training and trainers and to the way Part 2 (the 'how' section) is organised. The use of improvisation as a strategy of training is a way of developing the performer's resources, which as it is formalised or repeated develops into a methodology; improvisation as a way of creating or amending performance alters its nature and effect, inflecting its status and meaning. Pre-rehearsal involves the preparation of bodies and groups for *disponibilité* and play, and the exploration of the relationship between the body of the performer and the space of performance. Improvisation in and as rehearsal continues these moves with reference to the performance-text (the ensemble of signs and codes which constitute the performance); it develops the contexts and 'back-stories' of characters and situations through exercises like 'hot-seating' or affective memory work; and it works on strategies to energise relationships and intentions, by attempting to find ways to 'raise the stakes' and intensify the degree of attention to what is happening between performers and in the space. Improvisation in and as performance can be the most risky venture possible – for a clown courting failure, for a participant in a scenario whose parameters are known but whose detail, order and meaning is liable to be changed by any performer; or a subtle variation registering the receptive condition of the audience or the specific dynamics of the moment by a highly skilled performer; or uncensored or deliberately invoked interventions from spectator-participants to which performers respond supportively. In what follows we discuss both forms of training (process) and uses in performance (application or product), which often feature in parallel in the work of trainers and theatre-makers, or follow directly on from each other.

Precursors: Stanislavsky, Meyerhold and Chekhov

Improvisatory methods slowly began to percolate through mainstream Russian theatre. In St Petersburg in 1908, the idealising theorist Vyacheslav Ivanov (1866–1949) proposed a renovation of the theatre in which the actors would descend among the audience, distribute masks and costumes 'to everyone who wanted them … involving those present in a communal creative improvisation' (Rudnitsky 1988: 10). He sought to replace theatre's classical reliance on *mimesis* with a dionysian group *praxis*. His Symbolist poetic contemporaries were cautious, and they regarded Ivanov's proposals for a renewed liturgical theatre that would take the place of traditional religious ritual as utopian and unworkable.

Following Meyerhold's use of *commedia* techniques in *Columbine's Scarf* (1910), Alexander Taïrov's production of *The Seamy Side of Life* by Jacinto Benavente opened in 1912 at the Reineke Theatre. This too sought to explore the improvisatory essence of masked *commedia* and mime, though the young, inexperienced actors struggled to realise Taïrov's vision.

After the October Revolution of 1917, perhaps the first person to think of improvisations as more than idealist experiments, historical reconstructions or as training and rehearsal exercises was Meyerhold's protégé Sergei Radlov (1892–1958). Radlov founded the 'Popular Comedy' (*Teatr Narodnoy Komedii*, or People's Comedy Theatre, St Petersburg) in 1920. He argued that 'a genuine contemporary art form could be achieved only in one way – by means of "the actor's verbal improvisation"' (Rudnitsky 1988: 57). Where Meyerhold had stressed physical improvisation and mime, Radlov placed emphasis on the spontaneous creation of verbal text. Feeling that melodrama and tragedy depended for their power on a fixed, stable text, Radlov chose to work exclusively in comedy, often with circus performers and clowns such as Georges Delvari, creating half-plays/half-scenarios in which every one of the players

> was allowed, and in fact obliged, to say everything that came to mind. The main criterion for success lay in the audience response: the more often and the more loudly they burst out laughing, the better. Topical jokes about current events, remarks unexpectedly directed at the audience and informal, familiar banter with spectators were encouraged.   (1988: 57)

For Radlov, indeed, the playwright was seen as 'pernicious', and his aim was to free the actor from the writer's tyranny. He felt that the actor's enslavement to the words of others 'completely atrophies the actor's initiative, transforming an independent artist into an obedient and passive performer, practically a marionette, controlled by the writer's will' (57). He did, however, collaborate with Maxim Gorki, who found the idea of improvisation attractive, on a piece called *The Hardworking Slovotekov*, a satire on bureaucracy. The piece was considered a failure: the theatre's designer Valentina Khodasevich described Delvari's improvisations as 'crude and vulgar' (Rudnitsky 1988: 59) and recorded Gorki's displeasure at the way the actors turned sharp satire into broad farce and slapstick. Discouraged, Radlov began to direct more classical, less improvised comic pieces, and the circus performers decamped back to St Petersburg's Cisinelli big top. In 1922, the Popular Comedy closed.

Yevgeny Vakhtangov's last production, Carlo Gozzi's *Princess Turandot*, which opened at the Moscow Art Theatre's Third Studio (later renamed the State Vakhtangov Studio) in February 1922, saw his actors given freedom to improvise in performance. They were asked to imagine that they were playing Italian actors playing the Chinese roles of the play: they were encouraged to get into role, and to get out of role, and to show the transitions.

They were instructed 'to conduct complex, capricious and merry play with the character, simultaneously demonstrating the technique of transformation, the joy of metamorphosis and the ability to look at one's hero with irony "from the side"' (Rudnitsky 1988: 54). Vakhtangov's 'fantastical realism' style of performance anticipated Brecht, quoted from *commedia* as well as from Chinese theatre and remained in the theatre's repertory for a thousand performances. Revived in 1971, it remains popular to the present day.

We might assume that Constantin Stanislavsky (1863–1938) was the originator of the modern use of improvisation, at least as a rehearsal and training device. Many of the scenes described in his books, *An Actor Prepares*, *Building a Character* and *Creating a Role*, in which the director 'Tortsov' guides his young protégés through the processes of self-discovery, are improvisatory in nature. But these books are the product of Stanislavsky's later years, after a heart attack had forced him to give up acting. They do not necessarily relate to his own theatrical practice, particularly in the early days of the Moscow Art Theatre (MAT).

Stanislavsky did use a form of 'proto-improvisation', a kind of imaginative projection of oneself into a role, and began to suggest to his actors (*a*) that they might do this together, as a group, away from the pressures of actual rehearsals; and (*b*) that they do it continually, *outside the theatre*, while practising simple physical activities. The concentration required led them towards group outings, boating or mushroom picking, away from the bustle of 'normal' town life, so that the actors could slowly become immersed in their characters.

Although knowledge of Stanislavsky's practice has until recently been limited by lack of access to his writings in the original Russian, he seems in fact to have made use more consistently than hitherto recognised of exercises aimed at physical, emotional and intellectual integration in order to produce a multilayered spontaneous 'truth'. Some of these exercises resemble the kinds of energy work used extensively by Michael Chekhov (Carnicke 2000: 22); improvisation was particularly important in working on structure, rhythm, atmosphere and social context in Stanislavsky's last (posthumously performed) production, *Tartuffe* (1939).

It took a long time for Stanislavsky to come to the central conclusions of his early work: that a director should be interested in the actor's process rather than trying to dictate a result; that an actor should blend himself with the character he plays; that when playing a villain one should look for his good side; that it was not important that one played 'well' or 'ill' – what mattered was to play truthfully. But Stanislavsky was also, at this time, overimpressed by the externals of naturalism, by a scenic naturalism that gave the illusion that genuine emotions were being played out within it and also by the autocratic example of Ludwig Chronegk's practice with the Duke of Saxe-Meiningen's company. Only later in his work, after the famous vacation in Finland in 1906, would he consciously transfer the emphasis to the inner life of the character: in effect, the creation of the Stanislavsky 'System'.

It was not until 1911, when Stanislavsky founded the First Studio of the MAT, that improvisation became in any way central to the practical work (and even later before it became part of the theory). According to Paul Gray, improvisation was first introduced by Stanislavsky's trusted friend and associate Leopold Antonovich Sulerzhitsky, whom Stanislavsky had put in charge of the Studio's developmental work (Gray 1964: 25). Improvisation immediately became the rage among the younger generation of actors and actresses who made up the First Studio but was equally powerfully resisted by the older generation. For Olga Knipper and Ivan Moskvin – and even for Nemirovich-Danchenko himself – there seemed nothing practically useful in the Studio's work at first. But for Yevgeny Vakhtangov,[2] Mikhail Chekhov, Maria Ouspenskaya and Richard Boleslavsky, Sulerzhitsky's technique was a liberation.

It was really only in the last phase of his work, when he had ceased to act and when the translator Elizabeth Reynolds Hapgood had prevailed upon him to write down his way of working, that Stanislavsky himself began to consider seriously the techniques of improvisation, making the students work on scenes entirely without a text.

As David Magarshack points out, Stanislavsky had never really applied this purely theoretical idea to prove its efficacy in practice. It would be his successors who would elevate this experimental way of working into a central tenet of the 'Method'. Stanislavsky's work has led directly to that of modern America (both the 'Method' and the 'New York School' of improvisation discussed below) and to the plays of Mike Leigh, in which the *sine qua non* of performance is the truthful depiction of naturalistic character. His influence on the theatre of the twentieth century is still immense, but the naturalistic theatre's development of applied improvisation is due to his successors and emulators rather than to Stanislavsky directly.

Bella Merlin's books *Beyond Stanislavsky* and *Konstantin Stanislavsky* contain a full and more detailed discussion of, for example, the 'The Method of Physical Actions and Active Analysis' (Merlin 2001) and a short and very accessible account of Stanislavsky's life and work, with detailed discussions of *An Actor Prepares* (Merlin 2003). The latter also focuses discussion on three Stanislavskian methods: early 'round-the-table' analysis ('table work', which she stresses is active and fun rather than dry and scholastic) and the 'System' (117–25); an introduction to the 'Method of Physical Actions' (126–42); and an introduction to 'Active Analysis' (143–54). There's a useful glossary (157–62) that discusses key terms such as 'grasp' and 'communion' as well as the more obvious System terminology and relates them directly to the main text, and to Stanislavsky's own writings (see also Part 2).[3]

Techniques which emanate from Stanislavsky, such as 'affective memory', substitution, use of 'hot-seating' or improvised 'back-story' scenarios, proceed in stages from individual imaginative activity to mutually improvised dialogue. They aim for an internal sense or feeling of 'this is how it is'. In the 'finding the needle' exercise directed by 'Tortsov', the actress starts by demonstrating 'looking for a needle in a bewildered way'. It's an act. Stanislavsky raises the stakes, as subsequent practitioners would say, by telling her that there really is a needle and if she doesn't find it she'll be out of a job. She changes her behaviour completely and the dynamic shifts radically. In other words this is a nutshell version of getting inside, of solving a real problem in real time.

Meisner's second-level exercises build on repetition of banal mutual observations by introducing a task for one of the participants ('You have to fry an egg for your gran'; 'there's a bomb under the TV') to operate a similar process. Here then is another kind of sequence – increasing intensification, upping the ante, ramping up the stakes. So this kind of trajectory (simple basic version: 'your energy level when you did that scene was 5; now do it at 9 or 10') is a key procedural feature of this strand of improvisation as rehearsal and training; it signals that method is being employed to arrive at a point – I really have to find an actual needle, I have to fry an egg and keep throwing the dialogue ball back – where the actor is 'free' because he or she is experiencing diverse parameters of a situation and operating at a level of organic complexity where a different order of mental and physical coherence starts to kick in. (See discussion of Drinko on improvisation and consciousness in Chapter 2.)

If it can be argued that both Lee Strasberg and Stella Adler, though in different ways, pursue Stanislavsky's aim to enrich the actor's inhabiting of the present through their work on emotion, Sanford Meisner is particularly concerned to centre all exchange between performers in a developed sensitivity and openness to what is happening to them in the moment. Exercises which appear to consist of the banal repetition of surface observations are guided in such a way as to lead to acknowledgement and articulation of subtle shifts of attitude, and they also aim to engender a spirit of play between actors. (Nick Moseley's book (discussed in the Introduction, pp. xxii) frames Meisner's work well and presents a good selection of his exercises.) So this work is about taking from each other

(Keith Johnstone's 'yes-saying' as spontaneous verbal response initially) and playing; passing the ball back and forth, offering and accepting; developing a 'dialogue' between players as in, for example, jazz or Indian classical music, or between musicians and dancers in Indian work. Here the rhythmic patterns (*Tal* or *Tala*) used to structure the interaction between performers – dancer/musician, musician/musician and so on – are known as *jugalbandi* – there is a stipulation that this word is used when the artists are of equal standing, not one leading the other. The rhythmic 'subvocalisation' which goes on here – a kind of *grammelot* (see Chapter 3 on Dario Fo) – seems to incite spontaneous physical response, even within relatively 'closed' forms like *Kathakali* or *Kathak*.

What is improvisatory here – and has links with aspects of Copeau's, Johnstone's and Grotowski's work – is the way in which 'text' becomes a porous field of interplay and revelation, where actors begin to develop the kind of antennae which can pick up their own 'pre-expressive' shifts which are so essential, for instance, to the red-nosed clown, but also to sensitive acting in all kinds of performance. And this kind of subliminal or subtextual sensitivity seems to imply a psychophysical functioning of a somewhat extended kind.

The modern 'alternative' examination of improvisation 'begins' with Vsevolod Meyerhold (1874–1940), one of the MAT's leading actors during the early autocratic stage, who left Moscow in 1902. Stanislavsky invited him back to join the MAT Studio Theatre project in 1905. Meyerhold's disagreement with the MAT's 'realistic' concept of theatre soon became apparent. A conflict between him and Stanislavsky ensued; the Studio Theatre was closed before it had opened. For Stanislavsky, especially as his work developed, the actor was the focus of theatre. For Meyerhold, the focus was the director's art. The division between them was a formal one and should not obscure the great respect each had for the other.

In 1910 Meyerhold opened the 'Interlude House' at the former Skazka Theatre at 33 Galernaya Street, St Petersburg, to explore aspects of popular and street theatre and, especially, *commedia dell'arte*. Because he was working at the conservative Imperial Alexandrinsky Theatre at the time, he was asked by the management to conduct his experimental work under a pseudonym. At the suggestion of the composer and poet Mikhail Kuzmin, he took the name of 'Doctor Dappertutto', a character from E. T. A. Hoffmann's *Adventure on New Year's Eve*. Doctor Dappertutto was a real-life manifestation of the mask, a ubiquitous *doppelgänger* who assumed responsibility for all Meyerhold's experiments in the eccentric and the supernatural for the rest of his time at the Imperial theatres (Braun 1969: 115, 119–28).[4]

Although the Interlude House was short-lived, the Dappertutto experiments continued for many years. Meyerhold's fascination with *commedia dell'arte* had a number of levels. Where Stanislavsky's theatre explored the 'inner truth' of character, Meyerhold glimpsed the equally profound 'exterior truth' of the mask. He was also fascinated by the figure of the *cabotin* (which he regarded in a very much more positive light than Copeau later did). The figure of the itinerant, poor, professional actor, descended from the classical *mimus*, via the Russian *skomorokhi* (Russian equivalent of the *jongleur*) and *balaganschik* ('fairground booth-player') no less than the Italian *comici dell'arte*, attracted him powerfully.

His awareness of *commedia dell'arte* was conditioned by his acquaintance with a number of European sources: the drawings of Callot, with their grotesque and malicious, sexual and scatological figures; the *fiabe* of Carlo Gozzi, with their deliberate room for actors' improvisations, their poetic, magical delicacy; the plays of Goldoni, with their developing interest in psychological realism and their literary grace; the works of the Romantic Hoffmann, with their masked and transformed mysticism, their fascination with reality and its double; and, finally, his close association with the writer and director Vladimir Soloviev, whose knowledge of *commedia* stimulated his own (Risum 1996: 75).

Beyond his initial intellectual, literary and aesthetic interest, Meyerhold was engaged with the actor's physical skills: the extraordinary plasticity of the street entertainer would ultimately become the basis of the scientific bio-mechanics with which his name is associated, and which led to an investment in the *actor's* independent creativity. He returned to the idea of the *commedia dell'arte* scenario, set in advance by the *concertatore* or laid out by a master dramatist like Goldoni or Gozzi.

Michael (Mikhail) Chekhov (1891–1955) was the nephew of the playwright Anton Chekhov. He worked at MAT from 1912 to 1918, and later in Berlin, Paris, Dartington, New York, Connecticut and Los Angeles. Franc Chamberlain describes Chekhov as 'an outstanding actor and author of one of the best actor training manuals ever published in the European tradition' (Chamberlain 2000a: 79). His approach is now incorporated into the curriculum of many training establishments.

Over 100 of Chekhov's exercises have been published. Much of Chekhov's focus is on developing inner resources, and the exercises aim to:

- link inner and outer, psychological and material (via work on energy and focus)
- create and inhabit imaginative space
- locate and inhabit imaginary bodies and centres

- explore psychological gesture, archetype
- develop imagination and concentration
- activate higher ego
- explore atmospheres and qualities
- develop a sense of form, beauty and wholeness.

The general context of his work is towards the evocation of 'atmosphere, actors' creativity, physicalisation of inner experience' (Chamberlain 2000a: 80). It is important for the actor to 'become an active participant in the process of imagination' (86).

Rudolf Steiner's Theosophy and associated practices were useful to Chekhov in overcoming a personal crisis and leading to 'liberation from his self-indulgent and self-destructive tendencies'; from this Chekhov acquired a distance from the everyday self which he was able to incorporate into acting strategies, moving away from the Stanislavskian emphasis on personal emotion towards activation of a Steineresque 'higher ego' (the 'artist in us') (Chamberlain 2000a: 81), which has attributes such as detachment, compassion and humour. Chekhov also stressed the importance of the condition of 'two consciousnesses' – 'real acting was when we could act and be filled with feelings, and yet be able to make jokes with our partners' (Chekhov 1985: 102). This suggests parallels with Copeau's and Lecoq's work on 'neutrality', discussed below, and also with non-Western actor training rooted in particular understandings of mind/body integration and models of consciousness. Chekhov himself also used aspects of eurythmy (Steiner/Dalcroze) and worked with Vakhtangov to synthesise the approaches of Stanislavsky and Meyerhold.

According to Franc Chamberlain, 'the basic principles of his technique will allow as many variations and creations as there are creative individualities' (2000a: 113ff.). So exercises can be adapted; they should also be explored at length in order to allow new outcomes to emerge. Chekhov requires this openness and 'wanted an attitude of warmth, friendliness, freedom and ease in the workspace. Giving and receiving, underpinned by a sense of joy, is at the heart of the work' (115). Chekhov's 'Four Brothers' is a set of exercises designed to stimulate these kinds of experience. These criteria exemplify important improvisatory principles and form a link between the psychological and inner-directed end of the Stanislavsky spectrum and the kinds of spatial and element work partly derived from dance and *mime blanche*, also figuring extensively in Lecoq's sport-derived methodology.

The first person, however, to investigate improvisation as *the* means to explore the nature of acting, and the first man to grasp the full significance of this way of working, was Jacques Copeau. In Limon, in 1916, he wrote:

It is an art which I don't know, and I am going to look into its history. But I see, I feel, I understand that this art must be restored, reborn, revised; that it alone will bring a living theatre – the theatre of players.   (Kirkland 1975: 58)

Renovation and the development of drama training: Jacques Copeau and Suzanne Bing

Albert Camus said, 'In the history of the French theatre there are two periods: before and after Copeau' (cited in Saint-Denis 1982: 32). This judgement might be extended to the history of improvisation: Copeau (1879–1949) truly began the modern tradition. John Rudlin enumerates the many debts which the modern theatre owes to Copeau's teaching and practice:

In no particular order: drama games; improvisation; animal mimicry; ensemble playing; writers-in-residence; *commedia dell'arte* revival; mime; mask-work; repertoire rather than repertory; community theatre; theatre as communion.   (Rudlin 1986: xiv)

And not to Copeau alone. His assistant (lover, mother of Copeau's son, the writer Bernard Bing, partner in all but name) the actress Suzanne Bing (1885–1967) has been unfairly neglected, due largely perhaps to her own diffidence and deference to Copeau's memory. Much of the credit for discovery and invention in this new mode should rightly be hers.[5]

Copeau was not the first to use improvisation as a rehearsal and training technique: Stanislavsky, we have seen, used it at the Moscow Art Theatre Studio; Taïrov had employed it at the Kamerny, too. But Copeau, at Le Vieux-Colombier and in his teaching, was the first really to base a system of exploratory work upon it, and the impact of his decision is still reverberating.

Jacques Copeau was a drama critic before he became a full-time practitioner. He was part of the reaction against the realism of Antoine's Théâtre Libre (though he knew and admired Antoine and regarded Stanislavsky as a source of creative inspiration), against the false rhetorical style of the Comédie Française and against the crassness of boulevard theatre. He read and in many ways admired Craig and Appia, but disagreed with their proposed alternatives. Instead, in 1913, he published his own 'manifesto' – his *Essai de Rénovation Dramatique* – and founded his own theatre in the rue du Vieux-Colombier in Paris. Bing was a young actress, recently divorced from the avant-garde composer Edgard Varèse, by whom she had a daughter. She took Copeau's call for renovation of the stage literally and joined his new company that year.

She (like Copeau) became interested in the ideas of Émile Jaques-Dalcroze, which included music improvisation and its expression through the body, and had experimented with them teaching children with Copeau in Geneva before rediscovering them again via Margaret Naumburg in New York, where the Vieux-Colombier spent two important seasons during the First World War as part of the propaganda war effort.

Margaret Naumburg (1890–1983), then the wife of the novelist Waldo Frank, had been quietly instrumental in introducing the ideas of Dalcroze and Alexander technique to America. She was a passionate and devoted educationist, trained with Maria Montessori, whose ideas she refined. She wrote an article popularising Dalcroze's ideas in America and (when the Great War put his business at risk) personally invited Alexander to New York, where she introduced him to her former teacher, the Pragmatist philosopher and progressive education advocate John Dewey. Waldo Frank had written an account of the Vieux-Colombier (Frank 1918), and he and Margaret entertained the actors during their stay. Bing (then nursing a baby) was offered a teaching job at Margaret's Walden Infant School. Here she observed and practised Margaret's use of games.

Bing's resultant physical theatre training exercises – masks and animal games in particular, which derived in part from Naumburg's work – would be crucial to Copeau's project to eliminate *cabotinage* (the actor's reliance on a repertoire of stale tricks; 'ham' acting). She taught them first to the French actors at Morristown. They would contribute directly to the formation of *les Copiaus* – Copeau's experimental troupe in Burgundy – and, later, la Compagnie des Quinze under Michel Saint-Denis. It was Bing's personal tuition which directly led to the developmental mime of Etienne Decroux and through him to the extraordinarily influential teaching of Jacques Lecoq. If Copeau is the father of physical theatre, then Suzanne Bing is its mother.[6]

In the beginning, Copeau did not so much have a vision of a future theatre, as a certainty that such a theatre would be possible – if only the right conditions were fulfilled. His manifesto ended with the now famous plea *'Pour l'oeuvre nouvelle qu'on nous laisse un tréteau nu!'* (For the new work, just leave us bare boards!) (Copeau 1913: 72), and almost his first act, practical and symbolic, was to empty the stage of the old music-hall building. He ended the 'tyranny of the technician', leaving the stage open and free for the actor to perform and (just as importantly) to rehearse on. By 1921, he had stripped away the proscenium arch and replaced it with an open, multi-levelled end-stage.[7] Yet, with a minimum of technical means, Copeau's actors achieved a remarkable degree of realism when they wanted to – even astounding Antoine with Charles Vildrac's *Le Pacquebot S.S. Tenacity* (1920), in which a few tables, chairs and bottles were enough to create the ambience of a seamen's café in a harbour.

As a director, Copeau was renowned both for his fidelity to text and for his ability to train and develop actors. He employed an 'organic' approach, aiming to discern what the written text demanded of the actor. He came to improvisation in an interesting way. Copeau believed in ensemble acting. He believed deeply in truth on the stage. But he also believed in liberating the physical and vocal creativity of the actor. Acting in Paris in 1920 was still dominated by two highly contrasted schools: broadly, the classical (exemplified by the Comédie Française) and the naturalistic (Antoine's Théâtre Libre). The 'classicists' over-elaborated the text, using it as a vehicle for displays of virtuosity. The 'naturalists' stripped away the beauty of the text, 'deflating' it (in Saint-Denis's terms) and losing touch with the actor's essential theatricality.

So this great lover of the text resolved, for a time, to take away the text from his actors – to withhold it from them – in order to force them to rediscover the essentials of the craft of acting. He had no real idea, at first, of how to achieve his aims. It is possible that he was as 'thrown' by the withdrawal of the script as his students. But he had intuition and remarkable teaching skills (complemented by those of Suzanne Bing, his best actress), and he was a great risk-taker. He knew where the work should start; that was enough:

> Therefore in his teaching Copeau temporarily withdrew the use of texts and made the study of the expressiveness of the body – Improvisation – his point of departure. He led all the work in an empiric fashion, guided by experience, observation and experiment. With the support of his collaborators in various fields, he invented exercises with many progressions and developments.   (Saint-Denis 1982: 32)

Copeau and Bing developed a hierarchy running from immobility and silence through movement to sound and finally to words and text (Felner 1985: 38). This underpinned much of his work, particularly with mask, which Copeau regarded as of great importance:

> The departure point of expressivity: the state of rest, of calm, of relaxation, of silence, or of simplicity ... this affects spoken interpretation as well as playing an action ... An actor must know how to be silent,

> to listen, to respond, to stay still, to begin an action, to develop it,
> and to return to silence and immobility.   (Copeau 1955: 47–53)

This is the first expression of the central concept of *neutrality*, to which we shall return in Parts 2 and 3. This work on neutrality included what Bing called 'pre-formation of the expressive idea', a phrase which suggests strong parallels with the later work of Eugenio Barba on 'pre-expressivity'.

The scenic innovations represent one aspect of Copeau's genius. The other was his ability to teach actors. Many of his early collaborators later went on to become teachers of drama in their own right, especially Suzanne Bing, Charles Dullin, Louis Jouvet and, of course, Michel Saint-Denis. Their influence upon drama, in France and beyond, is incalculable. Suzanne Bing taught drama games, animal mimicry, mask work and mime. (She taught Etienne Decroux, who later taught Marcel Marceau.) Dullin founded L'Atelier, where Decroux also taught. Among their pupils were Jean-Louis Barrault and, briefly, Antonin Artaud. Both Jean Dasté and Barrault contributed to the teaching of Jacques Lecoq. Jouvet, Copeau's greatest actor in the early days, founded a company at the Théâtre des Champs-Elysées and later became a professor at the Paris Conservatoire, as well as a resident director of the Comédie Française. Michel Saint-Denis was responsible for founding no fewer than five major drama schools, two in London, the others in Strasbourg, New York and Montreal: Jerzy Grotowski referred to Saint-Denis as his 'spiritual father'.

Already in 1913, Copeau had dreamed of a new type of theatre school alongside the Vieux-Colombier theatre. He felt that actors were 'the enemy of the theatre'. More precisely, the enemy was *cabotinage* – we might translate it as 'ham' but it also implies a kind of clinging to habits of thought and action. The *cabotin* is fundamentally uncomfortable on the stage: he looks for things to do, for 'business' to hide behind (Rudlin 1986: 45).[8]

Jacques Lecoq – a spiritual descendant of Copeau – taught clowning at his Paris school. The centre of this work is learning how to be at home on the stage – even when the clown has nothing to fall back on except himself, his audience and what can be created between them in the moment of performance. Sending the clown out to amuse an audience, armed with absolutely nothing (no 'gags', no jokes, no script, perhaps not even speech) is a way of 'de-cabotinising' the student actor.

By 1916, Copeau had sketched out the prospectus of his ideal training establishment, and the school itself opened its doors in 1921. The prospectus is worth describing.

1. *Rhythmic gymnastics.* Based on the eurhythmics of Jaques-Dalcroze. (Later Copeau revised his opinion of this type of work.)
2. *Gymnastic technique.* Breathing exercises, sport, fencing, athletics. The aim was total possession by the actor of his physical resources. Copeau based much of this work on Georges Hébert's *L'Education Physique de l'entrainement complet par la méthode naturelle* – a series of books that revolutionised the French system of physical education. Copeau used Hébert's methods as ways of developing the *play instinct* through physical ability and instinctive action (see also, on Lecoq, Chapter 3, pp. 68–76 below).
3. *Acrobatics and feats of dexterity.* To give the actor suppleness as well as strength. Ideally taught by a clown, and of great use in comedy and farce work. (Copeau was impressed by circus clowns; he invited the Fratellini Brothers to teach at the school.)
4. *Dance.*
5. *Singing.*
6. *Musical training.* The actors were to be taught at least the basic skills of playing various instruments.
7. *General instruction.* For two hours a day, the children of the school (for Copeau believed that the future would lie with those brought up under this method rather than those retrained in it) would have academic studies. The adults would develop their cultural awareness through seminars and by conversation with artists and writers.
8. *Games.* Copeau and Suzanne Bing were perhaps the first drama teachers to recognise the value of *games* work (discussed further in Part 2). They recognised that children learn through play, and that the responses of play are natural and authentic. Copeau speaks here not of a system but of an 'experiential education'. He writes, 'Somewhere along the line of improvised play, playful improvisation, improvised drama, real drama, new and fresh, will appear before us. And these children, whose teachers we think we are, will, without doubt, be ours one day.'
9. *Reading out loud.* Copeau was a brilliant reader. He felt it was vital to inculcate in his students the ability to respond to a text immediately and fully; to be able to vocalise a text at sight required quickness and flexibility of mind as well as voice.
10. *Recital of poetry.*
11. *Study of the repertoire* (which, of course, meant mainly the French classical repertoire).
12. *Improvisation* (see below).

To this list Copeau added mask and mime work and (after a discussion with Craig) study of the technical crafts of the theatre. The Vieux-Colombier School operated from 1921 to 1924. Much of what is envisaged in this prospectus could not immediately be realised, but there was enough success eventually to move Copeau to close the theatre in order to concentrate on the laboratory work of training.

The prospectus of the second year, as taught by Copeau and Bing (and with movement directed by one Lt Georges Hébert himself), lays out the whole programme – not just for the Vieux-Colombier actors but in embryo the entirety of subsequent improvisation and impro-based training.

> Dramatic training ... cultivation of spontaneity and invention in the adolescent. Storytelling, games to sharpen the mind, improvisation, impromptu dialogue, mimicry, mask work. ... (Rudlin and Paul 1990: 43)

On improvisation, Copeau wrote in the same 1916 prospectus:

> Improvisation is an art that has to be learned ... The art of improvising is not just a gift. It is acquired and perfected by study ... And that is why, not just content to have recourse to improvisation as an exercise towards the renovation of classical comedy, we will push the experiment further and try to give re-birth to a genre: the New Improvised Comedy, with modern characters and modern subjects.   (Rudlin 1986: 44)

What Copeau envisaged in *la comédie nouvelle* was a twentieth-century revitalisation of the energy of *commedia dell'arte*. He understood that simply to re-create *commedia* was of no use: the masks, situations, *lazzi* of the Italian comedy belonged inextricably to their own time. Academic reconstruction was of use only as an aid to the generation of a New Improvised Comedy (as Rudlin translates it) – a new form for the present.

Copeau conceived of a company entirely devoted to such work. Each actor would develop and play one specific role, just as the performers of *commedia* had. At first, Copeau himself would be the wellspring of the work, providing scenarios and training. But, gradually, the new characters – the new masks – would become independent of him:

> Choose from the company the six or eight actors most appropriate to such an enterprise, the ones with the most go in them, the most self-confident, and the best assorted ensemble – who would henceforth

dedicate themselves almost entirely to improvisation. A genuine brotherhood: the *farceurs* of the Vieux-Colombier. Each actor would light upon a single character from this new *commedia*. He would make it his own property. He would feed it. Fatten it from the substance of his own being, identify with it, think of it at all times, live with it, giving things to it, not only from his own personality, external mannerisms and physical peculiarities, but also from his own ways of feeling, of thinking, his temperament, his outlook, his experience, letting it profit from his reading, as well as growing and changing with him.   (cited in Rudlin 1986: 96)[9]

The attempts to put this dream of a twentieth-century *commedia* into practice were, unfortunately, beset by apparently insuperable difficulties.[10] Where could he find such a troupe, willing to make the act of dedication he envisaged? What sort of character types would so vividly encapsulate the preoccupations of the twentieth century as Arlecchino, Pantalone and Pulcinella had those of the sixteenth? What should the scenarios be about? Copeau didn't know – but he was willing to find out.

There were willing actors, too, among them Jean Dasté, Aman Maistre, Suzanne Bing, Jean Villard, Léon Chancerel, Auguste Boverio, Copeau's children Pascal and Marie-Hélène and his nephew Michel Saint-Denis. In 1924 Copeau relinquished the Vieux-Colombier and withdrew with a dedicated group of actors (affectionately nicknamed *les Copiaus*, or 'Little Copeaus', by the locals) to Pernand-Vergelesses, a village near Beaune in Burgundy. There, for the next five years, he based his work in an old *cuverie*, or store for wine vats.

The work was developmental, ranging from the austere discipline of *Noh* drama, singing, dance, mime and acrobatics to comic improvisation, *commedia* work and, later, character improvisations with and without masks. Shows were devised for the region (e.g., a play based on the labour of the vineyard worker, performed before 2,000 such workers in the village of Nuits Saint-Georges after the wine harvest).

Our comic improvisations were instantly accepted by this audience. Because there was never any barrier between players and audiences, the spectators sensed how much they influenced the actors, how they could affect their performances, indeed, how at times they could lift the actors to a rare degree of exhilaration.   (Rudlin 1986: 26)

Throughout his work, from 1916 onwards, Copeau had been making notes towards the creation of *la comédie nouvelle*. Now it was possible to attempt it with the Copiaus. They worked in 1925 on classical *commedia*: Jean Dasté (Copeau's son-in-law) played Arlequin; Copeau himself played Pantalon; Jean Villard worked on Pedrolino; and Léon Chancerel worked on the Doctor. The group did evolve new, personalised characters, too. Chancerel developed the Mask of 'Sebastien Congré' ('archivist, timid paleographer, molly-coddled and ridiculous'). Jean Dasté created 'César' ('an old "quacker" with a keen nose for business'). Suzanne Bing created 'Célestine'. Boverio invented 'Lord Quick' (a 'thoughtless, fat old man, who delighted in recalling his entire past life, both literary and worldly'). Michel Saint-Denis created the Masks of 'Jean Bourgignon' and 'Oscar Knie': he made the latter mask himself, by hand, and found it to be 'a violent character who made great demands on him and became a parasite on his own personality' and who both hated and was inseparable from 'César' (Rudlin 1986: 102–3; Rudlin and Paul 1990: 232).

The Burgundy period with *les Copiaus* came to an end in 1929. The ensemble had reached a point where, in Copeau's opinion, it needed to return to the mainstream of French theatre – though without him.

> We could act, dance, sing, improvise in all kinds of ways, and, when necessary, write our own dialogue ... [We had] become an ensemble with a fertile imagination and the technical means to represent in our work many aspects and facets of the world. What we were lacking was, no doubt, a few more actors and, above all, a writer.   (Saint-Denis 1982: 26–7)

Copeau's closure of the Vieux-Colombier was itself a kind of 'instinctive' rather than rational act, in order to 'start ... over again, [to] learn what we did not know, experiment with what we vaguely felt' (Rudlin and Paul 1990: 168–70).[11] The work at Pernand-Vergelesses served to bring the actors 'back to a naïve state ... their natural position before a world of possibilities where nothing is corrupted by habits of imitation, nor perverted by an acquired virtuosity' (*ibid.*).

Copeau encouraged the group to return to Paris. Michel Saint-Denis reformed *les Copiaus* into the Compagnie des Quinze and the work moved on to a different level. Devoted to physical expression still, the Compagnie des Quinze nonetheless wanted to work with a writer. Basing themselves again at the rebuilt Vieux-Colombier, they continued to improvise,[12] but now in collaboration with the young André Obey. Together, they continued to evolve theatrical languages (including *grummelotage*, a mixture of real words, mime and silent improvisation derived from the study of *commedia* and popular theatre[13]). It was a creative tension between text and improvisation, with the constant danger that one would overwhelm the other. Plays such as *Noah*, *Le Viol de Lucrèce* and *Don Juan*, however, showed that the collaboration could succeed brilliantly.

From 1931 to 1934 the Compagnie des Quinze took Europe by storm. In Paris, though, the Vieux-Colombier was still regarded as an 'art house', distrusted by the traditionalists and (perhaps) not radical enough for the modernists. The company tried to repeat Copeau's experiments by retreating again to the country – this time to Aix-en-Provence. Within six months the company had disbanded, defeated by financial pressures and the strain of communal living.

But Copeau's vision of *le tréteau nu* had been realised. The experiments of the years 1920–34 had demonstrated that a way back to the simple power of the medieval trestle-stage was possible and that community drama based on improvisation could succeed where the sophisticated classics had failed, and had proved beyond doubt that improvisation itself could form the basis of a system of training that could reinvigorate and revitalise the whole craft of acting.

Some of the principal elements of Copeau's theory and practice can be summarised as follows:

1. Much of Copeau's work was directed not immediately towards performance, but towards *readiness for performance*, as an underlying educational and developmental goal for himself and his actors.
2. The company learned (with lots of ups and downs) about working for each other, functioning – even living – as a group (with, ideally, no emphasis on 'stars'). Copeau himself learned as he went along; his directing included large elements of responsiveness, intuition and adaptation. The principles of change and involvement in a process were more important than the need to conclude or arrive at a finished product.
3. Improvisation operated within the context of games, mime and mask work, *commedia* and so on, and could develop along with any of these towards new forms of theatre. Copeau started by using text-related improvisations but later developed a freer and more eclectic use of text in the search for *comédie nouvelle*.
4. Copeau's subsequent concern with theatre-as-communion can be seen retrospectively to illuminate much of his career, from sincere and passionate critic of sterility, via the function of *patron* of a group enterprise culminating in community-rooted performance, to identification of theatre as a shared creative act with para-theatrical significance for individual and society.

It is no exaggeration to say that practically every major initiative in modern theatre can trace its lineage back to Copeau in some degree. His influence is subtle and often very tenuous, but it persists. He worked at some time with virtually every major figure in the French theatre of his day, and his students and collaborators have spread that influence to succeeding generations. The Theatre Guild and the Group Theatre in America acknowledged his influence. Most of the major British actors of the late 1930s onwards worked with Saint-Denis. And, most important, Copeau and Bing's initiatives still permeate (often without conscious realisation) drama training at all levels (see 'Genealogy of Modern French Mime', in Felner 1985: 49).

Improvisation and 'traditional' theatre training

The decision of the Compagnie des Quinze to work with a writer seems in retrospect an almost symbolic act, representing a shift of emphasis – a movement from improvised back towards scripted drama. The collaboration of Saint-Denis's troupe with André Obey seems to symbolise a particular reaccommodation of the script-based play.

Of course, neither Copeau nor Saint-Denis had any desire to abandon the written play permanently. What was important about Copeau's experimentation was the creation of a new type of *performer*, out of which a new type of drama might one day emerge. It was a way of renovating the classical drama from within, rather than an abandonment of it. As Rudlin puts it, 'Actors of *parts* are sustained by a dramatic illusion of which they are part; performers of *plays* by a nothing-to-hide, open contact with the spectator' (Rudlin 1986: 60).

The relationship with Obey was a step towards that new openness, a true collaboration of creative performers with a sensitive and gifted playwright rather than a resubmission of the actors to the text. The collaboration showed that there was, indeed, a new way to create plays.

But the return to the Vieux-Colombier with Obey marks the reincorporation of improvisation into traditional forms of play-making. Improvisation becomes just one of the many means of theatre, valuable certainly as a process which develops the actor, and which the actor and writer may use explicitly to develop the final play, but no longer the primary method of creativity.

And that is what, basically, improvisation has remained for 'mainstream' theatre, under the pressures of time, the constraints of economic resources and the fear of failure. In the UK, neither the National Theatre (which has offered workshops on improvisation) nor the Royal Shakespeare Company, nor any of the major subsidised repertory theatres has ever mounted a fully improvised show. (Plays created by improvisatory means are a different matter.)[14]

One cause may lie in the *training* of actors and directors, who have been taught to regard improvisation only for its developmental value in actor training and for its occasional usefulness in the rehearsal situation. Virtually all modern drama schools, in varying degrees, use improvisation (just as they might use games, mask work, mime and so on) in the training of actors. In this they follow, consciously or unconsciously, the precepts of Michel Saint-Denis. After the collapse of the Compagnie des Quinze, he was responsible for the development of no fewer than five major drama schools. He set up the London Theatre Studio in Islington (1935–9), his experiences at the LTS and later in teaching or planning for the Old Vic Theatre School (1947–52), L'École Supérieure d'Art Dramatique, Strasbourg (1952–7), the National Theatre School of Canada (1960) and the Julliard School Drama Division, New York (from 1968) all laid down what we might call the 'invisible curriculum' of most drama schools in Europe and America with regard to improvisation.

Saint-Denis's principle for training was to 'stimulate the initiative and invention of the future interpreter by making him pass through the experiences of the actor-creator' (Saint-Denis 1982: 81–2). The search would be for the performer who could more successfully interpret a text than evolve one; and many of the students were, indeed, professional actors, already fixed in their habits of work and thought.

Accordingly, the training programme was primarily based on improvisation work. But now Saint-Denis added 'a carefully selected group of Stanislavsky's exercises: those which would not lead our actors to an excessively subjective concentration which might prove detrimental in acting a classical role' (1982: 48).

His own *ideal* four-year curriculum – which he describes in *Training for the Theatre* (88–99) – is very clear on the relationship of improvised work to formal rehearsal of plays. The first year is largely improvisatory, with no public performances. This is the 'Discovery Year'. Mask work, observation, transformation and solo and group non-verbal improvisation are stressed. But in the last term of the second year (called 'Transformation Year') we find that the Improvisation work is to cease to give more time to the Interpretational work – specifically a Chekhov play. In the third ('Interpretation') year, Improvisation work is suspended altogether (except for two weeks in the middle term on preparatory exercises in the Restoration style). He splits his curriculum throughout into two groupings: 'Technique' and 'Imagination'. Both Improvisation and Interpretation come under 'Imagination'. By the middle of the course, then, the imagination is entirely given over to interpretative rather than purely creative work. Improvisation has become the servant of interpretation. In the final ('Performing') year there is 'no improvisation work, unless something special is needed for the rehearsal projects for the repertory season or unless there is opportunity to offer a unique master class' (98).

The drama school curriculum is clearly designed to 'produce' actors and, in their final year, present them to potential employers in a series of public 'coming out ceremonies' (the 'showcase'). Improvisation in this context is one of the tools by which 'an actor prepares' for the job.

The two main uses of improvisation in traditional drama (including drama training), then, are (*a*) to do with the exploration of a character's inner nature and the accommodation of that nature to the actor's own, and (*b*) the further exploration of character within situations which extend beyond those contained within the play.

The director may set up an improvised situation in order to let the actors discover what they themselves, as human beings, might do or feel in such circumstances. The actors gain insight into the circumstances with which the characters in the play have to contend, and their responses become more authentic as a result. The actors can draw upon their own vicarious experiences at difficult moments in the performance.

Or it may be that an actor will use 'improvs' to explore his assumed character in situations outside those explored in the play. An actor may ask, 'What is my character like when he is alone? when he is with his friends? his boss?' Out of this kind of work the actor may build up a wealth of small, circumstantial details – how his or her character walks, talks, drinks and handles props. In rehearsal this work is developed and crystallized through the use of the well-known 'hot-seating' technique, where a character is interrogated by other cast members and has to stay in role while replying. In performance these details will inform his or her playing and lend it credibility. It will be nearer the truth since it depends upon experiential discovery via the body of the actor rather than upon imposed externals.

In developing the 'reality of character', Stanislavsky was concerned with 'inner truth': the performer needs to develop emotional and physical resources which clearly are his or her own, even though they are used to invite empathy with (or in Brecht's view, to signal) some specific or typical behaviour patterns which constitute a fictitious character to be 'read' by the spectators. Saint-Denis paraphrases it thus: 'It is only from within himself [i.e. the actor], and through physical actions inspired by or drawn from his own inner resources, that the character can be realised' (1982: 82).

This realisation has to be coherent, not a matter of bits and pieces stuck on (a collage of a style of walking, a tone of voice, an accent); even Brecht, who was not concerned with all-round characterisation, demanded a complete *Gestus*. Saint-Denis sees it emerging from an alternation between this 'subjective' work on oneself and a more 'objective' understanding, via the text, of the role. Balance between 'reality of self' and 'reality of role' is an important basis *either* for mainstream acting or for more exploratory and ultimately extra-theatrical work. The essentials of improvisation can underpin both strands, and it is only the difference of focus which separates them. Ultimately, theatre is a way of 'knowing ourselves' better, and improvisation energises that process, whatever channel it may take.

Many Conservatoires and Drama Schools now include on their staff a Meisner expert and very possibly a Lecoq expert, in addition to those who teach movement (Laban method, t'ai chi ch'uan) or work on psychokinetic preparation (Feldenkrais, Alexander technique). And audiences – and thus also potential trainees – have become accustomed to performance styles which work more overtly from the body, from rapid and daring interconnectivities and from the (apparently) more visceral and/or spontaneous – though of course these are in most instances the fruit of long rehearsal. These same trainees are likely (in the UK) to have at least some encounter with the work of companies like Frantic Assembly, Théâtre de Complicité, Propeller, Cheek By Jowl and others; they may well have participated in workshops given by members of these ensembles, since all professional theatre now almost inevitably includes – and requires to meet its financial needs – an extensive schools and/or community outreach mission. They are also more likely than in the previous century to have heard of or been able to participate in a site-specific or immersive theatre event like those created by Punchdrunk, offering more direct kinds of personalised experience to audience members. Rather than what we have described above (improvisation as a rehearsal tool for the still largely 'naturalistic' requirements of most paid acting work on stage, film and TV), the flavour of the improvisatory permeates much of this spectrum; it will inevitably continue to shape developments in training too.

In the USA, the main line of development of character work passes through Lee Strasberg, whose work we shall examine in detail below. In the UK, there is, however, one area in which improvisation and what we are here calling the 'traditional' theatre have formed a liaison in the field of play-creation. It brings together the concern for detailed and truthful characterisation as the basis of acting, the idea of the actor as part-creator of the work, the methods of improvisation and the traditional crafts of the playwright. The focus of this synthesis is the playwright and director Mike Leigh.

Improvisation and playwrighting: Mike Leigh

The son of a doctor, Mike Leigh was born in Salford in 1943 (Clements 1983: 7) and grew up 'as a middle-class kid in a working-class area', which gave him an ambivalent but deeply perceptive view of class relationships. He was also, as his play *Two Thousand Years* (2005) makes clear, born into a Jewish family, which stimulated questioning about identity. 'All my films and plays have in one way or another dealt with identity ... Who is the real you, and who the persona defined by other people's expectations or preconceptions?' (Leigh 2006: v–vii). The negotiation of identity and role within ethnic, religious, national, historical, linguistic or regional contexts is thus fundamental to his interrogation of what makes up a 'character'.

Leigh's training at RADA included virtually no improvisation work. Improvisation was simply not a part of actor training at that time, even though innovative theatre directors such as Joan Littlewood and film directors such as John Cassavetes were using it quite commonly.

> Two aspects of [Leigh's RADA] training did make an impression ... He became fascinated by some exercises with the director James Roose-Evans, who employed a method derived from a visit to Lee Strasberg's Actors Studio in New York. This was to do with expressing the inexpressible through the movement, and touching, of hands (Leigh has subsequently used this technique to allow actors to progress beyond the parameters of naturalistic improvisations). And he was touched, too, by one particular improvisation conducted by Peter Barkworth in which two talented students – Sheila Gish and Ian McShane – were separately briefed with incompatible information and then thrown together.   (Coveney 1996: 61)

With hindsight, one can see the indirect influence of Strasberg and, even more importantly, the principle of separation: the isolating of the actors before allowing their fully developed *characters* to meet on stage or screen.

Leaving RADA in 1962, Leigh worked as an assistant stage manager and bit-part actor in films before enrolling in the pre-diploma course at Camberwell Art School. Sitting one day in the life-drawing class:

> I suddenly realised what it had been that we hadn't experienced as actors. In the life drawing class there were a dozen or fifteen kids and everyone was making a serious and original investigation into a

real experience. Nobody was doing a second-hand rendering of something. I began to think that acting could be creative in the same way
that any artist is.   (Clements 1983: 10)

Leigh was impressed by Beckett's ability to make his audience share his
characters' time, to concentrate on the moment of performance itself, and
by Peter Hall's work at the Royal Shakespeare Company, which allowed
Brechtian values to creep into the English theatre. Hall also brought Saint-
Denis and Peter Brook into the RSC, and Leigh saw much of the work
being produced by them. Most interesting for us is Leigh's response to
Peter Brook's 1964 RSC production of Weiss's *Marat-Sade*, in which the
actors were asked to base their characterisations upon actual case histories
of mental patients. When some of the rehearsals were broadcast on BBC
Television's *Omnibus* arts programme, Leigh thought, 'If they can do all
that, why don't they take it a stage further and make up a play?' (Clements
1983: 11).

So Leigh himself began to make up plays with young amateurs. The first
of these, *The Box Play*, taught him a number of valuable lessons. Although
the play was highly successful – it was fun to see and to perform, and its
subject matter (a family of six living in a cage-like box in the middle of the
stage) worked well as 'cartoon' – Leigh wasn't satisfied with it. He regarded
it as 'force-bred' – the inexperienced actors had to be coached throughout
the improvisations. He created parts for everyone who came to the rehearsals, and he describes the methods as being fairly arbitrary ('you're the dog;
you're the dad; you're the mum – improvise'). Leigh felt that the work in
this play and in subsequent workshops was too shallow.

His second play, *My Parents have Gone to Carlisle* (1966), established some
of the basic principles which have guided his work ever since. The improvisations were kept private (to avoid the actors trying to 'perform' before
they were ready). The play started from an event (a teenage party) to which
the players could relate personally. The actors were encouraged to build
up biographical details about their characters, and improvisation extended
beyond the immediate situation of the play to look at those characters
in other contexts. He drew the final play out of the 'real events' of the
improvisations.

There remained the problem of the play's final organisation. The
improvisations were realistic and truthful, but not very communicative.
The natural tendency of such sensitive exploratory work without an audience is to be 'introspective and inaudible'. There is nothing wrong in this:
the work is for the *actors*' benefit. But the transition from private to public
had to be made, and Leigh felt the need to impose his own sense of order.

He shaped the final play out of the actors' work, but in order to do so he often had to work against the 'naturalism' of the rehearsals.

In 1967, Leigh joined the RSC as an assistant director. This allowed him to work with professional actors on *NENAA*. Here he realised that

> if an improvised play was really to be a totally organic entity, genuinely evolved from characters and relationships, then I had been wrong in starting rehearsals ... by stating plot or theme and then 'filling it in' ... I saw that we must start off with a collection of totally unrelated characters (each one the specific creation of its actor) and then go through a process in which I must cause them to meet each other and build a network of real relationships; the play would have to be drawn from the results.   (cited in Clements 1983: 15)

In some ways this type of work can be related to Copeau's experiments in the 1920s (though it merely echoes them unconsciously). The idea of a play evolving out of characters created by the actors is not so far from the ideals of *la comédie nouvelle*; though instead of *masks*, which the actors would develop throughout their lives, we have naturalistic *characters* evolved for the duration of a play's work period.

Leigh began rehearsals for *NENAA* by providing a series of receptacles, objects such as 'boxes, suitcases, egg-cups, a bucket, a coffin', and getting the actors to build characters suggested by one of the objects. This is analogous to mask work, responding to an object which gives the actor a starting point for improvisation. But, in Leigh's 'pre-rehearsals', where the actors work singly (and privately) with the director, the object (as in Stanislavsky's work) is to create the 'inner lives' as well as the external physical mannerisms of the characters. The job was then to structure situations in which the characters thus created could meet and interact. Finally, an overall situation had to evolve which would contain the action that developed between the characters. Between 1965 and 1969 Leigh created nine plays based on improvisational work. Until then (says Paul Clements in his book on Leigh, *The Improvised Play*) he still believed he would become a solitary playwright. It took him a long time fully to understand that working via improvisation was a way of being a dramatist.

Mike Leigh *is* a playwright; all the more so, perhaps, in that his plays are wrought rather than written. He is a writer of plays in the other sense too; though his plays are written *on* and *with* his actors. The early choices are all his. He asks his actors to make lists of potential characters, but they may never know what has attracted him, what possibilities he has glimpsed for future developments or why he has chosen one character for them to work on rather than another. The process of keeping the actors apart from one another until the characters have been formed is directly analogous to the mental compartmentalisation of the more traditional writer of scripts. One level of the play is very privately developed and, while the actors are never puppets, they never really have access to that level of the composition. When they are brought together and begin to interact, many of the fundamental choices will already have been made. The possibilities will have been narrowed down. The future pattern will not be predictable but its shapes will have been conditioned by Leigh.

The plays themselves are 'traditional' in two senses: first, in that Leigh has said he is not interested in 'happenings' and they are therefore not improvised in performance (although one knows that the depth of characterisation is such that, if anything accidental were to happen during performance, the actors would be able to accept and incorporate it *in character*); second, in that the result is always a tightly crafted and (usually, apparently) naturalistic drama.

In Leigh's best-known early works (the play and film *Bleak Moments* (1970–1), the film *High Hopes* (1989), and his published plays *Abigail's Party* (1977) and *Goose Pimples* (1981)) this is quite obvious – as the 'finished' and 'published' versions of the original performances make clear. The publication of the playscripts of these works, which were 'evolved from scratch entirely by rehearsal through improvisation' (Leigh 1983: 7), reaffirms Leigh's status as a 'traditional' playwright. The plays can be (and are) performed by actors other than their original creators without recourse to further improvisation.

At the time of Leigh's breakthrough success with *Abigail's Party* at Hampstead, the critic Sheridan Morley discussed Leigh's early career in more detail. By the time of *Abigail*, he points out, Leigh had already been responsible for over thirty plays in the previous ten years, many of them devised and improvised. The method had been established carefully, and by working with many actors in many types of theatre. Leigh himself was keen to stress that *Abigail's Party* had a socially critical *raison d'être*, and his conception of improvisation in the making of these works is rigorous and demanding in the extreme:

> [A]s soon as you start talking about improvisation people expect anarchy: in fact our objectives … the things we wanted to say about these people and their social habits and surroundings, remained rock solid from the very first: only the surface text is flexible.   (Morley 1977)

Mike Leigh's influence has spread: actors and actresses he has worked with have gone on to direct in their own right (Les Blair was in *The Box Play* right at the beginning; Mike Bradwell, the founder of Hull Truck, played Norman in *Bleak Moments*; Sheila Kelley was in *Babies Grow Old*, *Nuts in May*, *Ecstasy* and *Home Sweet Home*). Sara Pia Anderson and Phil Young are other deviser-directors who have essayed play creation in the improvised style after Leigh.

Paul Clements, however, makes the very telling point that it was not until after Phil Young's *Crystal Clear* in 1982 (televised by the BBC in 1988) that any major drama critic explicitly acknowledged that

> improvised plays are just as much plays as any other kind ... Indeed the tendency with improvised plays appears to be towards a much higher degree of accuracy in characterisation than with the average pre-conceived authorial script.   (Clements 1983: 57)

And the general critical tendency is still to regard the improvised play as somehow too 'loose', too 'unfinished', perhaps as not 'a real play' at all. Leigh's works are certainly 'real plays'. They are created experientially. They are based upon observation. They are authentic, carefully crafted and detailed examinations of character and social environment. They are drawn from life – 'serious and original investigations into real experiences', the crucial discovery of the Camberwell art classes applied to the theatre – but they are also shaped and purposive events, poetic and symbolic statements about the ways in which human beings live and relate and fail. Leigh and those who have collaborated with or learned from him have shown that improvisation need no longer be just a rehearsal device of the drama schools. With Leigh's plays (and equally his films, which are created by the same rigorous methods), improvisation has become the source and means of dramatic creation itself.

It was clear, even as we prepared the first edition of this book in 1990, that Mike Leigh had virtually ceased to work in the theatre. He had gradually been drawn into the ambit first of the television drama and then the pure film, although he continued to use his remarkable improvisatory techniques in much the same way in the new media.[15]

Improvisation in cinema is a study beyond our present scope (perhaps needing a companion volume!), but brief reference should be made here to those genres and pioneers whose influence can be detected in Leigh's cinematic work. Chief among these are the 1950s British 'Free Cinema' experiments – with hand-held cameras, improvisatory acting and documentary social-realist subject matter – of directors such as Lindsay Anderson, Karel Reisz, Tony Richardson and Lorenza Mazzetti,[16] which prefigured the British 'New Wave' films of the 1960s; and the American movies of John Cassavetes, perhaps problematically described as 'improvised' films.

Cassavetes (1929–89), a New York Method-trained actor, screenwriter and director, working chiefly with his wife Gena Rowlands, Peter Falk and Ben Gazarra, made and appeared in many films, over some of which he had full artistic control. These films are legendary for being made 'outside the system', often on 16 mm stock and on minimal budgets. In fact, as Ray Carney's detailed critical studies of Cassavetes's work have shown (Carney 1994, *passim*, 2001, *passim*) the improvised elements in them are quite circumscribed. It can be quite hard for a low-budget film to allow much improvisation, because it wastes film stock and costs time, and time is always money. The claim blazoned across the screen at the end of *Shadows* (1959) – that 'the film you have just seen was an improvisation' – should perhaps be taken under advisement.

In 1960, the film played to sell-out audiences in New York, Venice and London, where the Beat generation hailed it as a major breakthrough in film technique, and where its press material certainly fostered the idea that it was entirely improvised, and 'grabbed' from the New York streets rather than shot on a sound stage. Carney suggests that a largely improvised film (now known to scholars as the *Ur-Shadows*) was first made in 1957–8, previewed, largely rewritten (by Cassavetes and uncredited screenwriter Robert Alan Aurthur (1922–78)) and then re-shot: only about a third of the original film remained. Carney discovered a worn 16 mm print of the *Ur-Shadows* (and remains in dispute with Gena Rowlands over its authenticity and validity). In later films like *Faces* (1968), *Minnie and Moskowitz* (1971), *A Woman under the Influence* (1974, which Cassavetes originally wrote as a play, only filming it when Gena Rowlands persuaded him it would be too emotionally harrowing a central role to play night after night), *The Killing of a Chinese Bookie* (1976) and especially *Opening Night* (1977), the actors certainly improvised in rehearsal; but Cassavetes then scripted the films very tightly before shooting. In reality, Cassavetes himself – as screenwriter – was the principal improviser (which in no way detracts from his films' impact or importance). The result is an always very coherent and carefully plotted piece of work.

Cassavetes's own understanding of improvisation is filtered through the ideas of jazz. His various takes are riffs on the scene he is performing. This is wholly consistent with the Beat ethos: Allan Ginsberg claims that 'the entire Beat literary movement was based ... on Kerouac's estimate of be-bop as an improvised, spontaneous form' (cit. Sargeant 2008: 10).

All film actors improvise to some extent. Takes can never be identical. Directors often encourage stars to explore the role on camera; some film actors seem incapable of doing anything else. Directors like Martin Scorsese (who championed Cassavetes's work) and Mike Nichols (who began as an improviser himself, with Elaine May and Compass) are very likely to create improvisatory moments in shooting: stories like Nichols having Alan Arkin surreptitiously 'goosed' below the camera in order to film a shocked reaction on the actor's face in *Catch 22* abound. This is not the same as improvising a whole movie in the way that Leigh does. For this reason, critics like Amy Taubin rightly regard Leigh's 'lengthy, improvisory rehearsal methods' as 'more radical' than John Cassavetes's or Scorsese's. (Taubin 1993: 70; cit Watson 2004: 29).

Leigh's work in cinema, then, has a prehistory, of which he is fully aware. *Shadows* was one of the first films he saw on coming to London (Coveney 1996: 60); Anderson and Reisz were still major figures in the theatrical and cinematic scene during his formative years (and took an interest in his work). And Leigh, in turn, has an influence on successive generations of film-makers. His approach, forged in the theatre, has transferred fairly directly to the screen. Improvisation is still the main method used, and it is thoroughgoing. The films are worked out with, and 'written' through, the collaboration of a company of dedicated actors, who undergo a lengthy series of isolated exercises with Leigh before meeting and colliding for the camera. David Thewlis (who created 'Johnny' in Leigh's *Naked* 1993) explains that:

> When you work with Mike, you take a source character, who is someone you know and you build the character on top of a real person. It's not an impersonation but it's inspired by a real person. Of course, for any character you draw on all sorts of people. In Johnny's behavior there's bits of my friends, my brother, my wife, an old girlfriend. At the same time Mike is tweaking the character, pushing me in certain directions and pulling me back, influenced, presumably, by people he knows. And that's how Mike directs in terms of creating a character who is neither me nor the original person but someone entirely new.   (quoted in Watson 2004: 29)

Surprisingly 'one of Leigh's biggest worries is that audiences think the actors aren't acting at all' (Interview with Peter Brunette 1991, in Movshovitz 2000: 31). Leigh (speaking at the time of the film *Life is Sweet*) responded to this concern very carefully and with great determination to be understood:

> These people aren't playing themselves, they're creating characterizations. I cast in a very empirical, instinctive way, partly because I work

with people who are known to be highly versatile character actors. Gradually we begin to bring into existence, really, the whole world of the characters . ... I really don't know where it's going. My job is to be inventing it, and as I do so, I begin to discover, to create the premise for the film.

But all of this is only preparatory, and the real meat and bones of the thing is what happens when the shoot starts. I write a structure that is very brief, like three pages. ... And each scene is built and rehearsed on location and built up through lots of discussion and very thorough rehearsal until it's ready and then it gets shot.   (*ibid.*)

So how, he was asked, if there is no pre-existing script (as there certainly was with Cassavetes) is the piece given shape? Does he at least know where the story is heading?

Yes and no – this is really the most elusive thing of all. Yes, certainly, a substantial part of it, but I also keep my options open, and, invariably, I really don't know how it's going to end. This is normal in dramatic writing: Anybody can do the end; it's getting the beginning and the middle set up that's the problem. If you've got everything else going in the right direction, then the end is there like a harvest to be plundered.   (*ibid.*, 31–2)

But the fact of the actors' atomisation remains crucial to the process. The actors

don't actually know what I'm up to. In fact, the actors never know anything more about the whole thing than their characters do. ... That's important, because it means that you really preserve those tensions and get the reality of the thing.   (*ibid.*, 32)

Reality, as Peter Brunette points out, is central to Leigh's film work (and Watson, too, subtitles his book on Leigh, 'A Sense of the Real'). That three-dimensionality, the sense that the surface of the play or film is penetrable, and that we have somehow slipped through it into a world even more real than this one, underpins the work. Garry Watson follows Henry Krips's and Hal Foster's ideas that this penetration marks for an audience – especially those disturbed or made uncomfortable by the traumatic nature of the events relived and experienced – the irruption of the 'Lacanian Real'. That is to say, it creates 'a site of anxiety where the symbolic order [as defined by the psychoanalyst Jacques Lacan – the linguistic, socially created mediation of experience, as opposed to the "imaginary," which is its prior non-linguistic aspect] breaks down' (Watson 2004: 12, and cf. Krips 1999: 37; Foster 1996: 29). This rent in the fabric of the symbolic represents the 'traumatic real' and makes the immediate reception of the work highly problematic. Almost by definition (he argues, following Foster), avant-garde work requires to be viewed more than once: the symbolic order is not prepared for it, and the mind requires time to accommodate to it.

Leigh would perhaps find this too abstract – too 'film studies'. Instead of Lacan's inexpressible 'Real', he proposes a simpler notion of reality: that which surrounds us.

> [W]e should aspire to the condition of documentary. By which I mean that when you shoot documentary, you do not question that the world you're pointing a camera at actually exists in three dimensions and that it would exist whether you filmed it or not. And if we can aspire to that condition with what the actors are doing, so that it really is in three dimensions, and really does go around corners, then the bit that we actually see, the tip of the iceberg, is going to have that solidity to it.   (Interview with Brunette, in Movshovitz 2000: 32)

The arrest of 'Vera' (played by Imelda Staunton) in the 2004 film *Vera Drake* came as a huge shock to the actors playing her family. They knew nothing at that stage of shooting about Vera's occupation as a back-street abortionist, and their shock is registered on camera in precisely that documentary manner. Compare Thomas Vinterberg's application of a similar technique in *Festen* (1998), the first successful Dogme film. Vinterberg had the company improvise on site (not on set, this being Dogme) for some weeks. The guests at Helge's sixtieth birthday had genuinely grown to like their genial host. Once the (single, hand-held) camera was running, though, at the height of the festivities Helge's estranged son, Christian, rose to make a formal speech of congratulation to his father. Instead, he spilled the beans about the incestuous rape that shattered his childhood and caused his sister's suicide. The assembled actors (no less than their characters) greeted the revelation with stunned disbelief, even to the point of trying to carry on eating as if nothing had happened! In both of these scenes, what is revealed beneath the surface of the apparently real is a traumatic deeper reality, and does profoundly disturb. Our identification via the very banality of the representation – its ordinariness and its verisimilitude – leaves us unprepared for the incursion of a real against which we have no prepared defences and with which we, as receivers, now need to improvise.

There is an aspect of Leigh's work we have not discussed. This intense obtrusion of reality into the business of acting may be disturbing or destabilising for the performer as well as the viewer. Once the actors' scenes have been shot (remembering that, unlike plays, films are often performed out of sequence), there may be a necessity to complete the imaginary and often very emotional journey they have been asked to undertake: Leigh understands this need for what Schechner calls 'cool down' and allows for it. David Thewlis describes him spending a day after finishing *Naked* simply doing improvisations with the actress Lesley Sharp so that her character could come to terms with the rejection she had endured in the film (cit. Watson 2004: 29).

It is, therefore, possible to see Leigh's late work (from *Naked* onwards) as a clash of two 'reals': the observable, verifiable reality of the world around us, and the inexpressible Real that it conceals from us, apprehended by asking his actors to undergo a guided, self-revelatory process no less rigorous than Grotowski's.

Leigh has revisited the theatre on a number of occasions in recent years, and to popular and critical acclaim. Two new theatre pieces, *Two Thousand Years* (2005) and *Grief* (2011), were accompanied by a directorial foray which saw him revive *Ecstasy* at Hampstead (also 2011), where it had premiered in 1979, and later at the Duchess Theatre. The plays are now interspersed with the films (*Happy Go Lucky* 2008, *Another Year* 2010, *A Running Jump* 2012 short and *Mr Turner* 2014).

Two Thousand Years, self-described as his 'Jewish play', applies the original method of improvised creativity to the theme of the 'Jewish family' in its broadest sense. It encompasses the familial and domestic world of secular North London jewry, and also explores the generational and political differences within the broader family – issues of religious fundamentalism, the struggles for Israeli independence from British rule and the current divisions over settlers' rights and the treatment of Israel's neighbours are all woven into the play's dense fabric.

All my films and plays have dealt in one way or another with identity. Who are you? What are you? Who is the real you, and who the persona defined by other people's expectations or preconceptions? *Secrets and Lies* was about a woman seeking the truth of her identity; *Vera Drake* told the story of the heroine's hidden life; *Abigail's Party* explored received notions of social behaviour; *Topsy-Turvy* was about reality and artifice; and *Naked* and *High Hopes* were each concerned, in quite different ways, with the conflict between what we are and how we live, with what we believe in.   (Leigh 2006: v)

What better interrogation of identity could there be than the improvisational process, where everything is, and everything remains, provisional until it's ready to encounter the Other? Where every tentative statement about character is open to exploration, revision and confrontation until a credible persona emerges.

2   The Improv Scene (US)

The development of improvisational drama in America is complex and falls quite outside the pattern described so far, which is primarily European. *Applied* improvisation (as opposed to *pure* improvisation undertaken for its own sake) derives ultimately from Europe but has become so thoroughly naturalised as to be distinctively American. There is also a native tradition distinct from anything we have met so far in this study.

Because there is a geographical as well as metaphorical distinction to be made, we can categorise the former, naturalised tradition as the 'New York' school, while the latter, native impro is associated with the 'second city', Chicago.

In what follows, we will trace these variants and the kinds of performance they have given rise to, moving from performer training to new modes of performance which increasingly invite audience involvement and co-creativity.

New York giants

We noted that there was considerable traffic between Europe and New York in the early part of the century – one example being the meeting of Copeau and Bing with Waldo Frank and Margaret Naumburg. The interchange was fruitful, and Copeau's methods later attracted young Americans (among them actress Cornelia Otis Skinner and director Harold Clurman) to train with *les Copiaus* in France.

Michel Saint-Denis (through his influence on the drama school curriculum, especially at the New York Julliard School) added a great deal to American actor training, as he did to that of Europe. But the use of improvisation in American acting predates Saint-Denis, stems more directly from the Russian rather than the French tradition and is inextricably bound up with the development of American written drama. As Clurman put it, 'Copeau's attitude was creative ... but we believed we were on the road to learning a sounder technique for the actor ... the so-called Stanislavsky "system"' (Clurman 1975: 17).

Richard Boleslavsky (born Boleslaw Srzednicki in Poland, 1889, and edu-
cated in Russia) had trained at the Moscow Art Theatre since 1906. Like
Michael Chekhov, he had been a leading member of the First Studio under
Sulerzhitsky, remaining a member of Stanislavsky's company until 1920.
Boleslavsky fled, first to Warsaw, and thence in 1922 to New York, where he
worked as a director for an *émigré* revue company.

In 1923, following the celebrated tour of the MAT to America, there was
enough interest in Stanislavskian acting techniques for Boleslavsky to be
asked to run a Laboratory Theatre based on Russian rehearsal techniques.
He was joined by Maria Ouspenskaya, one of the MAT's actresses who had
chosen to leave the Russian company and remain in New York after the
tour. The new venture was christened the American Laboratory Theatre,
usually known as the Lab.

> There were three aspects of the total training: (1) development of the
> actor's body and voice, which Boleslavsky called the outer means of
> expression; (2) refinement of the inner means of expression which
> enabled the actor to live through – in his imagination – the situations
> conceived by a playwright; and (3) enlargement of the actor's intel-
> lectual and cultural awareness.   (Willis 1964: 113)

The first aspect was provided by specialists in ballet, interpretive dance,
eurhythmics, fencing, mime, voice, speech and make-up; the third by specialist teachers in theatre history, art, music, literature and 'ideas of Western
culture'. Boleslavsky and Ouspenskaya specialised in the second aspect,
and the work was derived from Stanislavskian practice, totally unknown in
America until this time.

The aim was to train an ensemble for three years before letting them
perform publicly, though this was eventually compromised. As the Lab repertory theatre occupied more of Boleslavsky's time, Ouspenskaya adopted
responsibility for teaching, focusing on small group improvisations,
one-minute plays and character work. Her improvisations, often animal
or object characterisations, stressed observation but also tried to explore
aspects of characterisation alien to the actor's own personality – something
the MAT had resisted. Her work was closer to Stanislavskian practice in its
use of given circumstances:

> Improvised situations, such as waiting at a train station, were
> often complicated by varying the given circumstances suddenly to
> force the student to adjust and react flexibly to different situations
> while remaining true to the basic *données* of his character. During

improvisations students were urged to connect with each other – to become sensitive to one another's subtlest changes in attitude or behaviour.   (Willis 1964: 114)

This is the core of the New York style: derived from Stanislavsky but with subtle differences, used in the development of characterisation and basically a system which functions *intra-actively* – between the actors in the scene. The Chicago system derives from a different, not originally theatrical tradition and stresses *inter-action* between the performers and the audience. The New York style, like its Russian original, strives to keep its intentions 'upstage of the footlights', inside the scene. The Chicago style crosses the boundary into the auditorium, both ways.

The Lab, which Boleslavsky ran from 1923 to 1929, was profoundly influential. Among its approximately 500 members were Stella Adler, Ruth Nelson, Eunice Stoddard, who studied acting; the critic Francis Fergusson (Boleslavsky's assistant for a while); Harold Clurman and Lee Strasberg, who studied directing and whose ideas were to profoundly affect the development of American acting, writing and drama teaching via first the Group Theatre and later the Actors Studio. Ouspenskaya ran her own school from 1932 to 1936: her work bridges Stanislavsky's understanding of the improvisational *étude*, based on the given circumstances of the play, and the simplified, naturalised version of his work that would later typify the work of the Actors' Studio in New York under Lee Strasberg.

Lee Strasberg

Whereas Stanislavsky's System emphasises the continuity implicit in a 'through line' of action and characterisation, Strasberg's Method produces emotion which 'erupts in explosive flashes' (Counsell 1996: 58), often startlingly powerful and conforming to the modernist sensibility of a fragmented rather than a coherent self.

> The Strasbergian character is fractured and schismatic, its inner self observably dislocated from its outer ... Method techniques inscribe their characters with what we term an iconography of neurosis. (Counsell 1996: 70)

The character's 'inner self' is revealed as a damaged, schismatic psyche which struggles to articulate its hypersensitivity against the restricting confines of the playtext. Actors often resort to paralinguistic means which are frequently in conflict with the overt text. There is recurrent recourse to minor improvisation or ad libbing in performance, with actors extending the script or truncating parts of it in favour of wordlessness. The result is often impressive: just as often it is unreadable. The neurotic inner self (in a recognisably American cultural way) is privileged over the social, inter-active self – even when carried to the extreme of inarticulacy and isolation (think of De Niro's 'Travis Bickle' in the film *Taxi Driver*) – and its inability to coherently express itself is, of course, a major sign of its veracity.

Central to the process of constructing and then expressing such a character is improvisation. Rehearsal of the scripted text is regarded as secondary, as an alliance with the process of covering rather than revealing the inner self. So

> both with the Group and at the Studio, Strasberg insisted on substan-tial improvisation in order to build for the character a detailed inner life. When rehearsing a play, for example, actors would immerse themselves in their roles by improvising scenes, acting their char-acters in situations that were not a part of the playtext and so build-ing more extensive 'inner circumstances'. Improvisation played an equally large part in general training, and a Studio practice called 'the Scene' is exemplary.   (Counsell 1996: 64)

'The Scene' was an unpolished presentation to the rehearsal group by one of the actors performing workaday activities (washing, cooking, etc.) *in character*.

> As with Strasberg's other improvisational techniques, the Scene was sometimes the focus of more creative activity than the playtext itself – indeed, improvisation was usually undertaken before practical work on the playtext was begun … Although Strasberg demanded that his actors root their work in the text, at a *procedural* level his techniques required them to regard the playtext's conception of the character as an obstacle; to address it, that is, like language, sociality and so on, as an obstacle to the expression of what the Method considers most important, 'true emotion'.   (Counsell 1996: 65)

Lorrie Hull, who worked under Lee Strasberg (not at the New York Actors Studio, but at the Los Angeles Lee Strasberg Theatre Institute) for twelve years, offers a more positive assessment and quotes Strasberg:

> The whole point is to learn to see behind words, to learn not to think of words as a safeguard, but always to look for imaginative

comprehension which will extend the actor's own avenue of thinking. The improvisation trains the actor's willingness to act without
knowing the end result and at the same time to permit fantasy. The
actor's imagination is trained to perceive possibilities of thought and
meaning. (Hull 1985: 147)

She points out that, like Stanislavsky before him, 'Strasberg always pro-
claimed that acting should appear to be happening for the first time. This
means the actor must create the illusion of spontaneity ... This is the Great
Illusion of the theatre, Stanislavsky's "sense of truth"' (131–2).

Lorrie Hull is adamant that improvisation 'in all phases of rehearsal must
have a specific aim. The theme or purpose should be properly defined' (Hull
1985: 133), at least by the director. To approach that clarity of objective,
she then goes on to outline very succinctly the major uses of applied improv work in the Strasbergian model. She asks:

Is the improvisation utilized for an actor or director to deal with a
psychological problem, to develop behavior to make a characterization more believable, to develop a better sense of the character's
physical life, ... to execute an intention set by the actor or director,
to check how one character feels toward another and how well this
feeling will work, or simply to note what instincts actors follow in
staging a particular scene? (133)

She lists certain obvious kinds of improvised exploration. In addition to
improvisation exercises in formal actor training (discussed on 140ff.), in
rehearsal for performance these include running scenes in the actors' own
words, exploring what has happened between characters prior to a scene's
commencement, exploring the 'given circumstances' of individual characters, playing out scenes not in the play which allow the actor to explore
particular feelings, continuing to running scenes ad lib when they first go
'off book' and are struggling to remember the script and, finally, taking
elements of improvisation into the finished performance (in film as well as
on stage).

Strasberg sensed the blockages in actors – indeed, perhaps the Actors
Studio began to attract blocked actors to it, craving liberation in personal
psychodrama. In the exercises, that release could be obtained, and creativity made to flow. When some exercises were presented publicly, irre-
concilable – and therefore risible – contradictions became manifest. The
baby was washed away with the bathwater. This was a confusion that the
Chicago school carefully avoided from its inception.

Chicago Bears

The first theatre in Chicago opened in 1847, and the city has been a theatrical centre since the turn of the century. In 1912, British playwright Maurice Browne and his actress wife Ellen Van Volkenberg opened the Chicago Little Theatre (following the Boston Toy Theatre of the previous year) in the vanguard of what came to be known as the 'little theatre movement' that quickly engulfed America:

> The influence of the new movement ... was also felt abroad. [...] Jacques Copeau ... found inspiration for the Théâtre du Vieux-Colombier from accounts of the Chicago experiment.   (Browne 1956: 165)

Chicago was and is still the source of a uniquely American dramatic energy, and the Chicago style of improvisation has its roots in the work of a number of different people, some of whom had little or nothing directly to do with the theatre.

Neva L. Boyd (1876–1963) was a teacher, sociologist and educational theorist. In 1921, she founded the Recreational Training School at Chicago's Hull House.[1] From 1924 to 1927 she had Viola Spolin as a student living in her house. Spolin writes:

> I received from her an extraordinary training in the use of games, storytelling, folk dance, and dramatics as tools for stimulating creative expression in both children and adults, through self-discovery and personal experiencing. The effects of her inspiration never left me for a single day.   (Spolin 1963: xi)

From 1927 until 1941 Boyd worked as a sociologist at Northwestern University (Evanston, Illinois), teaching play theory, leadership and group organisation. Margaret Naumburg and Boyd were advocates of Progressive Education, championed by John Dewey and Maria Montessori. Both had done work in the Projects (that is, tenement housing for immigrant communities) in New York and Chicago respectively and had come to similar conclusions about the validity of games in teaching communication and social skills. And both had gifted protégées: Suzanne Bing and Viola Spolin.

In the foreword to a collection of children's games published in 1945, Boyd writes:

> The educational value for so-called normal children of games dynamically played is unquestioned; their therapeutic value for

hospitalised children has been demonstrated beyond doubt; their use as therapy in the treatment of mental patients has proved effective; and their corrective value in the re-education of problem youth has been repeatedly demonstrated in schools and custodial institutions. (Boyd 1945: 6)

While the book in question deliberately does little more than list and describe about 300 children's games, Boyd is in no doubt about the sociological, physiological and psychological bases of games theory. Jean Piaget and Margaret Lowenfeld would, in various ways, continue to develop educational and psychological theory: the dramatic use of games was developed chiefly by Viola Spolin and her pupils in America, and Naftali Yavin, Albert Hunt and Clive Barker in England.

Viola Spolin (1906–94), trained by Boyd, began as a teacher and drama supervisor on the Chicago WPA (Works Progress Administration) Recreational Project during the New Deal years, developing a 'non-verbal, non-psychological approach' (Spolin 1963: xi) to help train students to use drama in community work – a remarkably advanced project for its time.

Her greatest single contribution was the development and systematisation of Boyd's insights about the use of games. Working with non-English-speaking immigrants and their children, she devised many non-verbal improvisations. Spolin, working primarily with children and amateur adults, was the first to open up improvisational work deliberately to include audience-suggested material. This would, in later years, become a feature of what we are calling the 'Chicago style'. Spolin uses the term 'player' in preference to 'actor' with regard to this kind of developmental work (and the term has great currency in the field of Chicago-style improv). The method centres on games: her definition of the term 'Improvisation' begins with 'Playing the game' (Spolin 1963: 383).

Her book *Improvisation for the Theatre*, first published in 1963, was the first to attempt to codify and to teach improvisational acting. The final draft had to wait until she was given the opportunity to observe at first hand the workings of America's first fully professional improvisational theatres. The central figure in the creation of both, back in Chicago, was her own son, Paul Sills.

From the New York angle then, we've seen the development of the Stanislavsky line into the Method, but with the interesting clarification that it quite consciously targets both outer (representational) and inner (psychological) kinds of 'truth' (Actors Studio) and then 'imaginative comprehension' (Strasberg/Hull). So there is a clear understanding here that improvisation is a force in the holistic development of the performer. Two other important things emerge from the Chicago scene: (i) 'performer' may now be a facilitator in social and/or pedagogic contexts; (ii) games and play are identified and validated as essential ingredients in those essentially interactive processes. Pragmatically and historically, this latter perception becomes the basis of the Chicago improv method (see below, p. 48–52); but what all this taken together indicates is that major elements of improvisation practice are perceived as developmentally productive for actors in society as well as those in theatre. We shall pick this up later in discussion of Augusto Boal's work, but it is worth signalling here that strong correlations between improvisational theatre practice and pedagogy are emerging. These will, as we shall see, continue to resonate in different ways and will bleed into expectations that performance may be a zone of experience in which the self and what it is capable of may be renegotiated.

Sills entered the University of Chicago as a student in 1948. Many gifted actors were attracted to the artistic environment blossoming around the University during the immediate post-war years; among the best known are Edward Asner, Fritz Weaver and Mike Nichols, while Elaine May and David Shepherd were among the many performers informally associated with the University Theatre.

Paul Sills joined the University Theatre group; then, in 1953, he was instrumental in setting up the Playwrights' Theatre Club, which, as its name implies, was intended to produce works of great playwrights. In 1955, Sills teamed up with David Shepherd to found the first performance group solely dedicated to improvised work: The Compass.

Shepherd's original idea was for a theatre derived (in inspiration) from the *commedia dell'arte*. Both he and Paul Sills were heavily influenced by the theories of Bertolt Brecht (Sills later studied briefly in East Germany and ran classes in Brechtian theory and practice). Shepherd wanted Compass to be a working-class theatre for culturally deprived groups in industrial centres of America, such as Gary, Indiana. In the end it was decided that Chicago University had its own cultural deprivation problem, and Compass settled in Hyde Park. The Chicago school adopted Brecht as its mentor, much as the New York school had appropriated Stanislavsky. Compass and its many successors derived their cabaret style from Brechtian 'Smoking Theatre'. Compass's political aspirations, though, were short-lived. An early associate, Andrew Duncan, describes the Compass clientele as 'lumpen-bourgeoisie' (Sweet 1987: 46), and Shepherd himself quickly became frustrated that the group seemed more concerned about fighting their Jewish intellectual parents than about fighting McCarthyism. Amy Seham notes that motives underlying Compass and its successors were always divergent:

Spolin was devoted to improvisation's spiritual and psychological release of human potential. Shepherd wanted a political community theatre that would fight class oppression through a dialogic interaction between actors and 'real people'. Sills was interested in both the spiritual and the political, as long as improv also produced authentic 'art'.   (Seham 2001: 7)

From the start it was agreed that Compass was to have no playwright, and no scripted play: its work would be based upon scenarios which could be hung up backstage like the 'platt' in an Elizabethan theatre. The first Compass production was *The Game of Hurt*, from a scenario devised and directed by Paul Sills. Like the *commedia*, this wasn't imagined as totally free improvisation:

> The original idea was to have a scenario which was – as we fondly imagined – the *Commedia dell'arte* idea. We wrote a story out, usually eight to twelve scenes written out on a sheet of paper, and we'd follow through the scenes by rehearsing.   (Sills 1964: 174)[2]

In addition to the main piece, the group also performed short 'Living Magazine' pieces (reminiscent of Moreno's Vienna experiments – see below, p. 93–7 – and rather more superficial than the 'Living Newspapers' developed by Hallie Flanagan's Federal Theatre Project in the 1930s) and most significantly considering Paul Sills's early training in his mother's TIE (Theatre in Education) work, *audience requests*.

The audience request, or the immediate incorporation of suggestions from the audience, is the most distinctive feature of the Chicago style. The troupe retires backstage and rapidly sketches out a scene or scenes in response, which they then perform. Mike Nichols and Elaine May, for example, astounded audiences and critics in 1960 by their virtuosity in using audience-determined material. John Monteith and Suzanne Rand still do the same kind of act (though not so often), and this style also formed the basis for the radio and television improvisation game, popular on both sides of the Atlantic, *Whose Line Is It Anyway?* It even underpins radio-improvised comedy, such as BBC Radio 4's cult success *The Masterson Inheritance* (starring London's Comedy Store stalwarts Paul Merton, Caroline Quentin, Jim Sweeney and Josie Lawrence, together with Phelim McDermott and Lee Simpson, later of Improbable).

In particular, the audience request characterises Sills's next venture, the famed Second City, established (by Sills, Bernie Sahlins and Howard Alk) in 1959 and still, nearly fifty years later, an important breeding ground for much that is best in American acting. A New York spin-off of Compass, Ted Flicker's The Premise (later involved in a row with the British censor), tended to concentrate mostly on one-line jokes, but Second City, under Sills's guidance, allowed 'long, complicated scenes, whole plays, to evolve ... all sorts of parodies and operas and musical versions' (Sills 1964: 175), while Alan Myerson's spin-off troupe The Committee (1963–73) would develop a more serious, politically involved type of improvised theatre in San Francisco.

The Second City original format involved the presentation of a main show (built up and rehearsed over a number of months). Regular 'characters' emerged over time because they were successful with audiences, who greeted their reappearance in the house shows or in 'spot improvs' with reincorporative pleasure. This amounted to an (more or less conscious, but untheorised) attempt to establish an American *commedia* (Seham 2001: 18–19), with recognisable type-figures (the blond all-Americans, the Jewish schlemiels, Alan Arkin's 'Puerto Rican drifter', Severn Darden's 'Madman') recurring throughout early Second City work. Funny though these characters were, they were *social* types, by and large, rather than *archetypes*, and lacked the enduring resonance of the original *commedia* masks.

The rehearsed show was then followed by audience suggestions which the players were allowed to think about and discuss for a short while; or by 'spot improvs' – suggestions acted on immediately, without reflection – treated by actors and audience alike as virtuoso feats (when they worked). At regular intervals, the best of the resultant material was then selected out, discussed, refined and rehearsed to form part of the next main show.

The 'Chicago style' (obviously no longer confined to that city) bifurcates into comic strip performance (typified by Shelley Berman, the late Joan Rivers and John Belushi, Dan Aykroyd and Gilda Radner) and quiet, totally credible naturalism (Barbara Harris, Alan Arkin, Alan Alda and Betty Thomas). The division has always been present in American acting, to some extent, with the conflicting Broadway paradigms of the musical and naturalistic drama. But the conflict was also part of Second City's make-up.

In its early days, many of the actors were university intellectuals, excited by the boundaries of their new form. But there were also those for whom improvisation was only a means of generating and developing performance material; they saw it as a form of play – or rather revue – construction. Improv was a product of the great period of satirical comedy, the era of Lenny Bruce and Mort Sahl.[3] Second City became increasingly a prisoner of its own success. It established improv classes early on, which attracted thousands of paying would-be performers, many of whom have gone on to found rival companies. Young talent was attracted to the theatre less because it was the home of improvised drama than because it was an excellent platform from which to launch a career in comedy or, increasingly, in television. Clever caricatures began to replace the more thoughtful 'people scenes' of the early shows.

Paul Sills left Second City in 1967; co-founder Bernie Sahlins took over and ran the company until 1984 when he, in turn, sold his interest to Andrew Alexander, the producer of the Toronto Second City. Sills and Viola Spolin opened The Game Theatre in Chicago, which was followed in the early 1970s by Sills's highly successful Story Theatre. The Game Theatre was centred primarily on Viola's exercises. Leaving revue behind, the idea was to have the *audience* play the impro games, becoming their own performers. The technique of Story Theatre was related to impro, though it usually used pre-existing narrative and textual material. Sills moved to Los Angeles and set up a small company under the title Sills and Company, which continued to play the theatre games devised by his mother from Neva Boyd's work. The company included his daughter Rachel, a fourth-generation improviser. In 1986 the company mounted a five-month off-Broadway tour, which was widely acclaimed by the New York critics.

For David Shepherd, the original conception had been political, derived from Brecht. He has since continued to experiment with proletarian theatre forms. Subsequently, he became (briefly) the mastermind behind the growth of 'theatre sports' – 'Impro Olympics' – in the US and Canada (see below, p. 49).

But for Paul Sills and Viola Spolin, the work passed (like Grotowski's) beyond the borders of the theatre, into the para-theatrical world of self-discovery and self-actualisation, the creation of 'free space' in man.

> All the people who have worked with improvisational theater know that there's a free space they can come back to and they like to come back to ... I'm not interested in improvisational theater *per se*. I'm interested in the establishment of those free spaces where people can do their own work, and I'm interested in the forms which begin to emerge in these free spaces.   (Sweet 1987: 18–19)

The basic difference between the New York and Chicago styles is that the giants of the New York theatre world confined improvisation, seeing it only as a rehearsal tool or play-writing device. The actor was confined, too; like Saint-Denis they imagined the actor as primarily the interpreter of a written script. Paul Sills is the inheritor of another tradition. An irascible and difficult director, by all accounts, and occasionally uncommunicative, he is nonetheless inspired by the *idea* of communication. In Chicago, improvisation games were a way of communicating between people, especially those disadvantaged and without a social voice, long before they were borrowed by the stage.

Amy Seham points out, however, that these ideals were not always lived up to. In no other area has there been so much explosive change since our first edition appeared. At its height, before the market became saturated in the early 1990s, there were a hundred companies offering improv in Chicago alone. Between 1990 and the present, the field of North American improv has been further revolutionised. Chicago remains the source of much of its energy, but the form has spread across the continent and beyond.

Seham documents disquiet about issues of 'gender, race and power in improv-comedy' (Seham 2001: xi), especially centring on Second City. Noting an increasingly visible tendency towards sexism, racism and homo-phobia in the Chicago improv field generally (in which women performers were frequently sidelined, blacks, Asian Americans and gays often rendered invisible or tokenised), she charts the emergence of a 'second wave' (later followed by third and possibly fourth waves). David Alfred Charles reports that the first all-women improv team, named 'Jane', which appeared on the ImprovOlympic stage in 1996, tackled gendered assumptions and reclaimed status and agency (Charles 2003: 187; and cf. Alissa Green's *World's Worst: Improv Magazine*, 2005 *passim*).

The second wave saw the creation of professionalised 'Theatre Sports', with major companies such as ImprovOlympic and ComedySportz, stem-ming largely from Keith Johnstone's Canadian initiatives at Calgary in the late 1970s. Seham notes (2001: 37) that sport had always offered improvis-ers useful metaphors for the experience of working together 'as a team', being 'in the zone' etc., though she adds that women often understood *teamwork* to imply cooperation, whereas men tended to see it as formal-ised group conflict. The idea of a team improv competition (synthesising both masculine and feminine views) was formalised by David Shepherd's 'Improvisation Olympiad' in 1981. Shepherd imagined friendly compe-tition between 'identity' teams, made up of players representing occupa-tions or age groups. He joined forces with Charna Halpern, a 29-year-old producer and actor, and together they established ImprovOlympic (now known briefly as iO or iO Chicago). However, before the venture got off the ground, Shepherd and Halpern fell out over their aims (his political, hers artistic), and he left. Halpern struggled to keep the idea going until 1983, when she met (and later married) Del Close. (See Chapter 3 below for more on later developments in Theatre Sports.)

Del Close (1935–99) had a background in writing comic books, liked recreational substances and was a legendary member of 'the first wave'.[4]

He was an original member of Compass, had starred on *Saturday Night Live* and had performed, taught and been artistic director at Second City from 1973 to 1981 (where he had been responsible for discovering many of the great comedy names like Belushi, Radner, George Wendt, etc.). Already known for the surreal quality of his improvisational work, Close's great invention (dating from his time with The Committee in San Francisco) was what has become known as 'long form' (also 'Long-form') improvisation and, in particular, the 'Harold'.[5]

Rather than the 'short-form' work of audience-galvanised multiple scenes, or 'spot improvs', which were the trademarks of Second City and its followers, the Harold takes a single suggestion from the audience. Players do not go offstage to discuss anything but respond immediately with short and initially unrelated scenes until, as 'the game' or underlying idea or pattern which links them is osmotically discovered, all the scenes begin to make sense (or perhaps don't, which may still be fun). The Harold can last from twenty minutes to two hours depending on inspiration. The key to Long-form, maintained Close, was the development of *groupmind*: relaxed attunement and memory – a pre-conscious sensitivity to underlying pattern leading to sustained group creativity, and the fundamental principle of reincorporation.

Clayton D. Drinko, a New York actor who has worked in Chicago with iO, writes in *Theatrical Improvisation, Consciousness and Cognition* (2013) about 'improv consciousness' and focuses mainly on Chicago long-form (Harold) improv and the development of that work from Spolin to Close. His book explores aspects of individual and collective consciousness in improv work ('flow', *pace* Csíkszentmihályi and 'group mind') in the light of creative experience and brain-functioning (neurological models in particular). Drinko quotes Spolin's claim that through spontaneity 'we are formed into ourselves'... and 'perhaps... to the human spirit itself' (both cit. in Drinko 2013: 20–2). This utopian or millennial perspective recurs in many places, as we have begun to document, and is strongly resisted by others (e.g. Lecoq).

In particular, Drinko develops Spolin's view that 'focus' (originally Point Of Concentration) is the essential factor, which shifts attention to other players, the situation and environment, etc., and thus reduces or phases out self-consciousness. This results in 'less self-consciousness and more intuitive playing, the true self over ego [sic] according to Viola Spolin' (9). 'What connects Spolin's work to [Neva] Boyd's is that their games require outward focus from participants' (15). 'Focus releases group power and individual genius' (Spolin, cit. 22).

For Boyd, games (a 'situation set up imaginatively') condense time and space to promote more rapid and freer learning. For play-theorist Gregory

Bateson, they provide structure, include frequent role-switching, and are clearly 'framed' – a criterion developed further by sociologist Erving Goffman. For Boyd and Spolin, they also provide a problem-solving dimension.

So consciousness is addressed here in terms of the business of relating and connecting (there are links here with analysis of Forum practice by Sanjoy Ganguly and Birgit Fritz; see below, p. 102) and is also conceived of as a movement of energy, a voluntary – though not necessarily solely rational – phenomenon. Drinko refers to neurological studies of 'creativity' (a famous one looked at jazz musicians – see Chapter 4) which indicate changes in activity in the dorsolateral prefrontal [reduction] and medial prefrontal [increase] cortices, and also links Csíkszentmihályi's 'flow' to Spolin's 'spontaneity' as a state which includes a heightened awareness of fellow players and the audience ('instant feedback'). This is also furthered through 'mirroring' (Spolin has several mirror exercises; Boal of course has the well-known 'Columbian Hypnosis'). Drinko links it to the function of mirror neurons ('unconscious imitation'), which, as Ramachandran indicates, 'could allow us to interpret other people's intentions and predict their actions' (cit. 27). This 'could be one of the reasons improvisers are able to be so in sync with their teammates' (27).

Drinko clarifies the structure of short-form (the 'focus on the creation of a scene within the rules of the game') (Leep, cit. 19, mainly based on Spolin and Boyd's model) as:

- Respect and Trust + Yes, And
- Be in the Moment + Encounter
- Let Go + There are No Mistakes

This establishes a pattern which is retained for the most part in long-form. Flicker and May's 'Kitchen Rules' (St Louis Congress Theater) are similar to Spolin's and are adapted by Close partly as a result of his experiments with drugs in search of altered states of consciousness (cf. Huxley, *The Doors of Perception*) (37); he was a Wiccan and introduced 'invocations' as one way of beginning a Harold – they are still taught at iO; he also began incorporating dreams into his long-form improvs.

The basic sequence of the Harold (later developed and varied considerably) is as follows:

- Word-association game (e.g. 'The Pattern Game' using a single word from audience to start different associations/versions, or 'organic opening', or 'invocation' or 'monologue')
- Three scenes derived from these (first version)

- Game
- Second version of scenes with shifts in time and/or addition of more character(s)
- Game
- Version 3 (conclusion) of scenes revealing connections between them

A key strategy in moving through the versions is 'editing', which includes the 'sweep edit' (change all components, preceded by players running around the space), 'tagging' (one character replaces another), 'pattern' (repetition of phrases or actions), 'callback' (recalling information from previous scene) and 'montage' (a series of scenes without any particular sequence). Often used is the 'rule of three' (three repetitions of phrase, situation, etc. – three may be the number when a pattern becomes perceptible).

The twin drives here are incorporation of the 'outside' material and collaboration between performers. Drinko's view that these institute an outward focus and that this is significant in the creation of 'group mind' is plausible; though it perhaps runs somewhat counter to some of the things that Close was also doing to 'expand' his. But both approaches, as well as their indebtedness to Spolin, Boyd *et al*, underline a similar trajectory in terms of the use of improv methodology.

In this discussion, consciousness emerges as (a) 'individual/internal': 'Altered States' (ASCs) giving rise to shifts/extensions/different functioning, whether or not this can be specifically connected to particular kinds or zones of brain activity; (b) 'group/interactive': heightened awareness and production of patterns, structures, links (between images, themes, people), again perhaps linked to some shifts in brain activity.

Both seem to engage a different sense of 'self' which is less ego-and-logos-bounded, more connected with and operating in conjunction with phenomena 'beyond' the narrow range of conception and perception. If we are talking about 'cognition' here (Drinko's title uses this but doesn't in fact define it), this would seem to include the psychophysical and the affective, the intuitive and the barely or subtly sensed.

Some of the aims and principles of this work are also found in forms like Playback and varieties of movement practice, including Contact Improvisation; we look at these briefly in Chapter 4. A not-altogether-dissimilar outgrowth is the Theatre Sports model, which dominated the late 1980s, and groups in and around Chicago grew exponentially as both Second City and ImprovOlympic offered training and created new 'teams' of 'players'.

A brief glance back across the pond is appropriate also here to mention Ken Campbell. Campbell ('British theatre's leading heretic', according to *The Guardian*) had a series of late-night shows scheduled for the Royal Court's Jerwood Theatre from March 2006 which were in part a tribute to the improvisation and mask work led by George Devine and Keith Johnstone in the 1960s and 1970s. He also helped to develop what might be termed 'ultra-long-form' in the shape of *Improvathon*, a 36-hour play hatched on the spot at Ladbroke Grove's Inn on the Green, using the talents of master improvisers Adam Meggido (of LAMDA, Extempore Theatre and The School of Night), Dana Andersen and Davina Stewart (from Edmonton, Canada), as well as some 25 other professionals and amateurs. This resulted in a complex plot involving Woody Allen, Islamic fundamentalist terrorists and the Russian mafia. In the spirit of Keith Johnstone, the guiding principle was not saying no or, as Andersen put it, 'Yes will make the world open up'. The marathon time-frame led, according to Campbell, and echoing some of Drinko's speculations above, to acceding to the 'lizard brain', whereby performers gain full access to some of the supposedly primitive but very useful areas of the human mind (*The Guardian*, 22 December 2005).

A figure we, and perhaps most commentators on Second City, have tended to overlook is the gifted improvisation teacher Josephine Forsberg (1921–2012). As her student Margaret Duffy warns, there is a danger that '…Forsberg herself is slowly being erased from improvisation's historical narrative' (Duffy 2011, *op. cit.*).

Jo Forsberg, born Pepita Raciti, was introduced to improvisation by David Itkin, a pupil of Stanislavsky; later she attended The Actor's Company, where she studied under Mini Gallitser and met budding actor and director Rolf Forsberg, whom she married. After seeing a play at Playwrights' Theatre in 1954, she met Sheldon Patinkin and Paul Sills, and later Sills's mother, Viola Spolin, who introduced her to improvisational games and exercises.

She acted in a number of Playwrights' productions and then, in 1959, was asked by Patinkin to join the newly formed Second City. She deferred for a year because she was expecting her second child (Eric Forsberg) but then, in 1960, agreed to join. It was at this point, working as an understudy with an improvisational company, directing the children's theatre activities, and the touring company, that she really engaged in detail with Spolin's training. She was so successful that Spolin took her on as her assistant, and Forsberg gradually assumed the role of company teacher. By the mid-1960s, Forsberg had taken over most of the classes and was directly responsible for the training given to players. Just about everyone who thrived at Second City had done a year's training with Forsberg (e.g. George Wendt, Betty Thomas, Bill Murray and Charna Halpern). Her son proudly notes that 61 of the famous alumni of the Second City's main companies between 1965 and 1989 were her students (and she gave work to many others, including the young David Mamet, who played piano for her children's shows).

In 1969, she took a 'hippy' sabbatical to teach in the mountains of Montana. By the time she realised that wasn't going to work and returned to Chicago, other teachers – among them Del Close – had come to prominence. So, in 1971, she opened Players Workshop at Second City in Chicago which, for a decade, was the country's only specialist improvisation school with a five-semester curriculum. She recruited her nephew Martin de Maat (1949–2001) and her daughter Linnea to teach there. When Alexander bought Second City, he wanted to run the training 'in-house' and the Second City Training Centre was opened in 1987. Originally, it only offered advanced classes, and Forsberg's school taught basic improvisation. Marty de Maat and former pupils Jeff and Michael Michalski ran the Second City courses, building on their knowledge of Forsberg's curriculum (cf. Duffy). Forsberg's teaching was a hybrid of her own and Spolin's methods, Stanislavskian technique and the insights of Transactional Analysis. It was through the Players Workshop that David Shepherd first began to develop ImprovOlympic, with one of Jo's most creative students, Charna Halpern. But in 1992 Second City offered beginners' classes (as did other offshoots) and effectively began to displace the Players Workshop.

Once the Second City Training Centre had been established (with Marty de Maat at its head), and despite still having over 500 students, the Players Workshop was no longer seen as the obvious route to join the main company and began to lose its central position. She had a consultancy role in the Training Centre, but eventually Jo Forsberg retired and the school was closed around the turn of the millennium, though she continued to be called on as a teacher and adviser. (For an extended genealogy of Chicago-derived work and organisations, see the notes to this Chapter.[6])

In 2008, former student Bill Murray invited Jo to come to New York to run improvisation classes for the actual New York Giants football team. It is worth noting that the Giants won the Superbowl that year – coached by one of the original 'Chicago Bears'.

In the 1990s the tendency to marginalise women, blacks, Asians and gays led to a domination of the improv field (often aggressive and competitive, despite its apparent championing of cooperation) by men and a swamping of more thoughtful and developed work in favour of the quick joke – the slow-developing Harold by the quick-fire short-form. Thus in 'third wave' troupes (such as the Annoyance, the Free Associates, Oui Be Negroes, etc.) two tendencies become visible. One is a deliberate political attempt to reclaim lost ground: to give voice to ethnic and sexual minorities via improv and to address issues of power, gender and identity directly. The other is a slightly weary, 'Generation X' postmodern deconstructionism of impro-visation itself, leading to 'meta improv' (Seham 2001: 117–18), in which 'calling it on stage' (reflexive and recursive drawing of attention to the techniques of improv themselves) has become normative.

Seham (writing in 2001) was unsure whether a fourth wave was gather-ing beyond the horizon, and it is possible to point to the over-commodifi-cation of improv as all-too-ubiquitous training classes and easily consumed undemanding entertainment. But we can certainly also point to possibil-ities outside the confines of Chicago theatre. One is the trend to partici-patory and 'immersive' performance (see Chapter 4); another, still using narrative drama as its basis, is the participatory form of Instant Theatre, as practised by the English company Word and Action, based in Wimborne, Dorset.

Audience-led impro

Word and Action (WANDA) theatre was founded in 1972 by R. G. Gregory, a former English and Drama teacher who had experienced participatory theatre as a language teacher in Europe and Africa and had worked with Stephen Joseph, the English originator of in-the-round work, and with drama-in-education specialist Dorothy Heathcote, from whose techniques he gradually distanced himself. Gregory stayed with WANDA for thirty years, retiring on his 75th birthday in 2003. The company itself has ceased, but former members like Pag Naylor, Tony Horwitz and Peter Graham con-tinue its work in the UK and abroad and specialise in 'Instant Theatre' (Johnston 2006: 229–3). Here the company describes its method of turning narrative into participatory theatre:

> An audience is seated in the round: on all 4 sides of the acting area. A well-known genre is chosen (folk tale, legend, horror story …). From an accessible and inclusive gathering technique, the audience cre-ates a story. In this unique theatre, everyone's ideas are included and no idea is rejected. Its rules and forms of organisation represent an egalitarian model of society. The parts are offered to the audience (for voluntary participation). Everything is represented by people, including inanimate objects and special effects. An innovative play [lasting an hour] begins to unfold, with the help of the Word And Action actors. This extraordinarily rich and unique theatre form uses no props, scenery, lighting or costumes.   (Word and Action website, http://www. wordandaction.com: the website was closed in 2005)

The company slogan sums up the point of the work, linking individual narrative with collective transformation via participatory drama.

> Out of nothing the story. Out of the story the play. Out of the play
> awareness. Out of awareness the power.   (*ibid.*)

Chris Johnston views Instant Theatre as a model of participatory theatre.
He writes, 'While the better known Forum Theatre is combative, Instant
Theatre is celebratory' (Johnston 1998: 229; and cf. Eva and Lorenz Hippe's
commentary on the form *'Alle Antworten sind wahr. Alles ist freiwillig'* ('All
answers are true. Everything is voluntary') Hippe and Hippe 2011: 12).

If, on stage, performers are becoming obsessed with their own techniques and practices, outside the theatre *audiences* have taken to a form of
improvisation which is far less commoditised. Called Live-Action Role Play
(known as LARP or LARPing) this form again reduces actors to the role of
supporters, while the true improvisers are the public themselves.

LARPing is remarkable as much for its widespread popularity throughout
Europe and North America as for its formal departures from other forms of
extra-theatrical improvisation. Styles of LARP vary from country to country.
German festivals can attract up to 7,000 players. Scandinavian countries
are noted for taking a more artistic approach. The key to LARPing is that:

> the player himself represents the role-played character, and the
> player's actions directly represent the character's actions. This dis-
> tinguishes LARPs from tabletop role-playing games, where character
> actions are described verbally ('My character says ...'), and from
> computer role-playing games, where characters are controlled by
> the player through a computer interface ... Role-playing at LARPs
> is similar to acting in theatre and cinema, though character actions
> in LARPs are always improvised. (http://en.wikipedia.org/wiki/
> Live_action_role-playing_game)

At LARPing events – which may last for a few hours, a whole weekend or
several weeks – players will typically spend most of their time 'in character'
(known also as 'IC', 'in-game' or 'in-play'). An essential distinction is made
between an active player in role and a player 'out of character' ('OOC',
'off-game', 'off-play', 'out-of-game', etc.). Players apply themselves between
LARP events to making or acquiring costumes, props and skills, which they
will use in the game itself. These costumes can be spectacular and complex
(some games represent non-human species) and there can be a definite
element of competitive display.[7]

Part of the fascination of LARPing arises from its simultaneous occupation of parallel, overlapped realities. LARPs ask their players to occupy two simultaneous realms: the actual physical location of the player and the diegetic 'setting', the world of the character. A theatrical set exists to allow the audience to visualise the setting of a play: the actors of a drama are generally aware of its falsity – they can see the backs of the painted flats. Improvisational drama uses settings in a slightly different way, to stimulate the imagination of the performer. In some impro exercises, for example, actors may be asked to reconstruct an environment into which they can imaginatively project themselves (such as the actor's own bedroom). The LARPing environment is of this latter kind. The physical events take place in a secluded rural setting (the real or extra-diegetic setting), where participants sleep in tents. Some effort may be made to simulate the game world scenically, but most elements will remain conventional (a rope may signify a castle wall) or be natural (a real wall may be used).

The diegetic environment, however, may be remarkably elaborate (considering LARPing's origins in fantasy board games and literature, this is hardly surprising). Depending on genre, it may represent an historical or counter-historical world (for example, a world in which the Roman Empire never fell), a science fiction or fantasy world, or a dystopic contemporary environment. Most frequently it represents a fantasy realm in which magic powers, spells, charms, swords and sorcery are active.

There are also many LARPing versions of the zombie apocalypse. One involved an immersive four-hour game staged by an English company called Zed Events in a disused shopping centre in Garrard Street, Reading, Berkshire in 2012. As far as we know, the Zed Events experience is the only one to take advantage of a specific and appropriate play environment (the disused mall, ultimately to be demolished) which celebrates Romero's original *Dawn of the Dead* vision: carnage amid the spoils of capitalism and consumerism (for which the punters willingly pay £139: 2012 price).[8]

LARPing is the most extreme form of audience-centred improvisation – one in which the audience completely replaces the actors, as it were, or uses them merely as adjuncts and facilitators (known in the jargon as NPCs or 'Non-Playing Characters') for its own imaginative self-expression.

Another model of this is Kaleider's *The Money* (Exeter 2013):

You buy a ticket to take part, choosing to be a 'benefactor' or a 'silent witness' (benefactors must donate a minimum of £10). On the appointed night you all turn up at Exeter's Guildhall, a space that lends real gravitas to the proceedings. The benefactors sit around the polished wood table on which sits the money that, together, they have donated. In the space of two hours, the benefactors must unanimously agree how to spend the money, and all must sign a document detailing how and when this will take place. If they fail, the money rolls over to another evening. Silent witnesses observe, but can say nothing. But at any point during the evening they can turn benefactor and join the discussion by adding £10 to the pile of notes on the table.   (Lyn Gardner, in *The Guardian*, 22 November 2013)

£10 here buys you the right to act – in the literal sense of being able to intervene, as well as in the subtler sense of giving a performance as yourself, improvising with others: it makes you a 'benef-actor', and witnesses can become participants at any point. Kaleider's Artistic Director Seth Honner calls it a 'show/game', in which some watch others dealing with the corroding power of money and finding a means to make a collective decision. As it goes on,

Natural leaders rise and fall while the collective politeness of the group mutates into both tension and synergy. Emotions bounce around the room; peace, passion, pain, power, pep, pride, panic. All within a space of two hours.   (Mudge 2013)

LARPing is fully participatory and co-creates imaginary worlds; the example above also involves decisive activity. Other formats cater to different degrees of this and all to some extent invite interaction. In recent years, the economic downturn in Europe has created cheap property rental in some city centres. The BBC online business correspondent Lucy Hooker describes the way Hungarian entrepreneurs (like Attila Gyurkovics, founder of 'Parapark' in 2011 and Zoltan Kovacs, who created the more elaborate 'Trap') have taken advantage of available premises to establish live, rather than online, *Escape Room Games*, based in Budapest cellars (Hooker, BBC News Online, 19 December 2014). The players – like those avoiding the zombie plague in England – simply have to cooperate to solve puzzles in order to escape from their locked dungeons and the game affords them similar thrills and satisfaction when escape is achieved within the 60-minute time limit. A London version, *Escape Rooms*, derived from the very popular Japanese online *Takagism* game (originally devised by Toshimitsu Takagi), has recently opened near London Bridge, and many other versions are springing up across the world. Tan Yifan, writing in the online *Shenzhen Daily*, 12 July 2013, describes the growing popularity and thematic diversity of live *takagism* games in China and across Asia.

Living History events generally have a strong investment in the creation of 'authentic', sometimes explicitly educational, experience and take place in historical sites (stately homes, museums, battlefields, etc.). Visitors are afforded something of the 'feel' of what it was like to live there at that time, by actors in role dressed in period costumes and speaking in appropriate language; they are asked to accept the created world to an extent actively by experiencing or taking part in situations which would have occurred there. At one end of the spectrum events may gravitate towards the more exotically imaginary and begin to resemble *Renaissance or Medieval Fairs/ Fayres*, which are more commercial or geared to 'entertainment'. Among the stalls providing reproduction articles and food, performers (musicians, jugglers, actors) create an ambience and may engage in interaction with the public, who in some cases can hire costumes and join in as 'playtrons'. There are many such events in the US and Germany (in the latter, more than 1,000 in 2010).

Streetmosphere is another, mostly American version, in which performers create an appropriate experience: the Las Vegas 'Venice' experience with classical singers and living statues, varied cultural offerings in civic centres and in-character actors recreating a period feel on Hollywood's Sunset Boulevard. Other forms of 'carnival atmosphere' or the wealth of street events at the Edinburgh Festival are not dissimilar. All these things involve both rehearsed performance (research on roles and period attire, attempts to recreate period dialect, highly tuned acts) and a degree of spontaneity involving performers and audience. The degree of experimentation for both is probably relatively limited, even specifically by comparison to immersive theatre events (see pp. 103–9), but there is a case to be made for such phenomena as part of a shift of performance towards the inclusion of the 'audience', which may sometimes be enabled to glimpse possible new potentialities. Equally, they could be seen as a retreat to rather obvious historical reconstruction or fancy-dress antics demanding very little except acquiescence and a certain surface bonhomie.

And in other formats too, improv shows are booming.

Improvising musical theatre

Despite the understandable nervousness of producers and theatre investors, improvisation can be used in the creation of full-scale and highly commercial theatre works. In 1998, *Musical! The Musical* premiered at the Royal George Theatre in Chicago, and it has toured widely since. Using the favoured local technique of asking the audience for suggestions (not only for plot ideas, but also for a three-note sequence which will later form the basis for a central musical number), the cast improvises a new two-act, ninety-minute spontaneous musical theatre piece every night. To date, the company has delivered new shows such as *Moby! The Musical*; *Jeffrey Dahmer! The Musical*; *Psycho! The Musical*; *Alamo! The Musical* and many others – including one show in 1999 about the India–Pakistan nuclear testing conflict called *Bomb! The Musical*. No show is repeated, though many are fondly remembered.[9]

The seven-member troupe was set up by actor and improvisation teacher Nancy Howland Walker (who began working with impro in 1989, was director of ImprovBoston and had previously worked on long-form improvised pieces with The Free Associates in Chicago) and musical director Luke Nelson, who improvises the score, complete with overture, on a plethora of instruments. Walker and her fellow actors have to be able spontaneously to create a narrative, act it, sing it, harmonise and improvise intelligent – and often surprisingly moving – lyrics.

Broadway experimented with the idea of multiple endings in a musical, in Rupert Holmes's 1985 Tony Award-winning *The Mystery of Edwin Drood* (based on Dickens's unfinished last novel), which ran for 608 performances at the Imperial Theatre. Since then, it has been staged in London (appropriately at the Savoy Theatre which had once housed Gilbert and Sullivan) and around the world. Holmes proudly claims that it has run, somewhere, every day since its opening.[10]

American writer and song composer Holmes initially struggled with the adaptation – how to convey the complexities of the Victorian plot, how to increase the number of female roles, how to find an ending (Dickens's novel doesn't have one) and how, of course, to make the whole thing theatrical rather than literary. But his crucial inspiration was that:

> as a performer, I knew that a live audience delights in anything that happens on stage spontaneously ... in the specific performance they're witnessing: an ad lib, an unscheduled song, a guest artist who drops in without warning, a genuinely unexpected unrehearsed encore. (Holmes 2001: http://www.rupertholmes.com/theatre/essdrood.htm)

From this he derived the realisation that the improvisatory principle could be *written in* to a full-scale work.

> I sat and typed the words, 'Victorian Vaudeville.' What if I didn't attempt a strait-laced musical adaptation of Dickens' *Drood*? What

if, instead, I introduced the audience to a motley British Music-Hall company who are bravely overreaching their traditional evening's fare to create what they hope will be their finest achievement: the premiere performance of their own *Edwin Drood*, to be concluded in the fashion most comfortable to them – 'Give the public what it wants.'   (Holmes 2001)

Rather than create his own ending, which would reduce the openness of Dickens's unfinished work to a fixed, closed form, and imply that only Holmes had intuited Dickens's original intention:

I'd let the audience decide who was the murderer, who was the Detective in Disguise, which pair of lovers had a happy ending, by writing an extra act's worth of material from which one of hundreds of combinations of endings could be created on the spot ... the traditional Music-Hall Chairman could ... be scripted to offer up candidates for Culprit, Sleuth and Lovers, and to host a series of genuine elections in order to create the audience's own customized conclusion to *The Mystery of Edwin Drood*.   (Holmes 2001)

Exploiting the source's incompleteness, he contrived a plot with multiple endings and presented as a play within a play, set in a Victorian music hall. The audience is asked to loudly vote on a number of things – Is Drood alive or dead? If he's dead, who killed him? – and thereby democratically determine whichever ending they want. It is, essentially, a choice of 'whodunnit', and the spectators are rewarded by a sense that they have completed Dickens's work. As, indeed, they have – for this performance. (The popularity of 'murder mystery' dinner parties, sometimes provided by ad hoc theatre companies, where the diners take the role of detectives as the actors play out key scenes from the mystery, confirms the appeal of this kind of participation.)

The cast have alternative scenes rehearsed; interaction is largely a matter of multiple-choice voting (together with much cheering of heroes and hissing of villains), and the actual improvisational content by the actors is therefore relatively slight. But the piece respects the experience of improvisation, of spontaneous decision-making in performance, and gives the audience the pleasure of making explicit the fact of its own co-creativity.[11]

3   Improvisation in the Creation of New Modes of Performance

Roddy Maude-Roxby/Theatre Machine

This chapter returns to Europe to discuss ways in which major figures used improvisation in the 1960s and 70s to create new kinds of work and develop new resources for performers, much of which has strongly influenced subsequent developments across the spectrum of theatre and performance. Almost everyone who has encountered improvisation has come across Keith Johnstone; a whole generation of performers has been influenced by Jacques Lecoq. They and the others we discuss here position the improvisatory at the centre of new approaches to making work which significantly reshapes the parameters of theatre.

Roddy Maude-Roxby, one of the members of Johnstone's Theatre Machine, remarked in conversation that 'the most important moment in improvisation is when you don't know what will happen next'; Eugenio Barba speaks of actors and theatres which 'live as if they were always in a *statu nascendi*, in an emerging state or in the constant condition of the new beginner even if they have many years of experience' (Barba 2014).

The genesis of Theatre Machine is outlined by Keith Johnstone in his book *Impro*. The company was actually formed at Montreal's EXPO 67 by Johnstone, as director, and four actors: Ben Benison, Roddy Maude-Roxby, Ric Morgan and John Muirhead. Primarily interested in comedy improvised in performance, the group had worked together at the Royal Court Theatre, London, in the mid-1960s. They had given lecture-demonstrations to schools and teacher-training colleges (educationalists were already becoming aware of the value of their techniques in teaching).

There followed a period in which THEATRE MACHINE established its improvisatory style with audiences at home and abroad and also produced scripted and unscripted plays: *Clowning, Brixham Regatta, Robinson Crusoe, Arabian Nights,* and the Sir and Perkins plays *The Martian, Time Machine* and *Moby Dick.*

> With the departure of their director in '71 Theatre Machine's four actors formed a performance group, self-reliant, without a director, designer or author, these roles being taken on 'in the moment' during the performance.   (Theatre Machine Programme 1987, Wells-on-Sea)

The company remained loosely organised, the four actors following separate careers and coming together to become 'Theatre Machine' at will. Among other events the 'company' was challenged – by Keith Johnstone from his base in Canada – to take part in one of the increasingly popular 'Impro-Olympics' contests.[1]

Theatre Machine emerged from work at the Royal Court Theatre with George Devine, who was closely associated with Michel Saint-Denis, as well as from Johnstone's own input. It was the only professional company to present performances which were 'totally' improvised (though in recent years work by Improbable has come close, and Secret Theatre has performed shows which use a similar aleatoric pattern of characters and *lazzi*); not only was its work linked to the use of improvisation in traditional theatre – if of an 'experimental' kind, given the Royal Court's emphasis on new writing for the theatre – but it also marked a limit which even 'fringe' productions rarely approach.

> *Clowning* was an improvised show: there was no written script of any kind – though there was an extremely loose structure – and all the actors changed parts for different performances ... although certainly related to the *Commedia dell'arte*, its more immediate inspiration is the English music hall tradition.   (Browne 1975: 46–7)

Clowning had to be presented officially as a *lecture* because of the Lord Chamberlain's inability to pass improvisational work. We nowadays tend to forget the dead hand of official censorship, which was not abolished in Britain until 1968.

With reference to Theatre Machine, it is necessary to define what 'total' improvisation means in this context. It does not mean a completely random and chaotic show. Rather it is a compilation of a number of *lazzi-type* ingredients: the performers have 'up their sleeves' a number of characters – some with appropriate masks or bits of costume – or fragments of sketches. Some sections may be familiar to them or quite fully rehearsed. But everything is open to change.

> If you don't know the show is improvised, or don't believe it can be, then the bits that work well will seem obviously rehearsed. The bits

that flop you will think 'obviously not rehearsed' – you'll think those
are the 'improvised' bits and you'll wonder why they improvise, if
it doesn't work.   (Theatre Machine Programme 1987, Wells-on-Sea)

The answer is that:

THEATRE MACHINE has throw-away form, it is disposable theatre,
ideas and memories get re-cycled and the best is really best because
it comes out of the moment; and sometimes you were just ahead of
them.   (*ibid.*)

This idea of 'throw-away' theatre captures the very essence of improvised
drama. The term is also used by Dario Fo and Franca Rame (*un teatro da
bruciare*), although in their politicised context, theatre is used, and then
disposed of, in the same way as a newspaper is burnt once it has served its
purpose of informing the reader. Theatre Machine's 'disposability' is simply
an acceptance and a celebration of the central fact of performance – the
ephemeral act of co-creation between actor and spectator 'in the moment'.

Theatre Machine's method of working depended on close mutual support by all performers. Timing is one important example: if something
threatens to flag, the actors on stage are dependent on one of their colleagues taking the responsibility of entering and changing the direction.
They must be sensitive to each other and to what is happening, 'present'
and alert, prepared to support each other and not 'block'; whatever happens has to be accepted and used in the on-the-spot construction of a
scene. Theatre Machine pushed the demands to the limit because there is
nowhere to hide on stage: ultimately, all acting is about being able to take
full responsibility for yourself and your colleagues. Improvisation is valuable both as individual training and as a way of enhancing ensemble work.

One of the key elements of Jacques Lecoq's training is the emphasis on
play: using and enjoying the moment and what it brings. Maude-Roxby,
like Viola Spolin, uses the term 'players' in preference to 'actors' in his improvisation work. This is part of a deliberate strategy, accompanied by a
relaxed and apparently non-directive manner, to help participants to feel
at ease. 'Playing' suggests a game in which everyone can take part, and in
which there are more rewards than penalties; it takes the heat off the rather
threatening nakedness of improvisatory situations. Maude-Roxby often
says that his sessions are about 'not acting', a maxim which is related to
Lecoq's work on clowning.[2] The basis of clowning is the ability to feel OK
about being yourself and making a fool of yourself. It necessarily includes
a passage through vulnerability, but it can't afford to get stuck in it. So,

too, 'play' admits the possibility of making mistakes or rather allows the chance for what we might think of as 'mistakes' (if we are thinking about 'giving a good performance') to be re-evaluated as possibilities of new directions. Everything in Maude-Roxby's work can lead anywhere, so there is no *a priori* categorisation of right and wrong. Rightness is more a question of *attitude*, not of what you do but of how you do it, whether you are prepared to play with what comes along. Andy Harmon, on the YouTube extract described below, says of Maude-Roxby: 'I believe it's fair to say that the classic "Yes … and" improvisation exercise comes from Keith [Johnstone] watching Roddy work.' 'Play' in this context also has the idea of interplay – development of the range of the possible.

Roddy's *Lecture From A Skip* (2011 www.youtube.com/watch?v=5D5Jvy 0NJk8) is apparently rambly and inconsistent, but he says, 'I'm an improviser, so I don't like to know where I'm going.' The lecture is on 'Transforming Trash', so it occurs in an appropriate site (Roddy has long been active as a performance artist, sometimes with overt irony); it features a snippet of 'real' lecture, that is, something being read, although what is read is a poem by Maude-Roxby about not being able to find the right way out of a pullover. So it also frames, reproduces and subverts the mode and structure of a lecture. During the event he quite often recalls times when he has felt rubbish, or felt like trash, and demonstrates some ways of standing in different places which signal this (or not). He mildly regrets not inviting his audience to throw things at him in order to make him feel a bit more like his subject, which he is clearly both delineating and inhabiting from several perspectives. And in the process of so doing that subject is transformed, since it becomes an art event and a demonstrably non-lecture lecture. His final recollection is of taking part in a reading of N. F. Simpson's last play (*If so, then yes*), written in his eighties (Roddy, who played the lead in Simpson's 1959 *One Way Pendulum*, was 81 at the time of the lecture), which he says was a demonstration of the enduring need for the absurd in the face of ubiquitous rationalism. This indeed is transforming trash, showing that he remains true to the spirit of play and the urge to explode the 'serious'. Very much in the Keith Johnstone mode, also strongly recalling the era of Monty Python and British farce of the 1950s and 60s – with many of whose personnel he has worked.

There are also similarities between Maude-Roxby's demeanour as teacher and performer and the 'non-theatrical' style of French company Philippe Quesne/Vivarium. They perform random-looking domestic episodes in an ironic, almost casual, but perhaps actually very subtle, attempt to 'catch' spontaneity; 'almost nothing seems to be happening' when they perform, but this 'almost nothing' may induce a kind of (Beckettian) mode of awareness, in which conscious volitional activity is (almost) switched off, but it remains alert, trawling at a deep level for the faintest sign of life. It's another of those ways into tuning up (or down) the mechanism so that it can operate from the onset of perception, from the ground up, from the 'centre of the eddy', as Beckett puts it in 'Proust and Three Dialogues': from *The Moment Under the Moment* (Russell Hoban's 1992 title) – before the improvisatory moment, that is.

Many of the exercises Maude-Roxby uses are similar to things discussed below in the section on techniques. It's his way of using them that is particularly interesting. He seems to be open to the developing sense of structure, seeking an organic form which emerges through the activity – collecting objects, talking about them, evolving a narrative; finding different ways of moving and building a 'scene' around their interrelationships; developing from one person/object/position to more and more complex collages or combinations, with or without speech; arranging a collection of bodies or masked players. All of these work off not knowing what will happen, building in the unexpected, allowing it to become an unforced part of a construction or meaning which emerges as part of a (group) process.

There is now a considerable range of performance events which share some or all of these characteristics. Writing about Lone Twin, who have created work in a variety of unusual modes and formats somewhere between happening, journey and performance art, Carl Lavery and David Williams say:

> Nothing is left to chance in Lone Twin's work; or rather, chance is planned for, summoned up in such a way that it can be acted upon productively when it appears ... Art is no longer a question of creating autonomous products but of manufacturing the conditions for what ... Bourriaud calls 'relationality'... the onus is placed on inventing the conditions for invention. (Lavery and Williams 2011: 19–20)

They also point out that

> Lone Twin's interest in impossibility, the amateur, everyday language and journeys ... reflect a wider set of aesthetic concerns that has dominated much of the best theatre and performance work in the past two decades in the UK and elsewhere. (2011: 18)

And they list companies and artists such as Desperate Optimists, Forced Entertainment, Goat Island, Richard Maxwell's New York City Players, Gob Squad, Jérôme Bel and Bobby Baker. Williams writes that Lone Twin's method functions 'to invite me into elsewhere and otherwise' (2011: 14).

There are strong links here, particularly in terms of the invitation to 'participate' in some way, with much of the work we discuss in Chapter 4.

This kind of work also gives free rein to fantasy – allowing it to bypass cliché – by linking it to physical events which don't have a specific, predetermined meaning. The shape which the body adopts, or the function of an object, is not interpreted as fixed notations in a set code, as they might be in naturalistic performance. There, for instance, a chair tends to be a specific sign in a particular context – it denotes economic or social status – or a bodily position is evidence of a particular psychological state (head drooping, shoulders dropped, hands clasped = powerlessness, depression). In impro situations, the chair could become an umbrella, a bicycle or the horns of a bull; the pose could suggest a child being told off, a person sheltering from a storm and dying to go to the loo or someone praying. The sign ceases to *denote* and becomes the possibility of infinite *connotation*: it opens out to the play of significance.

Even less specifically related to the parameters of 'traditional' theatre (settings, characters, narratives) is Al Wunder's 'Theatre of the Ordinary', which we describe in more detail in Chapter 4. Here, performance is totally improvised utilising movement, text, sound or song, without pre-planned ideas or suggestions of character traits given by the audience.

Absence of specific meaning allows anything to be imagined – but not in a total void, because the physical event ensures a physical memory-trace. The impulse to meaning is generated in conjunction with the physical event, as the body moves and relates to itself, other bodies or objects: the pattern of meaning evolves as a succession of such relationships and assessments. So this kind of activity is doing at least three important things at once: showing that signs are arbitrary, helping us to play with them and getting us to experience that we make meanings with the body as well as with the mind. It is also a mediation between structure and freedom, between memory and imagination, between the given and the created.

Theatre, of course, is about *physicalising* the sense-giving act, producing it as *performance*. Structuralist analysis has highlighted sense-giving as a central human activity and indicated how different codes of meaning and kinds of discourse are elaborated and given privileged status in different usages. Structuralists tend to view the symbolic and the mythological as processes of *encoding*, but, useful as this is, it to some extent ignores the role of the body. If symbolism, as Susanne Langer suggests (Langer 1959), is about giving form to *feeling*, performance underlines the equality of the mental and the physical in this process, and improvisation work particularly acknowledges that mind and body have to be treated in tandem. The work of Lecoq exemplifies this further.

Jacques Lecoq and the semiotics of clowning

Jacques Lecoq (1921–99) began by teaching physical education and sport, learned improvisation from Claude Martin, a pupil of Dullin, and worked with the Association Travail et Culture (TEC), which gave shows based on improvisation and organised spectacles for 10,000–15,000 people after the Liberation. In 1948 he went to Italy; he claims to have discovered '*le jeu de la Commedia dell'arte*' in the markets of Padua: '*Commedia* has nothing to do with those little Italian troupes who export precious entertainments. It's about misery, a world where life's a luxury … If you're thinking of *commedia*, forget about Italy' (Hiley 1988).

In 1951 Lecoq created the Theatre School of the Piccolo Teatro in Milan and worked as both director and teacher; here he developed his speciality in mime and dramatic choreography, and gained experience of many other theatrical styles, assisting on Strehler's early productions of Brecht and choreographing the young Dario Fo and Franca Rame in revue work.

In 1956 he returned to Paris to found his own Ecole Internationale de Mime et de Théâtre, which he ran until his death in 1999. Lecoq's Paris school has given rise to some of the most important developments in performance style to have occurred during the last five decades. His original interest in movement in sport has remained at the basis of his work. He worked with Michel Saint-Denis and Jean Dasté and thus has direct links with the tradition of Copeau. He represents, however, an important modification and development of what Copeau began, both in terms of approach and of the organisation of a coherent curriculum.

The overall aim of Lecoq's work is '*découvrir les règles du jeu théâtral par une pratique de l'improvisation tactile à tous les niveaux (du réalisme à l'abstraction)*',[3] which might be glossed as: to discover the essentials of play and interplay in theatrical performance by the practice of improvisation using the whole range of tactile possibility at all levels (from realism to symbolic condensation). The significance of '*règles du jeu théâtral*' and '*improvisation tactile*' – key phrases in Lecoq's method – will be touched on further below.

Four things figure prominently in most of Lecoq's courses: (*a*) the establishment of the 'neutral body', including use of the neutral mask; (*b*) the concept of 'play'; (*c*) observation and research, both of 'realistic' detail and of rhythm and movement; and (*d*) the *auto-cours*, or 'do-it-yourself', work, in teams or groups towards producing various kinds of performance.

The structure of the courses themselves typically involves work which can be classified into three areas: (*a*) basics of dramatic performance; (*b*) the play of styles; and (*c*) movement and plasticity in terms of the architecture of space.

Running through Lecoq's presentation of his work is a metaphorical complex related to the activation of space in performance, starting from '*la récolte de rhythmes moteurs*' (a gathering or harvesting of fundamental rhythmic impulses, dynamic rhythm or the basic rhythms of life), going on to suggest that moods and emotional tones can be identified according to the orientation taken by the body in space (melodrama is 'oblique', as is jealousy, whilst pride elevates and shame seeks to lower itself) and finally engaging with '*l'architecture invisible du drame*'.

Lecoq breaks down movement and gesture structurally, using anthropological and physiological criteria. For him, '*l'homme pense avec tout son corps*' (Lecoq 1987: 17), and these criteria enable him to offer his students a way of analysing and reproducing the dynamics of action. There may well be interesting parallels here with, for instance, the work of Laban[4] and the approach to movement teaching in other schools. But what we are concerned with here is the relationship to improvisation.

Impro work is a central part of Lecoq's courses: a typical four-hour session will contain one hour of movement, an hour and a half of improvisation and an hour and a half of *auto-cours* work in groups, which aims to use the results of the first two areas in building up group presentations.[5] So there is a very close fusion of movement and improvisation in developing the 'play' of performance. And perhaps nowhere else do we find such a precise intellectual and practical structure to movement work in the context of improvisation. For Lecoq, theatre is an '*acte essentiellement physique*', and it must thus deploy its range of meanings through the movement of bodies in space. Every organism has spatial coefficients of position and direction; each mood or style may also operate like an organism in this sense. Lecoq's method is directed towards the identification and physical assimilation of these relationships so that they come to form a 'vocabulary' on which the performer may call as appropriate. Lecoq calls it the '*saisie du réel qui se joue dans notre corps*' (1987: 17): performance always occurs as immediate experience within and across bodies and their emotional and physical sensibilities, be they of actors or spectators, prior to categorisation or assimilation into discursive categories. I know *only and directly* because I know 'before' what is conventionally defined as knowledge. It is the job of any serious actor training to get performers to that condition. In other words, real knowing always has to be a surprise, an amazed 'recognition' – for producers and receivers.

Simon Murray describes the major aim of Lecoq's school as 'to investigate the corporeal basis of creativity' (Murray 2003: 158). Fundamental principles of the exercises presented by Murray are (*a*) movement generates emotion and (*b*) the body remembers. So in targeting a 'site to build on'

(McBurney, cited in Murray 2003: 63), Lecoq is interested not just in the physical flexibility of his early sports training, but more crucially in the body's potential for engendering, registering and remembering experience at subtle and profound levels. For Lecoq, the body moves and speaks as it moves.

Its speaking is an act of memory and an act of creation, an invention of corporeal, imaginative and theatrical languages. To arrive at that capacity, which is in fact something like a 'pre-expressivity' prior to the 'physical score' sought by Eugenio Barba, Lecoq's practice adds to rhythm and flexibility the 'economy and simplicity of movement' of Georges Hébert (see Murray 2003: 165), which feeds into work with the neutral mask. (This is not 'affective memory' in the Stanislavskian sense, but the *production* of a psychophysical 'trace' which can be incorporated into a network of performance signs.) Neutral work opens to that sensitivity towards the least perceptible impulse or sensation; it is the most basic level of Lecoq's work of 'preparation'.

This preparedness leads to a 'read[iness] to be surprised' (McBurney, cited in Murray 2003: 106), which in turn stimulates the capacity to become aware of how bodies move in space (see exercise section on work with elements, pp. 174–5), how they play and interact with each other and how they produce meaning. Its rootedness in the materials of production enables performers to explore the relationship of their bodies to other kinds of body and to the ways these together can reconfigure the space in which they operate: both in the 'optional extra' LEM (*Laboratoire d'Etudes du Mouvement*) course which seems to have in many ways encapsulated much of Lecoq's most astute thinking and which has become if anything even more integral to the school after his death, and in the productions of the companies Murray describes in some detail, Théâtre de Complicité and Mummenschanz. The latter – Murray calls them 'sculptors of the imagination' (Murray 2003: 115; see 110–26) – use a vast range of materials to produce 'a redrafting of the boundaries between masked performance and puppetry' (115). Complicité's work in *The Street of Crocodiles*, *The Three Lives of Lucie Cabrol* and *Mnemonic* specifically produces a linkage of personal and cultural memory out of the interaction of bodies and the objects of daily life – desks, cloth, buckets, books and agricultural tools. *The Street of Crocodiles*, for instance, draws on the fragmentary and evocative narratives of Polish writer Bruno Schultz, and Complicité's transformations of themselves and their surroundings embody the experience and the location of threat, marginalisation and intense desire.

It is thus in this context that we need to see Lecoq's use of improvisation and the way in which the concept of 'play' is central to it. Lecoq uses the term to signify the energy that is shared between performers on stage and in rehearsal – the ball that the game is played with – which is why for him improvisation is very much a matter of physical activation. 'Play' also means the *inter-play* of this activity, emphasising the relationships which spark off or create new combinations: people, movements, moods or styles meet and collide, giving rise to different possibilities. Structuralism's 'play of the signifier' is relevant here, suggesting the idea of verbal play and inventiveness. Other appropriate shades of meaning include the hint of 'bringing into play' and the sense of 'possible movement or scope' as in the degree of play in a bicycle chain, for instance. This picks up another useful angle, namely the balance between freedom and restraint; 'play' here indicates a fruitful tension within reasonably precise limits.

All of these usages are underpinned by the sense that 'play' is a salient feature of mankind's capacity for the production of symbolic form, signalled primarily in Schiller's *Aesthetic Letters* and in Huizinga's *Homo Ludens*. Thus it also implies *playfulness* – the pleasure derived from discoveries in the moment of creativity. Thus for Lecoq 'play' is very much a question of developing the physical articulation of mimetic possibility; for him 'mime' signifies all the resources available to the actor including his use of text, and the function of improvisation is to set those resources in play. Therefore, the outcome is in and through performance, that necessarily improvisatory moment when imagination composes new shapes and makes active the knowledge that resides in the body.

'*Le style est un esprit de jeu*', says one of his course descriptions ('style is a way of playing/a sense of play/a kind of playfulness'): the body of the actor has to be 'disponible' (open, available, ready; see Part 3 below) to engage in different styles which demand that he or she be capable of '*changer l'espace, la vitesse et la matière de son jeu*'– that is, to transform the various coefficients of performance, whose 'content' (*matière*) then becomes something quite different. The 'spirit' of play which emerges is precisely the ability to *activate* a particular configuration, to enter the game of its structuring: an acute mental and physical condition permitting creation to occur ('*provoquant (l')imagination à inventer des langages*').

Lecoq uses the *masque neutre* as the first and fundamental stage in the development of this condition; through it he aims at a physical condition ('*état neutre*'; '*état de disponibilité silencieuse*'; '*masque du calme*') which is at the basis of dynamic extension in space (*l'espace*), time (*vitesse, rhythmes moteurs*) and matter (*animaux, éléments, matières, couleurs, lumières*).

His work then proceeds via the *larval mask*, which offers nascent expressive states, towards an incorporation of the passions in melodrama and *commedia*. For him, improvisation is less about psychological liberation (though that is, as it were, taken for granted) than a matter of building up resources of physical awareness about how people move, how the body develops certain attitudes when it is in certain modes, about the acquisition of precise mimicry which can then be activated in the construction of scenarios, at first more realistically imitative, then involving more elaborately imaginative forms.

For Lecoq, knowledge comes about *through movement*: so 'he attempts to return the mime to the precognitive state, freeing him to gather a new set of sensory impressions in a neutralised state of naiveté' (Felner 1985: 148). He works (via the neutral mask) towards what he calls *mime de fond*, the 'gestural rendering of the essence of reality' (Felner 1985: 153). This reflects an Artaudian belief in the ability to discover a pre-verbal level where, after passing through the *silence de fond* – the first phase of his work, Lecoq says, is about forgetting – one may begin to 'find the gesture of the word, the actions for the verbs in the profound silence in which they were born' (Lecoq 1967).

Anthropologically and anatomically, movement precedes language, and Lecoq seeks to return students to that situation where they discover emotion and meaning through gesture: the *mime de fond* is also the *mime du début* – of the beginnings of all knowing and all articulation.

The *disponibilité* Lecoq seeks is a situation of balance which can draw upon an extensive range of possible movement and action which has been internalised in the preparatory work. Here as elsewhere, then, 'neutrality', of mask and of the whole body, is not a kind of blankness; it is highly charged. The body has a wide range of available resources; neutrality engenders a state in which they are ready to go into play but not programmed to operate in a predetermined way. The 'waking up' exercise often used by Lecoq and others in neutral mask work (Eldredge and Huston 1978) indicates the desired condition: it's rather as if the whole body were 'full of eyes within' and they are all opening to an unfamiliar world.[6] The coefficients of action have to be drawn anew. But if it works, this kind of alertness as the basis of performance can produce inventive and delightful play.

Lecoq uses the Clown to illustrate this. (The Clown is the *'esprit de jeu' par excellence*: Lecoq says that clowns operate 'at a point where all is blunder' – where the unexpected is the rule, therefore.) The semiotics of clowning rate a closer look in this context.[7]

A clown emerges from behind a screen. S/he wears a red nose, but otherwise has no props. S/he looks at us. And for some reason we laugh. S/he looks at us again, pleased to see us. We laugh louder. S/he takes delight in our laughter, and that pleases us too. The clown has done nothing – except *notice* us. And yet we are laughing. S/he has told no jokes. S/he has performed no 'routine' to amuse us. So why have we laughed?

That red nose? It is iconic. It looks stupid, and the clown is not afraid of looking a fool. S/he is vulnerable, and happy to be so.

It is indexical. It draws attention to the eyes and mouth, the expressive parts of the face, pointing that expression and at the same time defamiliarising it. It is symbolic. The very entrance of that nose arouses in us the expectation of laughter to come, predisposing us to judge the clown's actions in a certain way, making us willing to laugh at the slightest provocation.

The fact that the clown was *aware* of our presence was vital. S/he made *contact* with us directly and openly. So the clown has included us in her/his game; right from the start we are implicated in whatever s/he is doing. The clown plays. The clown plays the realities of what and where and with whom s/he finds her/himself to be.

S/he cannot know these realities in advance, for so much of it depends upon us, the audience, that it cannot be pre-planned. Everything is *new* to the clown. Of course, the clown always has 'an act' up the sleeve, a sure-fire set of gags and jokes and routines. But in good clowning s/he may never have to use them. The clown has to 'find the play' in the immediate context. The work is hard and, especially in the early stages, fraught with fear of what Lecoq calls *la tasse* (the 'cup') – in other words, catastrophic failure.

Clowning in this (*ab initio*) sense is one of the purest forms of improvisation. None of the things the clown does is ever guaranteed. Everything is on the brink of *la tasse* – because everything is real.

> For several years now, the clown has taken on a great importance; not in the sense of the traditional circus, which is dead, but as a part of the search for what is laughable and ridiculous in man … We put the emphasis on the rediscovery of our own individual clown – the one that has grown up within us, and which society does not allow us to express.   (Lecoq, cited in Towsen 1976: 353–4)

Neutrality, play, rhythm and the offering of self, fraught at any moment with not just the possibility, but almost the necessity, of failing and looking silly: the clown incorporates all of these in the 'encounter' (to use Grotowski's term) with the audience and always underscores the frailty and the miracle of creation. At any moment the act is on the verge of dying, and yet somehow s/he rescues it, and another fragile construction of gesture or words is launched.

Beckett perfectly understands the condition of the clown, and that of the improviser. The final words of his novel *The Unnamable* express, though in the context of the writer rather than the actor, the fear of self-revelation, of being *true*, of finally encountering oneself:

it will be I, you must go on, I can't go on, you must go on, I'll go on, ... it will be the silence, where I am, I don't know, I'll never know, in the silence you don't know, you must go on, I can't go on, I'll go on. (Beckett 1979: 381–2)

What Beckett and Lecoq emphasise is the need to act (speak, write) *immediately* from the silence, from the unknowing.

Lecoq's work has spawned many exciting companies and solo performers whose style reflects his concern with plasticity and physical precision. Among them are Théâtre de Complicité, whose work relies on exact observation and subsequent stylisation of movement and mood, sharpened by the interplay between idiosyncratic rhythms developed by each performer. From this they construct a texture of emotional situations inscribed in time and space as shape and rhythm and counterpointed by expressive *grummelotage*: their show entitled *A Minute Too Late* deployed their impeccable timing via a series of reflections on attitudes to death – and was itself a comment on the improviser's art. In contrast, Footsbarn Theatre's inventiveness has led to a manipulation or restructuring of Shakespearean texts.

Lecoq trainees have produced shows based on a variety of mime styles and movement, using a range of masks and exploring to the full the possibilities of 'physical' theatre. All of Lecoq's protégés are different; and all of them work in differing fields of theatre. Ariane Mnouchkine, Stephen Berkoff, Peter Brook and Dario Fo have all learned from and with Lecoq. The British group I Gelati made a speciality of *commedia* work, yet a major project, for example, was a five-actor version of Brecht's *The Good Person of Szechwan*. The American Avner the Eccentric presented shows which were a mixture of circus skills and clowning (as Avner Rosenberg he now teaches Clown). Moving Picture Mime Show gained their greatest successes using 'larval' mask work and mime. What links these very disparate groups and individuals – apart from time spent with Lecoq in Paris – is not that they all follow Lecoq's precepts. They don't. In the end, like all students, they take from their training the things that have impressed them most; and, like all creators, they use the things that serve their own artistic needs and discard the rest.

What links them, then, is not a stylistic unity. Each group has its own artistic integrity. Each makes its own vision of a future theatre. They are not all, by any means, devoted to improvisational work: yet all of them share a common theatrical vocabulary and that internalised repertoire of physical and imaginative skills which marks the successful Lecoq graduate.

In some forty years Lecoq's school taught 4,000 students from more than sixty countries, and many of them are well known in Europe and the

US. They return occasionally to Paris, and Lecoq acknowledged with a certain pride the existence of a kind of 'mafia' of his graduates. Certainly they recognise and value each other's work and attribute much of its success to their training, which continues in much the same form after Lecoq's death (continuity is provided by several longstanding teachers and three members of Lecoq's family).

Lecoq himself occupies a major position in the history, theory and practice of improvisation in theatre, particularly in terms of the importance of clearly conceived and precisely executed physical expression. In his work, improvisation and mime become ways of developing highly focused capacities for generating richly iconic texts which articulate an extensive internalised vocabulary of gesture, shape, rhythm and sequence in continually inventive patterns and structures.

For Lecoq, the occasional resurgence of the improvisatory (that is, the *mime de fond*, for him) marks periods of redefinition when theatre returns to its roots. From here it can emerge, as does his own work and that of his students, in new forms, and it does so because his training most centrally focuses on 'pitting the student face to face with himself in a state of perpetual discovery' (Lecoq, n.d.: brochure of L'École Jacques Lecoq).

Philippe Gaulier (1943–) and Monika Pagneux (1927–) together and separately have continued and extended the work of Lecoq. Gaulier distinguishes his work from Lecoq's by saying that, while Lecoq's work centres in movement, his own celebrates *le Jeu*, the playfulness inherent in the moment, the child's game at the heart of acting. He has developed the work of the *bouffon*, and – where Lecoq teaches actors to find their inner clown – he aims to liberate their 'inner idiot'.

Gaulier founded his own school (L'École Philippe Gaulier) in 1980, moving it to London in 1991 for eleven years. It is now based in Étampes, outside Paris. Teaching is in English (Gaulier is fluently abusive in English!) and the school does not select either by interview or audition. Gaulier stresses the political origins of the *bouffon* during the French Renaissance; the 'ugly' (the deformed, leprous) were banished to the margins of society (the swamp, *le marais*), except at festival time when they were required to entertain the 'beautiful'. *Bouffonerie* is, therefore, more than comedy: it is an aggressive and subversive act, designed to take revenge upon the oppressors by satirising and insulting them under the guise of entertainment. Gaulier fantasises that 'the ideal performance for a bouffon would be one where the audience is wildly entertained, go home, realize that their lives are meaningless and commit suicide' (Wikipedia).

Like Lecoq, he employs the method of *via negativa*, and his rejections of whatever he considers to be unworthy or failed or pretentious are much harsher and more brutal than Lecoq's: John Wright has described it as being 'like open-heart surgery without anaesthetic' (quoted in Dominic Cavendish, 'From the sublime to the ridicule', *The Daily Telegraph*, 12 March 2001). (Other alumni include Simon McBurney, Annabel Arden, Marcello Magni, Kathryn Hunter, Cal McCrystal, Sacha Baron-Cohen, Emma Thompson, Roberto Benigni and Helena Bonham Carter: many of whom also trained with Lecoq.)

Monika Pagneux was born in Buckow, moving to France in 1951. She studied dance with Mary Wigman, and mime with Étienne Decroux and Jacques Lecoq. From 1963 to 1979 she taught *Éducation corporelle* at Lecoq's school. From 1973 to 1976 she was also movement director at Peter Brook's Paris centre and began to incorporate Feldenkrais work into her teaching. From 1980 to 1987 she taught with Gaulier at his school. Since 1991 she has lived in Grenoble and still teaches.

Le Théâtre du Soleil

Ariane Mnouchkine's Paris collective Le Théâtre du Soleil, formed in 1964 as a workers' cooperative, reflects a clear development of the tradition of Meyerhold and Copeau (Mnouchkine also attended Lecoq's school in 1966) both as aesthetic practice and as a form of politics of and in theatre.

In 1969 the company mounted *Les Clowns*, a production which was their first real attempt at group creation, the result of an investigation of the circus as a form of popular theatre, intended to break away from the constraints of socialist realism and what the company referred to as *psychologisme* (Kiernander 1986: 196).

Les Clowns continued the use of *lazzi*, together with the 'ebullient, physical style' and 'frantic rhythm' which had marked their production of Wesker's *The Kitchen* in 1967. This was followed in 1970 by perhaps their most famous piece, *1789*, 'a group creation based on improvisations'. *1789* was premiered in Milan at Giorgio Strehler's Piccolo Teatro and then performed from 1971 at their now famous base, the Cartoucherie, until 1974. By this time, the group had established their commitment both to popular theatre forms and to collective, improvised creation around a powerful political statement.

In working on their next project, *L'Age d'or*, the company (partially) succeeded in doing what Copeau had dreamed of, creating a contemporary form of *commedia* that could speak to the twentieth century. Not *la comédie nouvelle* exactly, for the actors of the Théâtre du Soleil had no intention of developing their Masks for the rest of their careers. But to the extent that the work addressed contemporary themes (exploitation, poverty, sexual politics) and did so via the reinvention of *commedia dell'arte* (without attempting any historicist reconstruction of it), Copeau's vision was fulfilled.

In the resultant play, Pantalone becomes a real-estate promoter and Abdullah-Harlequin a cheap construction worker who is bribed to work on a high scaffold in a fierce wind. He dances his death fall to Verdi's 'Requiem'. Pantalone tries to stop the show and tries to cover up the scandal (see Kirkland 1975: 97–100).

Like Copeau's own company, the Théâtre du Soleil went on retreat into the countryside, contrasting the reactions of the villagers of the Cévennes with those of the Parisian critics. Unlike the latter, the villagers simply accepted the work in its totality, making no distinction between the formal elements and the political content. The Théâtre du Soleil's discoveries about the creative relationship between a community theatre and its patrons via improvisation exactly parallel those of Copeau and Saint-Denis:

> The actors improvised every day in various village meeting places, both outdoors and indoors, around themes proposed by the people, who were very receptive to the masks, costumes and physical movements of the performers, as well as to the accuracy of what was expressed about their lives. (Williams 1999: 171)

Mnouchkine and her company read Copeau for the first time (as his *Registres* were being published) in 1974, during the rehearsals for *L'Age d'or*. But their inspiration also goes right back to Meyerhold's early conception of a reborn theatre of the *cabotin* and the *balaganschik* – and includes Meyerhold's political as well as theatrical fervour.

Mnouchkine (who is happy to be thought of as the artistic 'midwife' rather than director of the group) works almost entirely through improvisation. She provides visual materials, imaginative prompts and research materials; and the work grows out of lengthy discussion and careful repetition. From Lecoq, Mnouchkine centrally derived the early emphasis on *création collective*, the desire for performers to acquire a plasticity particularly in their relationship with space and bodies in it and some of her use of masks in rehearsal and performance. These principles – which, as we shall suggest in Part 3, emerge from much improvisation work to similar effect – underpin her concern to require performers and audience to validate and engage with the 'other', as artistic process and political imperative; they are also expressed in her transcultural explorations (*Les Indiades*; *Les Atrides*) and in the sharing of food with the audience at performances (see Bradby and Delgado (2002) and Williams (1999) for a fuller account of Mnouchkine's work).

Dario Fo and Franca Rame

The improvisational style that stems from Lecoq's work is well illustrated, in addition to the examples given above, by Dario Fo and his wife Franca Rame. But English-speaking audiences have a multiply-distorted view of Fo and Rame's work. We need to clarify those distortions – recognise them as such, at least – before proceeding to look at what the Fos' real achievements are.

1. We only know a relatively small fraction of their work, in spite of increasingly available translations and productions of their plays. Fo is one of Europe's most popular dramatists, with consistently more productions in more languages than anyone else over many decades. Still, it is true that most people outside Italy associate the Fos with a limited number of works: *Can't Pay? Won't Pay!*, *Accidental Death of an Anarchist* and *Female Parts*.

2. The plays do not have the political bite that they do in Italy. English versions, divorced from their original context, often seem cleverly satirical – but sometimes merely whimsical. There are, of course, parallels between political injustice or governmental corruption in Italy and in Britain, but translations do not always render specifics and may distort the sense by virtue of different cultural assumptions. British farce is almost exclusively a bourgeois form of lightweight sexual innuendo (except in the hands of Joe Orton), whereas for Fo the term implies a particularly acerbic form of satire readily accessible to 'the people' (the *'piccolo populo'* as he refers to them in *Accidental Death*). Fo wrote to the director of the Washington production of *Accidental Death*:

   Don't call my play a comedy. I call it farce. In current language, farce is understood as vulgar, trivial, facile, very simple. In truth, this is a cliché of Official Culture. What they call comedy today has lost the rebellious strain of ancient times. What is provocative and rebellious is farce. The establishment goes for comedy, the people for farce.   (Fo 1974: 121)

3. Non-Italian-speaking audiences primarily regard Fo as a playwright. Fo is not present to them in the theatre, any more than Shakespeare is. All they have of him are the plays which bear his name (though, as suggested below, they are the work of translators and adaptors as well as Fo). In Italy both Fo and Rame have long been celebrated as performers of their own works rather than as writers. Fo's primary aim is to create

> a throwaway theatre [*un teatro da bruciare*], a theatre which won't go
> down in bourgeois history, but which is useful, like a newspaper art-
> icle, a debate or a political action.   (Fo 1974: 58)

Like Theatre Machine, Fo and Rame produce disposable drama. Not in the
consumerist sense, but theatre 'to burn', like a newspaper when its purpose has been served: plays of the situation, activist responses to a social
and political context. The techniques are farcical, and the structures are
often loose – looser than would be the case if they were crafted only at the
keyboard rather than in the theatre. The 'play', for Fo and Rame, is not
finished when its author stops typing; in fact, it has only just begun its
process of being wrought. It will be rehearsed and will change and develop
throughout that period, as with traditional plays; but then the next, perhaps most important, phase begins. The play is offered to an audience and
will continue to change and develop in response to that audience's reactions during and after the performances. *Mistero buffo*, for example,

> always relied on improvisation, since the audience is involved in it
> and doesn't play a passive part, since it imposes its rhythms, and
> provokes off-the-cuff lines. This type of theatre is recreated from per-
> formance to performance, and is always different, and never repeti-
> tive.   (Fo 1977, trans. Mitchell 1984: 18[8])

Fo is much more than a playwright. He is a director, teacher, stage designer,
student of architectural and theatrical history and song-writer; most
importantly, he is a political activist and a theatre performer.

4. The act of translation itself means that the play becomes a fixed script.
    It loses its improvisational relationship to the audience. Stuart Hood
    writes:

> Franca Rame and Dario Fo work within a tradition of improvisation
> which means the texts of their plays are difficult to 'fix'; they change
> according to the changing political situation ..., different audiences.
> They are like living organisms but within them there is a hard skel-
> etal framework of radical criticism of our society and of relationships
> within it.   (Hood 1981: vi)

Accidental Death of an Anarchist, for example, was first produced at the same
time that Inspector Calabresi, implicated in the 'defenestration' of the
anarchist Giuseppe Pinelli, brought a libel suit against the left-wing paper

Lotta Continua. These court hearings were the immediate context against which the play was first received. The play was constantly updated, and each night included a report on the day's proceedings in the case. *Mistero buffo* was re-created from performance to performance. Franca Rame spoke of developing her one-woman show with audiences in the same way,[9] rather than having a fixed script to which her performance nightly adhered. When the play is translated (*a*) to another country, (*b*) to another language, (*c*) to a different political context and (*d*) to another performer, all that Rame has gained experientially is lost. The play may become by default a 'text' to be rehearsed and performed, alien to its original conception as having a living relationship to a contemporary theatrical and social context. Yet, despite these inevitable distortions, Fo and Rame's reputation grew. Enough of the spirit and theatrical power of their work remained to excite audiences and performers all over Europe and America.

Sources and origins

Dario Fo was born in 1926 near Lake Maggiore in Lombardy. His father, Felice, was a staunch socialist and keen amateur actor. As a child, Fo would repeat the tales of the local storytellers to his brother and sister and built a puppet theatre to act out stories. He also studied and imitated the gestures and techniques of the *fabulatori*, descendants of the medieval *giullari* – 'essentially *pre-commedia* ... popular, unofficial mouthpieces of the peasant population' (Jenkins 2001: 34) – and came to be regarded by the locals as an expert. Tony Mitchell points out how large a part first-person story-telling plays in almost all of Fo's plays (Mitchell 1984: 36), and Fo regards the techniques of the *fabulatori* as 'a structural storehouse' for all his later work – celebrating their love of paradox, contradiction and contrariness; de-sanctifying and demythologising – always and quite naturally political.

Fo believes his work goes back to a tradition of itinerant comedy deriving directly from the *mimes*. As an authority on *commedia* technique, he is perfectly aware of the tradition of the *comici dell'arte* (professional 'court jesters' taken up and given official recognition by the ruling classes) and consciously uses techniques such as *grammelot*, an onomatopoeic theatre language derived from *commedia* theatrical practice.[10] Such techniques develop the quality of *souplesse* and help the actor to discover physical ways of relating to his audience. But he always tries to relate the origins of those techniques to their social context.

Fo worked with Giorgio Strehler at his Piccolo Teatro, where he created *A Finger in the Eye* (*Il dito nell'Occhio*), a piece which broke new ground theatrically: zanier, more satirical and more political. Fo designed the sets and costumes. Franca Rame was in the cast (they married two years later); Strehler did the lighting. But, most important, it introduced Fo to a French associate of Strehler. The choreography for *A Finger in the Eye* was done by Jacques Lecoq.

Lecoq taught Dario Fo

mimic and vocal technique to shape his spontaneous improvisations. Lecoq trained Fo to use his physical defects (long arms and legs, uncoordinated body and flat feet) to advantage rather than hiding them, instructing him in the different forms of laughter, while also introducing him to *Grammelot* and character transformation, ingredients which were to come into their own in *Mistero buffo*.   (Mitchell 1984: 40)

Fo, a natural improviser, nonetheless needed to learn the theatrical skills of performance. Lecoq taught him how to find 'his' clown, his personal comic style. One might say that, although their encounter took place before the school was founded, Fo is the most distinguished alumnus of L'École Jacques Lecoq. Their acquaintance continued (despite various disagreements) with Fo giving special classes to Lecoq's students.[11]

Franca Rame (1929–2013) also taught Dario Fo: she, too, was a gifted improviser, coming from a touring theatre family (Teatro Famiglia Rame) with a repertoire of popular farces.[12] Fo attributed his education in improvisation to working on stage with Rame. She shared in the traditions of the *fabulatori* and the *giullari* – perhaps even the *cabotin*. David Hirst reveals that her attitude to improvisation was that of all strolling professionals: nothing is left to chance (Hirst 1989)! She recorded her performances and made detailed notes of which ideas and jokes worked and which did not. Her style (and hence Fo's) returns to the kind of improvisation that rests, like that of the *commedia*, on solidly prepared and rehearsed foundations. Fo directly credits Rame with teaching him how to improvise (Fo, cited in Jenkins 2001: 80):

The kind of improvisation Rame advocates is not a digression but a way of personalizing the text and creating intimacy with audiences by making them feel that the performer is responding to the specific circumstances of time and place in which the play is happening. (Jenkins 2001: 83)

Fo and Rame conceive of theatre as direct intervention in, rather than detached comment on, political life. That abrasive, urgent struggle, which has often brought them into conflict with leading figures at different points on the Italian political spectrum (most recently and repeatedly with Silvio Berlusconi), is rarely so visible in English versions of their plays, even when presented by left-wing groups. Sexual politics are central to Rame's self-expression, too. She was at the forefront of the women's movement in Italy, and her monologues are performed by actresses across Europe and America.

The jester of the people

The piece that exemplifies the style they have evolved together, and which ties together many historical threads, is Fo's long solo *Mistero buffo* ('comical mystery play'), a dramatisation of a collection of medieval texts deriving from the strolling secular performers and street entertainers of Europe. It is a *bouffonerie* – a grotesque spectacle – a carnival version/inversion of sacred events mingled with *lazzi, canovacci, grammelot* and mime – bound together by Fo's modern *discorsi*, which contextualise the pieces and serve as prologues and discussion prompters.

Mistero buffo is not a static text: it has undergone innumerable revisions, and there are several versions of it. The play is created every time it is performed. It is as if one man has created and performed an entire medieval cycle, an epic conception. The pieces cohere around the idea of undercutting the repressive structures of church and state; by taking an officially accepted form and casting it back into the language of the peasant, he reveals what is grotesque in those structures themselves.[13]

The piece with which Fo usually opened *Mistero buffo* is called 'Zanni's Grammelot' ('*Il Grammelot dello Zanni*'). Zanni, the prototypical *commedia* character, is here played without a mask (although in an *Arena* documentary Fo demonstrates how to play the traditional *lazzo* on which it is based in a mask. See 'The Theatre of Dario Fo'). The theme is peasant starvation, but typical of Fo (and his sources), it is treated as bitter farce: Zanni is so hungry he imagines he is eating himself. He then dreams of an enormous feast. Finally, waking, he catches and eats a fly. Each detail of the scenario is physically portrayed with great virtuosity, accompanied by the onomatopoeic sounds of cooking, eating and digesting.

The pieces were introduced by *discorsi* in which Fo – using the familiar *tu* form – addressed the audience directly, explaining, expanding and improvising. Fo's intended audience was the industrial working class, just as the *giullari* played to the rural peasantry. In Italy, he achieved this aim, playing in occupied factories as often as in 'art houses'. He listened to that audience both during and after the show. Listening during the show means responding to their laughter, shaping and reshaping the text, breaking the frame to incorporate topical or local allusions. Listening afterwards, in the 'Third Act', means incorporating political and social, as well as dramatic, criticism. He has been attacked by the Church for blasphemy in the way he inverts Gospel narrative to reveal the Church's underlying message of political servitude; he has been attacked politically from all sides. For the terrorists he was too moderate, for the PCI (the Italian Communist Party) he was too militant; for some other political dramatists (like the late John McGrath) his style was too disorganised to be politically effective and for the conservatives (in art as well as politics) he was simply unspeakable. But

> When I relate the origin of the *giullare* in *Mistero buffo*, I'm able to tell the story in a convincing way because I believe in it, I believe in the mission which the *giullare* originally chose for himself as the jester of the people. I also believe in it because I've experienced what it means to be the jester of the bourgeoisie. (Mitchell 1984: 21)

Dario Fo, the politicised clown, inheritor of the traditions of the *giullari* and the *comici dell'arte*, stands as the embodiment of the improvisational style of performance and audience relationship that grows from Lecoq's work. That relationship and that style are crystallised in Fo's use of *tu*. From the moment the clown enters, his relationship with the audience *is* a familiar one. What Lecoq's work centres on – above and beyond the acquisition of technique – is the necessity of *complicité*. Linguistic familiarity is more than cliché. The improviser's relationship to the audience (in Martin Buber's terms) is that of 'I and Thou', not 'I and It', because in this style of work the performer and his audience create the piece *together* (see Buber 1923).

Performance and the grammar of participation

The processes Fo employed are, according to him, similar to montage and cutting between cameras (the use of millimetrically precise gestural detail to create close-ups forms part of the grammar of his acting) or to the sixteen-line structure of blues:

> I also improvise in a sixteen-line structure. When I invent an action, you can count it out, and you'll see that it fits into that rhythm. If I insert a new gesture, a discovery for achieving a particular effect, I have to take out something else. I can't add a line with impunity. (Jenkins 2001: 135)

This quality of precision and rootedness in the specifics of place and situation is what enabled Fo to 'play' the interaction with the audience in musical terms. This is technically achieved by breathing – and that rhythm in turn determines the interrupted style of the performance on the micro-cosmic scale – which in turn leads naturally to the interrupted, epic style on the macrocosmic level:

> The tempo of breathing … comes from the necessity to listen to the reaction of the public. To be able to do this you have to interrupt the flow of the performance with a pause that allows you to observe the tension of the room. (Jenkins 2001: 136)

> I take the same breath you are taking. We breathe together so that you have enough breath to make the sound of laughter. You laugh and we continue on together … We are telling the story together. (Jenkins 2001: 145)

'Interrupting', like 'accidents', gives a clue to the generative mechanics of Fo's improvisatory style: it identifies the points of suspension and renewal at which the chance to make new sense is available. That is the only way to ensure that what you do is a new creation. The shifts of perspective, Jenkins claims, are intentionally Brechtian, in order to stimulate under-standing from a variety of perspectives: rhythm here is not just a musical device but a way of moulding a psychodynamic response. The gap, which is in many ways a crucial signal of the improvisatory attitude (What next? Where next? Who next? Why?), is used as a means of treating the audience democratically, inviting them to become co-creators. Jenkins continues:

> The theatrical jump-cuts in Fo's performances suggest a complex interaction between history, economics, religion, morality, and mun-dane current events. Fo's comedy exists at the overlap between the private and the public domains.   (Jenkins 2001: 266)

'Gaps' (rhythm is syncopation around silence) are structural holes or moments of in-betweenness which mark important opportunities for intervention and sense-making by the receivers; they offer the possibility of alternative vision, border-crossing, bypassing of taboos; they are the synapses of new connections, but these connections are not only per-formative and active (important enough in itself as a mode of engagement with the audience) but also moments of political and ethical recognition.[14] That political engagement has been real and sustained throughout the Fo and Rame era. In 1997, Dario Fo was awarded the Nobel Prize for Literature. The citation praised his emulation of the medieval jesters 'in scourging authority and upholding the dignity of the downtrodden'. Rame, who died in 2013, aged 83, spent the years 2006–8 as an Italian senator, representing the anti-corruption *Italia dei Valori* party (until she felt it had compromised *her* Italian values in supporting Romano Prodi's government). Both Franca and Dario were members of the *Partito della Rifondazione Comunista* (a breakaway Communist party) from 2010. Fo has been described as the chief ideologue of former comedian Beppe Grillo's Five Star Movement (*MoVimento Cinque Stelle*), promoting action on ecological as well as political grounds. His energy, humour and political passion remain undimmed as he enters his 90th year.

4　Improvisation for Change: 'Paratheatre', Participation and Performance Work beyond the Stage

The previous chapter situated improvisation as a key component in the renewal of performers and performance, with important reference to styles of acting, development of performance confidence and capacity and ultimately the deployment of the 'invitation' in a political as well as aesthetic sense. In this chapter we follow these trends beyond the stage as conventionally conceived and look at ways in which the improvisatory has underpinned work which aims to engage with personal and public worlds in a variety of domains and genres.

Jerzy Grotowski

Jerzy Grotowski (1933–99) came into contact early in his career with the work of Stanislavsky (at the Polish State Theatre School in Cracow, and at GITIS in Moscow, where he did a one-year directing course, learning also about Meyerhold and Vakhtangov). Visiting France in 1957, he learned of the works of Jean Vilar, his teacher Dullin and Marcel Marceau (a pupil of Decroux, who was taught by Suzanne Bing). Thus, he was open to the traditions of Stanislavsky, Meyerhold and Copeau, in addition to those of Polish writers and directors (for example, Witkiewicz, Słowacki and director Juliusz Osterwa, who founded one of the first theatre *communities*, similar to Copeau's and Stanislavsky's experiments and prefiguring those of Grotowski himself).[1]

In 1959 Grotowski became the director of 'the only professional experimental theatre in Poland'. The 'Theatre of the Thirteen Rows' had a small company, dedicated to ensemble work from the outset. It began in Opole with nine actors, three of whom were to remain to form the nucleus of the later *Teatr Laboratorium* group. These were the actress Rena Mirecka and the actors Zygmunt Molik and Antoni Jahołkowski. In 1961, these three were joined by Zbigniew Cynkutis and Ryszard Cieślak. (Stanisław Scierski joined in 1964, Venezuelan actress Elizabeth Albahaca in the late 1960s.) This group – together with Ludwik Flaszen as Literary Director – were the co-creators of most of Grotowski's work after that time. In January 1965 the company transferred to Wrocław, where it nominally remained until its final dissolution in January 1984, after twenty-five years of performance, teaching and research.

Jennifer Kumiega describes the theatrical situation in Poland at the time as being largely dominated by the director and (as with Western theatre) by literature (Kumiega 1985: 11–12). Right from the beginning (despite his increasing status as *auteur*) Grotowski wanted to re-establish the primacy of the actor and of communication via the actor's body:

> To create theatre we must go beyond literature; theatre starts where the word ceases. The fact that a theatrical language cannot be a language of words, but its own language, constructed from its own substance – it's a radical step for theatre, but Artaud had already realised this in his dreams.   (Flaszen 1985: 12)

The company moved gradually towards this goal, both through discussion with the 'Friends of the Theatre of the Thirteen Rows' and through performances such as Mayakovsky's *Mystery-Bouffe*, a stage version of *Shakuntala*, and *Dziady* ('Forefather's Eve', with words by Mickiewicz). This production saw the beginning of Grotowski's relationship with Eugenio Barba, later to found Odin Teatret, who came to see one of the performances, stayed on as Grotowski's assistant for two years and was largely responsible for popularising his work outside Poland. Then followed the major productions which established the Theatre Laboratory as an internationally respected group of theatrical pioneers and extended the frontiers of theatrical possibility in their use of space and their demands on the performers' bodies, voices and minds: *Kordian, Akropolis, Faust, The Hamlet Study, The Constant Prince* and *Apocalypsis cum Figuris*.

Jennifer Kumiega discusses four main areas of development during this period:

> (i) the emergence of the principle of 'poor theatre'; (ii) the attitude to, and treatment of, literature and text; (iii) spatial construction and relationships (environmental theatre); and (iv) the actor-spectator relationship.   (Kumiega 1985: 17)

These are the four main planks on which Grotowski's early work rests. In 'poor theatre', the actor's body is the primary resource. Everything else can be dispensed with: text, costume, lighting and so on are revealed as 'accidents' rather than 'essentials' in the act of performance. The actor can be and do anything and everything. (For instance, if a mask is needed, the actor's own facial muscles can create a mask.) Everything needed for the production is there in the performance space throughout; objects are transformed simply by the actors' use of them. Text is used but it is reformed, deconstructed and reconstructed text, displaced and given new meaning by the way it is employed by the performers.[2] The performance space envelops and includes the audience; they and the actors share the same space and time, the same event.[3] In the end, for Grotowski all performance is an encounter between the actor and the spectator – and between the actor and himself. Throughout the early work there develops the idea of the actor making a 'total gift of himself' – the 'total act'.

Grotowski's *theatre* practice – as distinct from the *paratheatrical* work which we shall discuss shortly – is implicitly based on a theatre of signs: a semiotic theatre, in which texts, objects and actors are infinitely redeployable. Words are relexicalised; texts are intercut and their intertextuality made evident – often blasphemously: the actor searches for the archetypal physical sign of the character's condition. But, beyond the semiotic, even in the early days we can see the quest of the actor to escape from role: to be himself. The theatre exercises (described first in *Towards a Poor Theatre*) and the daily training routines give a slightly misleading impression of Grotowski's aims. The exercises were not a 'training' for the act of performance. They used improvisation in training, certainly, developing remarkable physical and vocal skills, but the aim was not purely to develop bodily and imaginative *skill*, but rather to bring about the spiritual condition in which

> the body would not resist the actor ... For as long as the actor has the feel of his body, he cannot attain the act of divestment. The body must totally stop resisting; in effect, it must cease to exist.   (Grotowski 1979: 36)

Part of Grotowski's aim, then, was to *subdue* the flesh. The body is seen as an obstacle to be overcome, and the harsh yogic exercises are as much a means of fighting the body as training it. The same stricture applies to the mind of the performer (at least as it is evident in the teaching work of Rena Mirecka): the mind's desire to shape, to form, to 'script' the event, the intellectual ambition to create 'meaning' (by making intertextual references), hampers the ability genuinely to experience the event. The famous *via negativa* approach of Grotowski's rehearsals is an attempt to prevent physical or mental habits from interfering with the process of *giving* oneself utterly to the event (this is one interpretation of a process which, although described differently, is to be found equally in, for instance, shamanistic experience, the Harold's 'group mind', Ken Campbell's 'lizard brain' and indeed the goal of Nicolás Núñez's Castaneda-derived 'walk of power' exercise).

Thus for Grotowski, acting in 'poor theatre' is not dressing up and pretending: it is divesting – sometimes physically, always spiritually – and being. One is aware of the actor as an actor, not in the Brechtian manner of calling our intellectual attention to the fact, but in the sense that, beyond the matter of the play, the event is an encounter with the actor as a human being. He is not so much a *character* of the play, as the *subject* of the play. His skill may amaze us, but what moves us is the actor's gift of himself.

Grotowski believes we use art 'to cross our frontiers, to fill our emptiness' (Grotowski 1969: 21). For him this is a slow process in which we 'peel off the life-mask', and the theatre thus becomes (as, in somewhat different ways, for Artaud and Brecht) 'a place of provocation'. Workshops and performances are a confrontation with the vulnerability of feeling and experiencing which lies behind public and private roles. We often avoid this exposure: we screen ourselves by adapting our feelings to the image we have of ourselves or that we would like others to have of us. Actors, even or especially in (dangerous) impro situations, are prone to this: it's much easier to adopt a stereotyped role. This easy route out is tempting precisely because the alternative is frightening: facing up to the fact that I don't know who or what 'I' *is* or how it might respond if it abandons all *a priori* models. Before filling our emptiness we have to experience it, and that is uncomfortable. But until we do this we can only go on 'acting' what we think we ought to feel.

> We arm ourselves in order to conceal ourselves; sincerity begins where we are defenceless ... if a method has any sense at all it is as a way to disarmament.   (Grotowski 1973: 121)

Grotowski's 'obstruction exercises' aimed at locating and neutralising individual blocks or tendencies to hang on to comfortable habits; one technique used by Rena Mirecka in workshops illustrates this. As soon as the participants become aware that they are no longer fully 'with' whatever they are doing (that is, starting to decide what they ought to feel or do instead of doing it), they must immediately do a backward roll (without looking behind) and come up facing in a different direction. This physical breaking of the situation allows a fresh start.

In Grotowski's process, we find many of the basic assumptions of improvisatory work in theatre and outside: work on actors and audience, in the awareness that their relationship creates theatre, and centred on the establishment of a state which may be called neutrality, being wiped clean, deconditioning. This last aspect is comparable with Copeau's neutral ('noble') mask work mentioned earlier and involves an element of fear and crisis. It is only moving through this that allows us to experience without the familiar filters of habit. (When you put on a theatrical mask, especially a neutral mask, the body suddenly 'sticks out', all its awkwardnesses revealed; you can't 'hide' it behind the attention-catching expressions of the face.)

If we *do* move through, if we abandon ourselves to what may seem like chaos, to the totally unknown, we may find that there is an unsuspected order to feeling. In the backward roll exercise, people rarely bump into each other: the body orientates itself in space without conscious thought (just as blindfold trust exercises, or the 'eunuch/pauper' game described in Part 2 may produce an extension of spatial awareness and other subtle operation of the senses). We may begin to 'know' and to 'behave' in different ways, which change our patterns of relationship to others and to the environment.

Grotowski's work – with performers and audience – thus implicitly moves beyond the boundaries of what we conventionally designate as 'theatre' and seeks to set in play fundamental physical and psychological capacities. But it arises in the first instance from a concern to establish a more acute experience *in* the theatre and from an understanding of what that involves. In his later Theatre Laboratory performances, the audience (strictly limited in numbers) is assigned a role (accomplices, judges and so on) which inhibits the passive or detached gaze. Provocation is physical and psychological, and thus personal and political. It affects the audience as a whole, making them uneasily aware of collective responsibility and, as individuals, making them confront the limits of their capacity to understand and respond. What is created first is the sense of panic at being cut off from familiar behaviour, which is exactly paralleled by the demands on the actors: Grotowski 'stresses the moment of surrender ... the extinguishing of individuality, and then the elation and regeneration involved in the recognising of "another" reality unobtainable in everyday life' (Grotowski 1973: 121).

Grotowski's work with the Theatre Laboratory, in its various phases, always focused on small groups (of actors and audience members) exploring or being subjected to very intense experiences and sometimes reaping rewards in the form of profound personal 'breakthroughs', revelations of suddenly liberated or unblocked capacities for doing and understanding. There is, in addition to the emphasis on psychological process, something slightly esoteric, hermetic and elitist about this kind of activity, necessarily largely self-selecting in terms of participants. Of course, all intense work with actors requires relatively small groups, and improvisatory work is certainly no exception: but there are many instances in which that work aims to open itself up to a wide public and to formulate its presentation in a 'language' of directly accessible physical or symbolic signs. Grotowski's approach is even more 'difficult' than, for example, *commedia* or Lecoq's work. But it's clear that Grotowski himself was aware of this and that this awareness contributed to the move towards 'paratheatre'. In the course of this move, the boundaries between performers and spectators are broken down; thus, although the total number of participants at any one event is not necessarily very different, their function and relationship to each other change significantly. *Performance* as psychophysiological process opens itself to a wider clientele, but in doing so performance as theatre is left behind.

The charge could be made that by moving out of theatre, and ultimately out of Poland, Grotowski confirms the 'solipsistic' or even 'narcissistic' direction of his work as opposed to practitioners like Kantor and Różewicz. Grotowski's response to the political situation can be seen as a form of retreat. However, that should not obscure the significance of his work with actors, within the contexts of bodies, links between mental and physical action and the importance of focus, generosity and openness.

After *The Constant Prince* in 1969, the search for technical mastery becomes less important, and the exploration of personal authenticity through group activity becomes central.[4] The major focus is on the discovery or disclosure of the full self (or Self, to give it its Jungian emphasis) through group activity. In its various phases and locations (for example, the US, Australia and France), the work is seen as 'research' (the 'University of Research' operated in Warsaw in 1975), sometimes with a small select group, sometimes with participants from a slightly wider public, though these too were carefully screened and selected. The aim is to achieve a condition of personal and interpersonal behaviour where 'a man does not impose himself ... He comes forward and is not afraid of somebody's eyes, whole. It is as if one spoke with one's self: you are, so I am' (Kumiega 1985: 144).

Activities include work on aspects related to acting (release of vocal and physical blockages); the use of language to penetrate to, rather than conventionally mask, the personal; exploration of the 'oscillation between game and play' and workshops leading to interpersonal contacts. The experience of paratheatricals directly fed the later work of the Laboratorium: in 1981 Ryszard Cieślak directed *Polish Thanatos*, in which the audience was informed: 'It is possible for those present – without constraint – to enter the action. Your participation in the particular life of this group may be active, vocal, or simply by being with us' (Kumiega 1985: 208).

From 1976 onwards, Grotowski's attention turned towards a new focus, which he called the 'Theatre of Sources': a multicultural exploration of the ritual, communal roots of the theatrical experience and an attempt to study their foundation techniques or sources. In many ways, his study of non-Western ceremonies, liturgies and ritual forms seeks a return to the original, shamanistic experience of inner transformation – of making over one's body and one's self.

The latter two phases especially work towards this 'meeting' between ancient modes of performance score (song, dance) and the highly personal associations which these evoke in the performer through physical response. This process raises lots of questions – for instance about how particular stimuli, which are necessarily culture-specific, may resonate with performers from other cultures. Does this quest for some kind of (historical or material) 'origin' in the realm of the pre-expressive resemble Barba's claims for 'universal' kinds of extra-daily balance across cultures? (Schechner 2002: 297). But it is a form of 'improvisation' which fits into the spectrum of work which uses impro to engage with kinds of otherness or extension of the self.

The work of Nicolás Núñez also engages with this dimension and similarly opens up possibilities that extended modes of sensing or feeling represent a form of 'participation' which has ecological implications. Núñez's *Taller de Investigación Teatral* (Theatre Research Workshop – TRW), founded in Mexico City in 1975, engages in practical research in theatre and ritual. The group worked for a year with Grotowski during his Theatre of Sources period; they developed 'anthropocosmic theatre' – a theatre of the human in the cosmos. Núñez's book describes the TRW's work as 'devices of "participatory theatre" which give back to our organism its capacity to be the echo box of the cosmos' (Núñez 1996: xvii). Deborah Middleton reports that 'the work consists largely of interactive "dynamics," structured sequences of psychophysical actions in which participants play an active part and through which they may access altered states of experience' (Middleton 2001: 42–3).

Although there are some parallels, the use to which Grotowski puts improvisation is, in the long run, clearly different from that of Copeau and Lecoq and even, though to a lesser extent, from the direction taken by Johnstone and Maude-Roxby. For all of these people, theatrical performance is still the issue, whereas for Grotowski and Núñez it has been superseded by other concerns, however much these arise originally in the context of performance. But Grotowski's way of thinking and working has had important effects on developments in theatre and perhaps most of all on the theorisation of theatre and performance – thinking *about* it and developing an aesthetic and a range of theoretical approaches which account for its influence in various spheres. Improvisation is now used widely in other contexts, ranging from 'psychodrama' as a recognised form of therapy, to various educational and developmental applications (role-playing in language learning, in project-centred work in schools, in the acquisition of interpersonal skills in counselling, in training for management or negotiation situations in business). The Bibliography lists publications which deal with some of these areas. Part 2 sets out some of the techniques and exercises available, and we will discuss the implications of the use of improvisation in a wide variety of contexts in Part 3, as well as picking up the ramifications of the essential change in *status* of improvisation (from a tool to what Bakhtin would call a genre or mode of operation) which we have signalled frequently. First, we shall consider a range of examples of its use in the situations we mention above.

Jacob Moreno: Stegreiftheater and psychodrama

Jacob Levy Moreno (1889–1974) was, among many other accomplishments, a renowned confabulator. He liked to embellish the story of his life, making biographical statements about him at best somewhat provisional.[5] As far as can be discerned, he was born as Iacob Levi into a Sephardic family in Bucharest; he preferred to claim he was born aboard ship during a storm on the Black Sea. His mother moved the family to Vienna, where he studied medicine – hearing Freud and Jung lecture – and began his career. He was for a time a tutor to the family of Elisabeth Bergner, later a leading Austrian actress. At medical school,

> he became interested in social issues and started to experiment with ways of facilitating social change, most of which were either weird (he grew his beard long, wore strange clothes and gave up worldly goods) or revolutionary (he worked with prostitutes), or both.   (Gale 1990: 85)

After graduating, he divided his practice between lucrative paying clients and the poor, whom he treated without charge.

His association with theatre began while tutoring the Bergner children. There are accounts (perhaps true) of his attracting a crowd of children in Vienna's Augarten park and regaling them with stories which he improvised dramatically for them. And when they told stories of family problems, he would encourage them to act them out.[6] In 1921 he founded *Das Stegreiftheater* (the 'Theatre of Spontaneity', located in Vienna's Maysedergasse) which operated as a prototypical improvised 'Living Newspaper'. The actors – among them future international stars like Elisabeth Bergner[7] and a youthful Ladislav (László) Löwenstein (who later changed his name to Peter Lorre) – would improvise in public upon the day's newspaper articles. According to one source:

> *Mit seinem Theater der Spontanität schuf Moreno ein Forum, in dem aktuelle, tagespolitische Fragen, aber auch persönliche Probleme der Teilnehmer nicht nur erörtert, sondern unmittelbar verkörpert und erfahren wurden.*

(With his improvised theatre Moreno created a Forum in which topical socially relevant questions could be examined, as well as personal issues of the participants, which were not simply mentioned but directly embodied and experienced.)[8]

According to Charles, Moreno's agenda for the Stegreiftheater 'reads as a blueprint for the improvisational endeavour: there is no text, an inclusive mode of performance is sought that breaks down divisions between player and spectator, the event is creative rather than reproductive, and environmental and innovative staging practices are sought' (Charles 2003: 98).

The painter and actress Anna Höllering was a leading member. Her husband, the writer Georg Kulka, told Moreno that she was difficult to live with, though sweet and charming in public. Moreno noted that Anna tended to avoid seedier, darker, riskier roles in performance and suggested to her that she consciously try to confront them. In analysing her responses, they noted that the more she acted out anger and violence on stage, the happier she was at home. This is the key observation from which grew the psychodramatic cathartic process, which Moreno took to America when he emigrated in 1925.

In 1931 he founded Impromptu Theater (more or less a translation of *Stegreif*) and the review *Impromptu*; he was naturalised in 1934. In 1936 he opened Beacon Hill Sanatorium in upstate New York, the site of his most famous theatre of psychodrama, and became associated with New York University (where one of his colleagues was Margaret Naumburg). In 1942 he founded the Sociometric Institute and the Theatre of Psychodrama in New York City. Most importantly, he married his third wife, Dutch-born Zerka Toeman Moreno, in 1949. Derek Gale believes the method:

owes as much to Zerka Moreno as it does to J. L. Moreno. It is no insult to Moreno's memory to say, that he was the visionary and thinker and that Zerka tidied up and developed his vision. (Gale 1990: 88)

The principal techniques of therapeutic psychodrama – often confused with other practices, both psychiatric and dramatic – require a private space. Beacon Hill had a circular undecorated stage; some chairs, seating blocks and cushions; a reinforced back wall covered in carpet (against which chairs, etc. could be harmlessly thrown if necessary); a balcony above and behind it and seating for the spectators. The formal stage is regarded as necessary to form a therapeutic boundary between participants and audience, but its actual shape matters little. Sessions are only ever facilitated by a trained, experienced therapist called the 'Director', who, after a warm-up, elicits from the watching, participating group by a variety of techniques someone who wishes to work on themselves, a 'Protagonist'. This protagonist, the client at the centre of the psychodynamic transaction, tells their story and is then helped by the director, assisted by volunteer 'Auxiliary Egos', to act it out. The director effectively 'interviews' the protagonist, encourages the re-enactment of a 'scene' and instructs him to 'role reverse': in other words, to play the other pole of a problematised relationship, while an auxiliary takes his role. In a dramatised conversation with a deceased mother, a daughter may be encouraged to put herself in the mother's role for a time. By an intuitive and empathetic process which Moreno called 'tele' (pronounced 'tay-lay'), the facilitator knows when to intervene and when to suggest role reversal or invite a soliloquy from the central actor and guide the protagonist safely towards 'catharsis' – usually the liberation of affect in tears – after which there is a cool-down period of 'sharing' in which the significance of what has transpired may be discussed and realised cognitively.[9]

Moreno's beliefs and practice are linked to a network of artistic and theatrical work spanning more than a century, whose key points might be Jarry, Brecht and Boal. He begins in resistance, disagreeing with the emphasis Freud – whom he met while at university in Vienna – places on the (bourgeois) individual and instead construing humans as social beings, working with prostitutes and refugees, and, like a cross between Zürich Dada and Alfred Jarry, mounting an All Fools' Day carnival in the Vienna Komödienhaus in 1921, in which he appeared 'in [his] king's boots, king's beard, and king's hat' (Pörtner 1967: 11) and invited the audience to join in creating a 'sacred apocalypse'. In 1923, as well as his manifesto

Das Stegreiftheater, he published *Der Königsroman* (*The King's Novel*), which denounced the deadening influence of Fathers, Kings, Prophets, God and Therapists.

His legacy might also conceivably include Artaud and the Situationists, both of whom influenced the body in performance and the nature of the performance event in significant ways, but for our purpose there are two more immediate and interlinked lines to pursue. They are his work on spontaneity and his attitude to the spectator.

For Moreno, the sign of being fully alive is to be a complete player, to *play* your life to the full. He who plays is most powerfully himself: '*Die Lebensmächtigsten müssen die Spielmächtigsten sein*' (Pörtner 1967: 12). So the spontaneous is a mark of the ability to escape inculcation and all forms of social programming and indoctrination, manifested both externally and internally (for example, as super-ego, for which Moreno constructed the balcony in his psychodrama theatre). *Stegreiftheater* aims to articulate the unconscious, and in order to do so it needs to overcome both gestural/ physical and verbal inhibitions: it thus goes further than Freud's 'talking cure' and is closer to the kinds of process Keith Johnstone targets in work to overcome conventions and taboos. (Moreno viewed *commedia* as too stereotyped and conventional: he said it tended to cover up the 'free space for improvisation' with events.)

Playing requires people to join in. Moreno asked Rudolf Königsfelder to design him a 'theatre without spectators' for the 1924 Theatre Technology Exhibition in Vienna, and his intention here was '*die Wandlung der Zuschauer in Zuschauspieler*' (Pörtner 1967: 11), which, with a degree of hindsight, might be translated as 'to change the spectators into spectactors'. Like Augusto Boal (see below, pp. 99–103) too, Moreno saw the 'safe' fictional space of theatre as affording '*Freiheit des Handelns*' ('freedom of action') and the possibility of articulating what it has not been previously possible to speak. Although the emphasis in Moreno's case is more immediately on the therapeutic than the communal or political, there is a progression in the work of both men, although in a reverse direction. Where Moreno starts with individual process (not forgetting however that he conceives the individual as a group member in a social context), Boal finds a need to address this dimension when concerns which might initially be thought to be only 'public' reveal their roots in the experience of individuals. Moreno's scenarios are usually developed by using a number of co-performers to assist the protagonist in materialising his or her situation, often in rapid (staccato, succinct, 'image'-like) succession; Boal's 'Cop in the Head' and 'Rainbow of Desires' techniques similarly use a 'row of bodies' (Pörtner

1967: 12). Moreno particularly emphasises the need to play not the passage of time, but the 'moment'.

The liberating function of spontaneity and play and the injunction to engage the spectator in the theatrical process, conceived as both social and individual events, mark an important understanding and practical use of the methods and implications of the improvisatory: it can, as many of its practitioners recognise, be simultaneously an aesthetic, a psychodynamism and a politics.

Jonathan Fox and Jo Salas: Playback Theatre

Playback Theatre was founded (also in upstate New York) by Jonathan Fox and Jo Salas in 1975 and has become an international success, with major branches in Australia, Germany, the UK and around the world (the International Playback Theatre Network has over 100 companies in some 40 countries). The form acknowledges debts to both Moreno and Augusto Boal, and both Fox and Salas were briefly connected with a Connecticut 'improv' group called 'It's All Grace' as well as having experience of travel in the Far East, thus synthesising from many of the different strands of improvisational work we have discussed (Salas 1993; Fox 1994).

Playback is distinguished from psychodrama and from Boalian methodology. Its format as public performance is ritualised. The 'Director' of psychodrama is replaced by a 'Conductor' who facilitates the event and solicits stories from the audience. The 'Protagonist' becomes the actor who plays the 'Teller', the storyteller from the audience. The auxiliary egos of psychodrama are here formalised into professional actors. The space is kept deliberately open and simple and reflects the psychodramatic arena (though without the reinforced back wall and balcony of Beacon Hill). The public nature of the event distinguishes it clearly from psychodrama whilst also posing ethical issues concerning performance and autobiographical storytelling.

Lucy Smith of ThreadBear Theatre (Huddersfield, UK) says:

Playback Theatre has connections with other improvised theatre, using 'Short Form' for brief moments and 'Scenes' or 'Long Form' for fuller narratives.[10] The 'Short Forms' help the audience and performers to become connected and warmed up to the interaction required for a Playback Theatre event, where the actors are entirely reliant upon the audience to share personal stories. The Conductor leads the event and develops a rapport with the audience, asking initially for short moments from their day, their journey, or a feeling connected to the performance theme. As the event progresses the Conductor encourages longer moments and stories to be shared, inviting audience members to come onto the stage to do so. Whilst the performance of a 'Scene' or 'Long Form' takes place the Teller remains onstage and so has a specific viewpoint of the onstage action, as well as being viewed and witnessed in this position by actors and audience. (Smith 2014)

The actors sit upstage, on chairs or on boxes. There may be a rail with a selection of coloured scarves, which are the basic props of Playback. The Conductor sits downstage right, with the Teller on a chair beside him or her. When a Teller has been chosen, and has recounted a personal story (the story must belong to them in some way), the Conductor will assign actors to roles and say 'Let's watch'. Smith continues:

> A Musician, who sits downstage left, often with an array of percussive and melodic instruments laid out, will begin to set the atmosphere as the Actors step into an opening tableau. The actors will then enact the events which have been recounted with an emphasis on metaphorical exploration using dramatic image, symbolism and music. The actor playing the Teller leads the improvised action, ensuring that the point of view of the Teller remains the central axis for the performance. Other actors take on various and flexible supporting roles as characters, objects, environments, atmospheres, inner thoughts/emotions etc. The actors work in combination with the Musician to provide a sense of atmospheric sound, and will use a Chorus structure at times to comment on the action or highlight underlying themes.   (Smith 2014)

The actors will then enact the events which have been recounted – sometimes from the Teller's point of view and in a naturalistic mode; sometimes in a more stylised form or from a perspective that the Teller lacks. The events are referred to the Teller for confirmation ('Was it like that?') and may be adjusted or reviewed, before an aesthetic closure is conferred on the performance by the troupe, which functions as an 'Act of Service' to the Teller (Fox 1994).

For Chris Johnston, Playback is relatable to Keith Johnstone's *Lifegame* (with which Phelim McDermott and Improbable have had such theatrical success) in which improvisations cohere around the life stories of a particular individual, rather than to psychodrama (Johnston 1998: 240).

However, in contrast to *Lifegame*, says Smith, 'Playback Theatre remains committed to being a form of social interaction by inviting anyone to tell a story, and it is precisely the variety of people and stories with contradictory and complex experiences that allow an event to act as a vehicle for community interaction and reflection'. *Lifegame,* which derives from Keith Johnstone and Loose Moose, 'is considerably more narrative, a signature feature of Johnstone's work. Performances progress in a linear fashion throughout the life of one volunteer' (Charles 2003: 146). Playback Theatre has often been used in areas of conflict: the Tel Aviv Playback Theatre troupe (Rowe 2007: 24–5) created an auditorium for opposing stories and experiences; they could be heard and considered with the aid of both emotional connection and the 'safe' distancing of the Teller. Other areas of engagement include education, human rights, work with refugees and corporate applications.

In fact, Fox and Salas's key insight has been to position Playback away from the psychodynamic pole of therapy towards a cooler, cognitive affective approach – from personal, emotional action centre-stage to a more detached, observational stance at stage-right. The Teller does not violently re-enact (with all the potential problems known to therapy of transference and reinforcement) like the Protagonist but instead watches a skilful re-enactment, avoiding metaxis, but gaining the ability to redirect problematised experience from the sidelines. 'It is in the role of witness to one's own story that the crux of Playback Theatre lies, having a connection made visible to both actors and audience, in fact becoming part of the performance and the ritual. This sense of honouring the story and the Teller places a degree of responsibility on the performers that can differentiate it from other improvised forms' (Smith 2014).

Playback Theatre thus offers the individual the same chance to rescript personal experience that Boal's Forum offers social groups and requires instantaneous verbal and kinaesthetic response from its actors; it usually doesn't however provide the chance to take this forward to specific action beyond the event or to subsequent revisitings of the situation.

Augusto Boal

Boal (1931–2009) conceives of theatre as a politics, a practice which unites performers and receivers in an interactive and dialogic mode of engaging with the personal, social and ideological parameters in which we live, in order – as with Bert Brecht, but in a manner more reliant on the process of making theatre than with analysing its product – to open up possibilities for change.

Boal's well-known *Games for Actors and Non-Actors* is a compilation of games and exercises (sometimes referred to by Boal as 'gamesercises' – as in much improvisation work, the two things tend to merge). It is extensive and has become widely used in many countries and many forms of what might be called theatrical process work in which participants are encouraged to articulate their situation. Paul Heritage speaks of 'the most systematic and widely used techniques by which non-actors can discover a means of making theatre' (Heritage 2002: 151). Ultimately the games aim to enable actors and 'spectactors' to engage in the various forms or stages of activist theatre promoted by Boal – image theatre, invisible theatre and forum theatre, which later develops into legislative theatre. In the process, however, they draw on improvisation, on an understanding of the liberating personal and collaborative effects of theatre games and the exploitation of the ability to signify and express through and with the body; in short, on an awareness of the outcomes of impro not dissimilar to those suggested by Johnstone, and a sense of its importance in actor training, which itself can be made available to 'non-actors' as a kind of personal empowerment, development or therapy in ways similar to those promoted by Barker, Lecoq, Grotowski and others.

In Boalian practice, improvisation is also a necessary ingredient of Forum theatre, in which a short play or sequence of scenarios depicting a situation of social or political 'oppression' is shown once and then repeated with an invitation to the audience – who ideally recognise the situation as one affecting their own lives – to intervene and speak or act out alternative responses in order to work towards a potential improvement, thus becoming 'spectactors'. The second (and any subsequent) run is compered by a 'Joker' who engages the audience, helps volunteers to make interventions and decides how far to let each one continue. S/he will also further engage in debate with the audience about the effectiveness or otherwise of the intervention and lead them in recognising each spectactor's contribution through applause. This is the first example of the need for improvisation skills: a high order of interaction with both audience and performers is required, and each intervention demands a different response. The second example relates to the performers in the scene. Normally the victim of oppression is replaced by the spectactor, though it is also now not unusual to allow the replacement of other characters, so long as this does not result in an unrealistically 'magic' solution (for example, an unmotivated change of attitude on the part of an 'oppressor'). The other actors need to respond in character to the intervention and to play the scene out in order to test the effectiveness of the suggestion. Here they will naturally have done some preparatory rehearsal of the most likely kinds of intervention to occur in each particular situation; but how the spec-tator produces this is largely unpredictable, and they will be required to improvise appropriate responses on the spot. What is required therefore in Forum are two forms of improvisation skill: semi-rehearsed but remodelled character work, rather like that used in 'hot-seating' exercises, and spon-taneous interaction with audience, play-situation and play-event. Frances Babbage says, 'Forum Theatre is playfully combative' (between actors and spectactors), and 'elements of unpredictability and creativity make Forum Theatre at its best highly entertaining and challenging' (Babbage 2004: 69).

So the games and exercises which Boal suggests lead towards both of these, in similar ways to those which we outline in Part 2: they develop the ability to respond rapidly mentally and physically, to be alive to the dynamics of the play situation, to work together as a group and to be able to develop the substance of a character to the extent that it is possible to respond to modifications in the 'script' without being thrown. Babbage indicates the following categories of preparatory work (see also Part 2):

Theatre of the Oppressed	*Games for Actors and Non-Actors*
Stage 1: Knowing the body	Feeling
Stage 2: Making the body expressive	Listening
Stage 3: The theatre as language	Dynamism
Stage 4: The theatre as discourse	Seeing
	Sense memory

Key features of Boal's method set out clearly in Babbage's book, which con-textualises his development and both explains the principles behind the training methodology and offers a clear track into his process, have al-ready been indicated in terms of links with Moreno (see above). They in-clude the belief in the power of theatre *process* as personal and psychosocial liberation, which is grounded in the awareness of the role of play in the sense both of group dynamic and of observable modelling of a situation which may subsequently be changed. The use of short scenarios (images, snapshots) to encapsulate key transactions and situations and the role of a 'facilitator' ('Joker' for Boal and 'witness-director' for Moreno) to construct, comment on and solicit reflection or contribution from audience-partici-pants are common to both (it may however be more accurate sometimes to speak of a 'difficultator', since his or her role is often to prevent easy out-comes and open up alternative possibilities) (Boal, cited in Paterson 1997). Both are noted for their aggression towards what they saw as the repres-sive or pacifying function of conventional theatre practice – Moreno in his antagonism to 'historical theatre' and Boal – following Brecht – for accusing Aristotelian catharsis of being a repressive mechanism, a kind of passive opiate; and both believe that theatre can be a personal and public/political form of 'therapy', though Boal might also be suspicious of the use of this term, and Moreno's work becomes almost entirely centred on the dynamics of groups and individuals in social, rather than political, contexts.

Boal's work connects many strands of improvisational practice. It emerged during the Latin American 1960s aesthetic and theatrical revolutionary scene and has links with the *Creación Colectiva* of Enrique Buenaventura (Fritz 2013: 277–86). Here, improvisation first meant articulating the unspoken reactions and feelings provoked in the performers by the text; later it became a process of identifying the conflict structures in the material. The group also worked by building up an iconography or sequence of images. Aspects of both of these techniques are visible in Boal's practice. Buenaventura however emphasised the supremacy of the aesthetic where Boal shifted towards the politics of collective creation. But Boal's last book is *The Aesthetics of the Oppressed*, which, in its full Portuguese version (the English is different), deals at length with the kinetic and relational aspects of performance.

In this light, theatre (process) is understood as 'a creative ritual', whose parameters are biological and neurological; Birgit Fritz details Boal's contact with Feldenkrais's work (via Brook and Schechner) which he saw as serving his aim to produce a 'whole human being' (Fritz 2013: 324), and there are strong links between the somatic awareness of Feldenkrais's system and the fundamentals of sensory awareness in *Games for Actors and Non-Actors*, as outlined above.

For Sanjoy Ganguly, who runs India's foremost Boalian company, *Jana Sanskriti*, 'Theatre of the Oppressed' is empowering because it develops relationship and agency through aesthetic means (Ganguly 2010). Crucially, Ganguly believes that it enables participants – actors and spectactors and the communities to which they belong – to 'script the play' rather than 'play the script' (2010: 128–9): and the play is the play of their own lives and socio-political realities, as well as the playing out and unfolding of their expressive potential. The improvisatory in Boal's practice thus spans a spectrum from the development of sensory and relational awareness ('sensory thinking', the aesthetic potential of embodied sensitivity, see Fritz 2012), to the production of blueprints for engagement and action – what Ganguly refers to as 'rational collective action' (Ganguly 2010: 87–9).

Boal's work is conceived as personal and political liberation as a means of activating response to environmental, social, cultural, doctrinal and political restrictions: a theatre of, by and for the oppressed. The fact that a large part of the training he envisages is made publicly available as 'games' indicates his place among significant practitioners of the improvisatory in theatre and establishes the link between the personal dimension of theatre-based work and its insertion in social and political life. In particular, his concept of 'the cop in the head' identifies oppression as internal as well as external, signalled also in the development from *Games* to *The Rainbow of Desire*, in which Boal focuses on methods of liberating suppressed emotion as a fulcrum of personal and subsequent collective empowerment. The penumbra of Boalian work is now very extensive, both geographically (well-known groups in France, the UK, Germany, Scandinavia, Austria, India, Brazil, the US, etc.) and generically, and in terms of the impact on the perception of interventionist theatre practice around the world as an ethico-political praxis.

Doing it with you: participatory, immersive and movement-based work

As we have mentioned earlier in several places, there is a considerable body of work, both in the UK and globally, which seeks to enable *all* participants, including or indeed especially those who would in more traditional scenarios have been assigned the role of audiences/spectators, to experience directly for themselves through participation in performance, to whatever degree, physical, psychic, imaginative, affective or cognitively radical, possibly transformative events. We have been at pains so far to indicate that there is a very strong strand of the history and application of improvisatory work which allies it closely with what on the one hand might be seen as a phenomenological view of the proactive, desiring, connection-making and self-creating subject, and on the other as a pedagogy of liberation and innovation. Particular markers would be Heathcote, Boyd, Spolin and Johnstone; their vision meshes with aspects of that of more recent thinkers like Bourdieu, Badiou and Deleuze as well as many practitioners who have attempted to change the relationship between 'stage' and 'audience' or, like Boal, to explore possibilities of interactivity and empowerment by breaking down the divisions between performers and receivers. Alongside this, and perhaps as another facet of it, has gone an increasing availability of the 'workshop' event and situation: from educational settings (virtually all theatre companies offer such opportunities, and many school and college students have experienced them), to social/therapeutic contexts (prisons, work with particular client groups, e.g. homeless, asylum seekers) and to an alternative model of development practice (PAR – Participatory Action Research); and a raft of workshop-style activities focused around dance and movement, some of which issue sometimes as public performance, others not at all. This as it were closes the circle with where we began this paragraph: in some ways a lot of 'immersive' performance, although offered to a paying public, is less a public than a private experience. What we are interested in here is the degree to which all of these activities draw on elements of the 'unexpected', 'spontaneous', 'free' and 'interactive'; in short, how they fit into the spectrum of the improvisatory and what this says about it in the current situation.

This work embraces a number of forms. We can't deal with all of them here, but we will look at some examples of paying-audience-oriented work, which links with aspects of what we have discussed above (particularly the Chicago style) but also takes it further, exploring more actively the kinds of 'offer' and 'risk' which are involved for participants from both 'sides'; open a side-door into a short discussion about stand-up, which also involves risks and has ways of dealing with audiences; interrogate the phenomenon of 'immersive theatre', which tailors experiences to discrete small groups – sometimes to a single individual – and thus accepts multiple constructions of its own work; pick up some further dimensions of Theatre Sports and look at several kinds of movement-related interactive/improvisational practice which seek to offer participants ways of finding kinetic forms of self-expression, physical and psychic liberation and ease of communication, including Contact Improvisation, Butoh and Movement Medicine.

Gareth White's *Audience Participation in Theatre: Aesthetics of the Invitation* (2013) and Josephine Machon's *Immersive Theatres* (2013) address work which pulls notions of performance beyond the frame of the stage and targets the embodied and active – and sometimes at least spontaneous, if not fully improvisatory – engagement of the 'audience' (who are therein redesignated as participants or co-makers of the event, which itself is likely to escape the confines of 'conventional' theatre).

We don't have room here to chart all the origins and routes of this work, but some of the *points de repère* in the US signalled by Machon would be Allan Kaprow, Happenings, Richard Schechner and the Performance Group/ Wooster Group; contemporary/recent work in the UK, for instance, would include Punchdrunk, WildWorks, Coney and Nimble Fish and also Brith Gof, Forced Entertainment and Lone Twin; we have also briefly discussed French company Philippe Quesne/Vivarium. Here, perhaps more than anywhere else in the book, it might be appropriate to invite readers to compile their own list.

Being a participant quite often involves wearing headsets (we have for instance experienced this during quests, animations of neighbourhoods or memory-scapes and a form of guided movement-and-exercise exploration done inside a large hall with occasional contact with other participants): so people will spend some or all of the event undertaking an individual (imaginary and/or actual) journey, probably responding to suggestions or 'orders' transmitted by the recorded messages they are receiving. Their progress is thus to some extent externally controlled (for 'health-and-safety' reasons this applies equally to many events where participants are invited or persuaded to tour cellars, large rambling buildings, underground passages, varieties of outdoor settings, etc.), but they may be able to make choices from a menu, and they are always free to respond imaginatively in their own way or indeed to terminate the interaction or switch it off temporarily. As often, the questions are: is this reactive or proactive? Are they controlled or empowered? Can both things happen simultaneously or at least alternately? How much 'improvisation' really occurs? Do people who go to these events to a large extent 'self-select'; for example, are those who undergo Punchdrunk's *Masque of the Red Death* (2007–8) predisposed towards receiving *frissons* of Gothic horror?

Machon's subtitle is 'Intimacy and Immediacy in Contemporary Performance'. Immersion, she points out, invokes rites of passage and may be 'comforting or potentially dangerous' (Machon 2013: xiv). The Index for the *Immersive Theatres* book doesn't include 'improvisation' or any references to practitioners of it (not even to theatre sports or the Harold). But it has extensive reference to 'site-specific', to 'play', to 'interactive' and to 'empowerment'. From this, it is clear that immersive theatre aims at intimacy, interactivity, play, participation and extension of direct experience. These are similar to key goals of improvisatory work. In interviews with performers and creators words like 'collaboration' (between performers and audience, with the site, etc.), 'democracy' and 'empowerment' come up a lot, as does *communitas*. The summary picks out the following:

- 'A more open response to the experience'
- Focus on how space and place are vital to the form and choreography of the work
- 'Allow[ing] a participant to make genuine human contact; to feel alive'
- '"*really being*" in the moment of the event' (Howells); '*attend[ing] to being*'
- 'Encourag[ing] the audience to become playfully curious'

- 'Focus on the full sensorium of the human body'; 'giv[ing] credence to the intellect of the body'
- 'Respect for the audience member as participant and collaborator'; [operating a] 'contract' [which] 'ensures safety and enables agency for the audience-participant within the work'. (Machon 2013: 149–50)

Punchdrunk operates 'a form of immersive theatre in which roaming audiences experience intimately epic storytelling inside sensory theatrical worlds' (Machon 2013: 3): 'audience-participants are [sometimes] required to wear a carnivalesque mask that encourages liberation' (*ibid.*). Work by them and other companies includes Punchdrunk: *Sleep No More, Faust, The Uncommercial Traveller*; Nimblefish: *Einstein's Dreams*; WildWorks: *A Very Old Man with Enormous Wings*; BABEL, *The Passion, Wolf's Child* and Wilson+Wilson: *Mapping the Edge, House*. All these events were produced over about ten years between 2003 and 2013, because they were frequently recreated for different spaces. (Nimble Fish's Samantha Holdsworth studied with Gaulier, Silvia Mercuriali, who runs another 'immersive' company, and Marina Spreafico, a Lecoq teacher.)

Consciously participatory processes 'make the audience members into material that is used to compose the performance: an artistic medium' (White 2013: 9). Notions of participatory engagement here are derived in part from performance art, which has exerted an influence on the shift towards the 'performative'. Machon's book deals with 'immersive practice that arises from the fusion of installation art and physical and visual theatres of the 1980s' (Machon 2013: xv); White points out that '[p]erformance has a register that comes before the theatrical or the artistic, in which we manage our presentation of ourselves, and in which we find the materials which allow us to become ourselves' (White 2013: 5).

This connects with an understanding of the politics of participation: 'the recognition of the participant as a subject within the field of activity of the performance with the potential to enter dialogue with it' (White 2013: 26). The underlying insight is (*pace* Bourriaud/Guattari) that 'participatory engagement with artworks promotes the fluidity of subjectivity in positive ways' (2013: 24). It may lead to a view that '[a]rt's job in this process is to resist the neurosis produced by capitalism, ideology, supplier-client relations and all those forms of otherness that press us into rigid, narrow and frozen assemblies of subjectivisation' (2013: 24). Art, according to Bourriaud, 'has the capacity for thermodynamic effects: melting the frozen relations produced by homogenizing culture' (quoted in White 2013: 25). (Keith Johnstone would buy that.)

This could be a manifesto for the improvisatory; and this and other recent work on audience participation/immersive theatre/performance events have begun to redefine or give alternative versions of the nature of 'audience' in a theatrical situation. It validates smaller, more consciously 'experimental', collections of spectators/participants and thus suggests – however questionably – that the nature of the theatrical event is shifting. Whatever the socio-historical reasons for this, it coincides with an aspect of much of the work we consider in this book, namely that it is concerned less with providing a 'group' entertainment than with offering opportunities for individual experience/expansion, that is, with shifts of state, in terms of sensory alertness, receptivity, response and stimulation of conscious reaction. It also, of course, opens out vast dimensions which we cannot possibly enter into here, by including *audience* – quite correctly – in any consideration of what happens in a performance event. This book has enough to be going on with looking mainly at performers and trainers and trying to chart what they do, how and why they do it and how it has manifested across forms and genres of performed work in many parts of the world at many different times. We gladly take up the issue of extending the interrogation to the 'invitation' to the audience and some aspects of the reconfiguration of this phenomenon, but we can't peer under all the stones which conceal what audiences have got up to.

One angle which is raised by White and which meshes with an idea we have mooted in our discussion of Copeau and Lecoq, among others, is that of the 'gap ... between performer and audience' (White 24), which is also that (Freirian, one might say[11]) gap between teacher and learner. 'Preparation', which is a vital component here, refers to the business of making ready the participant's capacity to create, rather like Copeau's definition of neutrality. What is emphasised is that performance is an event in which the interactive element is prepared 'so that it has gaps to be filled with the action of ... audience members ...; gaps that require the thought and felt response of the audience to make sense of [the] material' (White 30). Iser's ('Reader-Reception theory') model of the *Implied Reader* (Iser 1974) is more fully embodied here. Gaps stimulate agency: 'Aesthetic experience ... is a multiplication of connections and disconnections that reframe the relation between bodies, the world they live in and the way in which they are equipped to adapt to it. It is a multiplicity of folds and gaps in the fabric of common experience that change the cartography of the perceptible, the thinkable and the feasible,' says Jacques Rancière (Rancière 2009: 72). White asks, 'Does the audience participatory event consist of the structure or the action that happens in the gaps that it creates? The answer must be that it is both ...' (White 2013: 30). If it does change the 'cartography' in this way, it has a lot going for it. (A somewhat oblique but rather appealing parallel might be found in Stoppard's 'England? It's a conspiracy of cartographers!' from *Rosencrantz and Guildenstern Are Dead*. Changing our view on nationalism and ownership might not be such a bad thing from time to time, though it does prove rather risky for Ros and Guil.) This desire to activate the receiver, to persuade them to go on a journey – often quite literally – means that they have to inhabit the world of performance in and for themselves, as opposed to observing it vicariously in others. (Of course, as White points out, all spectatorship is participatory to some degree and Boal, for one, is too quick to write this off.) The implied assumption is that this offers participants a more direct access to how meaning is made. The improvisational element here is the coefficient of uncertainty and unknowability; although this is present in any performance, here – and in much of the improvisatory practice we describe – it is the touchstone and sweet spot of the event.

Much immersive theatre is designed to get the participant to 'become the event' (Machon 2013: 28). In many cases this means in a sense 'becoming' the environment, experiencing a different, more intimate imaginative and sensory relationship with it. So there is an ecological aesthetic at work here which activates a shift in the relationship between 'self' and 'environment', contests their separation and resituates their components in the direction of what Morton (2007) calls an 'ambient poetics' – a kind of liminality, a moving across accepted boundaries/borders. 'Walking is now an artistic language', says Machon (240), and this suggests an 'immersive' relationship to the environment. Spaces are frequently evocative and immersive or participatory events aim to make use of that. On an obvious level, they evoke real or imagined memories or associations of the location itself. *Masque* and many other shows use 'spooky' cellarage; one of us took part in an event about drovers in a cow-barn in rural Wales; Punchdrunk's *The Uncommercial Traveller* activated 'Dickensian' bits of East London. Agreeing to be in that place at that time means that you are opening yourself to the possibility of this kind of 'evocation': it's not improvisation *per se* but it's giving yourself permission to operate in the zone where it arises. Coney's *A Small Town Anywhere* (BAC 2009) recreated the experience of being in a French village in Nazi-occupied France, in which countless people were denouncing their neighbours to the authorities by letter. Audience members played a part in developing the story and thus became responsible for its outcome (*The Guardian* 19 October 2009).

Spyros Papaioannou, writing about immersion, explores 'the energizing potential that fragmentary and incomplete experiences create in performance' (Papaioannou 2014: 160). He identifies the interaction of destabilisation and loss of subjectivity and role as central to the creation of 'new agential possibilities' (165) for spectators. Papaioannou suggests that 'this potential of the audience is made possible by experimenting with, and sometimes blurring, the boundaries between normality and irregularity; that is, between the safety of spectatorial distance and the unpredictability of proximity' (166); spectators also 'become part of the choreographic land-scape by means of what they do' (*idem*), thus reconfiguring the conventions of theatrical space. A major feature of immersive theatre, he points out, is 'constant movement *in between* established coordinates' (167), which turns the audience into 'deterritorialised' Deleuzian 'nomadic subjects', as they negotiate the 'intermezzo' or path between different events, encounters, roles and locations. They thus 'float' within 'sites of mystery' (165) as spec-tators, performers, performance and site are continuously reconfigured. '[D]ramaturgical structures... hinge on networked spatiality, rather than on linear teleology' (McGinley 2010: 12; cit. Papaioannou 162).

In general then, there's a narrative in much of what we have been discussing here which is about extending into the 'unknown' or the 'other', about making and accepting offers, about taking and maybe managing risk and about redefining self and the contexts in which it operates, which links back not only to the (pedagogic, political) avatars we have noted above, but also to the sense of a quest through time which takes us back to the shaman. We need to examine pragmatically and critically claims about 'risk' – are we talking about self-indulgent sensation-seeking or a form of bourgeois escapism, or is this a fully inhabited personal and social undertaking? And what about the case of Forum, where the risks may be quite specific, local and actually in some cases life-threatening (see Ganguly 2010: 81–3)? But it looks as though impro-related activities might put on the line the 'self' in many of its roles and spheres of activity: is this a motive for doing as opposed to simply observing?

With all of this in mind, we will move a little further along the 'partici-patory' spectrum and look at some familiar and not-so-familiar forms of 'free movement' work.

Freeform as kinetic being: contact improvisation, Butoh, Movement Medicine

Contact improvisation is a dance technique characterised by exploration, mostly in pairs or threes, of continuous interactive movement, weight sup-port, shifts of position and rhythm; the focus is on maintaining contact within an improvisational structure which constantly skirts with falling off balance.

It developed out of the (American) tradition of modern dance in the 1960s (drawing on work by Merce Cunningham and Anna Halprin, among others). One strand – 'East Coast' – is more open-ended and experimental, 'a redefinition of self within a responsive, intelligent body' (Novack 1990: 3); 'West Coast' work moves more in the direction of (professional) public performance and applications to teaching, therapy and theatrical experimentation. Contact improvisation consists of 'spontaneous physical dialogues' practised by two or more people (either as a dance practice or as a social event) who attempt to keep a physical point of contact between their bodies while moving freely with or without music. The focus is on bodily awareness and physical reflexes, responding to and working with a partner or partners. There is some degree of crossover with Five Rhythms Dance, Alexander Technique, Feldenkrais, Laban, martial arts and so on.

Steve Paxton, a dancer with a background in tumbling and martial arts, was a member of several modern dance companies in New York in the 1960s, including that of Merce Cunningham and his longtime collaborator, composer John Cage; Contact Improvisation emerged from his exploration of improvisation with the dance theatre collective, Grand Union (1971–6). During the same period San Francisco's Mangrove collective performed extensively in the US, Canada and Europe.

Contact Improvisation has been applied to choreography, to dance training and to working with children, seniors and disabled populations, in therapy, visual art, music, education, environmental work and social activism. Many people do it for pleasure and personal development. Its key features include the need to 'yield rather than resist', an interest in 'the ongoing flow of energy' (Novack 8) and the goal of tuning into 'a dialogue... between sensations of activity and receptivity' (Novack 153). Novack's identification of this as 'seeing through the body' and 'listening through the skin' chimes with the principles underlying Boal's games (see p. 100–101). There are also parallels with dance therapy work which guides students in 'focusing inwards and outwards using movement to sensitise and heighten personal body awareness and to stimulate receptivity to others' movement' (Hayes 1996: 29).

The focus is on a number of tactile practices and sensations: generating movement through the changing points of contacts between bodies, sensing through the skin, rolling through the body (segmenting the body, moving in several directions simultaneously), experiencing movement from the inside, using 360-degree space, going with the momentum and emphasising flow and weight (derived from Novack 115–21).

Paxton was interested in 'finding out how movement could arise' (Novack 54, n.22), which suggests a parallel with Lecoq's and Copeau's work; the aesthetic of Contact is concerned with developing an internal awareness of movement, relationship in space and with others, giving and receiving and the co-creation of continuously altering patterns of bodies, energies and forms.

Butoh originated in Japan with a performance by Tatsumi Hijikata in 1959. Originally named '*ankoku butoh*' or 'dance of utter darkness', an amalgamation of influences fed it: German expressionistic dance (Mary Wigman and Harald Krautzberg), Surrealism and Dada, Marcel Marceau and Flamenco. Butoh is 'an attempt to uncover the dance that already exists'. It uses reduction, stillness and slow motion, which heighten presence: the dancers ideally are aware of everything going on around them and within their own body. Butoh loosely translated means stomp dance (there are parallels here with African and Indian forms and with the practice of Tadashi Suzuki) or earth dance. Hijikata believed that by distorting the body, and by moving slowly on bent legs, he could get away from the traditional idea of the beautiful body and return to a more organic natural beauty – an understanding which does not assume that 'nature' is simply an anthropomorphic reflection.

Butoh is a dance of utter darkness. Although it would claim to be very different from its ancestor, *Noh*, the same concept underlies both. If Noh's aim is to create *hana*, 'the moment when the flower blooms', what underlies *hana* is *kugen*, darkness. In *Noh*, stillness is more crucial than movement and silence more so than sound – and some of the chief characteristics of Butoh ('highly charged stillness and very embodied slow motion') reflect this too. The energy which creates new form can only be accessed in its fullest kinetic reach if the awareness first comes to a point of rest (Copeau, Eldredge, Lecoq and the neutral mask …). That rest is properly a tiny blip of nothing. No sound. No movement. No light. It hasn't started yet. The task is to start the world again from the darkness. All good shamans are up for that.

Movement medicine. Susannah and Ya'Acov Darling Khan's *Movement Medicine: How to Awaken, Dance and Live Your Dreams* (2009) charts the basics of Movement Medicine, which is a combination of free dance, guided 'introception' (sensitivity to physical and emotional activity) and shamanic practice. It evolved out of Five Rhythms Dance (Gabrielle Roth) and shamanic teaching and, like the former, is participatory rather than performative. The work targets development and integration of body, heart and mind, the liberation of movement and the ability to intuit and respond to feeling as directly as possible through spontaneous gesture, rhythm or movement, singly or in collaboration with others. The principle is to free up the 'inner dreamer', the intuition of what to do: not planned, but letting it arise from whatever condition you are in, giving it permission to be free. It thus has strong affinities with the patterns of development targeted through theatre games and with the underlying assumptions about mind/awareness/body/expressiveness which Keith Johnstone and others have articulated.

There are similarities of taxonomy to other participatory performance work: exercises tend to be cumulative in structure (first on one's own, with awareness of body/space/movement/sensation etc.; then moving/dancing with one other person, then in 4s ...). Another pattern (cf. Gaulier) is moving back and forth between 'macro', 'medio' and 'micro', always attending to the process but with different degrees of energy and expression – sometimes sharing with partner/4s, sometimes moving back into individual dancing, with eyes open or closed. Some exercises include observing others, noting spontaneously what comes out of their movement.

These could be stages in actor-training and improvisatory process. Past/present/future is also explored as intuitive/bodily connections, so for instance a sequence may be about recognising (accepting) where you/the idea/the shape 'comes from' [ancestors, past], engaging with it (playing) [fully who/what/where you are in present] and developing together with it (co-crea-tivity in a historical sense, new configurations or combinations) [what will be, what you leave behind, future]. Looked at like this, 'realisation' is also relevant – it's a recognition of the potentiality of self through time, of the essentially creative nature of being and of the enjoyment of it as process.

There are other practices we could mention here. Many of them, like Mary Overlie's **Viewpoints** (a structure for working on movement and gesture developed by Anne Bogart and Tina Landau), appear in the cur-riculum of performer-training establishments (in the above case, NYU). They represent a wide span, ranging from professional and for-the-public to amateur and personal, from the gymnastic to the contemplative or imaginative. But people who participate in one – to whatever degree – would be unlikely to find themselves alienated from others. Maybe that is because *at this historical moment* they represent a menu of embodied, transcultural, participatory practice – largely accessible for middle-class explorers, operating through largely non-verbal, kinaesthetic channels. So also *synchronically*, they point to a desire or felt need which seems to be similar to that articulated by participants and practitioners of immersive theatre, and which perhaps also says, impro is *now* (as well as at many other junctures in the history of performance).

Theatre Sports

Theatre Sports is a trademark/format developed by Keith Johnstone and operated by the Theatre Sports Institute; it provides training, coordination and information and also licenses 'Maestro' (known in the USA as 'Micetro') and 'Gorilla' – two other short forms. There are companies throughout the world (see Theatre Sports Institute website for more information). Its method is essentially Keith Johnstone-derived short-form. Megan Kruskall, who has been running Theatre Sports in South Africa for over two decades, distinguishes this from Chicago improv short-form (Del Close) by saying that Johnstone's focus is on *narrative*, whereas the Close/Chicago version targets *emotion*, in the form of striking experience. Kruskall describes what she does as 'slightly competitive short-form improv' in which the audience is the key partner. She agrees that major principles are offering and accepting, being available for spontaneity and surprise and being prepared to play (this holds for both performers and audience) (Kruskall 2012).

Events work as a contest between two or more teams. The audience or some audience members may function as judges (with large scorecards). Games include:

- Story in a literary mode (audience selects)
- Interview with 'expert' plus sign language interpreter
- 'Emotional roller coaster' (play scene, switch emotions on cue)
- Shared memory (characters interact around this stimulus)
- 'Come again?' (any character can use this phrase to stimulate new tack)
- 'Dreaming': audience member recounts day's events which are replayed by impro team as dream
- A 'who/where/what' scenario based on audience suggestions

Principles include spontaneous acceptance of stimuli, rapid switching of role/mode/style narrative. Scenes last about five minutes.

'Theatre of the Ordinary'

Al Wunder's 'Theatre of the Ordinary' rejects the *via negativa* approach of Lecoq, Gaulier and others in favour of a 'positive feedback', affirmative approach (Wunder 2006: 122. And see below Chapter 10, n.7). He sees the danger of creating a negative mindset in which the performer knows that something isn't working, but isn't being given help to find an alternative.

> [What] distinguishes the performances of *Theatre of the Ordinary* from most other forms of theatre is that they are totally improvised utilising movement, text, sound or song to communicate to an audience. There are no pre-planned ideas or suggestions of character traits given by the audience ... The first sounds, words or movements become the genesis for a theatrical event that has not been rehearsed and will never be seen again.   (Wunder 2006: v)

This openness extends to Wunder's teaching style: 'The teaching itself is improvised. I haven't planned a class since I stopped teaching dance technique in September 1971' (2006: vii – though, as his book makes abundantly clear, there is a methodology, an approach, ultimately derived from his training with Alwin Nikolais, which underpins the teaching). His collaborators are generally non-professional performers (although they do include dancers, musicians and actors among their number, among his students in California were Terry Sendgraff, who would develop a gymnastic, aerialist dance style she called 'Motivity', and Ruth Zaporah, who would found 'Action Theater' – see below, Chapter 7). Wunder claims improvisational performance '... is a *showing of* ourselves rather than a *showing off* of what we can do' (2006: vi., our emphasis). He says, 'I won't teach you what to do. I'll inspire you to evolve your improvisation style and help you to develop your self-teacher and inner-director by creating guidelines for you to explore various aspects of performance. I'll offer practical ways of being more articulate with your movements, voice, and the spoken word. I'll create a non-competitive, playful environment that encourages you to be impulsive with your physicality and vocality' (http://www.artsatlas.com.au/wunder/; accessed 24 May 2014).

   Ruth Grauert describes a session led by Wunder back in New York (he has been based in Melbourne since 1982) in 2006. He began with a very brief comment on three types of motion (axial, rotary and locomotive) and then invited the group to begin, starting with their fingers and developing rapidly to full body engagement, then to working in pairs and small groups, all without further prompting. Another session began with a simple exploration of directional gaze: the eyes are the primary sense in his system of work. He talks little, until a session is well underway, saving discussion and feedback to the end (Ruth Grauert at http://bearnstowjournal.org/al_wunder-rev.htm; accessed 6 May 2014).

   Al Wunder speaks of his discovery of Belly Dancing (2006: 30) as taught by Jamie Miller in California, which he later used as the basis for much of his own teaching in Melbourne. This should not seem as strange as it does. Wunder had been an accomplished dancer and dance teacher, although

plagued by a back injury. And Belly Dancing is itself, at root, an improvisational form from Egypt (sometimes called *raqs sharqi*, literally 'oriental
dancing': a hybrid modern form that grew out of the older *ghawazi* style).

Improvisation in poetry

The ubiquity of improvised poetry is easy to demonstrate. There are almost
too many examples from which to choose, and they can be selected from
the Arab world, Africa, the Caribbean, India, Japan, South America, many
parts of Europe and the United States. Here too we are talking about improvisation in the live compositional process, not just – as in 'performance
poetry' – in the delivery and inflection, which also has an improvisatory
element.

   To substantiate the claim of ubiquity, we have examples from Yemeni
and Palestinian poets, from Xhosa-speaking South African *iimbongi* (improvising praise poets and their poetic form, *izibongo*), West African *griots*,
to the *extempo* of Trinidadian calypsonians, with forms ranging from the
Indo-Pakistani *mushaira* and *ghazal* to Japanese *haikai no renku*, *la paya* of
Chile and *la payada* of Argentina, Uruguay, Paraguay and Southern Brazil.
From Europe we can point to the *spirtu pront* ('ready witted') style of *ghana*
in Malta and the equally competitive *bertsolaritza* of the Basque country,
while from Italy we have the *canto a braccio* of Lazio and the *stornelli* and
improvvisazione in *ottava rima* of Tuscany; from the Balkans comes the major
epic tradition of the *guslari* (described by Milman Parry and Albert Bates
Lord) and there are or were many parallels from the Greek and medieval
periods of our common history. From America, most recently, we could
cite Freestyle rap. The list offers a great diversity of forms, each adapted to
its local culture, but employing remarkably similar means – improvisation
controlled by adherence to metrical and musical rules and shaped by traditional verbal formulae.

   And obliquity is easy to demonstrate, too. Many of the forms described
encode a resistance to controlling or repressive authorities which improvisation enables the practitioners – and their audiences – to sidestep, just as
we saw in the case of theatre improvisation in times of censorship.

   Each of these words – *calypso*, *bertso* and *ghana* – encapsulates a cultural and usually political history. 'Calypso' encodes a condensed history in
which the West African *griot* is slowly remade into a Trinidadian 'chantwell'
(or *chantuelle*) and then into a calypsonian by means of slave trafficking and
French, Spanish and latterly English colonialisation and linguistic oppression – and the form embodies and performs aloud the resistance to them as

well. It reclaims and celebrates West Indian verbal competence and speed of wit, even as it may at times speak to its audiences on more than one level. During the Second World War, for example, Trinidadians laughed at calypsos mocking Hitler's tyranny, while simultaneously being aware that the same lyrics encoded their resentment of British colonial rule.

Bertsolaritza records the struggle simply to remain Basque but also retains a memory of a tradition of female troubadours, the itinerant *profazadoreak* (profanesses) whose existence is attested by the Arab historian Al-Makari (who writes in the fourteenth century of female Basque slaves noted for their elegance, education, excellent voices and cultural attainment in ninth-century Al-Andalus) and the early Basque historian Esteban de Garibay y Zamalloa (1533–99), who writes during the reign of Philip II of the 'women improvisers' (*damas improvisadoras* or *improvvistraces*) of the region. The Church had a hand (unsurprisingly) in suppressing the tradition, the Bizkaia (Vizcaya) Council Laws of 1452 banning traditional mourning rites (including sung laments) and defamatory songs (*profazadas*) sung by women. These women were perhaps the first *bertsolaris*. There is much dispute about the antiquity of the form, with some claiming a vast but unrecordable antiquity and others pointing to the historical emergence of the modern form only since perhaps 1900. As frequently happens, the suppression of an oral tradition gives rise to the emergence of a literary replacement, and Basque poetry tends for a period to be male-dominated and written. Only in the early twentieth century does *bertsolaritza* emerge in its modern form, and only since the death of Franco and the resurgence of Basque nationalism has the *bertso* regained its fully improvised and ungendered nature. There are again women *bertsolaris* (such as Estitxu Arozena and Maialen Lujanbio), and they are again successful. The maturity of the improvised *bertso* is attested by the ability to address complex politics (e.g. assassinations by ETA, Spanish oppression) within the form. The obliquity, the awkwardness of the improvisational form, is what kept *bertsolaritza* alive and has allowed it to thrive. Academicism is a great danger: the theme setters wanted to make it ever more complex, at the risk of alienating the public and the *bertsolaris* themselves (see Garzia 2007).

The word *għana* (pronounced *aana*) derives, like the Maltese language it helps to keep alive, from the Siculo-Arabic that survived on Malta long after it became extinct on Sicily, overlaid with Italian, French and English, and it may reflect a practice akin to those of the Palestinian and Yemeni poets spoken of above – testament to Islamic expansionism and the lasting impact of Arab culture – and in its modern form may well be an outgrowth of a simpler spontaneous form, the songs hummed or chanted to accompany work. In recent times, in the period leading up to and following Malta's accession to the EU in 2004, its improvised poetic duels between rival *għannejja* have placed the form directly at odds with the middle classes and indeed the majority of Maltese, who think of it as a vulgar remnant of an Arabic past long since superseded by a European rather than Middle-Eastern world view and who would rather speak English or Italian than Malti. *Għana*'s survival, therefore, is a statement of minority discontent and resistance to the homogenising influence of mainstream European culture (see Ciantar 2000).

Originally referring (in the early days of hip hop, say the 1980s) to a pre-composed rap verse on no particular subject, a demonstration of pure skill, 'Freestyle' has since come to mean improvised rap lyrics, with or without instrumental beats. It has its origins in the black communities, heir to a long history of slavery, disenfranchisement, racism and impoverishment, from which they are not yet free. Like the *picong* of calypso (and like the *sanankuyo* of the Mandé peoples of Mali and elsewhere and the medieval *flyting* of Scotland and Scandinavia), it takes the form of an improvised but often formulaic game of insults between the participants in front of an audience. It inherits the African-American tradition of 'the dozens' and sets it to an implicit or explicit music.

Dirghām Sbait describes performance of Palestinian improvised poetry, principally improvised *debates* undertaken by professional poets at trad-itional Galilean eve of wedding celebrations (Sbait 1993: 93–117).

Sanjoy Ganguly similarly talks of a 'poet's spat' in West Bengal, in which, in either *kabigan* and *tarja*, two folk art forms, one poet presents a series of arguments against the opponent through recitations and songs, accom-panied by music (Ganguly 2010: 131). What could be more important for a West Bengali village community, situated relatively close to the border with Bangladesh, than the debate between Hinduism and Islam? What better way to conduct it in the right spirit than to ask two poets to put forward extemporaneous arguments in such a way as to awaken the specta-tors' sense of critical judgement? The form allows the negotiation of highly contentious material as well as the appreciation of poetic skill and quick-wittedness. The audience is a crucial component. Ganguly recalls a Bengali poem by Rabindranath Tagore ('*Gaan Bhanga*') which expresses the beauty of the singer's melodious voice paired with the equally beautiful song of the listener's 'sensitive mind' (2010: 132).

The form achieved mass popularity across Bangladesh as well as West Bengal, though it has declined somewhat in modern times. It is some-times transliterated as *kavigan* or *Kabi gan*, meaning 'poet song' or *Kabir*

Larai, which means something like 'poet fight'. The non-professional minstrels, known as *kabiyal* or *sarkar*, each supported by a troupe of musicians, *dohars*, who also act as a chorus, always represent oppositions (not only Hindu and Muslim, but also Capitalism and Socialism, or Science and Philosophy) and can also be women. The Bengali performances traditionally begin by offering prayers – to the Hindu deities, and to Allah and the Prophet if the villagers are Muslim. First one troupe puts forward questions and the other troupe replies. The sarkars always end the performance by sharing the performance space and resolving their differences.

There are many other Indian improvisational poetic forms including *ghazal*, consisting of 'a series of [sung] two-line couplets, with the second line making a commentary or a surprise twist on the first' (Rockwell 2005), and *khayal*, which

> leaves the words behind and uses *taans* or *sargam* (musical ornamentations: fast, dextrous musical improvisations, and singing the notes instead of the words respectively) to create variations on the *raga*. [But] in *khayal* you can never use notes outside of the *raga*. In *ghazal* you can. (Singer Kiran Ahluwalia, quoted in Rockwell 2005)

The Urdu term *mushaira* denotes a Pakistani or North Indian poetic symposium. There are many forms, some (like *Tarahi Mushaira*) are competitive, and *ghazals* are composed on the spot using a given *misra* or starting line. However, as practised in Bengaluru (Bangalore) in Karnataka by Yours Truly Theatre – founded by Nandini Rao and Ranji David in 2003 – the term acquires other meanings. As well as *mushaira,* this largely improvisational theatre company also performs new plays, Harolds, Masala Theatre (locally flavoured short-form improv), enjoys Theatre Sports and uses Forum Theatre, Theatre of the Oppressed, Complete the Story, Perspective Theatre, Black Rainbow (blindfolded acting for blind audiences) and Playback techniques. To quote from their website:

> **Mushayara Theatre**. This format emerged from our theatre lab. Done in an improvizational format where the audiences share a poetry/ *Shayari* written by them and these are then taken by the actors and converted into stories and composition on the spot. The actors speak to each other in poetry/*shayari*, which is done on the spot as well. (www.yourstruly-theatre.com/morestyles.htm. And see also: http:// www.youtube.com/watch?v=p1AV5gTb23s)

Jazz

The question of whether jazz is improvisation is surprisingly difficult and opens a very wiggly can of worms. It applies not only to jazz and other forms of improvised or semi-improvised music, but to all art forms in which the performer makes use of prepared material as part of the apparently spontaneous act of creativity. Are they, truly, improvised? Is 'prepared improvisation' an oxymoron or a self-contradiction?

Jazz is regarded as reliant on spontaneous composition, differing in its early days from other forms of musical improvisation by its complex use of cadential chordal progressions (descending from supertonic via dominant to tonic) in multiple keys. After *Kind of Blue* (Miles Davis 1959, Columbia Records), jazz improvisation became 'associated with modal harmony and improvisation over static key centers' (Wikipedia, on 'Jazz Improvisation'). It changed again with the later work of John Coltrane which featured 'jazz improvisators that are atonal, formless and avant garde' (ibid). Later, 'free improvisation' since the mid-1960s features 'improvised music without any rules beyond the logic or inclination of the musician(s) involved' [Wikipedia, 'Free improvisation'].

Innovation occurs then through (i) chords and intervals, (ii) modal harmony, (iii) keys and (iv) rhythms (cf. Dave Brubeck's 'Take Five'). Central to the technique of modern jazz improvisation is the use of 'cells' and 'lines' (also called 'licks') – defined as 'pre-planned ideas for re-use' (often derived from transcriptions of what great improvisers have played on their recordings). All these and other techniques are aimed at creating a moment of surprise and shifting the quality and effect of the piece overall. To paraphrase the words of jazz guitarist Elliott Sharp, no improvisation is ever truly 'free' unless performed by amnesiac musicians [*ibid.*]. But this does not devalue the activity in the slightest, any more than we would disallow the *comici dell'Arte* their use of pre-learned verbal *concetti* or physical *lazzi*.

Perhaps the best contribution to an understanding of the problem comes, not from jazz studies, but from the work of musicologists specialising in improvisation in Iranian and Indian music, Laudan Nooshin and Richard Widdess:

> The distinction between composition and improvisation is ... artificially rigid, as in practice there is a sliding scale between the spontaneous and the pre-planned, and the same performance may draw on elements from different points along that scale. ... [Many commentators on Indian music, for example] have observed that what appears

to be spontaneously improvised music may in fact be based on memorized or rehearsed material: *what is spontaneous is the decision to use a particular phrase or sequence of phrases at a given moment in the performance.* (Nooshin and Widdess 2006: 104–19; our emphasis)

See also below, 'The fixed and the free' (Chapter 6).

Jazz research: the improvising brain

Charles J. Limb (a saxophonist who also happens to be an otolaryngologist at Johns Hopkins University in Baltimore) and Allen R. Braun have researched the activity we call jazz improvisation and are currently undertaking similar studies of Freestyle rappers. Designing an entirely plastic MIDI keyboard allowed them to place jazz pianists in a fMRI scanner and set them repeatable tasks (scales, learned passages and improvisations). During improvisation, they consistently noted focal activation in the medial prefrontal cortex (broadly speaking, Brodmann Area 10), widespread deactivation of the dorsolateral prefrontal cortex, together with sensorimotor activation. Or, in lay terms, a reduction of pre-planning and self-censoring activity and a rise in self-expressivity – which conforms very nicely with what we think improvisation should be (see Drinko above). Interestingly, similar patterns are associated with REM sleep and dreaming. Preliminary results from work with Baltimore rappers suggests a rise in both verbal *and* visual activity (even when the eyes are shut) when they are improvising.

It would be impossible to play a Harold in an MRI machine; and to wire up actors (or audiences, as some German researchers have done) with electrodes to measure physical changes during actual performances would distort the nature of their activity beyond useful measurement. But it's not impossible to image the effects of creative impulsivity in the brains of musicians and performance poets and to extrapolate some of the results to actors. And some forms of impro – such as word play, storytelling and singing – might be measurable in the fMRI suite, if the subject were in communication with fellow improvisers in the control room. Limb and Braun have shown that it is possible to map, and therefore begin to scientifically study, the creative brain at play.

Stand-up and encounters with impro

John Kearns (winner of the Best Newcomer Comedy Award at Edinburgh in 2013 and Best Show Award in 2014) says 'you can get stale or stuck if you just keep doing the same thing – it's quite a lonely business'. So for the stand-up comedian it may be useful to change the pattern and face some new challenges. Kearns did a clowning course, which meant that he had to focus on other things than text – timing, rhythm, facial expression, being ready to fail, etc. He also recounted working with someone who created a two-character scene in which the comic first played both characters and then invited someone from the audience to come up and be one of them and repeat the scene with him (a bit like Forum for comedy) (Kearns 2013).

One of the key things about stand-up is how you engage with the audience, and it is clear that doing that can involve taking risks, being open to the unexpected, and allowing at least a degree of co-creativity. Kearns's show works like that and involves a lot of 'acting' (pauses, facial expression and mime) rather than just comic patter or telling stories; it creates a character who reflects the mood of the piece and represents a bizarre perspective. In this and other ways it challenges the boundaries of the form itself.

Stewart Lee is a stand-up, a playwright, a music reviewer, a broadcaster, a novelist, a reluctant director and a performer. His on-stage persona is complex, ironic and self-reflexive: he has been described by Clare Brennan (in *The Observer* 10 November 2013), as 'the most Brechtian of comedians, exposing the mechanics of his art at every turn'. In addition to co-writing and directing the multi-award-winning *Jerry Springer: The Opera* in 2005, and delivering his often acerbic one-man shows and his televised *Comedy Vehicle* show, he performs randomly ordered readings from John Cage's anthology, *Indeterminacy*. Cage (1912–92) first performed and recorded these 'short stories, epigrams and mini-essays' in 1959 'while his regular collaborator, David Tudor, performed improvised music in another room' (*Guardian* online 30 March 2014). He follows Cage's instructions – in collaboration with musicians Steve Beresford and Tania Chen who improvise on prepared pianos and found objects. Cage's directions, which accompany the 90 cards of 90 stories of varying lengths (reduced from an original set of 190 for Cage's 1959 recording), state, 'Read the stories aloud, with or without accompaniment, paced so that each takes one minute. A stopwatch or watch with a second hand will keep time. Read all 90 stories in order or select a smaller number, using chance procedures or not.' Lee uses 45, and the cards are shuffled by audience members before he begins (*The Observer* 16 September 2012).

Lee is deliberately uncategorisable, and his book *How I Escaped My Certain Fate: The Life and Deaths of a Stand-Up Comedian* (Faber 2010) gives a wonderfully unreliable and yet totally authentic account of the rise of what for a time was called 'alternative comedy'. It has been described (by

Andrew Male, caughtbytheriver.net) as 'Brechtian autobiography', and it explores – among many funnier and more interesting subjects – the tension between the scripted and the improvised. Describing fellow comedian Eddie Izzard's skill at making his prepared material seem spontaneous, and thereby involving audiences, large and small, in the illusion that they are present at an unrepeatable improvised event, he writes, 'And, when you've tried to do it, you realize why he doesn't. It's hard. It's hard to do. It's much easier to just go "er" in every sentence and give the illusion of spontaneity' (Lee 2010: 64; but see also Double 2014: 351ff. for another view). Following this up in one of his wonderful footnotes (which outweigh the main text by a substantial margin and which exponentially increase the likelihood of him misdirecting the reader) he adds, 'I can't fake things. I have no acting skills. I have to build actual improvisations in to achieve the effect, and over the course of a long run I can feel the scripted sections of a show ossify and stiffen.' (*ibid.*)

The American journalist and comedy writer David Spark regards the relationship between 'Improvites' and 'Stand-Ups' as akin to that between the Hatfields and McCoys, or the Montagues and Capulets. Hired in the late 1990s to write corporate humour for Second City Communications, he was (he says) forced to do improv classes – which he hated. His article about it, 'Improv Confessions of a Stand-Up, or, Why Won't Improv in Chicago Die?' (1997: online at http://www.davidspark.com/bestfunny. html), argues that 'Improvites dislike stand-up because they believe its preparation lacks challenge. Stand-ups hate improv because it's not funny'. He argues that (Chicago) audiences are only forgiving of improv because they have invested in the material and are prepared to pay themselves back by laughing at what they have co-created, even if it's often quite feeble. A stand-up – whose quick-wittedness and imagination may be just as great during the writing process as any improviser's – has to earn laughs every minute from a demanding crowd.

One recent development which aims to reconcile the feud that Spark depicts might be the show created in 2011 by Troy Conrad and Paul Provenza, called *Set List: Stand-Up Without a Net*, designed to work live at festivals and comedy clubs around the world and to be aired on TV. In essence, the show aims to create a situation in which the stand-up comedian can't simply refer to a memorised library of jokes. Some comedians, like Ross Noble, are happy to go on stage with 'four words on a scrap of paper' and trust to their wits and a rapid stream-of-consciousness inventiveness fuelled by responsivity to the audience (see Double: 2014: 356–63). Others, like the late Bob Monkhouse, have a prodigious store of jokes and collect many books filled with gags. Given almost any topic, Monkhouse could search his memory and respond within seconds with an appro-priate one-liner or adapted joke. *Set List* aims to by-pass that reliance on memory by using short audience suggestions (live, or e-mailed, or tweeted) which create an unfamiliar or unpredictable topic to which the comedian has to respond without preparation. (One such topic in an early show was 'genocide note'.) Hundreds of well-known comics – from the USA, UK, Australia and some European countries – have now taken part in this form of theatre sport for comedians, eager to show that they can, as it were, perform 'un-plugged'. British stand-up Phill Jupitus has called this synthesis of instant response and comic skill irresistible: 'catnip for comedians'.

5   Improvisation in Non-Western Performance

Japan, China and Indonesia

Improvisation is a worldwide phenomenon.[1] Though not always acknowledged, and sometimes vigorously suppressed, it underlies dramatic forms in all cultures at all times and is recognisable even where no formal term for it exists. The work of ISTA (the International School of Theatre Anthropology), led by Eugenio Barba and Italian scholars Nando Taviani, Franco Ruffini, Nicola Savarese and Mirella Schino, was one of several streams which signalled the improvisatory principle underpinning the actor's scenic *bios*, the pre-expressive potential of the actor.

This selection from non-Western theatres illustrates the ubiquity of improvisation. Some aspects display (post-colonial) traces of the European drama or define themselves in relation to it. Others – usually dramas with a strong sense of tradition and heavily codified form – admit no use of 'improvisation', at least officially. Here we are talking about largely 'traditional' forms where it may be supposed that, for instance, the very strict imitative and rhythmic mode of training performers, allied to the strong communal and historico-cultural nature of the forms themselves, leaves no room for individual 'creativity'.

In *Noh*, for example, only the *iemoto* (head of a clan/school, functioning as a professional super-ego) has the right to invent, to introduce, new elements into performance (Rath 2004: 248). This does not mean that *Noh* is not innovative, and there have been many examples of experimental crossovers; contemporary Japanese directors such as Yukio Ninagawa have specialised in applying the traditional forms of *Noh* or *Kabuki* to Western classics such as *Medea* and *Titus Andronicus*. But when *Noh* actors perform in their official style, they do not normally consider that improvisation in the liberal European and American sense of freedom to change anything applies. It is, however, the case that a *Noh* performance only occurs *once*: musicians and performers do not rehearse together in a European manner; knowing their roles intimately, they do a single walk-through before the event, which may then itself produce (or not) the 'Flower' or *hana* of spontaneous perfection. In the words of the great theorist of *Noh*, Zeami

Motokiyo, even though improvisation in our Western sense is discouraged, it is still the case that

> [a]n actor who has grasped all the styles will insert his own inventions and devices, giving the performances a hundred nuances ... [and] the audience will still have a sense of the unique if it's kept fresh in this way. (Zeami 2013: 115–6)

Improvisation also happens *historically* and thenceforward defines a new epoch or a new school in the art. And it happens subtly, almost invisibly, in the way a *shite* or *waki* breathes and feels their part on stage, or the *shite*, sitting in the mirror room, contemplates the mask he is to animate. That is to say, it is manifested in the investment of energy, focus and expression (the *abhinaya* of Indian performance) in the moment of production. The supreme characteristic of *Noh* is, as George (1999) notes, its production of the Buddhist cognition of performance as the locus of generative action. What is 'improvisatory' here is not so much the *what* but the *how* of doing: the recognition that, most fundamentally, the improvisatory moment is that in which one accedes to the basis of form which is then produced as action. Lecoq's 'invention of languages' is exactly parallel (see above, p. 71).

The consummate *Noh* artist Akira Matsui (demonstrating at the 14th ISTA in 2005) clearly found it psychologically immensely difficult to permit himself to improvise freely in front of an audience, yet was always totally in the moment, every moment. Given (by Eugenio Barba) the stimulus of the Bob Dylan song *Tomorrow is a Long Time*, Matsui's tendency was to consciously, very deliberately, *translate* the verbal images and feeling of the music into the terms of his art – to recodify it and use the learned codes to express it. He knew no *kata* for the fan he carried through which to symbolise the exact emotions of the song, but he could approximate them and turn the coded gestures of his tradition into symbols that reflected Dylan's themes ('there's beauty in the silver, singin' river / there's beauty in the sunrise in the sky'). Shored up by these symbols, he again knew how to perform and to suffuse them with energy.

Improvisation in Asian forms ranges from comic business, repartee and interaction with the audience to the subtle, but significant, shifting of parameters in highly stylised work like *Noh*, *Kathakali* or *Beijing Opera*. The latter is a highly conventional form and one that is learned apprentice-like in a very hard school to which improvisation would seem very foreign. Nonetheless, Mei Lan Fang writes:

A friend who had seen me playing the lead role in these two operas [Mei's favourite roles in *The Drunken Beauty* and *The Maid who Feigned Madness*] several times commented that I like to keep changing my gestures and movements. Actually, I do not do so purposely. As I perform a part, new understanding of it makes me alter my gestures unconsciously. (Mei 1986: 32)

His improvisation is based not on casual ad-libbing, but on a deep absorption into the role and its 'genetic' stage history (see Riley 1997, *passim*) as well as on an endless process of self-education, technical refinement and response to criticism.

Unless you really understand a character, even if you are taught how to act it, you cannot interpret it correctly. The technical skill of a performing artist improves with the years; it cannot be forced. I admit that I have improved my art by constantly revising my technique.   (Mei 1986: 32)

This *is* improvisation, but not as Western actors normally understand it; however, the development of such things as movement and flexibility, particular qualities of attention and availability and so on, to which we refer throughout this book, indicate that there are more parallels than may at first be imagined.

Balinese *Gambuh* and *Topeng* performers claim there is no term for improvisation in their language – the nearest equivalent means simply 'to react' – or in the lexicon of their theatre style. *Gambuh* is an ancient form, the progenitor of the better-known (and freer) *Topeng*, dating back to the fifteenth century, with fixed masks and codified gestures and dances, strongly linked to the *gamelan* music that accompanies it. *Topeng* is simpler, but no less codified and no less impressively complex in performance. Yet these players, as *penasar* (clowns), have an obviously improvisatory aspect, particularly in their relation to the audience, with whom they joke and chat in everyday language. Ron Jenkins and I Nyoman Catra draw attention to the subtle and 'invisible' training that a *penasar* undergoes (Watson 2001: 85–91). Clowning (as *penasar* connotes) is the 'foundation' of Balinese theatre, and a *penasar* needs three skills (in addition to the highly disciplined corporeal ones). The first is *lingkungan* (attention to the environment, in the sense of observing one's predecessors, other actors and, of course, the immediate natural and social world). The second, *sastra*, refers to scriptural knowledge, especially of religion, history and the Balinese repertoire and its epic sources. The third is *penonton*, which they define as 'an ongoing interaction with the audience':

> The actors continually change their improvised dialogue in response to the moods and needs of the audience, so that no two performances of the same story are ever equivalent. Each performer is obligated to tailor the evening's story to the specific needs of the event. (Watson 2001: 89)

The actors have to be responsive to the social and personal situation, the environment of the performance. They will eat and talk with their village hosts before performing, and the show will move freely from fifteenth-century epic to the most contemporary concerns (for example, tourism, politics and rude jokes about individual dignitaries attending the show). The result of the successful integration of these three 'invisibles' with the technical skills of the performer is that he is said to have *taksu*: 'receptivity', 'inspiration' and 'flow'.[2] *Topeng Pajegan* requires the portrayal of a number of different characters by the same actor, what Keralan forms call *pakarnat-tam* (multiple transformational acting) or Lecoq would characterise as *disponibilité*. Although there is no Balinese word for improvisation, *penonton* is clearly an articulation of the same underlying principle and a reminder of the fundamental psychosocial importance of clowning.

And there are other ways in which improvisatory forms can have social impact. Barbara Hatley describes the modern popular Central Javanese form of *ketoprak* (which has affinities with other forms, like the West Javanese *sandiwara*, and the *lenong* of Jakarta). Clifford Geertz (Geertz 1960: 289) dates the invention of *ketoprak* to 1923. These forms are by no means exclusively female, but they do privilege the participation of women – as characters in the drama, as performers and as spectators – in a way which more traditional forms do not. As well as being more given to the use of humour and contemporary, colloquial language, performances

> are created 'on the spot', without a script, by a process of adjustment between the details of a particular story and a standard framework of scenes, passages of dialogue, and character types. This framework continues to be strongly influenced by the dramatic structure and rules of characterization of traditional Javanese theater, most highly elaborated in *wayang kulit* and associated forms. (Hatley 1990: 188)

But *ketoprak*, while largely retaining an affinity with traditional *wayang wong* and *wayang kulit* (the *dalang* of *wayang kulit* also improvises freely), differs from them in drawing its materials from contemporary and historical Javanese society – rather than the Indian epics that inform the older styles. It adheres to traditional female roles (such as the shy, demure princess or the more talkative and sharp-tongued village woman) and types (such as the 'refined' *luruh*) but it has also introduced more *moderén* (modern) types, with female characters who are more

> glamorous and flirtatious, spirited and vivacious, direct and assertive of speech, [a type]... defined as both *branyak* ('strong') and *kenès* ('coquettish, charming'). (*Ibid.*)

Such assertive types are absent from the more male-dominated dramas, such as *ludrug* (or *ludruk*).

The *lenong* form (produced by the Betawi people of Jakarta, and using the Betawi dialect) also uses female performers (known as *ronggeng*). This form evolved at the start of the twentieth century from the earlier *Gambang Rancag* and betrays a strong ethnic Chinese influence. Early narratives glamourised the exploits of bandits, in the Robin Hood manner, and stories tend to fall into *lenong denes* (exploits of the nobility) and *lenong preman* (stories about common people). Performers tend not to be well educated, and this may explain the use of improvisation in ways that may also illuminate for us the practices of the Italian comedy:

> Stories are not memorised from a script. Rather, performers will memorise an orally-presented outline and follow that, with improvisation as necessary. (Loven 2008: 142).

Some ways in which something which has similar processes, goals and outcomes to what we may call improvisation or the improvisatory can be seen, for example, in:

1. Clowning (above; also in *Kathakali* and other forms), which has aspects of the interplay with audience discussed in the Chicago section above – and therefore of the kind of focus this requires, and may have political or cultural resonances, response to immediate issues, banter, dialogic framing of events or situations, passages of poetic exchange in a recognised form but with improvised content (see also Chapter 4).
2. Subtle modifications on the basis of total command of the base 'score' (similar to the 'Western' practice of modifying scenes in rehearsal over a period, but more likely to be done individually in solo or presentational forms like *Kathakali*, *Noh* and *Topeng*).
3. Interaction with musicians, other performers, audience and environment (which may be an important ritual event).

4. Forms of preparation: for example, getting made up (*Kathakali*) or addressing oneself to the mask (*Noh* and *Topeng*); fasting and other psychophysical preparation over days.
5. Attainment of a condition of ease, flow and spontaneity (*hana*). See references to Csíkszentmihályi above, pages 50–1.

It's worth noting too that much recent work (by Phillip Zarrilli, Margaret Coldiron, Richard Schechner, Sreenath Nair, Arya Madhavan, Paul Allain and many others) has made it clear that the vocal, kinetic and psychophysical preparation of performers in India, Japan, Mexico, Brazil and South Africa (to mention but a few places) very often aims to bring them to a condition of performative readiness (Barba: extra-daily functioning, precarious balance; Copeau: state of neutrality; Lecoq: *disponibilité*) which we think is one characteristic of the improvisatory. The long history of performance training in countries like this may not always have identified 'improvisation' as such, but it has for a long time known what it is and what its contribution may be to performance.

Proto-drama: the Gimi of Papua New Guinea

There are emergent forms of drama which anthropological fieldwork (of a more traditional and scientific nature than Barba's or Schechner's) has revealed, and whose seeming *naïveté* is often only apparent. The *harukaru* ritual dramas of the Gimi people of Papua New Guinea are a case in point. Their 'theatre' is made of disposable materials – bodies and living spaces temporarily decorated and transformed. There are no specialised theatre buildings. Masks, make-up and costumes are sometimes very elaborate and colourful, but made only from local, natural materials, and generally made quickly rather than kept and stored and practised with. Their stages are spontaneously created around the central fires in smoky thatched houses, lit only by firelight. Gillian Gillison comments:

> Gimis possess an elaborate performing art, staging short dramas and farces with costume and props made from feathers, marsupial furs, leaves, flowers, berries, mosses, barks and coloured clays. Though these materials are discarded or dismantled after use, leaving no collectible artefacts, Gimi theater is … an art form as complex and full of interest as the fabulous lowland sculptures now housed in the world's museums. (Gillison 1993: 147)

There are no rules of dramaturgy for either performers or audiences. The actors are amateur, and rehearsal is brief. There is of necessity much improvisation. There is a rich song culture, but no extensive, normative standard of performance, other than a general sense of what plays can be about and that they are usually brief. This means that some dramas are awkward, overlong and inadequately produced by Papuan as well as Western standards. Actors may lack control. There is no codified and centrally adhered-to alteration of balance to produce a performance style; yet the performers are fully *present*. There is none of what Eugenio Barba would call *luxurious balance*: indeed, sometimes, balance fails altogether, and the actors tread on the audience in their enthusiasm. The same lack of rules applies to the spectators, who are free to interject or interrupt a performance – or, in a most fascinating way, to respond to it with a rapidly rehearsed or improvised play of their own.

While we can trace elements of the *fictive body* (the clay-daubed faces and limbs, the ornate natural decorations), there is no consistency (and no *consistent inconsistency*) to this. Make-up and visual transformation – and thereby the beginnings of a system of semiotic codification – are visible and clearly felt to be important. The use of immediately available, natural materials is no barrier to the evolution of highly codified systems of costuming and make-up, as examples of Indian village drama amply demonstrate. While there is clearly *extra-daily activity* being expressed, it is equally possible to represent daily life as the Gimi experience and choose to represent it; however, there is no centrally acquired extra-daily *technique*.

This is early – but not 'primitive' – drama. Though it is formally undeveloped, and non-literate, it would be utterly wrong to think of Gimi drama as unsophisticated. And just as wrong to think of it as purely ritual or shamanistic. It offers a model of a theatre only a few steps away from its birth yet is already able to deal with the most difficult and complex issues of its society. The subject matter of the plays ranges from cosmic to domestic: Gillison saw 'portrayals of Gimi myths, old stories, and even household dramas and scandals' (Gillison 1993: 141). Interestingly, she adds, 'Those involved in the squabbles may be in the plays but never play their own parts.' This sounds very like a basic psychodramatic mechanism, the participants using drama to gain some perspective on the events dominating their lives.

What emerges is a drama that is consciously *used*: made to order for the society that consumes it, enlarging traditional themes, confronting traditional dreads, dealing with traditional conflicts. It dramatises the essentials of Gimi life, beginning with the division of *gender*, a deeply contested field in the society. Culture is highly gendered, with boys being removed from women's company at an early age and initiated into men's society, with separate houses and separate social jobs. Many men and boys live in the central barracks-like men's house at the village centre; only as performers can women transgress the taboos against entering there. But dramas can and do also occur in the peripheral and private women's houses as well as in the central and communal men's house. Men hunt, clear land and build fences. Women work in the gardens. Drama offers a space in which that separation, formalised in the laws of taboo and the rituals of pollution, can be temporarily dissolved.

> When plays are risqué, the sexes do not act together. But Gimi theater is a place where tabooed subjects can be broached, relations between the sexes ridiculed, and tensions eased. (Gillison 1993: 163)

This is not ritual, though it happens on ritual occasions: it is clearly drama. Equally, it is not *just* drama but an already sophisticated mechanism of social and psychological transaction, fully susceptible (in Gillison's work) of psychoanalysis, born out of and wedded to its entire anthropo-logical and cultural context.

An essential element is the acting out of the unseen and unseeable – what Brook called 'the Theatre of the Invisible-made-Visible' (Brook 1968: 42). For Western theatre the invisible and intangible elements are nowadays psychological and profane, but in cultures like that of the Gimi, the invisible world is describable only in the vocabulary of spirits. So, of necessity, some dramas enact spirit visitations. Gillison tells of one powerful play which dramatises an encounter in the past between a white Australian officer and a Gimi ghost. The spectators respond directly. Men in the audience leave and return some hours later with a newly created play which dramatises another such encounter between Papuan coastal natives (speaking in appropriate dialect) and the white men arriving in their boats like the ancestors coming from across the sea that separates life and death.[3] Gimi theatre, apparently simple and naive, is obviously very capable of re-rendering experience as complex metaphor and of exploring passages across borders of role, space and time: an important function of the improvisatory.

Orta oyunu and *ru-howzi:* improvisation in the context of Islam

The principal *indigenous* Near Eastern forms of comic drama are varieties of *taqlīd* (Arabic: 'imitation' or 'mimicry').[4] *Taqlīd* forms generally involve a degree of improvised or semi-improvised clowning, always involving the comic depiction of human or, occasionally, animal 'types'. There is no indigenous Islamic drama which sets out to copy the world of reality – *taqlīd* is not Aristotelian *mimesis* (Papadopoulo 1979: 53). The traditional Islamic understanding of drama substitutes for comedy and tragedy the laughter-raising mimic forms of *hijā* ('invective' or 'satire') and the panegyric, encomiastic art of *madīh* ('eulogy') (Frost 2000: 55). But *taqlīd* does not imply, merely, an external (or racist) mockery of type figures. Rather, it is a clear example of how a humorous and indigenous dramatic form has accommodated itself successfully to the religious demands of Islam which, strictly speaking, forbids representation.

As Clara Brakel and Shmuel Moreh note, 'Medieval Arabic theatre was a popular, oral and mainly profane art, which apparently made use of improvisation in performance' (1996: 35). Early 'comic scenes' performed by itinerant clowns are sporadically recorded from the ninth century and accounts can be found from all over the Muslim-influenced world (see And 1975; Banham 1988; Moreh 1992). The origins of the, often proscribed, modern Arabic theatre are found in a fusion of the colonial European drama (e.g. translations of Molière) with the indigenous Arab performance style of the *muhabazeen*, originally Egyptian travelling players who had hitherto not used scripts but relied on improvisation derived from audience interaction. Forms such as this spread across the Muslim world.   A seventeenth-century Iranian example illustrates:

> Entertainers in *taqlid* would normally imitate the accents and personal characteristics of well known people in the towns and villages in which they performed. These people would be seen meeting and greeting each other. After a short while they would fall to arguing and making fun of each other's accents and behaviour, and the story would end with the two characters fighting and chasing each other.
> (Beeman, quoted in Banham 1988: 667)

There are many recorded versions of such entertainment. But the most developed forms of *taqlīd* comedy are the Turkish *orta oyunu* and its Persian cousin, *ru-howzi*.

Early accounts stress the rough, improvised or half-improvised and often animal-based nature of the farces which would develop into Ottoman *orta oyunu*. Turkish scholar Metin And has pointed out that in Central Asia, the word *oyun* denotes the shaman's exorcistic rite, and this may suggest a mediumistic origin. *Orta oyunu* has sometimes been seen as a Turkish fusion of the classic mime of Byzantium with *commedia dell'arte*: there was constant commerce between Byzantium/Constantinople and the Adriatic, particularly Venice. *Orta oyunu* certainly employs its own stock characters and uses improvisation. But, if anything, *commedia* took its birth from the refugees streaming *out* of Constantinople and towards Venice after 1453.

Orta oyunu[5] is primarily an open-air form, played in an oval or rectangular earthen stage area – the *meidan* – some 20 by 30 metres in length. Usually the theatre site was a public square or a city park. Originally, the acting space was just the middle of a circle made by the spectators. Later, the staging was slightly more defined, and the spectators were roped off from the actors and seated on wooden benches or rush chairs. A raised acting area was never used until after the influence of Western theatre forms was felt.[6]

Onstage there are only two items, a low screen or a chair (*dukian*, meaning a 'shop', the locale which these objects frequently represented) and a higher two-winged screen, the *ev* ('house' or 'dwelling'). The shop and the house recall the street origins of *orta oyunu*. Sometimes two such *ev* screens are placed together to make a three-dimensional structure which the actor can go in and out of. Scenery is highly schematic; crude illustrations representing castles, doors and gardens – whatever scenic locale was required – are painted on paper and pasted onto these screens.

All Turkish performances (like most in India and Africa) are accompanied by music. The orchestra (visible and seated to the side of the playing area) integrates and, as it were, stage-manages the performance. The play is largely improvised: a known scenario can be expanded or compressed by the actors at will, with rehearsed set-pieces cleverly worked into the drama. The repertoire is occasionally written down but is mostly transmitted memorially from generation to generation.

There are three main characters. Pişekâr, the 'leader' (whose name also implies 'conjuror' or 'clever man'), also known by the personal name Tosun Efendi, wears a parti-coloured hat, yellow robe and red trousers, begins the play proper and rarely leaves the performance space, sometimes sitting on the ground or among the spectators if not actually in a scene. It is as if his entrance 'conjures up' all the other characters.[7] Much of the play consists entirely of Pişekâr's improvised *muhavere* (dialogue and punning comic crosstalk) with Kavuklu ('Big Hat', from his comically huge turban). Usually the latter represents a comic trader, servant or porter who often breaks the few illusionistic conventions of the genre and enjoys talking to the audience.[8] Kavuklu's comedy is often physically adroit but not as gymnastic as that of the *commedia zanni*: some acrobatic elements are introduced by the younger, minor actors. Plays often end with Kavuklu being comically beaten. Zenne is the generic name of the 'woman' character who represents a variety of 'dames' or female characters ranging from rich lady to Arabian slave. Zenne is always played by a man, speaking in a high register and wearing special make-up. The central trio are supported by minor actors playing (with much doubling) a host of clearly identifiable regional, social or racial types.

Actors generally face each other and move around the space while they speak so that an 'in-the-round' audience can see all the action clearly. The acting style is presentational:

> The actor does not lose his identity as an actor and shows his aware-ness of this to the audience. The audience does not regard him as pretending to be a real person, but as an actor.   (And 1975: 14)

This accords with the Islamic proscription on representation, while cleverly infracting it. It is not an abrogation of Allah's sole right to give life, because such characters are not to be thought of as 'alive' (as naturalistic characters in Western drama might be). The audience comes to see the storytelling skill of the *meddah* and the presentational skill of the actor. The guiding principle of *orta oyunu* is *taklit*. One of the principal sources of laughter is the accurate mimicking of these recognisable regional and social types (not to mention animals in the early farces).

Under Western influence *orta oyunu* declined. In the 1870s the form modulated into *tulûat* as a challenge to the influence, and official mon-opoly, of the Armenian director Güllü Agop (Agop Vartovyan) who was modernising and Westernising Turkish theatre as part of the *tanzimat* ('reorganisation') movement. Returning to the street roots of their form, the *tulûat* actors took a vague storyline and elaborated it with gossip, local events or current affairs taken from the day's newspapers (a street parallel with Moreno's later 'Living Newspaper' and the better-known American Federal Theatre version). Part of their success was their ability to address, through comic improvisation, contemporary political issues – always an important strand of *orta oyunu* and of Turkish entertainment generally.

But *tulûat* had little chance to grow. In 1884, Agop's theatre was dissolved and its building demolished by order of the last autocratic Sultan, Abd al-Hamid II, who was disturbed by the actors' traditional freedom to express political criticisms from the stage. All other theatre forms found themselves equally eclipsed. The theatre was heavily censored, and specta-cles often prohibited until the revolt of the Young Turks in 1908 curbed the power of the Sultanate and Kemal Atatürk's modern constitution in 1926 set Turkey on the path to Europeanisation.

Nowadays versions of *orta oyunu* or its modified descendant *tulûat* can still be seen, although in Turkey the tradition can no longer be described as a living one. In Iran, however, and elsewhere, the form thrives. An Azeri language version operates in Azerbaijan while, in Iran, a related form, *ru-howzi*, thrives, even in the turbulent period since the Revolution.

Ru-howzi is similar to *orta oyunu*, but with particular differences worth mentioning. Improvisation plays a much greater role in the Persian form. Whereas *orta oyunu* is often at least partly scripted, in *ru-howzi* nothing is written down and the entire transmission of the form remains oral. Its original actors were craftsmen and shopkeepers rather than full-time professionals. Iranians believe it predates even Greek drama (though there is no evidence for this) and claim it originated as entertainment for wedding feasts. *Ru-howzi* performances are generally paid for by wealthy patrons to celebrate weddings or birthdays. It is at root an entertainment for a private party.

Most well-to-do Persian houses used to have a large circular courtyard pool (*howz*) about 30 centimetres deep, where servants would wash clothes or prepare food. The lower-class actors would set up their makeshift theatres *on* and around these pools (*ru-howzi* means literally 'on the pool'). The audience sit on all sides of the pool, and the colourfully costumed actors act in their midst. The acting style is very rapid and highly verbal, switching from literary to colloquial registers and back again with great fluency. Scene changes are purely nominative: to enact a journey actors take a few steps on the Persian-carpeted stage floor and announce they are in a new location. As with *orta oyunu*, musicians sit visibly to the side of the acting area and accompany the whole performance.

Classical *ru-howzi* was originally played by men to men. In big cities, the performers and their shows were often associated with the local brothel quarter. As recently as the fall of the Shah, *ru-howzi* could be found in the old walled city, or 'red light district', of Teheran, with many performances actually taking place in brothels. The version seen by Peter Brook's mixed-sex company in the early 1970s, and described by A. C. H. Smith, however, was actually 'designed particularly for women, the most salacious audience of all in Persia, because most confined' (Smith 1972: 149).

A recent innovation – one which can only have increased clerical antipathy and which is believed to have been extirpated since the Revolution – has been the use of actresses:

In relatively recent years, women, often prostitutes, have performed with the *ru-howzi* when they travel to wedding fetes, which often last from sunset to sunrise. In ancient times, women were excluded from these performances, which were done specifically for an all-male audience. (Ryan 1974: 114)

This is attested by Brook's company, too, who were taken into the old quarter to see the *ru-howzi* players in their natural habitat. The company responded to what they had seen by taking their own improvisational form, a 'carpet show', out to an Iranian village – though the Iranian company members had proper misgivings about Western eclecticism and the 'theft' of indigenous theatre forms by outsiders (Smith 1972: 167).

Troupes traditionally tailor their performances to the taste or concerns of their patrons: wedding feasts would naturally call for a different subject matter from brothel plays. The actors may learn what the subject of the play is perhaps only half an hour before the performance and therefore need to call on a huge repertoire of jokes and stock scenes and to rely on humorous interchange with the audience throughout the show.

Subjects can be literary or legendary, drawn from incidents in the national epic, the *Shāhnāmeh* of Firdowsi, or they can be purely comic and slapstick scenes packed with risqué jokes. The clown is, once again, the central figure of *ru-howzi*. He has no specific name, but since his face is blackened he is usually called the '*Siah*' ('Black': *siah-bāzi* implies 'playing the black', 'clowning'). Often he plays servant characters and is known by the personal name 'Rajab'. The second character is the *hajji* (making a similar dyad to Pişekâr/Kavuklu: Karagöz/Hadjeivat). The *hajji* is an elderly merchant, who represents respectability and traditional morality (for example, as a strict father whose daughter is in love with a boy of whom he disapproves), against which the *Siah*'s clowning is set in relief. Here, as elsewhere, the Iranian clown fulfils a Bakhtinian, liberative function with regard to *authority* (textual as well as social and religious; for example, the clown can even burlesque the heroic and pathetic story of Rustem); to the physical *appetites* and, especially in this fiercely macho country, to *sexuality*: actors introduce themselves as 'workmen of joy' (Ryan 1974: 114).

The success of *ru-howzi* – and all similar forms – is summed up by an old Iranian performer: he could speak for all improvisers. The form's energy, its endless ability to renew itself and to survive oppression and threatened religious censorship:

derived from continuous group work, with an emphasis on instant creativity. We just love our work. We are only interested in putting on a comic performance that people can enjoy for its honest good fun. (Ryan 1974: 115)

West African 'concert party' and South African theatre

The most distinctive indigenous popular form of West African drama (for example, in Togo, Benin, some parts of Ghana and Western Yorùbá-speaking Nigeria) is the 'concert party'. It occupies a liminal space between traditional forms (masked dance drama and storytelling) and modern, Europeanised theatre, alluding to tradition while addressing modern, and particularly colonial and post-colonial, issues and using hybrid, eclectic techniques. It is defined as 'popular, modern, commercial, traveling, musical theatre which combined elements of indigenous and imported culture in a creative and innovative fusion' (Barber *et al.* 1997: 1).[9]

Concert party's chief mode is improvisational and humorous. No scripts exist but, as Karen Barber suggests, it is as if 'the actors themselves worked with a kind of virtual script' (1997: xiii), a discernible characteristic of most other professionally improvised forms. Its improvised elements are 'yoked, ambiguously but vitally, with literacy [in Akan or Yorùbá]: an orientation which has profound effects on the actors' notion of what a play is' (1997: 5). She insists, however, that having got rid of a chiefly script-centred view of these works, we should resist 'merely replacing it with an exclusive emphasis on their immediate, emergent, provisional, and improvisational character. This would be to fall back on a sentimental valorization of "orality" which the theatre companies themselves would not recognize and which would fail to account for central features of their practice' (*ibid.*).

For Alain Ricard 'dramatic improvisation … [here] cannot be described as disorderly. The use of space and time was governed by definite rules, accepted by the group members and recognized by the audience' (Barber *et al.* 1997: 126). To be a successful performer in this style requires an ability to abide by the plot 'and at the same time provoke the audience', sticking to the story and yet being able to 'take advantage of the emotions triggered by a song to pocket the money which the audience will throw to you on the stage' (1997: 131–2).

In Ghana, concert party was for a long time the only professional form. Groups are known as 'Trios' (whether there are three players or not), the actors as 'Comedians', and their improvisations as 'Comic Plays' (whether they are serious or humorous). The form is generally dated from 1920, when 'Bob' Ishmael Johnson started a youthful company called the Versatile Eight. His 1930s company, Two Bobs and their Carolina Girl, reveals the interpolation of American vaudeville and minstrel show, as well as the advent of Jolson in *The Jazz Singer* ('Carolina' was, of course, played by a man; and the African actors 'blacked up', or at least outlined lips, eyebrows, moustaches and noses with blanco to perform in that borrowed style). Trios flourished particularly in the 1960s and 1970s and still continue although, as elsewhere, they face competition from the encroachment of cinema and television.

Performances can take place in a formal theatre space or on a fit-up stage in a village. The actor-manager assigns roles, taking account of individual performers' strengths and aptitudes in improvising and singing, and dictates the pace in dialogue with the chief musician, while the actors themselves agree on the scenes to be performed. The show itself depends entirely on the improvising skill of the actors who resemble the collaborative ensemble of a good jazz band. There are four sections, all associated with music. The first three units comprise a twenty-minute or half-hour build-up of energy (although it used to be much longer). The last section, known as 'the scene', forms the play proper and lasts about an hour. There are considerable similarities here with the south Indian *Yakshagana*, similarly 'compered' by an on-stage manager (*Bhagavata*) and featuring warm-up routines and songs and dances interspersed with 'naturalistic' scenes, often of domestic conflict or around local political issues, though the Indian 'frame' is an episode from one of the great epics.

Concert party features compressed use of time, non-illusionistic style (make-up 'masks'; traditional use of a female impersonator, which distinguishes concert party from other forms of, for example, Yorùbá popular theatre), explicit address by actors (and characters) to the audience to provide plot information, encouragement of audience participation (jeering and throwing coins onto the stage), and, crucially, linguistic diversity (Barber *et al.* 1997: 84–6). The original concert parties are performed in English, the colonial language. In Ghana, the plays have increasingly used Akan and are now likely to include a lively assortment of dialects and languages (Fanti, Twi, Ewe, Ga, English, etc.) as the actors improvise. Language is largely the point. Barber quotes one spectator's remark: '*Inú eré lèdèé kù sí*' ('It's in the plays that the language survives'), meaning the language 'in its fullest sense – its idioms, archaisms, innovations, slang, dialectical peculiarities, and its sacred and secret registers' (Barber 2000: 2).

> Concert actors know they are going to stage the mythologies of everyday life, that they are going to speak the language of cultural domination and represent the cultural and linguistic alienation of their coastal cultures. This is not an easy venture ... The actors must therefore prepare themselves for the task. They wait for nightfall because 'masks only go out at night'. They mask themselves; they protect themselves against the spells cast by dead actors. A sort of

symbolic armor is constructed which will allow them to withstand the shock of representing cultural beings from their inner world. (Ricard, in Barber *et al.* 1997: 140)

Margaret Thompson Drewal characterises all Yorùbá performance, formal or informal, as ritual: 'moment to moment manoeuvring' in which 'each move is contingent on a previous move and in some measure influences the one that follows' (Drewal 1992: 7). West African theatre artists, like the renowned Nigerian playwright and manager Chief Hubert Ògúńdé (1916–90), would take concert party as their starting point for the development of a completely new and politicised aesthetic, where, in the tradition established by the concert party, 'every moment and every level of production is a site of creative potentiality' (Barber 2000: 9).

A great deal of African, and particularly South African, theatre incorporates in large or small measure the improvisatory, both in terms of physicality and of language. As in Indian and other Asian forms, the plasticity of body and the understanding of performance as involving dance/movement, rhythm and music enable particular kinds of flexibility; traditions of storytelling and repartee extend this to verbal language. (A lot of contemporary Indian performance, for instance, involves kinds of fusion – between music and text, between traditional and modern, between dance and theatre. Examples include Amit Choudhury's mix of text, image, Indian classical music and jazz; and work by the Keralan theatre company Abhinaya (*Siddharta*, *Macbeth*) which involves text, rhythm, choreography and moving images.) Negotiation between different forms, structures and languages is a crucial hallmark of the improvisatory, indicating that it operates across familiar boundaries and in the spaces 'in between' versions of identity, ethnicity and expression. Add to this the predominance of collaborative/co-creative work during 'resistance' periods[10] and there are a number of important streams feeding into this spectrum. Even a cursory and oversimplistic account of South African work of this kind would have to point to monoacting and stand-up, to environmental theatre, to mime and physical performance, to relatively 'naturalistic' formats, to ensemble and co-creative work, to theatre of the absurd, to declamatory and protest work, to celebration and resistance, to bearing witness and interrogating the past, to intertextual and metatheatrical moves and to the incorporation of dance and song. Athol Fugard specifically acknowledged a debt to Grotowski's concept of 'poor theatre' and the subsequent realisation that precisely the enforced poverty of political oppression renders the nakedness of the actor's physical resources a site of resistance; the ability of improvisational work to escape censorship and closure, to make do with reduced and easily transportable appurtenances and to require and cele-brate the multi-dimensional, multi-role and multi-linguistic facility of the actor as an active example of liberation in practice are key qualities. In a world where, as John Kani put it, 'you never knew whether by waking up you weren't breaking the law' (Open University Recording: *The Island: An Historic Piece*), shape-shifting characteristics were both pragmatically necessary and also an act of conscious defiance, claiming a form and place to be. The improvisatory touchstone of play takes on the quality of a pol-itical act.

Recent South African work, which is increasingly cross-racial in cre-ation, production and casting, has continued and extended the practice with blends of physical theatre, dance, shadow and other puppetry, music and song, often in conjunction with inventive multi-linguistic scripting sometimes including aspects of *grammelot* and also featuring highly flexible acting in which performers play multiple – often cross-racial and cross-gendered – roles. Examples include the work of Magnet Theatre/Jazzart: Mark Fleishman and Jennie Resznek (*Onnest'Bo*; *Cargo*); Greg Coetzee (*White Men with Weapons*) and Brett Bailey (*Ipi Zombi*); the originality and high per-formance quality of Andrew Buckland's both scripted and co-created plays (*The Ugly Noo Noo*, *The Well Being* and *Makana*) and the highly physical, environmentally oriented productions of Nicholas Ellenbogen's Theatre for Africa (*Horn of Sorrow*) – which has also spawned high-quality street theatre work by Ellis Pearson and Bheki Mkhwane. The improvisatory mode also to some extent reflects in the more conventional form of the 'township' musical, popularised by Gibson Kente, but drawing on jazz, itself a plur-alistic collaboration of various historical moments of 'Africa' as cultural other, refracted via the US and the UK/Europe and fused with indigenous modes. South African jazz is itself also both a central part of the music scene and one which gives rise to fertile collaborations and exciting new work across musical and cultural boundaries.

In the programme note to *Onnest'Bo* ('Upside Down'), Fleishman and Reznek claim that their work frequently 'explores the terrain between per-formance and historiography' to create 'moments and experiences that they transform and interpret through theatre'. *Onnest'Bo* uses a combin-ation of movement, the spoken word in several languages (some of it improvised), music and set (a collection of boxes) to present experiences of forced removal, of which the most notable under apartheid occurred in Johannesburg's Sophiatown (1955) and Cape Town's District Six (1985). This is theatre on the borders of history, fiction and memory – recreated by the original directorial and performance team in collaboration, together with input from researchers attached to the District Six museum, which 'address[es] the gaps and spaces between facts' and may 'stumble across a moment in history that is porous, fragmented, a hole in the archive', in order to 'imagine, fictionalise and represent the *possibility* of the lived experience at that time'. These 'moments' represent a crossover point between the diachronic narrative of history and the synchronic in-depth illumination of a multi-dimensional performance event.

Such work archetypally positions itself 'between', and from the 'gaps and spaces' of this in-betweenness uses the ephemerality of theatre to engage with both history and theatre as practice. These gaps – nodal points in the location of imaginative possibility within historical narrative – function in the process of the creation of performance as junctions between sequences and episodes (Fleishman 2005), rather like the repeated pauses which punctuate Vladimir and Estragon's attempts to fill up time in *Waiting for Godot*: where you ask? what now? where next? Borders, junctions, gaps and hybridity offer the chance for what Maude-Roxby calls 'new combinations' and illustrate Fleishman's view of 'theatre as a crossroads' – in a conscious reference to Patrice Pavis's title. It's perhaps no coincidence that the terminology is reminiscent (but in no sense derivatory) of post-colonialist theorists like Deleuze and Bhabha, who also locate 'in-betweenness' as crucial to the production of new modes which can acknowledge the complex otherness of multicultural societies. Greg Homann, in *At This Stage*, quotes Ashraf Jamal's assessment that the 'formal hybridity' and 'liminal impurity' of theatre position it well to interrogate the contradictions and ambiguities in any model of 'national unity' (2009: 2). These factors suggest that the improvisatory in performance defines a mode and a space in which body, language and identity can be dis- and re-articulated, and that this is an important indicator of the possibility of theatre as a mode of re-engagement in democracy.

There are, in addition to the examples we have discussed here, many other instances of the improvisatory occurring within and beyond forms and conventions in many parts of the world. David Alfred Charles discusses some in which it functions essentially as a means of creating work in its own right rather than as an 'applied' technique for rehearsal. They include: 'Japanese renga poetry, South Korean madang, South American Newspaper Theatre, the Mexican carpa, Nigerian Apidan Theatre and Kenya's Kamīrīīthū Cultural Center' (Charles 2003: 10).

PART 2

What? The Practice of Improvisation: Improvisation Exercises

Introduction

This section describes in greater detail the kinds of practice outlined in Part 1 and is intended as a summary and source of reference for both students and practitioners.

There are a number of techniques commonly used by teachers and directors of improvised performance. Individuals place different emphasis on different exercises. Some are important only for specific types of work (for example, for creating a very structured piece); others are fundamental to all acting. One thing is certain: techniques cannot be adequately learned from books. Improvisation is learned experientially, in the rehearsal room and on the stage. The improviser learns from his or her mistakes (and, if he or she is clever, from other people's mistakes).

What follows, then, is not a DIY manual on 'How to Improvise', but a discussion of techniques and approaches: those we consider to be part of the improviser's repertoire and others central to the work of some of the most distinctive teachers of drama and practitioners of improvisation. The techniques fall into a number of groups, although they ultimately run into one another, so that distinctions of grouping soon dissolve. Equally, many of the techniques discussed are by no means specific to improvisation work but are common to all types of theatre and performance training. The first group, in Chapter 6, is about *preparation* for work:

Relaxation
Games
Balance and 'body/think'
Space and movement
Concentration and attention
Impulses and directions
The fixed and the free

The second group, in Chapter 7, is about *working together*:

Working in pairs
Trust and respect
Making a machine
Showing and telling
Entrances and exits
Meetings and greetings
Blocking

The third group, in Chapter 8, is concerned with more difficult exercises, *moving towards performance*:

Senses
Tenses
Status
Masks
Structures, rhythms, atmospheres

The last group, in Chapter 9, is about improvisation methodology applied to work on scenes, characters and narrative:

Who/where/what?
Objectives and resistances
Point of concentration (focus)
Memory
'Set'
Character
Narrative as generative structure

The exercises lead towards particular *objectives*, which develop psycho-motor, cognitive and affective skills in individuals and group relationships. These objectives imply an underlying network of processes and significa-tions inherent in improvisation work. These *active meanings* are generated through impro activities, indicating that improvisation keys into fun-damental ways of creating the structure of human existence. In the fol-lowing chapters we outline the practice; in Part 3 we will follow up the implications.

An *Index of Games and Exercises* is located at the end of the book (pp. 277ff).

6   Preparation

Relaxation

Experimental work in drama has always been underpinned by movement theory, by a fundamental system explaining how the body is organised and how its performance can be rendered more in harmony with nature, or more efficiently controlled. A line (exactly parallel to our history of improvisation) links François Delsarte to Émile Jaques-Dalcroze, to F. M. Alexander, to Rudolf Laban, to Georges Hébert and to Moshé Feldenkrais. Each innovator in theatre or dance improvisation has been influenced by a leading movement specialist or has adapted their own movement training from a pre-existent movement tradition, such as yoga or t'ai chi ch'uan.[1]

Beginning with Stanislavsky, an insistence upon relaxation is the prerequisite condition, the starting point, from which to improvise or perform:

> One of Stanislavsky's first discoveries was that muscular tension limits the actor's capacity to feel as well as move. A body totally free from tension is essential for stage creativity. (Gordon 1987: 241)

The actor's primary resource is the body. It has to be fit, flexible and capable of a great range of expressive movement. Everything the actor communicates is expressed through the body, through conscious and unconscious tensing and relaxing of the musculature, which controls posture, gesture, movement, breath and vocal expression. If the body is inappropriately tense, the channels of communication will be interfered with or blocked altogether.

Relaxation does not mean 'to go limp'. Going limp means that the actor falls over and lies like last week's blancmange on the floor, without the energy or the inclination to get up and do anything. Tension is necessary for balance: the calf and neck muscles are contracted (that is, under tension) when we stand naturally, with the head in its normal, raised position.

The principle of *relaxation*, therefore, in Feldenkrais, gives way to the idea of *eutony*:

which doesn't mean lack of tension, but directed and controlled tension with excessive strain eliminated.   (Feldenkrais 1966: 121; see also Callery 2001: 39)

Clearly, what is implied by 'relaxation' is the elimination of *unwanted* tension – or habitual and inefficient muscle use. This can be temporarily relieved by a **draining exercise**, where physical tension is imagined as a liquid pooling in the body's extremities and is made to 'flow' towards the centre, from where it is 'drained away'. Laban- or Alexander- or Feldenkrais-based techniques for understanding and correcting posture are extremely valuable, as are yoga or t'ai chi exercises. They leave the actor physically composed and mentally refreshed – in the perfect condition to begin work.

Currently the most significant theorist and practitioner of movement is probably Dr Moshé Feldenkrais, whose practice has somewhat eclipsed Alexander and Laban in actor-training establishments. The two methods that bear his name are Functional Integration (a direct manipulation technique used to assist with injury or disability) and Awareness Through Movement (a verbally guided system which liberates students from habit in order to increase self-perception and free movement). His ATM work was introduced into contemporary theatre practice largely by Monika Pagneux in the 1970s; and through her it has come to support the practice of *inter alia* Peter Brook, Jacques Lecoq, Philippe Gaulier, Jos Houben and John Wright – and through them generations of physical theatre companies (for example, Complicité, Trestle, Told By An Idiot and many others). Augusto Boal also drew on Feldenkrais in developing his aesthetics of the oppressed.

Games

Theories of play, and the usefulness of games in actor training, are major studies in themselves. Arising in the philosophical ideas of Friedrich Schiller, John Dewey and Johan Huizinga, we can trace the practical impact on Copeau and, especially, Suzanne Bing of the time spent at Margaret Naumburg's school in New York and, at approximately the same moment, the development of Neva Boyd's play work in Chicago. Both Naumburg and Boyd can claim to be originators in the use of play-based methods in drama teaching worldwide. From their pioneering work – through Bing, Copeau, Spolin, Barker, Yat Malmgren and countless other teachers of drama – games have become a standard, orthodox approach to drama training and to rehearsal. (In all that follows, it is important to stay attuned to the situation of individuals and groups and to their specific situation. Adjustments may need to be made in particular circumstances.)

Clive Barker, in *Theatre Games*, speaks of 'taking the pressure off the actor' (Barker 1977: 69ff.). The ideal way to do this is through game playing. One of the primary functions of childhood play is the acquisition and development of motor skills. Games are a heritage we all share, a language we can remember with the minimum of prompting. Most of all, games are *fun*. **Opening the pelvis**, freeing the pelvic joints to facilitate movement, is very difficult to learn and painful to practise. But sit the actors in a ring, legs outstretched and wide apart, feet touching those of the people on either side, and let them roll a ball at each other's feet, scoring and losing points if the ball makes contact, and the exercise is accomplished automatically. Actors and students *will* stretch their arms, backs, hamstrings to prevent the ball touching them, or to sweep it away to score off someone else, without complaint.

The game takes away the pressure of formal training and replaces it with a focus which is external and purposive. It *socialises* the training. The body becomes more supple; but so does the awareness. The actor's energy is directed outwards, towards the world and towards other actors. The work is in harmony with the body, and the body responds by flowing naturally. The spine stays erect, the head lifts, the posture straightens and the actor laughs rather than grimaces.

Chris Johnston offers a practical definition of play as:

> Directed activity, engendering liveliness, interaction, imaginative excite-ability and the reduction or removal of conventional spatial and temporal boundaries, in an exercise which is releasing and rewarding, often merely for its own sake. (Johnston 1998: 5)

Games can be played over and over again. The more proficient the players become, the more they become free to experiment and to develop. Games have myriad uses in actor training. Barker's book (subtitled *A New Approach to Drama Training*) offers a wealth of examples of ways to tackle difficult scenes, to encourage social interaction or to release the imagination.[2] Most of the well-known **warm-up** games, although they may be adapted to a variety of uses, target alertness, focus, participative engagement and fun as well as a degree of physical and/or mental agility. Other examples include:

1–6: Six directions in space – left, right, front, back, up and down: as a number is called participants must move/stretch/run towards that direction.

Cat and mouse: pairs stand one behind each other and form a circle; front row = cat, back = mouse; one pair is designated to begin. Cat chases mouse in defined space (e.g. outside circle); if cat catches (tags) mouse, roles reverse. Mouse can only escape by finding a 'home' behind any pair. When this occurs, front player in that pair becomes the cat and the previous cat becomes the mouse.

A cautionary note: Games, as noted above, have become so much an accepted part of group work of many kinds that participants/players may be familiar with them and/or may anticipate the 'correct' outcome. For the purposes we are dealing with here, the game is played for the process it instigates, rather than to 'win' or even to 'play it well'. What is most important is attention to the particular: to what you are doing *now*, with each move or response: in other words, with being present in the moment, not anticipating, and working off what is happening to you and between you and the other players.

Balance and 'body/think'

Eugenio Barba speaks of the 'extra-daily' or 'luxury' balance central to all performers of codified form (the Western ballet danseuse *'en pointe'*; the Indian *Kathakali* dancer poised on the outside edges of his feet so that his soles partly lift from the ground; the *manis/keras* duality of Balinese and Javanese movement; even the less obviously codified, apparently naturalistic balance of Western actors, nonetheless trained to erect and centre the posture, orient themselves towards the audience and, sometimes, hold unnatural reserves of breath). He asks:

> Why do all codified performance forms in both the Orient and the Occident contain this constant: the deformation of the daily techniques of walking, moving through space and keeping the body immobile? This deformation of daily body technique, this extra-daily technique, is essentially based on an alteration of balance. Its purpose is to create a condition of permanently unstable balance (Barba and Savarese 1991: 54)

The answer is that this deformation, this flirtation with instability, dynamises the body and charges the performer's being with energy in the eyes of the spectator. It creates a 'dilated body' – which Barba also terms 'a body-in-life' (Barba and Savarese 1991: 54) – a perception of the performer's presence and readiness to perform.

The practitioner who has perhaps most developed this principle into a training and performance technique is Tadashi Suzuki (*b*.1939), whose essay 'The Grammar of the Feet' suggests:

> (t)he way in which the feet are used is the basis of a stage performance. Even the movements of the arms and hands can only augment the feeling inherent in the body positions established by the feet. (Suzuki 1986: 6–8)

Suzuki suggests exercises for contemporary actors which energise the feet and legs (stamping to rhythmic music, squatting, moving in crouched positions and walking pigeon-toed or on the insides of the feet). They are partly about exploring different forms of balance; but equally they concern the apportionment, direction and reservation of the performer's energies. The lengthy **continuous stamping sequence**, for example, which is often regarded as Suzuki's trademark exercise, targets the relationship of the upper and lower body, the transfer of energy between them and the conservation of breath. It is a way of teaching the performer to self-organise, in order to make the whole body speak (Suzuki 1986: 8–9; Allain 2009: 102–5, 107–111 and accompanying CD).

Two very simple games can be used to develop balance, and that awareness of the self in space that Clive Barker calls 'body/think' or the *kinaesthetic sense* (Barker 1977: 29). Barker was one of Joan Littlewood's Theatre Workshop actors and worked alongside the Laban-trained Jean Newlove, who offers a fuller explanation of kinaesthesis.

> Information is relayed to the brain about the state of the body and its ongoing relationship with the outside world. This constant awareness of the current 'state of play', enables the brain to assess the situation and take appropriate action, i.e. unity of mind and body (gestalt). (Newlove 1993: 63; cf. also Drinko's comments on mirror-neuron activity in Chapter 2 above.)

Balance is essential to the improviser who cannot prepare to change direction in advance but must instinctively respond to each new impulse fully and openly. Japanese swordsmen long ago realised that there is no ideal, preset position in which to stand before a fight. To adopt any one stance reduces the possibilities of all other stances and therefore creates a potentially fatal weakness. The ideal position is 'no position' – a condition of alert or 'armed' neutrality – containing all potential within it. If the attack comes from the left the sword *sensei* can move right and counter-attack instantly and vice versa. For the improviser, too, balance is that 'armed neutrality', expressed physically as well as imaginatively. The best game for developing it is itself based on the idea of swordsmanship (though Chinese rather than Japanese): **the Fight in the Dark**.

The game comes originally from a favourite scene of the Beijing Opera. Two men armed with lethally sharp swords hunt one another in a room supposed to be pitch-dark. The actor has to convey to the spectator the idea of darkness, though his eyes remain open throughout. The swords slash the air centimetres away from the opponent's body and face as the actors manoeuvre in a terrifying and wholly credible dance of danger.

The game version of the Fight in the Dark (under the title the **Pauper and the Eunuch**) is a little safer. A square or ring of chairs facing outwards forms the outline of the room, perhaps 5 m × 5 m, with a single chair missing somewhere around the circumference to provide the only entrance and exit. On the chairs sit all the members of the group except for the two players. (Alternative without chairs: 'audience' sits on floor in a circle or other closed form; they hiss whenever a player risks bumping into them to signal the 'walls' of the 'room'.) In the space lies, somewhere, a bunch of keys – which the players are told represents 'a jewel of great price'. The room is 'totally dark', and in the room, guarding the treasure, which he is unable to see, waits a Eunuch armed with a scimitar (the lights are on, and the 'scimitar' is a rolled-up newspaper). Into the room comes a Pauper – sometimes armed, sometimes not. The Pauper is starving and desperate enough to try to steal the jewel. He knows the Eunuch is there, and he has to find the jewel and then find his way out again without being 'killed' (that is, dealt a hefty whack with the rolled tabloid). Those are the rules.

The game is played in three stages, with other group members watching in total silence (as far as possible) and commenting later on what they have seen. First, Pauper and Eunuch try to imagine themselves in the dark room, with their eyes open. They *act* the darkness. Then they play the game again, after hearing the comments of their peers (or they can watch two others play), but this time the combatants are blindfolded. They *experience* the darkness. The third stage repeats the first, assimilating what has been learned. When the players are blindfolded, there are a number of marked changes. (Playing just stage two is also instructive. The important thing is to keep the tension, which requires controlled attention from both players and 'watchers'.)

The actor's personal space extends to include the other player. The head is raised, the posture of the spine naturally corrects itself, balance improves, the actor tunes in to the slightest vibration in the air around him. The distance between the two players becomes very clearly defined as dangerously close, and the watchers thrill as the 'swords' come ever closer to the players' bodies. The tension generated is often cathartically discharged as laughter in the culminating collision. In the open-eyed version the actor is concentrating on a *result*, on playing the darkness. Blindfolded, he is forced to enter the *process*. His body relearns how to 'think', how to balance and how to wait, poised and still for the slightest betraying rustle. The audience cannot help but be drawn into the same process, holding their breath with the actors. The final version tries to use what has been learned, with the eyes open once again.

Play is innate. It links directly to the actor's experience and has pleasurable associations, lessening the actor's resistance to the exploration process. Sometimes, though, it is essential to contextualise the use of play and games. This should always be done *after* the practical session rather than during it, unless absolutely essential. To explain what a game is useful for actually changes the objective of the game: the players begin to strain after what they now see as the desired results, instead of just playing the game and letting the process provide that result naturally and organically. Sometimes students and actors do need to know why what they see as precious rehearsal time is being 'squandered' on games, however pleasurable. Once they understand the intrinsic value, and are aware that there is a justification for each and every game, this resistance vanishes.

The second exercise can, like many, be used in a variety of ways for different purposes but is particularly good at initiating rapid interaction and response, using a two-person dialogue of bodies and rudimentary improvised text. It's called **What are you doing?** Player 1 does an action – anything, from scratching her nose to dancing a jig. Player 2 asks, 'What are you doing?' Player 1 responds with a description which can be anything *except* what s/he is doing, for example, 'I am making pancakes for my Gran's birthday'. Player 2 then has to do *that* action; when immediately asked by Player 1 'What are you doing?', s/he must respond with another different 'heading'; and so the game continues. Here there are several kinds of balance and 'call-and-response' in play, and immediacy of response is encouraged.

Space and movement

The individual actor's space intersects with that of his fellow performers, and with that of the audience, however large that may be. The skill is to

fill the space, to inhabit it fully: to be *there*, totally, in the moment of performance. This is what relaxation and 'body/think' enable to happen and
allow to be seen happening. The performer is aware of all the potential
space around and wants to fill it: his or her energy level is geared to this.
Basic movement exercises are useful to begin to engage with this; for
instance, exploring the space around the body as fully as possible whilst
keeping the feet in the same position; experimenting with the speed, direction and weight of walking via the basic **Laban parameters** (sudden/sus-
tained; direct/indirect; light/heavy; bound/free) and moving all together in
the space and responding to (clapped or spoken) commands to 'go', 'stop',
change speed, etc. whilst maintaining as open as possible an awareness of
others (see also p. 156).

Improvising pure movement in space is difficult. The body quickly loses
orientation, and movement becomes aimless, unless some way of imaginatively coping with the surrounding void is internalised. Up and down
present few problems, movement works with or against gravity and the
floor is the primary reference point. Now imagine a large, invisible **cube**,
centred on, and moving with, the performer's body. A movement can be
seen to grow from the actor or dancer's centre and flow outwards towards
a given point (say, the top right-hand corner of the cube). The idea of the
cube encourages both spatial precision and the fullest possible gestural
extension: it formalises the idea of the **kinesphere** and gives it clear spatial
coordinates – angles, diagonals and diametrals – towards which the body
can reach. Every movement, every foray out into the void, is accompanied
by a *recovery*, a return to inward poise and stillness preparatory to the next
exploration or offering.

This Laban-derived work is totally compatible with Lecoq's teaching,
which also centres on the actor's body in space:

> You can't talk about movement unless you have equilibrium. You
> must know about the horizontal to undertake being vertical. What
> we give the public comes from within. There's a link, a reverberation
> between inner and outer space. If I make a physical action – pulling or
> pushing – it's analogous to internal emotion, love or hate ... I indicate
> passions in space.   (Lecoq 1988: 40)

Both methodologies get students to observe things with and in their own
bodies and thus to develop an active vocabulary of appropriate signs in
movement.

Once you have extended the ability to work in and with space in these
ways, it can more easily become a zone for play. The familiar (rehearsal
room or studio) or the confined (naturalistic conventions of dimensions,

levels and orientations) can be transformed imaginatively into anything/ anywhere. Charles says, '[s]pace is... highly generative and fluid during the process of improvisational performance'; performers can engage in 'creatively exploiting the entire site' (2003: 12–13). Just as many sets of drama exercises progress from developing motor skills to opening out imaginative correlatives (see Snow, below), many of the exercises which follow in subsequent chapters seek to instigate this flexible reinvention of the space and the bodies in it. (See particularly Chapter 7: 'Showing and telling'; 'Entrances and exits'; Chapter 8: 'Senses'; 'Structures, rhythms and atmospheres'; Chapter 9: 'Who/where/what' 'Set'.)

Concentration and attention

The central principle of 'presence' is mental and imaginative. It is a matter of concentrating without straining, attending and behaving in accord with the situation. Copeau's and Lecoq's work with neutral masks, or relaxation exercises, are ways of tuning up in preparation for this. Stanislavsky, in *An Actor Prepares* (better translated as 'An Actor's Work on Himself'), underlines the importance of the principle of 'concentration of attention':

> The eye of an actor which looks at and sees an object attracts the attention of the spectator, and by the same token points out to him what he should look at. Conversely, a blank eye lets the attention of the spectator wander away from the stage.   (Stanislavsky 1937: 78)

Stanislavsky's **Circles of Attention** exercise is very useful for overcoming this. Using first a spotlight in a darkened room, he placed objects within the circle of light, allowing the actor to examine them. The surrounding darkness contrasted with the brilliant illumination of the objects makes it easy for the actor to ignore everything but the objects of concentration. Using a larger circle, including other objects, the actor finds it at first more difficult to concentrate, to attend only to the illuminated area. The largest 'circle' is the whole space, fully illuminated. Now everything competes for the actor's attention, and focus is dissipated, unless the actor learns how to regain the original sensation of 'public solitude', imaginatively selecting the smaller circle out of the large one and concentrating wholly upon it. The actor's *attention* replaces the spotlight. As soon as concentration wavers it can be regained by this act of imaginative focusing.

A related but slightly different exercise can be done with **sound**. The participants lie still on the floor and listen. First they listen to the sounds emanating from their own bodies, their breathing perhaps, or the noises of digestion. Imaginatively, they are listening to the sound of their own heartbeat. The actor is still and silent, but concentrated and aware. Next, without losing the first set of sounds, if possible, they expand their awareness to include other sounds from within the room – the sound of others breathing, most especially, as well as the incidental background noises of the plumbing and, from time to time, the quiet, reassuring voice of the teacher or director. Then, they listen to *all* the sounds from within the audible range. They admit into consciousness the noise of traffic from outside the room, birdsong and people talking along the corridor, whilst trying not to lose the original sets of sounds. This magnified consciousness is too diverse at first, and so the participants are asked to come back to the middle stage, of listening to all the sounds within the surrounding room, and stay at that level for some time, making occasional forays into the smaller and larger regions. Actually, it is the middle level that students must learn to operate in. They have to be aware, albeit subliminally, of the whole space within which they operate and of all those who share it. Whenever concentration is destroyed, or misaligned, it can always be pulled back by regaining the sensation of alert stillness or 'armed neutrality'.

Stanislavsky's **Grasp** or **Empty Space** exercise involves each actor getting the other in his or her *grasp* (Merlin 2003: 65–6, 159). Every facial gesture, every physical movement and every sound is instantaneously noted and responded to by each actor, leading to a constant state of inner (and outer) improvisation. If the actors are 'in each other's grasp', the audience will be drawn – like magnets – towards the on-stage action. In this way, they also become part of the communion or grasp of the live performance.

For Michael Chekhov, the working definition of concentration was simply 'being with something' (Chekhov 2000: 30). Franc Chamberlain summarises a sequence of his exercises in developing and maintaining concentration. Picking any object in the room, the student *pays attention* to it, taking in its shape and colour and imagining 'a current of energy' connecting them to it. They then imagine that they are close to the object and can physically touch and manipulate it. Severing this imaginative connection with the object, the student notices the different quality of interaction when they do not maintain the imaginative focus. Working with a partner, imagining a **current of energy** linking them, the students explore the range at which they can maintain their connection and what happens when they break it and resume it. Finally, they work on concentration's opposite, distraction. One partner tries to listen to an internal melody, while the other sings aloud to try to distract them (Chamberlain 2004: 120–1). The exercises themselves are simple, but they operate on the recognition that the connection between self and other (whether person or object) has to be made visible, to each other and to the spectators. It can be imagined as visible and tangible; and the act of imagining this helps to reify the connection.

Impulses and directions

Direction in movement and speech once begun can be worked on. But what starts the movement? Every movement starts with an impulse to move. Whether voluntary or involuntary, all physical movement originates with nerve impulses that activate the muscles.

There are exercises which develop the motoric and impulsive functions, like **The Starfish**. The actor lies on a mat, curled up, closed and protected. On some agreed signal – say, a sharp noise – she instantly (and without thinking about it first) flings herself into a starfish shape, arms and legs fully outstretched. It doesn't matter whether she is face down or face up. At the next signal, the exercise is reversed. A soft fall-mat is essential if the actor is to feel confident about this.

In this exercise, the impulse to move is both controlled and liberated. The actor knows what movement is to be made, but the random timing of the signal means that the impulse has to be generated and obeyed instantly, without the intervention of 'insurance policy' thoughts of personal safety (which is taken care of for her by the mat and by having properly warmed up first!). She learns to obey the impulse. The **backward roll** exercise used by Grotowski's actress Rena Mirecka (described in Part 1) is another example of impulse work, involving a sudden shift of relationship.

Jacques Lecoq's structural analysis of movement includes the principle of *éclosion* (the term is derived from biology: the emergence of an insect from its pupa), a more controlled and fluid movement training sequence, which

> opens up from the centre. It starts from a crouched position down on the ground, the body occupying the smallest possible space, and opens up to finish on the 'high cross' position, upright, legs together and arms extended above the horizontal. Éclosion consists in moving from one position to the other without a break and with each segment of the body following the same rhythm. Arms and legs arrive simultaneously at the extended position ... The difficulty is to find exactly the right balance and an unobstructed dynamic. Too often the upper part of the body reaches the end before the arms, simply because more attention is being given to it. Éclosion is a global sensation which can be performed in both directions: expanding or contracting. (Lecoq 2000: 78)

Other key exercises in movement are derived from Lecoq's own experience of sports training, where he identified '**undulation** as the principle of all physical effort ... the human body's first movement ... underlying all locomotion' (Lecoq 2000: 75), and 'inverse undulation', which leads from the head rather than the feet, between which two poles éclosion is situated. The use of such primal exercises in drama training is to 'lay down circuits in the human body, through which emotions flow' (75). Lecoq, even at this preparatory stage, allows the performer to make a *liaison* between the external and physical and the internal and emotional, because 'in the theatre making a movement is never a mechanical act but must always be a gesture that is justified' (69): movement contains meaning, and movement liberates meaning. *Tout bouge.*

> I ask the students to adopt these positions one after the other ... to experience passing through the different ages: infancy, adulthood, maturity, old age. The body in forward position, back arched, head thrust forward, suggests an image of childhood or the figure of Harlequin. The vertical position, with the body upright, takes us back to the neutral mask, to the mature adult. The autumn of life, or digestive phase, makes us incline backward from the vertical axis. We fall back into retirement. Finally, old age hunches us up so that we become, once more, like a foetus.   (Lecoq 2000: 77–8)

Once moving, the performer can explore and, by exercising, extend what Rudolf Laban called the 'kinesphere', the space that surrounds and is reachable by the performer's body. The improviser has to be able to react within the space to any stimulus, changing direction instantaneously – literally and figuratively. An exercise which prepares for this is to ask the group to walk rapidly across the space and then, on a given signal (a clap or a whistle), always careful to avoid collision with others, abruptly and increasingly radically change direction. This can be modulated into Chris Johnston's **Walk, Clap, Freeze** exercise, which enhances concentration as it develops spatial confidence:

> The group walks around the space at will. Their task is to respond in different ways to different commands. The commands are given by clapping or verbal instruction. One clap might mean 'walk', two claps 'stop'. Three, 'reverse direction'. The purpose is to fulfil the commands with speed and discipline.   (Johnston 1998: 119)

Finally in this section, a couple of Strasberg exercises which promote spontaneity of response in the individual.

The ***one-word improvisation*** teaches the student spontaneity in acting. Here the student is told that he will be given a word [either by the instructor or by members of the group] in response to which he must stand up at once and react to the word with action, speech or both. The reaction may be silent or verbal, so long as it is brief, impulsive and unplanned. The word should be a noun: perhaps the name of a country or a word with broad implications such as 'religion' or 'politics' ... This exercise helps the actor follow his impulses to achieve a feeling of true spontaneity that can be applied to a script. (Hull 1985: 146)

Augusto Boal uses a similar game, specifying that the response must be in the form of a body image.

Hull describes at length Strasberg's invention of the **Song and Dance** exercise, originally devised for teaching acting to singers but later used to deal with all manner of acting problems (Hull 1985: 117–30). She quotes Strasberg's often-repeated 'Anyone who can do the Song and Dance exercise can do anything on stage' (119) because it is designed to release and make the actor aware of blocked impulses and emotions which it links with vocal and physical expression. It is a strange exercise, quite unlike any of the others we have looked at.

The 'Song and Dance' exercise (which actually has nothing to do with singing or dancing) deliberately disrupts the habitual connection 'between music and the verbal pattern, between rhythm and movement' (Hull 1985: 117). It begins with the student standing still and alone, balanced and relaxed, centre stage. Hands by sides, the actor begins a simple song (a nursery rhyme or 'Happy Birthday' is fine) in a monosyllabic fashion. Syllables are given roughly equal time ('reduced to rhythmless, single sustained tones', 117), and the song may use the melody or be in a monotone, with the relaxed singer aiming for a full and resonant, open-throated tone. Each tone should be stopped before the breath is exhausted. Once the song is finished,

the student executes a spontaneous movement [which] should be larger than life and should involve the whole body, if possible, though the feet usually remain still. The relaxed arms will naturally follow the body movement. The movement may be explosive. The first movement lasts only a few seconds, but the student then repeats it five to eight times. During this repetition the actor vocalizes syllables of the song fully [sounds, not words] in an irregular, explosive monotone, letting the sound erupt occasionally through the movement ... After several repetitions [with directions from the instructor] ... the student initiates a new movement, which can involve the feet moving (jumping, marching, skipping in place or whatever).   (Hull 1985: 117–18)

The student initially responds to commands from the instructor: with practice, he or she initiates his or her own changes. The new movement is also repeated five to eight times, with the student continuing to erupt the sound as before, and the exercise continues until he or she has worked (or been guided) through at least three different movements. At that point, the instructor halts the exercise and asks the student, still centre stage, to relax and 'to think about what he is *now* feeling' (118) and then to share the thoughts and feelings with the rest of the group.

Given the mechanical disruption induced by the exercise, it is not surprising that the request to examine and discuss one's own feelings often produces 'a flood of feeling and expression connected with the student's own life' (Hull 1985: 118). The exercise appears closer to a psychodynamic therapeutic intervention than a conventional actor-training technique – clearly related to the Method's fascination with 'true emotion' and 'psychic fracture' (of the actor rather than the character). Its benefits are that it encourages the actor's self-awareness, releases inhibitions and liberates blocked affect, opening a dialogue between the student and teacher, or actor and director. It can work diagnostically to identify a student who finds it difficult to let go of habitual physical movements, or whose jerky, involuntary movements may reveal an inner conflict 'between spontaneity and repression' (Hull 1985: 120). The exercise is good at identifying motor problems, physical tensions in stance or motion and body habits.

The principle underlying all such basic preparation work relates to what Eugenio Barba calls the *pre-expressive*, by awakening and strengthening the performer's body and establishing scenic *bios*, the actor's presence. Style is a creation of the performer's culture; it may therefore involve highly specific training in a particular performance form. But the *condition* of performance requires a universally identifiable preparation, an internal organisation of physical prerequisites, which training can address.

Theatre anthropology postulates that there exists a basic level of organisation common to all performers and defines this level as pre-expressive. ... It is the doing and how the doing is done which determine what one expresses.   (Barba and Savarese 1991: 187)

The activities we have here classified as 'preparation', or 'training', then, open out physical and mental skills, get the system balanced and alert, begin to work on focus and presence and leave the actor in a state of readiness to work for himself and with others.

Birgit Fritz, introducing Boalian exercises with closed eyes, makes points about their goals which are relevant to much that occurs in the initial stages of improvisation work: '[T]hey serve to dynamise, to enliven conscious awareness of the senses, stimulate awakening of body memory and the holistic functioning of human thinking and feeling' (Fritz 2012: 61).

The initial examples and categories we have given here and extend below have been selected particularly because they are appropriate to the development of different facets of improvisation work. Both in the text and in the Bibliography we refer to numerous books which provide collections of games and exercises, many of them from a similar perspective (e.g. Barker, Boal, Callery, Johnston and Johnstone) and some more generally relevant to performer training. A particularly useful example of the latter is Jackie Snow's *Movement Training for Actors* (Snow 2012), which sets out in very clear detail the movement curriculum of RADA (The Royal Academy of Dramatic Arts, UK). This arranges practice into very similar categories to those we have used, beginning with work to engage and animate individuals and groups and going on to lay out exercises incorporating the imagination and those aimed at generating a condition of neutrality – specifically referencing Copeau. The book also moves through sensitivity and awareness training to observation (as with Lecoq) and to specific forms of characterisation and historically contextualised dance and movement; it includes a DVD demonstrating many of the exercises and sequences.

The fixed and the free

One issue repeatedly arises in discussing improvisation. Is it proper to repeat an impro? If one does, is it still an improvisation, or has it become merely an exercise? Clearly, there is a problem of nomenclature here, which would be solved if such a repetition were called by a different name. But there are more important points to make. Improvisation is frequently used as the basis for choreography or in rehearsal for dramaturgical discovery, devising and so on. It therefore *needs* to be repeated, and practised, and polished for simply pragmatic reasons. And, at the level of training, there are those groups and institutions who make repetition of originally free form work central to their programme.

Considering the Brechtian emphasis inculcated by successive principals, even after the reunification of Germany, it may be interesting to note how much importance is attached to training in improvisation – and to its repeatability – in the pre-eminent German drama school, the 'Ernst Busch' *Hochhschule für Schauspielkunst* in Berlin.

During the first semester of study at the *HfSK*, students are enrolled in a course entitled the *Improvisations-Seminar*, a class which has been in existence under various titles since the Reinhardt era [the great director Max Reinhardt, who established the original school at the Deutsches Theater in 1905]. The course meets every day for four hours. ... Throughout the seminar, the dialectic between improvisation and the fixed score is explored, as it is felt that the creative process, invented during improvisation, can only be captured when the actor learns to repeat it unmechanically, and therefore creatively. Only by repeating the improvisation many times until it is fixed does the actor develop a rehearsal methodology. The methodology is realized through the creation of an improvisational process, which later can be transferred to the creation of a role from a written text. (Watson 2001: 38–9)

It's useful to reflect on the deliberate tension here (*dialectic* is the appropriate term) between the fixed and the free and the difficulty inherent in their reconciliation. An improvisation repeated mechanically is not an improvisation, but the aim is to find constant newness within the performance even as what is performed becomes fixed and repeatable, and dramatic form concretises from seemingly nebulous improvisation. An account of Odin Teatret's Iben Nagel Rasmussen performing a rehearsal and training sequence of movements extends this idea:

Her improvisation is a pattern of repetitions. She explores a score that has not been quite fixed yet. Each gesture is born anew, as in an improvised solo by a jazz musician. She is working on that project which is perhaps the core of the group's work: how to keep the improvisation impulses alive in a repeated pattern.   (Watson 2001: 104)

In the East Berlin school emphasis is placed on the realisation of the objective, material world rather than the fantastic or metaphorical. 'Settings should be from the real world and problems should be dramatized in a psychological manner.' (Watson 2001: 39)

The entire improvisation process is characterized as: '**observe-evaluate-react**'. ... [T]his process is also described as the development of a 'thinking act'. Students utilize the basic rule which breaks down dramatic action into easily palpable sections, thereby focusing their thought processes and thus their stage behaviour. (Watson 2001: 39)

The concept of observation is paramount. The improvisations are as analytical as they are experiential, and are backed up by reading associated literature, leading to a de-personalized but highly intelligent (as well as highly physical) style.

> Another important concept which is stressed in the improvisation seminar is the idea of a pivotal point. This is the point when the actor makes a discovery, is faced with the necessity to make a decision, and follows a course of action. Each pivotal point constitutes a block of action separated by the 'observe-evaluate-react' rule. The changes of action at pivotal points are the results of decisions, or of new attitudes towards the situation. Therefore the dialectic between attitude and action becomes the actor's smallest building block. (Watson 2001: 39)

As the semester progresses, students move from these unattached group improvisations to extended work based loosely on playtexts (but without reading the scripts), gradually approaching the desired condition of applying the training to small-group scripted scenes and finally a *Wahlrollenstudium* (personal work on a chosen role). The dialectic between the fixed and the free is inculturated during the training period. At the end of this (first semester) course, the actors-in-training are, like Iben Nagel Rasmussen, ready to use and re-use discovered material and to build and extend a personal score (Barba calls it a personal dramaturgy) in the approach to a role. Purposive repetition is no more a mechanical action than revisiting the house of an old friend. We make that journey with eager anticipation because, no matter how many times we have been there before, we will always find something new awaiting us.

The sequence identified here also signals that *the improvisational* is the bit in-between. The process of *improvising* and the structure of *an improvisation* will both contain, in roughly equal parts, the 'fixed' and the 'free'. To take the next step, you need to have at least part of one foot on the ground. It is the business of finding out what moves from there, where and how it moves, that determines what comes next.

To balance this relative caution, it's also worth noting Tim Etchell's comments on Forced Entertainment's working method. Often devising and the improvisational process which moves it along mean being prepared to throw away much more than what is retained (Dario Fo's *teatro da bruciare* fits here). Etchells says:

When it comes to improvising, a good half of what we do is useless – misplaced people, silly costumes, tangled-up texts, ideas that don't come to anything. It's a matter (as we say, rather drily) of 'eliminating things from our inquiries'. (*The Guardian* website, 21 December 2009, modified 10 July 2013.)

See also the 'Improvisation and writing' section in Chapter 11.

7 Working Together

Working in pairs

It is often useful to grade the process of working together by working first in pairs. In some games or exercises the pairs can then combine into groups of four or more. Basic pair exercises include **telling a story by turns** (a word or a sentence at a time) and **body shapes** (often used as the initial phase of image theatre work by Boal): A makes a shape with her body, B makes another which responds to it and suggests a relationship; A then responds to B's and so on. These begin to develop a sense of exchange and familiarity. Philippe Gaulier predictably has some more zany offerings, from mutual slapping to stylised dancing 'in major and minor' (i.e. less or more stylised) – use with caution with people who are comfortable with each other!

Another Boal and Théâtre de Complicité favourite is **Sculptor and Clay**: A is the sculptor, B the clay, as malleable as possible. Neither can speak. A must create a sculpture using B – gently bending and placing limbs, showing expressions or directions of glance, etc. The partners then swap roles. Although this forms the beginning of a sequence for Boal (all participants look at the 'statues', comment on what they see and what they interpret, and move towards reading social metaphors from this; Jana Sanskriti in particular use this trajectory very productively to begin Forum work), it is also a good way of encouraging mutual responsiveness and careful cooperation.

We now move on to exercises involving more people.

Trust and respect

When an improvising actor gets into difficulties, he or she has to *know* that somebody will come to their rescue, take what they are offering and develop it. Every member of the group is responsible for every other, a step further than the interactive process of Meisner work highlighted by Moseley (p. xxiv).

One way of developing this is the use of 'trust games'. In the **Trust Circle**, the group stands in a circle, facing in, shoulders touching. Each member in turn (and all of these exercises include the director or teacher) enters the circle, closes their eyes, relaxes and leans in any direction. The surrounding circle takes the person's weight and passes him or her upright across the circle. The one in the middle has to do precisely nothing; the group takes the weight and the responsibility for not letting him or her fall. The person in the middle gives up responsibility to the others. Birgit Fritz notes, 'Trust exercises are not meant to be used to manipulate the group dynamic, they are a way in which to encounter our sensitivity, as well as our own limits, and thus to reorient ourselves ... more takes place inside people than outside' (Fritz 2012: 54).

The necessary corollary of trust is respect. So much of this work is personal and difficult to learn. The group – and it is almost always *group work* that we are talking about – has not only to trust its members equally, but to have respect for them, the work and the ultimate goals of that work.

An exercise which is partly about meeting, partly about trust, partly about respect for each other, is Augusto Boal's **Glass Cobra**. The group makes a circle and turns in through 90 degrees, so they are one behind the other. They close their eyes and gently, with their hands, explore the head and shoulders of the person in front of them. Still with eyes closed, they are asked to break the circle and walk around the space carefully. Then, keeping eyes closed, whenever they meet someone as they walk, they explore to see if it is the person who was in front of them in the circle. If it isn't, pass on; if it is, join together and seek to build up the original circle by finding or being found. When the circle manages to reform itself and the facilitator says, 'Now open your eyes'. It is usually both a surprise and a joy and a great way to start or finish working together. Something more than the individual, that fragile but beautiful glass cobra, has come into being.

Making a machine

One of the simplest ways of getting a group to start working together is the **Making a Machine** improvisation. One member of the group is asked to make a mechanical and repetitive movement; others join in, fitting in with the original movement one by one, adding their own until the whole group is physically involved; then they each add an appropriate sound, one by one, to build up a sound-and-movement-scape. The machine can of course be specified (a tar-spreader, a bottling plant, an automated franking machine, etc.) and/or related to a textual context as appropriate. What we are highlighting here is the way it helps performers to look at and listen to each other, to overcome inhibitions, to share ideas and to build things together.

As well as being about personal responsibility, and following impulses, the 'Machine' exercise encourages listening and observing and the practising of rhythm. The combined noises are often very musical. If the exercise is repeated, and the students or actors are encouraged to relate physically to one another, by contact as well as by isolated movements, the exercise helps to break down tactile inhibitions. If the first person to begin, once the entire 'machine' has been assembled, is told to move or adapt within it (followed by all the others in sequence) then the 'sterile' machine can suddenly become an organically living 'monster', sinuously writhing and moving as one. This can lead to a whole series of related tactile explorations involving the whole group, which can evolve towards emotional work (victory, joy, anger, control, love, violence, etc.) as the group nears performance.

Another example of this is the **Laughing Snake**. Everyone lies on their back on the floor with their head on someone else's stomach. If they haven't done it before, don't tell them what it's about. It takes time to get everyone arranged (either in a serpentine diagonal line or, if possible, in a circle, or two lines or circles if it's a big group), so ask them to do nothing, just lie still and compose themselves. After a while someone will giggle. When people lying on their backs giggle, their abdominal muscles vibrate. The head resting on their stomach begins to bounce up and down. The owner of the head usually begins to giggle, too, infecting the next person in the chain. The sound of giggling is enough to set off some of the others and, in no time, there is a room full of people cackling away dementedly, heads bobbing up and down on each other's stomachs. It goes quiet, and then somebody's stomach rumbles, right beneath someone else's ear – and the laughter bubbles up again. It's an excellent exercise for de-inhibiting a group (and, when necessary, for stopping a workshop becoming too serious).

Work with *sound* can extend the feeling of interconnectedness. A group can build up a **rhythmic weave** from different individual noises (percussive, vocalised, clapped and so on) or explore relationships between the close proximity of sound and physical distance (start far apart, with a range of different pitches and notes; move closer together, shifting through harmony towards unison). The effects of chanting and choric work can be very powerful, and specifically in terms of improvisation they create a strong physical sense of unity, as well as freeing the voice – a significant method of de-inhibiting and relocating the sense of self and its potential.

Another option is **Sun and Moon**: the group sits in a circle, facing out-wards, shoulders touching. They make sound together: each person can use all the sounds in the words 'sun' and 'moon' (in no particular order) three times (Fritz 2012: 186).

Exercises from teachers of musical theatre (who use improvisation too) are useful here. A simple **group clap** exercise very rapidly establishes con-centration and a sense of unity. Standing in a circle, relaxed, everyone touches the tips of their middle fingers to the person on either side. 'The object of the exercise is for everyone in the group to clap at the same time' (Burgess and Skilbeck 2000: 54).

The actual object (or 'destination' in Burgess and Skilbeck's termin-ology) of the exercise is relaxed concentration. The cue for the clap can be overt or subtle, or completely absent, and the game can be played with eyes open or shut. Their **Concert** exercise explores 'aural awareness', via 'rhythm, vocal improvisation, relaxation'. Singers lie on their backs with the soles of their feet flat on the floor, their heads towards the centre of the room. Everyone simultaneously vocalises an 'ah' sound at any pitch until breath runs out. Each time a new breath is taken, a new pitch is randomly chosen. When the leader calls 'Concert!' the group finds its way to a single note; then, on another signal, the group again returns to random pitches (Burgess and Skilbeck 2000: 61). **Jets and Sharks** (the name deriving from *West Side Story*) splits a large group into subgroups of between three and six. Each 'gang' devises its own 'code' (a sequence of 'vocal sounds, claps, stamps etc. ... to last exactly eight steady beats'). The groups have to cross the space, passing through other groups, while maintaining their code as a group at all times. The game teaches 'co-ordinating complex rhythms using the whole body' via 'imagination, co-operating, eye-contact' (2000: 90–1).

Dymphna Callery details a number of rhythmic exercises, citing Fo's maxim that 'Theatre is rhythm' (Callery 2001: 118). It makes sense to unify a group through musical means, and she stresses the usefulness of Meyerhold's tripartite structure of *otkaz/posyl'/tochka* (Pitches 2004: 76); *otkaz* is the preparatory counter-movement or 'recovery', *posyl'* the action itself and *tochka* the completion, preparatory to a new sequence. The arrangement is used to develop the inner rhythmic sense of the actor, or the group, and Callery also lists clapping and sound exercises ('body rhythms', 'clap-clap' and 'rhythmscapes') which employ the Meyerhold structure and lead on to more advanced work on character rhythms.

Franc Chamberlain very usefully digests many of Michael Chekhov's psycho-physical exercises. Chekhov was concerned that we are afraid of our-selves and of each other and devised exercises – simultaneously imaginative and physical – to overcome this barrier to cooperative work. One sequence which is helpful for group work is that headed (by Chamberlain) '**Making Contact**' (Chamberlain 2004: 117). The sequence begins with holding hands in a circle, looking calmly about the group – opening oneself to being looked at as well as gazing at others. When ready, the hands are released, but the feeling of contact is maintained. The group is asked to imagine a giant golden hoop on the floor inside the circle. They squat together and lift it, stretching upwards to release it skyward. Next, the group chooses a variety of energetic actions to perform:

> (e.g. jumping three times in the air, quickly touching all four walls of the room, sitting on the floor, standing still or shouting nonsense loudly). Without planning, and keeping a sense of open-ness and contact, the group should try to sense which action to do as a whole. (Chamberlain 2004: 117)

The sequence of actions and interactions continues, building and dissolving groups and partnerships and exploring tempi and rhythmic movements. Throughout, performers are asked to invest imaginatively in the situation, location or action and to 'radiate' warmth and acceptance to each other, as they attempt to attune themselves as a group and as creative individuals.

> Chekhov suggested that we need to keep this sense of contact in performance, even when we're offstage. If we stay in touch with our partners, we'll enter the scene at the correct tempo. But we can also have this sense of contact with the set, props, and audience.   (118)

A more energetic game with a similar collaborative focus is played with a ball – either a large, very soft one in a big group or smaller versions. The ball is propelled into the air, rather as in volleyball; the group has to take responsibility individually and collectively for keeping the **ball in the air**, whilst all together counting out loud each time it is kept up. What is important is not so much how many you score – though that can be fun and useful – but how you help each other and how each person reacts to what is necessary in each situation in order to further the group effort.

The **Chair Game** sets out one more chair than the number of players randomly across the space. All players sit on a chair. The facilitator places herself at the opposite side of the space and begins to move towards the empty chair. The group has to come to a mutual agreement to occupy the chair before she reaches it and then to cover subsequent moves as on each occasion another chair becomes free. Sooner or later someone will panic and move from a chair close to the walker (or, as the group begins to work out a strategy, the jogger or runner). Other successive stages can limit the kinds of communication permitted between players, eventually to a 'no speaking' and 'no gesturing' rule. This game very rapidly develops wide spatial awareness, combined with strategic imagination and communication, thus establishing very useful ground conditions for productive group work.

Showing and telling

One of the hardest things to grasp is often the difference between 'showing' and 'telling'. 'Telling' avoids the full physical involvement of the body. It substitutes codified signs (words or pantomimic gestures) for full body response. An actor can 'tell' the audience he is 'walking through a doorway' by miming reaching out and turning a door handle and stepping forward (or by saying 'Oh look, here's a door. I wonder what's through here …'). The audience understands what is happening, but they won't *believe* it. The actor 'shows' us the doorway by first imagining the door (creating its reality in his mind) and then changing his whole posture as he steps from one visualised space into another. When a person steps from a small room into the open air, the spine lifts, the head rises and the eyes change focus. This happens naturally in life. As long as the actor imaginatively re-creates the circumstances and obeys them (creates the 'set' – see below – and conforms to it imaginatively), he will 'show' the audience where he is. *Kathakali* performers work from facial expression and the direction of the gaze to body position and gesture – and, if required, to gait and movement – so that each part is animated and becomes a 'whole-body *mudra*' through which the body, as Lecoq would say, 'speaks'.

Exercises to develop the imagination of mind and body are primarily non-verbal. Roddy Maude-Roxby and others use variations of the **Mime-stick** exercise. The student is given a simple stick (or equally basic object, such as a jumper) and has to assign it a reality other than its own. The stick may become a telescope; the jumper may become a baby. But, whatever the transformation, the new reality of the object has to be conveyed physically, and truthfully, within the improvisation. In early stages, transformations tend to be signalled rather cheaply (we read the stick held to the eye as a telescope almost without the actor needing to do anything else). Notions of 'showing' and 'telling' can then be brought in, and the actor's encouraged to use the object as an imaginative trigger for a scene. When the actors whole body begins to conform naturally to the imagined reality, 'showing' replaces 'telling'. At that point the prop itself will be subsumed into the scene which has been created from it. The audience's attention, like the actor's, will no longer be on the sign but on the signified. We will forget the telescope and, with it, see the ships in the distance.

Entrances and exits

The entry of a new character signals an intensification of energy. The audience knows that the playwright has sent him or her on to *do* something – that is, a new action is about to develop. (Hence the neoclassical system of scene division in playtexts.) So entrances are vitally important. In improvisation this is equally true. In rehearsal, the group watches a scene developing and is encouraged to join in as soon as possible with it. As each actor joins in – that is, enters – the energy of the scene lifts. As soon as it begins to flag, someone else *must* come in to help out. The actors mustn't be left stranded. That is the First Cardinal Sin in improvisation. The new action doesn't have to be highly significant, as long as it's sensitive to either the demands of the developing scene or the energy level of the situation. If this is learned as a principle, then there is very little difficulty in sustaining the spontaneity of improvisation. Actors learn to look after one another and to take the pressure off each other rather than increase it. ('What are you doing?', described above on p. 151, can be a useful way of re-energising a scene at key moments like this – a couple of interactions will be enough to launch things in a different direction.)

Entrances physically signal a change of space. In a development of the 'showing/telling' exercise, placing two chairs in the centre of the rehearsal space, about three feet apart, creates a natural **door-way**. Stepping back and forth through this doorway, the actor must imaginatively see and respond to new environments each time (a railway station, a cathedral, a classroom, a bar, etc.). This can also be linked to status work (see next chapter) or character work – entering with the appropriate attitude or characteristics – for example, leading with a specific part of the body, at a certain pace, with a particular gait, with an intention or attitude, in a specific rhythm and so on. The exercise can be done alone, first, so that the actor simply feels the impression of each imagined space. Later, the exercise can be done with onlookers, who should be able to understand from the bodily expression of the actor what kinds of environment are being traversed. **Wrong Room** asks participants to leave the space and re-enter, one by one; after a moment, each one recognises that s/he is in the wrong room; then they have to leave appropriately. Not only does this show the watchers how the body and expression signal a recognition, but it also asks participants to explore entering and leaving in very different states of mind.

It also makes it clear that exits, too, are important. They finish the scene, ending the action for the person departing (though not necessarily for those who remain). Encourage people not to hang around once their contribution has run out, but to think up a good reason for leaving and to play it. This can develop a sense of shape in the actor's mind, making the actor work through every moment of a scene. Sometimes, of course, this will be used as an excuse to get off as fast as possible, but just as often it will open up a whole new reason for staying on.

Meetings and greetings

All theatre is an act of encounter. Characters meet each other and we understand from their meeting how they relate to one another: this is a husband greeting his wife upon awakening; that is an underling receiving his boss into his home; these are two lovers who have been apart. But there is also a deeper level of encounter implicit in the act of theatre. Clive Barker writes:

> The theatre is the art of human relationships in action. This definition will apply to modern unstructured forms of improvised drama and rituals as well as to older established forms. In the theatre people meet, and plot is the result of their interaction. At the end the situation is not what it was at the beginning, because human beings have experienced a process of change. Change takes place in the audience individually through their meeting with the actors/ characters/dramatist.   (Barker 1977: 124)

There are a number of implications here. On stage, *people* should meet, not machines repeating the fixed formulae of lines learned in rehearsal. In one type of theatre (say, the Chekhovian) the implication is that *characters* encounter one another. In another (say, in *commedia*) the *actors* meet – and so do the *masks*.

Exercises about **meetings and greetings** abound. They include sitting in a circle and introducing the person next to you to the rest of the group; walking around the room and stopping first to acknowledge silently, then to greet and finally to introduce oneself to each other person; throwing a name (maybe accompanied by a ball) across the circle, focusing total attention on a chosen person for an instant. Here the idea of meeting is enhanced by a directing of energy and purpose. In Lecoq's school (just as in Copeau's) the neutral and other masks are used to facilitate genuine encounter. The openness of the neutral mask (discussed below) and the childlike curiosity of the expressive masks make them (and of course their wearers) especially apt for exploring and meeting the world around them because they encourage the laying aside of preconceptions and emotional 'armour'.

An interesting way of preparing for this kind of encounter is a Maude-Roxby exercise which could be called **Meeting the Object**. Participants are asked to find any object from nearby, inside or outside – a leaf, a twig, a stone, a bag, a rubber band, etc. – then to spend some time 'meeting it', enquiring about its contours, its consistency and its capacities, building a relationship with it. As a further extension towards narrative they can be asked to tell the story of this encounter and relationship; but for the purposes of the exercise we are discussing here it is enough to take time to explore, to be curious, to construct the possibility of a two-way encounter. The aim is to trigger an openness to the world and to imagination.

These exercises tend to progress from name games to partner work and then to working in small groups so that ease and familiarity is built up. At the pivotal phase of working with a partner, two activities are particularly helpful. One is Boal's celebrated **Columbian Hypnosis**. Here one partner holds his or her hand flat and close to the other partner's face and then *slowly and carefully* moves it in any direction. The partner follows the hand as though hypnotised by it, adjusting feet and body, place and position as necessary. It's important to develop a sense of reciprocity; in particular the 'leader' needs to be sensitive to the response and comfort of their partner. This is in a way akin to proto Contact Improvisation work and aims to develop a similar kinetic interactivity based on sensing and responding.

A second useful exercise is **Blind Leading** or creating a sensory experience for your partner. One of the two players closes their eyes. The other guides them by touch and/or sound around the agreed space, introducing them to as many different sensory experiences (touch, taste, smell, sound, but not sight) as possible, by inviting them to interact with things encountered and, perhaps, exploited by the leader. Again this involves care, sensitivity, imagination and attention to the other, all of which serve the goal of creating a 'new world' in an unforced and spontaneous way. Both these exercises usually swap the roles around after an agreed length of time. Both could figure in the section titled 'Senses' in Chapter 8 because they target the extension of openness and sensory awareness.

But in performance work the audience, too, encounters the actors and, through them, the characters and beyond them the dramatist or the idea of the play. This is the deepest level of encounter; here, the audience meets itself, touching physically (at the elbows if nowhere else) and touching spiritually via the play's depiction to the audience of their own concerns. And the individual audience member encounters herself and recognises some truth about herself in what she sees. The participatory or immersive work we discussed earlier foregrounds and intensifies this.

The vulnerability this involves (and highlights and celebrates) is an essential basis for these kinds of encounter, whose nature is fundamentally 'improvisatory' in that they are based in availability/disponibility/not being closed off. The ability, the willingness, to *meet* is necessary for actors and 'non-actors' (or other kinds of actors) alike; it forms part of a life strategy.

Blocking

'Blocking' – the Second Cardinal Sin of improvisation – is a denial of the possibility of encounter (Johnston 1998: 190–2). Blocking occurs when a performer tacitly refuses to accept what another is offering (or, indeed, when s/he refuses to accept the impulses and ideas of his/her own psyche). Keith Johnstone calls it 'a form of aggression'. He sometimes uses video to record improvisation sessions. It's difficult at first to show people (even those watching) how the blocking is inhibiting the development of a scene. On video it becomes obvious what has been offered and either missed or denied:

> Each actor tends to resist the invention of the other actor, playing for time, until he can think up a 'good idea', and then he'll try to make his partner follow it. The motto of scared improvisers is 'when in doubt, say "NO"'. We use this in life as a way of blocking action. Then we go to the theatre, and at all points where we would say 'No' in life, we want to see the actors yield, and say 'Yes'.   (Johnstone 1981: 94–5)

There's a good reason for wanting to hear the performers saying 'yes': it offers us a chance to experience those aspects of our 'character' and those possibilities of action which we do not feel confident about trying for ourselves in normal situations. The freedom of the stage action allows us to live a little more fully, and that is also what can happen through improvisation.

As Johnstone says, good improvisers develop action, even when they aren't sure where it's leading; bad improvisers block it. And in blocking action, they deny the possibility of any kind of encounter happening between the actors, and between actors and audience.

Some useful exercises which promote unblocking (though almost every-thing done in impro works towards this) focus on response situations: making machines and body sculptures, telling stories one word or sentence at a time and adding noises or gestures to a partner's story. In **Yes/Yes, but** scenes, one actor is allowed to say no more than 'Yes' (twice in succession) and then 'Yes, but' every third response. There is a version of this which figures in Indian folk-theatre such as *Yakshagana*, where the narrator-cum-director (Bhagavata) (or another character) intersperses 'comments' into an actor's speech, for example, 'Um', 'Ah', 'Eh', 'Oh' and so on. With very little or no vocabulary, the interlocutor can incite all kinds of interesting possibilities depending on tone of voice, timing or inflection.

Gibberish exercises may also be useful here. One used by Strasberg is playing a scene in an invented nonsensical language which has to make sense. A good way to begin is to ask one student to give **a gibberish talk** on a subject, which another student will translate for the audience. The translator does not invent the meaning but attempts to derive it from the gibberish speaker (Johnston 1998: 125; see also Fo's *Grammelot*; this kind of exercise figures quite frequently in Theatre Sports). In full scene work, importantly, the aim is to communicate with the acting partner: it encourages the rest of the body to become involved in signifying; and it makes the actors listen to each other. Each participant forces the partner to become clearer before the scene can proceed.

Strasberg noted that gibberish exercises were particularly useful when working with actors who could feel the emotion of a scene, but found its expression difficult. One actress, experiencing such a blockage, was encouraged to play through her emotional scenes in gibberish, 'and in using sounds and words that broke away from her conventional and habitual tightness, she exploded' (Hull 1985: 115).

Blocking is both a physical and a mental problem (discussed in Part 3 as censorship and psychodrama), and everything from gentle warm-ups to the most intimidating Grotowskian encounter strategies can be appropriate to tackle it, depending on the context. Ruth Zaporah speaks of 'countering' and 'blocking': for her, blocking is a physical check to another improviser, pulling them back or inhibiting their movement, while countering is 'a substitute for connecting to yourself' (Zaporah 1995: 92), expressed by breaking the other's concentration in some way, pulling the other performer 'out of his fantasy' (*ibid.*) or observing rather than fully participating in the improvised moment.

The things we have referred to here relate mainly to working in pairs or groups, that is, to the importance of unblocking in developing the ability to work together, which is basic to all performing.

8   Moving Towards Performance

Senses

The actor's senses are of paramount importance in order to be fully responsive to fellow performers and to the audience. They are the only means of experiencing and contacting the world around. Sight and hearing are crucial, of course, but smell and taste and, particularly, *touch*, are equally important. Sight is the primary means of spatial location; remove sight (with a blindfold) and the performer has to reorient physically and reach out through space. Learning to extend oneself spatially with eyes open leads automatically to becoming more physically expressive – less 'bound' or 'closed' (as the 'Fight in the Dark' game demonstrates).

But the senses also have an imaginative dimension. We have sensation memory, which Stanislavsky used as the key to 'emotional recall' – allowing the actor to get in touch with memories of childhood, say, by recalling the smell of soap or the roughness of school clothes. It is impossible to say whether 'emotional recall' is actual recall – or an imaginative creation of the present.[1] But the use of recalled sensory information is certainly central to the process, personalising and concretising the imaginary reconstruction. The group can be taken on a **mime journey**, for example, through an imaginary sensory landscape, ideally one which includes several stages and environments – through water, up a hill, lying on a beach and so on.

Lecoq makes the journey involve a **passage through each of the elements** – water, fire, air and earth – and an exploration of how the body functions in relation to weight, speed, balance and so on.

> The four elements … are approached through their different manifestations. When it comes to water, we have to discover ponds, and lakes, and rivers, and the sea. For example, we observe the movement of a body in relation to the sea: it is lifted by the water, thrown back by the waves … Water is a moving, resisting force, which can only be experienced by struggling with it. It is only from the pelvis that this overall sensation can be transmitted to the whole of the body. We emphasise the involvement of the pelvis so as to avoid arm- or

hand-gestures which would tend to 'signify' the sea without experiencing it. (Lecoq 1997/2000: 87–8)

Lecoq's work is rooted in movement; in mime, he directs the performer away from 'telling' and towards 'showing' through experiencing. The exploration of the elements has far more to do with the performer's body than with the external world, with sensing inner, physical realities than imagining external ones, and it is a highly systematised, structural, even structuralist, approach. Snow (2012) also describes exercises with elements in Chapter 14 of her book.

> Fire is born from within. It flows from breathing and from the diaphragm. In fire, two movements can be distinguished: combustion and flame ... Air is found through flight. Running across the room, arms outstretched like a glider, we can sense the possibility of getting leverage on the air, which is not a vacuum but an element that can give support. The whole body is drawn in ... Finally we work on earth, in the form of clay which we can compress, smooth, stretch. Here the sensation begins from the hands, before spreading to the whole of the body. (Lecoq 1997/2000: 88)

Michael Chekhov's training scheme – disciplining the body to liberate that 'higher ego' which he feels to be the core of the actor's creativity, sensitivity and morality – also makes use of the four elements, but with different nuances. He speaks of 'moulding' (earth), 'flowing' (water), 'flying' (air) and 'radiating' (fire). In the **moulding** exercise, for example, the mime of moulding clay (in fact moulding the air itself around the actor) is enlarged, and repeated, step by step, so that it becomes less naturalistic and involves the whole body. Each movement is precisely delineated by the actor, and performed without tension, ruled by the 'sense of ease' which underpins Chekhov's work. The actions are then reduced again, until the smallest of gestures conveys the sensory idea perfectly.

In the **flowing** exercise, movements lose their isolation and begin to merge into each other, while in the **flying** exercise, the body seeks a sense of lightness, and the movements continue outwards from the actor's centre as if continuing indefinitely. The **radiating** exercise – deriving from Sulerzhitsky's *prana* yoga work – asks the actor to imagine him- or herself radiating, projecting and receiving energy. Franc Chamberlain, in his book on Chekhov (Chamberlain 2004: 64–8), considers these exercises at proper length and notes that, once the basic physical forms have been mastered they are then also connected to the 'ideal centre', located for Chekhov in the actor's chest (as a Chinese performer or martial artist may speak of *chi*, or energy, being centred in the solar plexus). Through such exercises:

> Chekhov hoped that students would develop a sense of the import-
> ance of form for the actor and learn to be dissatisfied with 'vague and
> shapeless' work in themselves and others.   (Chamberlain 2004: 65)

For Ruth Zaporah, 'presence' has something of the 'decided' quality of the Barba body but little to do with charisma. Zaporah uses it in a more Buddhist sense; her work is concerned with 'how to focus attention on the body's awareness of the present moment' (Zaporah 1995: back cover). The exercises she presents in this book are in themselves relatively familiar – work on time, space, shape, dynamics, sound, movement and rhythm via **moving and freezing, mirroring** and **pair work** and exploring properties of phenomena like rocks and leaves. Each set culminates in a 'performance score', and 'we must notice what inhibits our freedom, be willing to give up all preconceptions, be truthful, and relax in order to act from lively emptiness' (1995: xxii). What characterises her work – as a teacher and per- former for over thirty years, starting in late 1960s California (as a student of Al Wunder) where impro was part of 'the march toward feeling' (xx) – is a focus on being aware of what you are doing and how you do it and letting impulses, emotions, movement, interaction and a degree of verbal interchange emerge from the attention to nascent sensation: 'clear, spon- taneous expression is not the result of how much you do but rather of the quality of attention you give' (41).

Tenses

Acting occurs in the present tense. It is experienced in the moment of its creation – the 'now' of the performance. That is another reason why we speak of the good performer as having 'presence'; his or her concentrated attention fills the space and fills the time. It doesn't matter whether the play is set in the remotest past or the farthest reaches of some imagined future: in order for it to be experienced it has to be performed in the pre- sent. This is particularly so with improvisation which, as Moreno insisted, is always 'now'; the illusion of the first time (in rehearsed performance) is replaced by the reality of the first time (cf. Charles 2003: 88).

So we always *act in* the present. But we can also *act* the past and the fu- ture. Clive Barker (following Brecht) has importantly qualified the process of acting 'in the present' in a way which throws light upon one of the basic principles of improvisation: the actor's use of the imagination. The performer can **vary the tense – and the person –** to produce a clearer mental and physical narrative of the action being portrayed. The actor moves from the understood 'I, the character, am doing this', via 'He, the character, is doing this', to, ultimately, 'The character did this' – which the actor then *re-enacts*. Barker explains it thus:

> The activity of the actor is not the illusory *reliving* of an imaginary event, but the *re-enactment* in the present of an event which we accept as gone for ever, in which we personally had no part, and which is no longer a direct issue. Whatever terms we work in, the actual event is the performance of a play by actors.   (Barker 1977: 162)

Another angle on acting in the present is highlighted by Richard Schechner. He is concerned with 'restored behavior' or with 'strips of behavior':

> Restored behavior is living behavior treated as a film director treats a strip of film … [It] is used in all kinds of performances from shamanism and exorcism to trance, from ritual to aesthetic dance and theater, from initiation rites to social dramas, from psychoanalysis to psychodrama and transactional analysis. In fact, restored behavior is the main characteristic of performance.   (Schechner 1985: 35)

The behaviours themselves, originating outside the performer in society, are the material with which the performer's process concerns itself (whether a Broadway actor in rehearsal or a shaman).

> Because the behavior is separate from those who are behaving, the behavior can be stored, transmitted, manipulated, transformed. The performers get in touch with, recover, remember, or even invent these strips of behavior and then rebehave according to these strips, either by being absorbed into them (playing the role, going into trance) or by existing side by side with them (Brecht's *Verfremdungseffekt*). (1985: 35)

That is to say, the means with which we work, whether on scripted plays or via improvisation, are drawn from a repertoire of pre-existent and remembered behaviours.

> Restored behavior is 'out there', distant from 'me'. It is separate and therefore can be 'worked on', changed, even though it has 'already happened'. Restored behavior includes a vast range of actions. It can

> be 'me' at another time/psychological state as in the psychoanalytic abreaction; or it can exist in a nonordinary sphere of sociocultural reality as does the Passion of Christ or the reenactment in Bali of the struggle between Rangda and Barong; or it can be marked off by aesthetic convention as in drama and dance; or it can be the special kind of behavior 'expected' of someone participating in a traditional ritual ... Performance means: never for the first time. It means: for the second to the nth time. Performance is 'twice-behaved behavior'. (36)

Actors can discover for themselves the 'tenses of acting' and have little trouble with changing person from first to third or tense from present to past. But how do you act in the future? Through dreams, prophecies, visions and desires which take you forward into the future, just as memory takes you back into the past. They can all be experienced (as strips of behaviour) and expressed (as facial or bodily signs).

Past and future are available as present in all kinds of performance. Moreno is also right that in one sense, in pure impro there is no past, only the immediacy of the present. There is only action, not re-enactment. Improvisation, however, is never entirely 'pure', in the sense of being created *ex nihilo*; it may still be spontaneous and unplanned and draw upon inculturated repertoires.[2]

And more specifically, 'Impro' makes the situation of performers and audience, the 'here and now', its subject. This encapsulates a central concern, to which we will return in the theoretical section of this book, that, when I 'act' in theatre (as performance, rehearsal or improvisation), I both cause something significant to happen in the present and repeat something which has already happened (either historically or conceptually). Improvisation, like all theatre, is both past and present – an enactment of that conjunction. Every time we 'repeat', 'rehearse', 'restore' or 're-enact', we make present the significance of what is repeated but we also, crucially, change it (we *re*-make it, *re*-present it) and render it alive in its new incarnation. The improvisatory partakes of and underlines this quality of liveliness, and that's why it's central to much, if not all, inventive performance.

Every performer is the sum of his or her experiences (real and imagined) learned from other situations in life and on the stage – the collection of behaviours to which he or she has personal and cultural access.[3] To draw upon them (often unconsciously) is not to submit to cliché: every actor does it. If the performer is responding genuinely, truthfully, to the here and now of his or her situation, improvisation can be divorced from the preparation process and become the performance itself. In a more discursive and situationist sense, too, improvisation often draws upon what is happening 'here and now', via the incorporation of current events and/or an engagement with the current state of audience and players in improv, 'Living Newspaper', 'Newspaper Theatre', Playback, etc. as well as through interactions in immersive theatre.

What improvisation games or exercises, then, lead towards this imagining and embodying of another temporal dimension? One route is to draw on Stanislavsky's **affective memory**. The performer may have a tactile, rhythmic or positional 'trace' of what a state (being a baby or being 10 years old), a condition (being ill) or an event (passing an exam or getting married) feels like for him/her. The ability to locate and create that instantaneously may generate a tone of voice, a bodily position, a look and a whole-body attitude. So many of the areas of work discussed so far will help (imagining places and elements; exploring sensory awareness; responding to a partner's offer verbally or physically). **Hot-seating** may assist in the creation of a sub-text, a narrative over time of what has contributed to the present condition. These resources may constitute a 'bank' of Schechnerian 'strips' of restored behaviour. The ability to access them is developed by 'playing' in many of the ways we have suggested. The shape they take each time, like the shape of a Theatre Machine scene, has to arise in the moment: that is the actualisation of the 'past' situation.

As a director, Beckett was not a fan of improvisation in the loose sense. He worked extremely precisely, even obsessively, on each nuance of tone and rhythm. But in so doing, what he targeted in his performers was an extended sensitivity to the possibilities of ambiguity. Each of his numerous and calculated pauses sets up different avenues of interpretation: they identify a nexus, a neutral place. By keeping this place open for the space of a breath, that sensitivity is enabled to flow in. When Krapp ironically recalls his younger self, he is both past and present. The imaginative act, for performer and audience, by which we see and hear this, is dependent on the flow. The flow depends on the preceding pause, and what comes up depends on all the work the performer has done previously. Or, as the woman in *Rockaby* puts it with delicious and excruciating ambiguity, 'Time she stopped'.

Status

The two chief sections of Keith Johnstone's *Impro* are devoted to *status* interactions and to *masks*. Both are extremely complex subjects and the reader is advised to consult Johnstone's book directly.

Status, for Johnstone, implies far more than just given power relationships or questions of submission and dominance. The word 'status' is best understood as both noun and verb. It does not simply define a state or condition, the social status; it is something one *does* or plays.

TRAMP.	'Ere! Where are you going?
DUCHESS.	I'm sorry, I didn't quite catch ...
TRAMP.	Are you deaf as well as blind?

Audiences enjoy a contrast between the status played and the social status ... Chaplin liked to play the person at the bottom of the hierarchy and then lower everyone. (Johnstone 1981: 36)

Status is a dynamic interactive process of continual adjustment. One can work to raise or lower oneself and those around one – what Johnstone calls 'the see-saw principle'. In Johnstone's view, people train themselves in life to become 'status specialists', manoeuvring themselves in any social situation into their preferred position and feeling uncomfortable when asked to play the alternative position. So a lot of his work consists in training his students to recognise and to adapt their preferred social positions. His exercises often centre around scenes in which pairs work together on **status transactions**. First both will lower status, then both will raise it, then one will raise while the other lowers and finally status will be reversed during the scene. He emphasises that the chosen position should be just a *little* bit higher or lower than the partner's; this means careful observation and delicate modulation. The actors have to learn the subtle dynamics of transition.

Status can be played to the space and to objects as well as to people. One can, for example, play high status to an empty room – rubbing a finger over surfaces and finding dust will raise one's status and lower the room's. Or one can play low status to a chair – avoiding it because it looks too posh lowers oneself and raises the chair. A development of this is Boal's **Great Game of Power** (Boal 1992: 150). In its simplest form, this involves participants entering the space one by one, each seeking to find the most powerful place/ position/attitude. Sometimes a few bits of furniture or props may be added.

One very important point about status information is that it may be all an actor needs to begin improvising. Talking of the 'Method' actor's wish to know all the 'given circumstances' in detail before attempting improvisation, Johnstone says:

In order to enter a room all you need to know is what status you are playing. The actor who understands this is free to improvise in front of an audience with no given circumstances at all! (Johnstone 1981: 47)

There are many exercises which explore **status relationships**. Simple ones using distributed numbers or playing cards work well. A large group is divided into players and watchers. Players are dealt a card face down. On it is their status: King is high; Ace is low. As an ensuing improvisation (say, a playground scene or a courtroom drama) unfolds, they have to play their relative status and defer to characters they imagine to be higher than themselves while acting high status to their presumed inferiors. At the end of the improvisation, the watchers have to come on stage and line up the players in their status order. It's easy to get the King and the Ace right and trickier for audience and actors to get the subtler distinctions between five and sixes without practice. (Max Stafford-Clark's *Workpack* describes a similar exercise in detail on page 24.)

Variations include a number of 'party' games in which participants have a status allocated by the facilitator and spelt out on a card stuck on their back or on a post-it note attached to their forehead. They can see other people's but not their own, and each player has to guess what s/he is from the reactions of the others.

A similar exercise works extremely well for **exploring status with creative writers** (or for re-animating a scene that isn't working). Cards are dealt to the writers, who are then given a fairly neutral but dynamic starting line to which they have to write a single-line response, for example, 'Read the note and give me the money'. If the card is a high number, then the 'bank teller' plays high status to the 'bank robber' (for example, 'Your spelling is appalling, young man: you should be ashamed!'). The scene can be developed with further lines/cards. If a scene isn't quite working, then asking oneself abstract questions about the status interactions *might* help: reaching for the cards and writing a high or low status response *will* animate the scene or clarify the issues within it.

The basic status game is **Master–Servant** (Johnstone 1981: 62ff.) in which each plays the status of his respective role to the limit so that the interaction becomes a battle (by grovelling to the utmost, the servant implicitly attacks the master, who has constantly to reassert himself). It's useful to remember that status can be shown by a range of different factors, which may be built up in stages: discourse, bodily attitude, gesture, facial expression and so on. This game and its variants allow actors to recognise and begin to use status as a part of their repertoire. Like other improvisation games dependent on a rapid response, it liberates the player from any one habitual mode and moves him towards becoming a kaleidoscope of available choices. Important for actors, of course, but equally so for actors as people, because it produces an extension of the range of existential choice, which is the most serious and far-reaching effect of the play element in culture.

Masks

Masks are used in various ways in improvisation and related forms of teaching. Copeau, Lecoq, Johnstone and Maude-Roxby all made extensive use of them. We have described some of this in Part 1, particularly from the point of view of the aims of mask work. In what follows, aims are naturally also relevant, although here we are more concerned with different techniques or ways of working. Of all the teachers we have mentioned, Lecoq is most systematic in this, since he incorporates work with five different kinds of mask into his training, although recently Sears Eldredge has systematised his own mask training into a complete course (Eldredge 1996).[4]

In his curriculum for studying and teaching mask technique, Eldredge says:

> Mask improvisation training is an actor training method that sensitizes and frees the imagination stored in the psychophysical being of the performer.   (Eldredge 1996: 17)

The intention behind it is 'to train actors to be more effective in their acting *without* masks', and it starts from 'the ... "breaking down" of the actor [as suggested by trainers like Clive Barker, following Rudolf Laban] as a precursor to learning methods of transformation' (1996: 18–19).

Eldredge sees the mask as operating this 'freeing of the imagination' in five ways: he lists 'The Five Major Functions of Masks' as: '*frame, mirror, mediator, catalyst* and *transformer*' (4–5). Both the Lecoquian scheme or progression – moving from neutral to larval mask and then exploring character masks and finally the red nose – and the ritualistic use of mask to assist shamanic trance or access the ways of being of 'gods' or 'demons' are covered by this taxonomy. Eldredge suggests that the bi-polar either/or view of trance obliteration or acute self-consciousness might be more profitably regarded as 'an experience of convergence' – that is to say a new, synthetic condition to which the transforming mask gives access: the creative '"both/and" duality of divided consciousness' (8). Eldredge is emphatic that

> work in the Neutral Mask always underlies the work in the Character Masks – and, in fact, all performance work, with or without masks. (19)
>
> For all mask work, external 'coaching' or observation is useful to remind the wearer to 'keep the mask up' and present it to the watchers (see also below, p. 189).

Neutral mask

Lecoq starts with this; in *The Moving Body* he writes:

> The neutral mask is unique: it is the mask of all masks. After our
> experiments with it, we go on to work with a great variety of other
> kinds of mask, which we group together under the heading of 'ex-
> pressive masks'. While the neutral mask is unique, the number of
> expressive masks is infinite. (Lecoq 1997/2000: 54)

It is the mask most fundamental to improvisatory work because learning
to wear it is learning to achieve the state from which new creative structure can arise. It works as a kind of 'unlearning', liberating the performer
from preconceived notions, from any 'recipe'. It requires – almost like a
Grotowskian *via negativa* – a complete letting-go in order to reach a condition of unprejudiced being, whilst at the same time one must remain
acutely focused and alert, ready to respond with the whole organism.

Lecoq regards the process as a *via negativa*, a process of discovering 'the
"yes" of neutral by a series of "noes"' (Eldredge 1996: 50). The neutral
mask

> depersonalizes the wearer [while at the same time] it essentializes the
> wearer. You discover more of what is distinctly 'you' … what is elic-
> ited is actually your *individual* neutral. (1996: 50)

Lecoq uses this mask as part of the process of 'forgetting': 'Neutral … means
without a past, open, ready' (Felner 1985: 158). He aims for 'a liberation
that permits the mime to rediscover the world in a newly attained state
of nonknowing' (158). In this condition 'the individual becomes a blank
page … Everything is erased so he can start from scratch, seeing things for
the first time' (158).

The typical exercises on **Waking Up** (in which one imagines waking on
the ground, without memory, without fear; then slowly rises, looks around
and explores), or the improvisation **Farewell to the Boat** (in which the
actor rushes to the end of a jetty to wave goodbye for the last time to a dear
friend (Lecoq 1997/2000: 40–1)), ask actors to explore movement and expression from a situation of no prior knowledge, evading preconceptions.
Although the features of the mask itself are simply of a male or female in
repose, without particular characteristics (latterly, Eldredge has challenged
this Amleto Sartori design[5]), it is actually almost impossible to 'behave neu-
trally' – and this is the first discovery one makes. The body 'sticks out';
one's habits of stance, movement and energy are thrown into relief by the

mask's simplicity even in these first, basic exercises. Out of that self-discovery, with patience, the ability to recognise and discard habitual postures and gestures begins to emerge.

> You take on the neutral mask as you might take on a character, with the difference that here there is no character, only a neutral generic being. A character experiences conflict, has a history, a past, a context, passions. On the contrary, a neutral mask puts the actor in a state of perfect balance and economy of movement. Its moves have a truthfulness, its gestures and actions are economical. (Lecoq 1997/2000: 38)

True 'neutrality' is, of course, unobtainable: 'The image of the individual neutral figure, like the concept of neutral, is obviously an intellectual construct – a compelling and powerful image that can function as an agent for the psychophysical transformation of the actor' (Eldredge 1996: 55). Eldredge suggests **six characteristics of the ideal neutral body** which would unite the body with the neutral mask:

1. symmetrical
2. centred
3. integrated and focused
4. energised
5. relaxed
6. involved in being, not doing

and, when observed in motion, the neutral body would appear:

7. economical in its use of energy, and
8. coordinated, with every part of the body engaged. (See Eldredge 1996: 53.)

This is the all-important process of getting back prior to habitual reactions and fixed notations, including language. Acting comes later. Lecoq goes on to use exercises derived from Copeau and Bing:

> We play people, elements, plants, trees, colours, lights, matter, sounds – going beyond their images, gaining knowledge of their space, their rhythm, their breath through improvisation. (Lecoq 1972: 41)

All Lecoq's work on rhythm, matter, plasticity and relationships in space is rooted in the improvisations he does with the neutral mask, examining or refusing to allow each *dérive* (detour or digression) that emerges. It is interesting that he also uses this mask for work on the Greek chorus, both in terms of the way it responds as a single organism rhythmically and spatially balancing the protagonist and because he regards it as incorporating a neutrality that is 'all-knowing'. What Lecoq sees in the neutral mask is precisely this leading into a kind of total and potent organic knowledge.

> Once [the actor] has achieved this freedom, the mask can be removed
> with no fear of falling back on artificial gestures. The neutral mask, in
> the end, unmasks.   (Lecoq 1997/2000: 39)

Expressive mask

All masks envisage (rather than embody) expression. The *Noh* mask – seemingly serene and neutral when not extravagantly demonic – awaits only the slightest tilt of the actor's head to reveal a full range of emotions rather than the single frozen one we might expect. The masked *shite* tilts the *omote* (face/mask) slightly upwards (*terasu*) to convey smiling or even laughing: tilting the same mask slightly downwards (*kumorasu*) produces an impression of frowning or sadness as the mask catches the light differently and is experienced differently by the onlooker.

The historic power of such masks was noted in Europe; Edward Gordon Craig's 1910 article 'A Note on Masks' had awakened interest in the mask as a theatrical vehicle. The Polish-American illustrator and mask-maker W. T. Benda (1873–1948) was perhaps the first in America to articulate similar theoretical discoveries to those Copeau and *les Copiaus* (newly returned from New York) would make in France after 1921 with the 'noble mask' (which would become Lecoq's *masque neutre*). Benda, who became an expert on the history of masks, noted this innate expressiveness in his early experiments, particularly in his designs for the improvising dancer Margaret Severn. In a 1926 article for *Ladies Home Journal* entitled 'Masks On the Stage and Off', he wrote:

> There is a general idea that all the expression is in the face of the
> person, but this is not so. The position of the head means even more
> than any change in features. A mask is of course immobile, but,
> when worn, every tilt or turn of the head will suggest to us a cer-
> tain expression of the face which we are used to seeing with that
> particular position of the head. A certain mask, which has the eyes
> looking down, appears very demure when the head is inclined; but
> the same mask will look extremely haughty when the head is raised
> and the eyes remain still looking down... The smile of one mask

gives it an appearance of shyness when the head is inclined; but when the head is raised the same smile becomes an arrogant sneer. A martial frown on another mask when worn high becomes a painful grimace when the head is well inclined by the wearer of the mask. (Benda 1926)

The expressive mask as used by Lecoq represents a fixed psychological type – rather like Pirandello's *Six Characters*. Wearing this full-faced, unspeaking mask forces the body to find gestures and emotions in direct response to the stimulus it offers. (Some *commedia* masks may be of this type: the difference lies in the degree of intensity with which they are invested.) Masks should never be form-fitting, argues Lecoq:

masked performance requires an indispensable distance between the mask and the actor's face ... [and so, including the neutral mask] the mask must be larger (or smaller) than the wearer's face. An expressive mask tailored to the exact dimensions of the actor's face or, even worse, a mask moulded onto his skin, precludes playing: it is a dead mask. (Lecoq 1997/2000: 55)[6]

The expressive mask is allowed its detours and digressions:

Anything that is not neutral is the beginning of a characterization – a turnout with the left foot, or a cocked-back pelvis, a head tilting down, or a loping walk, a movement centre in the chin, or a shallow chest with hunched, curving shoulders. Each of these is a character. (Eldredge 1996: 55)

Lecoq also uses this mask for *contre*-masque; perhaps Eldredge's greatest contribution to mask acting is his use of the **countermask**: not a distinct type of mask, but a method of playing counter to the 'givens' of the mask one is wearing (only, of course, after the actor has discovered them in rehearsal or training).

Beginning with the **nested mask** exercise – wearing one mask on top of another and shifting one's performance between the two (Eldredge 1996: 97) – actors are taught to use this doubling imaginatively when carrying only one mask: they are asked to play the visible mask and then switch to playing an imagined, invisible, opposite mask: the countermask.

Observers unite the two contradictory systems (that derived from seeing the visible mask and that derived from watching an opposed physicality carrying it) into a successful synthesis: a more complex character.

From the performer's perspective, rather than developing two separate characterisations, the actors quickly discover that there is an unsuspected relationship between the inner and outer masks.

> The actor can use the work in the countermask to develop different characterizations or a synthesized, single characterization …
>
> Mask/countermask is therefore a useful technique for creating characters based either on Stanislavsky's psychological model or on Brecht's dialectical model.   (Eldredge 1996: 99)[7]

Impro work with this mask thus leads to the experience of what it feels like to be a 'split' character with an internal conflict – one whose inner sense of himself is always at odds with his appearance, for instance. The multiple possibilities of self-regard and self-deception begin to emerge as physical experiences.

Commedia *masks*

In Lecoq's teaching, the essence of *commedia* lies in the fact that it takes stereotypes to the extreme and is always played at the highest level of intensity. Here too 'fixed external movements and the mask create the internal character' (Felner 1985: 164) so it's a matter of working off the mask through the body, not of thinking up suitably typical actions (or words, since the *commedia* half-mask has a voice; it uses language) in advance. Lecoq progresses towards use of *commedia* masks both through work on breathing and through exercises which raise the level of intensity of expressing emotion: each feeling, for instance, can be progressively 'scaled up' by every new character entering a scene.

Working with expressive or *commedia* masks involves particularly energetic preparation; it can even lead to trancing, as the writers can testify. Fifteen minutes under the Mask of Arlecchino can seem like hours of relentless pressure. When the mask is removed it can take an hour or two to 'come down' from the high induced by intense physical and mental concentration and perhaps also by changes in breathing due to the mask's demands. This type of work is, in the end, a validation of Johnstone's claims for Mask states of consciousness rather than a negation of them. However, where Keith Johnstone and Roddy Maude-Roxby's work is relaxed and exploratory, this style of mask improvisation is intense, physical and highly technical.[8]

The first half of a three-hour session consists of a devastatingly thorough physical warm-up, designed to inculcate professional discipline and to work on all parts of the body, especially the legs and the torso. The exercises stress coordination, flexibility and rhythm. The aim is simple. Under a mask, it is the rest of the body which must be expressive. The thorough bodily warm-up aims to awaken each part of the body, leaving it ready to become expressive, preparing it to help to *carry* the mask in an appropriate way.

Having selected a mask, the actors are asked to walk around the acting space. At first it is evident that the masks do not 'belong' to these bodies. There seems to be a discrepancy between the mask and the body that is failing to 'carry' it appropriately. So the work proceeds by requiring instantaneous organic response. Snap changes of bodily position, direction of gaze, gesture and so on have to be found in response to the beat of a drum or tambourine. Then the actors are asked instantly to assume a posture which (*a*) involves the whole body and (*b*) seems to suit the mask. As the actors adopt specific, grotesque positions and freeze them, the masks do seem to flicker into life. With the masks 'alive', and all the group working together, the session proper begins. The method is simple enough. Verbal instruction, coaching, comes continually from the sidelines, punctuated by cues from the drum: the group is at a zoo, looking at the exhibits. Over *there* is a magnificent **bird of paradise** on a high perch. At first the actors imagine the bird and 'pretend' to see it. But then the description from the sidelines becomes more precise.

The imagined bird has a sharp crest with three upright feathers. The actors' heads begin to lift three times in unison as the eyes of the masks – and the *always open eyes* of the actors (for to close the eyes for longer than a blink is to close out the watchers, to introvert the mask) – begin to trace the imaginary plumage.

The beak is long and angled down to the left, ending in a sharp point. The heads and bodies turn, following the line; noises begin to come freely from the masks, expressing the shape vocally and ending up in a sharp point of sound. The actors are beginning to show us, physically, what it is that they are imagining and responding to.

The bird has a magnificent swirling tail that reaches the floor. The actors' heads swirl downwards and then bob back up again so as not to lose the whole image and to lose contact with the watchers.

The bird of paradise exercise illustrates a number of key ideas. The mask is a *frontal* medium. It is often difficult to see properly when wearing a mask, and improvising in one is made more difficult by the fear of losing contact with the audience – letting the mask 'go dead' – while trying to keep contact with one's partners on the stage. The answer to this problem lies in a 'whole-body awareness' of the other performers, rather than in the 'eye contact awareness' appropriate to other forms of improvisation (for example, the exercises of Michael Chekhov alluded to above) and, indeed, naturalistic acting.

The whole body listens: it isn't necessary to look at one's interlocutor in order to convince an audience that one is paying attention, nor to establish and hold eye contact in order to communicate with a fellow actor. It *is* necessary to give one's attention totally and to communicate; but in the frontal style that communication is always mediated via the audience.[9]

The mask has to *show* the audience what it is seeing, with the whole body. It is carried by the physical being of the actor – which starts from a physical posture in some way appropriate to that mask (Il Magnifico's beaked nose is naturally avian and everything else is consonant with that; Arlecchino's mischievous agility goes with the feline smile on his black face). In Dario Fo's famous master-classes, Pantalone (the impotent Magnifico) is rendered as a fantastical kind of chicken, an ageing rooster whose power has gone forever.[10] Thus the mask comes instantly alive for the spectator but, as Fo (and Bertolt Brecht) would remind us, there is also a powerful political *gestus* inherent in that incarnation. It is part of the conception of the role, not a gloss upon it. Together with the physical there is also a mental set and a specific attitude to the character. The mask remains dead without it.

Physical considerations matter a great deal. The half-mask (or buccal mask), for example, may depress the actor's upper lip, or the large cavity behind a grotesquely extended nose may create an extra resonator, both of which will naturally transform the sound of the voice, adding and subtracting tonal qualities, and these changes have to be accepted, used and developed. To do anything else is to attempt to deny what the mask is demanding of the actor. Finding this physiological quality is a measure of integration of actor and mask.

Once the technical skills have been inculcated, the teachers home in on each mask in turn, providing the performer with a constant source of stimulation. They instruct ('Keep that voice'; 'Look at us!'). They ask questions ('What's that you're holding? Show it to us. Do you like it? Aren't you proud of it?'). Sometimes they cajole and flatter; at other times they seem to want to belittle or humiliate the mask ('You're boring!'), until the mask responds with something new, or something true. Sometimes the sideline coaching is more belligerent; they refuse to accept an explanation, say, or demand that it be sung first, or spoken like Shakespeare, or danced (while keeping the basic posture). This serves to renew energy and continually to pull the focus outwards, away from any relapse into introversion.

They pick up on every little thing the mask is doing, or failing to do, and instantly suggest a way of extending or developing what is happening. 'Camera Two has packed up and we didn't quite get that, love. Could you do it again for Camera Three over there?' The mask loves being the centre of such attention and happily repeats and enlarges the activity. Or they suggest that the mask freezes certain moments ('A few shots for the publicity people'). The mask, happy to oblige, naturally begins to find those fixed points, those moments of stillness which allow the action to be clearly read.

This form of mask work is difficult and initially scary, in that it involves overcoming resistance (arising from a lack of trust in oneself, but liable to be transferred to the teachers and the work) and operating at intense pressure under constant 'nagging'. It also requires discipline: once the mask is on, the actor has to stay within that mental set.

But if these conditions are accepted – and in the end they represent that willingness all improvisation work aims to initiate, to prise open the protective shell of the narrowly conceived self – the results can be exhilarating. Some students reach and sustain a high level of creativity very quickly. One mask, on trial for the theft of a can of soup (from a soupermarket), spontaneously made up and performed a rhyming aria on the merits of various brands of broth, while another operatically demanded the soup-reme penalty for the malefactor. Students who find it difficult to give their whole body to a performance (scripted and rehearsed as well as improvised) can be coached through a revelatory learning experience while wearing a mask.

Larval mask

Larval masks are abstract forms. A subcategory of the expressive mask, naive and non-human yet evoking psychic and emotional states, they lead, like the neutral mask, to a kind of precognitive situation where physical gesture precedes emotion and both precede conceptualisation. Larvals usually focus facial characteristics on one feature – a bulbous nose, bushy eyebrows – which thus stands out and 'speaks' for the whole face/personality: wearing them, actors experiment with the position of different parts of the body and discover that emotional changes may result. Lecoq's hierarchy, similar to Copeau's, runs from gesture through emotion and then to thought and finally language. The *mime de fond*, which Lecoq also calls *mime du début*, arises at the gesture level. The Lecoq-trained Swiss company Mummenschanz use larval masks (which derive in part from the masks of the *Fastnachtspiel* of Basel) which are powerfully evocative, working at a kind of pre-verbal level. The English troupe Moving Picture Mime Show also centred their work on the larval mask, as do the celebrated Trestle Theatre Company.

Trestle have used masks, particularly larval masks, since their inception (the company was founded in 1981 by three of John Wright's students at Middlesex: Sally Cook, Alan Riley and Toby Wilsher). Gill Lamden's book on devised drama has a useful section on Trestle, describing their working processes and use of masks (Lamden 2000: 19–29). Toby Wilsher ascribes importance in devising to 'letting go' and explains that 'what masks do best is interact'. Painstaking choreography results in freedom to play; scenes are built around kernels, called '**coathangers**', with minimal verbal description (Lamden 2000: 20, 21, 27, 29).

Callery comments that, despite a drift towards whimsicality in later years,

> Trestle's highly legible, visual style forces the audience to 'read' the thoughts of the character in movement, as the masks do not speak … [Their] genius has been to see the connection between the emotional charge of mask work and naturalism. (Callery 2001: 51)

Whereas working with a neutral mask involves exploring nascent sensation and its relation to movement, without invoking a particular type or character, and *commedia* masks require an energetic physical investment precisely in stylised type, the larval seems to summon up a combination of the two processes. Very often in Trestle's work the mask gives off an air of vulnerability, as though it were somewhat hesitantly seeking its own reality; so the working process swings between internal and external modes of inhabiting the persona. Having said that, the somewhat similar masks used by Geese in their work in prisons (see below, p. 192) tend to inflect the 'single characteristic' more aggressively, as a statement of defiance or protection. But in both cases what performers are being invited to explore is how they experience their own bodies responding to the suggestions – emotional and physical – implied by the mask.

Clown (red nose)

For Lecoq, this smallest mask is the ultimate in self-revelation: 'self-humour is the only true alienation effect' (Felner 1985: 166). Here one confronts and confesses by sharing what one normally represses: brings out one's 'shadow', as it were, and lets it dance in the light. As with all mask work, the 'technique' has to do with *not* acting, with letting the mask speak. Here, it speaks for the self, and the actor is most naked, most offered to the audience. (See also Chapter 3 above.)

Uses, problems and methods

Dymphna Callery ascribes much of the resurgence in British mask work to the influence of Lecoq-trained John Wright (Callery 2001: 51) as well as to the influx of other Lecoq trainees. Companies like Trestle, Improbable and Geese exemplify the uses to which masks can be put in devising shows.[11] None of these companies can easily or reductively be described; masks and improvisation are creative means rather than ends for all of them, but all are distinguished by the inventiveness with which they use them.

Geese use masks whose form lies between the larval and the expressive for their work with offenders; each signals a single psychosocial 'attitude' ('it's not my fault'; 'don't give a toss') and enables the wearer rapidly to explore its effects on the group. Improbable's work is rooted in Keith Johnstone; they define themselves as 'yes-sayers', leave unscripted gaps in their productions and are often deliberately cavalier about learning lines in order to maintain the sense of excitement about being on stage (Lamden 2000: 30–1): their work 'blurs the distinction between process and product'. Co-director Phelim McDermott claims that the use of masks was revelatory:

> To play someone from a totally different culture and learn about their story can be a real honour. In San Diego we used Julian [Crouch]'s techniques of building masks on people's faces quickly and we got this guy to play his Great Grandmother who used to tell him stories about the American Civil war when he was a kid. It was spooky ... like she was there. It is the closest I've come to experiencing some kind of channelling experience, being connected to this point of history generations back.   (Svich 2003)

Masks may take the actor back to the original state of transformation – the shamanic act of self-annihilation. They allow the transformation to happen safely, providing a format within which a new, creative self can appear. Thus they are crucial in improvisation work. But there can be problems. Johnstone in particular uses a kind of 'magical language' when speaking of the power of Masks – implicit in his capitalisation of the initial 'M' (Johnstone 1981: 143–4). It is perfectly possible to put on a mask (small 'm') and pretend to be someone else. But Johnstone is concerned with the induction of trance states in the performer via mask work. For him, it is almost impossible to define the changes wrought in the performer by the assumption of a mask without resorting to terms like 'possession'. For most European and American actors, it is probably more useful to refer to the understanding of John Emigh, who documented masked performances of all kinds throughout Papua New Guinea, India and Indonesia, that the masked state is paradigmatic of the 'relationships between self and other (and self and self) that lie at the heart of the theatrical process' (Emigh 1996: xvii; see also Emigh's demonstration of a succession of *Topeng* masks on his Insight Media CD 'Acting Techniques of Topeng Masked Theatre of Bali').

It is true that in some non-Western theatre, the mask is still frequently seen as the repository of something not entirely human. Despite this, and in spite of often lengthy ritual preparation and/or make-up processes designed to induce a trance-like state, performers are often surprisingly matter-of-fact about what they do, freely inhabiting two quite dissimilar worlds simultaneously. Issues about trance and transformation are too complex to explore further here (see, for example, Coldiron 2004 for an extended discussion); but the crucial thing from our point of view is that however you work with a mask – meditatively, as with the neutral or in *Noh*; dynamically, as in *commedia* or 'shamanistically', as with McDermott's description above or the Balinese performer who searches 'for the meeting place between himself and the life inherent in [the mask's] otherness' (Emigh 1996: 275) – you are targeting a mode of extended being, knowing and acting. So it is appropriate to be matter-of-fact but also precise and disciplined.

To begin it is helpful to let the masks do the talking, as it were. Actors can be asked to encounter the masks as characters, encouraged to find out about them – what they like to do, whom they like to be with and so on – treating them rather like intelligent children, perhaps. The actors could be childlike (never childish) too and begin simply by putting them on and seeing what the mask suggests to them. Mirrors can stimulate and later 'recharge' the masked actor but should not be overused. Far more essential is for the actor to work off the *feeling* experienced in the mask and the *feedback* received from the audience. Too much gazing in the mirror tends to trap the wearer into unproductive narcissism.

Too little respect, and the masks will remain lifeless cardboard props; but too *much* respect – treating the masks as if they were truly the repositories of ancient demons – can stifle creativity altogether. Masks begin work by ambushing their wearers. If the atmosphere is good and the work respectful, open, honest and good-humoured to begin with, the mask will animate the actor rather than the reverse. But it is essential that the work be undertaken with care, so as not to stifle the emergence of that new self. A good way is to encourage the actors to make and to decorate their own masks – and from as many materials as possible (paper, papier mâché, leather, wood, plaster bandage and photographs stuck on cardboard). What is important here is the emphasis on working *with* the mask, developing a relationship with it from which the new self can emerge, as a seamless – but never entirely *comfortable* – 'fit' between mask and actor's body.

Eldredge's book presents a training in mask improvisation.[12] The programme includes the following:

The learning objectives

- Experiencing release from the tyranny of the analytic, the critical and the logical in the flow of the improvisation
- Discovering that masks demand total commitment (physical, mental and emotional) to make them come alive
- Discovering how to use the total bodymind economically and appropriately, and therefore effectively, to communicate
- Discovering and utilising the techniques of playing with and against the mask (text), thereby creating and developing mask and countermask, public face and private face. (Eldredge 1996: 22)

Ground rules for mask improvisation

Many of these are appropriate to all forms of drama training and to improvisation exercises.

1. Have respect for the mask.
2. Work on yourself and for yourself until told to do otherwise.
3. Work in silence.
4. Avoid touching the mask while wearing it.
5. Keep the separation clear between your Self and your mask. (A participant should not speak in her own voice in the mask. The mask does not talk with her voice: it has its own voice.)
6. When you are told to stop and come out of the mask, you will do so. (Eldredge 1996: 42)

Ultimately, the 'trance' or power to change is not in the *mask*: it derives from the conjunction of mask, actor and audience. The wearer responds to stimuli both from the mask and from teachers and/or audience: what is involved is a dynamic process of co-creation.

In this chapter we have looked at a variety of ways of developing whole-body awareness, opening up the actor's resources and developing his or her performance vocabulary. In the process the imagination is liberated and re-chanelled to offer the possibility of new physical and intellectual invention and expression.

Structures, rhythms and atmospheres

The processes described in this chapter are thus also examples of ways in which improvisation exercises lead into the elaboration of embodied imaginative worlds. They also all, in some degree, begin to assemble the parameters of those worlds in terms of structures, rhythms and atmospheres. So we will think back to some of the ways improvisation helps to set these up.

Structures are about relating parts to each other: parts of me as a performer, parts of roles I may play, parts of scenes or stories I may be involved in or co-responsible for developing. Many of the types of games and exercises we have mentioned in the last four chapters offer paths into this. Exercises on meeting and work with partners and groups gets people used to *doing* relationship: it becomes an embodied learning methodology. The work on senses and status extends awareness of the performer in relationship to the performance space and to other characters/performers; exploring tenses opens up the diachronic axis and links with back-story and hot-seating activities discussed earlier; working with mask focuses attention on the path from inner sensation and imagination to the full range of embodied expression and movement. So all these activities take the practitioner forwards and outward, building on the flexibility and openness which the exercises referred to in Chapters 5–7 have targeted.

Some key aspects of structure are *dimensions, sequencing, relationship of parts*; and *vectors*. Games from the extensive menu we've identified (Babbage, Barker, Boal, Boyd, Callery, Fritz, Heathcote, Johnston, Johnstone, Wright *et al.*) can be used 'neat' or adapted to help students to be active in these areas.

For example:

Relationship of parts:

- Compose an image of how the characters in the scene relate to each other (Boal image theatre).
- Dynamise it and freeze the action at intervals to show the *development/ sequence* of the action (Buenaventura, Ganguly). (This is a kind of moving storyboard.)

Dimensions:

- Condense or expand a scene or segment into a very tiny or very large space and explore the results.
- Play actions or text in slow or fast motion.

- And (more style than dimension, but a good exercise!): Play a scene or segment in a style or mode: melodrama, Western movie or Noh theatre; do it in spontaneous verse or sing it.

Vectors:

- Change the angle of the action to the audience.
- Find a directional focus for each character's movement in a section.

To begin to find **rhythms** for a character, interaction or 'beat', Laban dynamics (quick/sustained, heavy/light, etc.) and 'efforts' (wringing, pressing, punching, slashing, etc.) are useful when combined with an improvised walk or action; verbal or physical interaction can be explored by asking performers to use rap rhythm for repartee or internalise a 3-, 4- or 5-beat pattern to which they move or speak – perhaps dancing to it as well. Cicely Berry, who worked extensively with the RSC, used an exercise where participants would recite a Shakespeare speech whilst walking in the space and **changing direction at every indication of punctuation**. The key here is not to get locked into one pattern, but to be prepared to experiment. Choric work, singing 'rounds' and dividing a speech between different speakers or an action between different bodies are also good ways in.

Neutral mask work is one point of entry for **atmospheres**: it starts the performer listening to her body and exploring sensations, perhaps connecting physically with memories. It might take her into affective memory or to the Lecoq imagination exercise where the performer explores the body's response to a space – a garden, a cathedral or a railway station. In a group, steps on from here might involve creating a soundscape, layering it (near/far, loud/soft) or asking members of the group to create an experience of the relevant atmosphere for one or two players who keep their eyes shut.

In any or all of these zones of activity – and especially the latter two – playing music may sometimes be a good addition. The improvisatory here is the willingness to experiment, to insert something different and to cut up and reformulate. That takes us on to looking at the development of scenes in the next chapter.

9   Improvisation for Scene-Building

Who/where/what?

The '**who/where/what**' exercises stem primarily from the work of the American teacher of improvisation Viola Spolin (Spolin 1963). Keith Johnstone finds this techhnique unhelpful (Johnstone 1981: 27), but this is because his aims are different. We have found it most useful in the creation of a consistent piece. It concentrates the attention and removes distractions, without limiting creativity. It gives the actor something to start with and to build upon. Given either a 'who', a 'where' or a 'what', the actor can create the other two. Given nothing, the actor can still choose one of these and generate a consistent and coherent piece of improvisation – and a writer faced with a blank page can use the same exercise to initiate a scene or an entire play (*Hamlet* begins with *the* fundamental stage question: 'Who's there?'). For example, the 'who' might be 'a farmer': this suggests the 'where' (in a field) and the 'what' follows quite naturally (planting potatoes). But the 'who' might as easily be 'yourself', in the same field doing the same thing – or some other 'where' doing something else – 'drawing the short straw', for instance (see Callery 2001: 166). Or the 'who' might be the character that one is developing in a formal, scripted play (or an action or a location) – which can then be examined carefully in another context. The exercise asks that the imagination remain constant to the 'set' chosen or specified. If the 'who' is a king, the actor has a constant imaginative focus to return to: he must behave consistently like a king (which implicitly involves status work too) or consciously choose to alter the imaginative set.

The 'who/where/what' exercise can overcome the automatic tendency of any group of inexperienced improvisers to 'play for laughs' at inappropriate moments – to make the scene as absurd and laughable as possible. The reasons for doing this are fourfold. First, the actor hasn't entered fully into the piece, either through not concentrating or not listening to what the other actors have created. Second, it's a subtle but very aggressive form of 'blocking', which rejects the creativity of the other performers (effectively saying 'no' by ironising their work). Third, it's an easy way out, avoiding the responsibility of having to remain consistent and 'true' to the situation. Fourth, it evinces a deep insecurity about this type of work felt by the actor.

This fourth type of response is very common. In a scripted play, the actor has a set of reassurances to rely on: the rehearsal process, the learned moves and gestures and the other actors doing preordained things. Above all, the actor *knows where she's going*; she knows what the outcome should be like and works towards that.

In improvisation the actor doesn't know where she's going and isn't always comfortable going there. She isn't sure that she doesn't look very foolish. Her defence against this can be to make the scene funny. It disarms criticism and, at the same time, gives the actor the reassurance that those watching accept that what she's doing works (they laugh). Del Close warns, 'The most direct path to disaster in improvisation is trying to make jokes' and stipulates, 'Don't try to make jokes in improv! ... the most effective, satisfying laughs usually come from an actor making a connection to something that has gone before' (Halpern *et al.* 1994: 26).

The 'who/where/what' discipline helps to remove actors' anxieties and blocks. It gives the performer a reassuring and familiar structure within which to operate and insists that the creativity keep within the bounds of the initial idea. It's another way of taking pressure off, without losing genuine spontaneity.

Spolin's 'disciplined' approach doesn't preclude the fantastic: action, characters and setting can be as absurd or outlandish as the imagination can make them, and the exercise is always a useful generator of narrative capacity, zany physical humour and enjoyable group process. Dymphna Callery documents a number of instances where devising groups have implicitly worked in this way, tracing its heritage to the *commedia* starting point of given characters (Callery 2001: 165). Make one of the constituents odd or frame-breaking, and there are invitations to stretch imaginative response in other ways (examples we have used in urban and rural environments in the UK and India include: patients, pineapple, waiting room; fisherfolk, dinosaur, river). But Spolin's formal method is less purely generative, less likely to overcome internal censorship, than Keith Johnstone's freer 'impro' work; it is perhaps best applied, therefore, to specific exercises on plays, to play writing, and to the improvised creation of sustained and 'true-to-life' scenes.

Objectives and resistances

Improvisation workshops and rehearsal situations are great ways of teaching fundamental principles of acting *and* dramatic theory. A group of students will 'discover' many of the major theories of acting for themselves – among them the Stanislavskian idea of the 'want' or 'intention' and how to play it against the conflicting wants of other characters. This playing of 'objectives and resistances' can work in some very strange ways, and not only ways connected with Stanislavskian theatre.

For example, an actor wants to pass through a doorway. What might happen if the doorway (played by another actor) chose to resist him – or if he imagined that it did? He would have to talk or fight his way through or invent a way around or over the obstacle. Almost any set of circumstances can be dramatised by the idea of **resistance**.

Exercises to discover this may start with an individual actor walking in different **imaginary physical circumstances** (through waist-deep water, through treacle, on ice, over hot sand, through a shrinking space, etc.), which problematise the simple act of walking. Lecoq's guided exercise through the elements extends this into a developmental sequence of physical actions. This may proceed to simple physical group improvisations with one member attempting to achieve a simple task while the rest find ways to baulk him or make the task difficult. The resistance serves to make the stakes clear: how important is it to achieve this task, action or sequence and to articulate this idea or make this request? Spoken improvised scenes can explore performance modes (melodramatic, absurdist, political, naturalistic) in which a series of basic interactions are similarly problematised. Melodramatic: hero wants girl, but villain abducts her; absurdist: hero wants girl, girl loves an aardvark; political: girl and boy want each other, but the world is out of joint; naturalistic: they want each other but each thinks the other is gay.

The principle of resistance can be utilised in the generation of improvised speech and in the process of writing. It's implicit in the idea articulated by Halpern and Close that 'finding the action' of a developing improvisation is dependent on recognising the *event*: 'the situation that makes this day different from all the rest' (Halpern *et al.* 1994: 81–2), which they relate to Keith Johnstone's idea of the **interrupted routine**. Red Riding Hood's encounter with the wolf, in Johnstone's terms, is an interruption of the routine of taking goodies to Grandma, which the audience responds to as eagerly as she does. Johnstone sees resistance functioning to disrupt routinised narrative and avoid what he calls 'cancelling': the unfortunate gravitational tendency of actors – and writers – towards closure in scenes, cancelling out the energies they have liberated and failing to move the narrative forward. Scenes (improvised or written) which go nowhere can be transformed by the simple discovery that there is a routine at their root which needs to be disrupted, made difficult and looked at afresh (Johnstone 1981: 138–40).

Whenever a scene is flagging, or lacking in impact, it helps to devise or strengthen a resistance and make the actors overcome it. This invariably produces new improvisations. The Stanislavskian terminology is very useful, keeping the 'want' active by shaping the idea (always using the most active verb possible, in a version of the 'actioning' method used by Max Stafford-Clark) and getting the actor to concentrate on physical objectives.

A somewhat similar structural model is the sequence of **frozen image** and **dynamisation** developed by Sanjoy Ganguly from Boal's 'image theatre' work (Buenaventura's model noted in Chapter 4 has some elements of this too). A performer creates an image with his or her body; the partner responds with another image (the images can be spontaneously derived or created as an encapsulation of a moment from an existing score or script). They freeze the joint picture. The rest of the group offers titles for the situation they think the image represents ('you are not welcome here'; 'help me!'); someone may be asked to tell the story; then the two performers are asked to dynamise the image and take the action forward; at any point the image may be frozen again and the procedure repeated. Additional or alternative strategies may be inserted: the actors are asked to make (non-verbal) noises; they can be requested to start to verbalise their situation – individually but simultaneously – as a stream of consciousness or 'inner monologue'. So the development of the scenario proceeds through freezes and activations, adding layers of significance built up from improvised image, movement and speech (scenes with more than two people can also move through these stages) (Ganguly 2013).

Point of concentration (focus)

Viola Spolin uses the term 'points of concentration' (abbreviated to **POC**) as the focal point of her system. She regards it as the 'ball' with which the game is played. It relates to concentration of attention as already discussed but disciplines the work and enables each exercise – and moment of performance – to be worked on in isolation. Most of her exercises have a specific POC to which the performer can attach herself, enabling the aspects of acting to be separated out and put together afresh (she also provides for evaluation of each exercise and gives the session leader a 'point of observation'). For example, describing an 'orientation session' in which a single performer becomes involved with a large, entangling object, she writes:

POINT OF CONCENTRATION: on the selected object.

EXAMPLES: spider web, boa constrictor, tree branches in forest or jungle, octopus, parachute, man-eating plant.

POINT OF OBSERVATION: Watch the wording when stating the POC to be certain that the player's concentration is on the object and not on disentangling himself from the object. This is an important difference and one which comes up continuously throughout the work. (Spolin 1963: 77)

Many of Spolin's exercises evoke and liberate the emotionality inherent within a situation. Her '*theme-scene*' exercises exemplify this. 'Theme' she describes as 'the moving thread (life) that weaves itself into every beat of the play and unifies all the elements of the production' (1963: 394) in terms clearly reminiscent of Stanislavsky's 'through-line of action'. 'Scene' is defined as 'an event that grows out of the POC' (390). A scene is

[t]he results of playing; a fragment; a moment in the lives of people needing no beginning, middle, or end ... The scene is the game coming out of the rules; playing is the process out of which the scene evolves by involvement with an object (the POC) and relationship with fellow players. (390)

The theme-scene exercise takes as its starting points a given theme (an 'activating phrase', often randomly selected or distributed to acting groups) and a place (a 'where' or setting). The group's point of concentration is the 'constant repetition of the theme'. She gives an example theme, 'The World Owes Me a Living', and sets the scene on a city rooftop.

Two sweethearts on a New York tenement roof during a hot summer night. They are tense over the problem of her pregnancy, for he is not willing to take the responsibility of marriage and parenthood. He feels himself to be an artist, and nothing will make him take a drudging nine-to-five job. He is 'special' and feels indeed that 'the world owes me a living'. The girl commits suicide by jumping off the roof. (219)

By no means all Spolin's improvisations are as emotionally fraught (or as melodramatic) as this, and she clearly recommends that the theme-scene exercise be introduced only after several months of preparatory work. She is also concerned that the theme-scene implicitly privileges narrative and can 'lapse into group playwriting'. But, at its best, the theme preoccupies and moves the players (as object), rather than them manipulating it (219). The totality of *structure* (Who/Where/What), *object* (POC) and the imaginative essential of group *agreement* (a consensually established reality between players, and between players and audience, 'our guests') Spolin defines collectively as 'The Rules of the Game' (390).

Spolin's work is highly systematised and at first may hardly seem to relate to Johnstone's pure spontaneity of response. But she is concerned with focusing the individual performer – child, student or professional – very tightly onto the work at all moments during training in order not only to liberate, but also to *channel* that spontaneity.

Memory

Andrea Perrucci wrote in 1699 about the internal consistency of improvised comedy:

> The actors must, above all, be careful not to make a mistake with regard to the country where the action is going to take place; they should realise whence they come, and for what purpose; the proper names must be kept well in mind ... actors must pay attention to the distribution of the houses, so that each player may know his own house, for it would be too ridiculous for anyone to knock at or enter into somebody else's house instead of his own: one would regard such a person as a booby or a drunkard.   (quoted in Nagler 1952: 258)

In any kind of consistent piece, memory plays a large part. It stores the 'rules of the game' and allows the player to improvise within them. **Memory games** are, therefore, very useful as 'mental warm-ups'. The most basic examples are the numerous name-games found in all handbooks and manuals, which rely on a combination of movement, rhythm, sound, attention and recall. Slightly more demanding but still simple games of mental concatenation can be great fun. Player 1 announces that she's going to a party and taking 'some yellow jelly'. Player 2 announces that he, too, is off to a party and is taking 'some yellow jelly and a trilby hat'. Player 3 (by a great coincidence) also has an invitation to a party and plans to take 'some yellow jelly, a trilby hat, and a dustbin full of red knickers'. The game passes to Player 4 and so on around the circle until it arrives back at Player 1 who has to reel off the whole string of unlikely objects. It's good, too, if the players can relax into this and have an attitude to what they are taking (maybe 'yellow jelly' is yummy!). If anyone breaks down, or goes wrong, the game starts all over again from the beginning with new objects. After a few breakdowns, the relationship between concentration, memory and the body is quickly learned. The mnemonic tricks for learning which we all possess are sharpened in an enjoyable way.[1]

Set

A paper by the Georgian psychologist R. Natadze poses the following question:

> When, with a spontaneity convincing to the spectators, the actor acts in conformity not with a real, but with an *imagined* situation imposed upon him by the play, embodying thus in his stage performance experiences and conduct not his own – what is the psychological mechanism of such behaviour? (Natadze 1962: 421)

Natadze implicitly recalls Diderot's *Paradoxe sur l'Acteur* and the controversy between the ideas of 'real feeling' versus 'cold virtuosity'. His hypothesis is that it is

> *fixated set* evolved on the basis of picturing to oneself the particular imaginary situation imposed by the play that constitutes the foundation on which stage impersonation rests. (1962: 421)

His experiments with gifted actors and promising students of the Tbilisi Theatrical Institute, as well as with non-actors and a comic performer, strongly suggested 'a high correlation between the ability to evolve a set on the basis of imagination and the capacity for stage impersonation' (421).

'Set' means a mental construct, a set of rules which apply to the world of the play, which then becomes 'fixated' through rehearsal. The actor has the ability to behave in conformity to that 'set', even though it isn't real. The non-actor finds it difficult (and the comedian finds it downright impossible!).

Natadze's work implies that actors have a combination of a powerful imagination allied to strong concentration (which enables them to hold onto the construct and to shut out perceived contradictions). His work rewrites Stanislavsky in psychological terms. But Natadze's 1960s purely psychological experiments have since been given empirical validation (cf. Barba and Savarese 1991: 46). Actors and athletes were placed on a machine which responded to alterations in balance. Left or right, forward or backward alterations in equilibrium were measured, with and without a heavy weight, such as a filled suitcase, in one hand. When asked to repeat the experiment while only imagining the weighty suitcase, athletes showed little or no alteration from the normal, vertical distribution of weight. Actors consistently did. In other words, the actors' bodies responded to the imaginary stimulus exactly as if it were real.

The improviser makes use of Stanislavsky's **magic If** all the time. And he does so without the benefit of rehearsal to fixate the evolved set. He plays the set *as it evolves*. So the improviser must be trained in the evolution of set, of imaginary and self-consistent worlds. His training must encourage him to accept and act upon them – to go with the products of his imagination 'as if' they were real and to accept their rules and statements as if they were not fantasies – which bleeds out into the key rule for acting in farce, which is for the performers to behave as though everything taking place is entirely normal.

Character

Although in *pure* improvisation ('impro'), character is not key, in *applied* improvisation, rehearsal 'improvs', character is the dominant concern. Actors undertake improvised explorations about **previous circumstances**; for example, meetings between characters that have happened before the action of the play begins.

This exercise puts the *actor* in a situation where he has to respond 'as if' he were the person he portrays. It allows the actor to develop what Natadze calls 'set' and practise being within it, with other actors, exploring its rules and its boundaries. And as Stanislavsky (in the person of 'Tortsov' guiding the student 'Kostya') wrote:

> Now I hope you realise the difference between approaching and judging a role in your own person and in that of another, between looking at a role with your own eyes instead of those of the author, or director, or drama critic.
>
> In your own person you live your role, in the person of someone else you simply toy with it, play-act it. In your own person you grasp the role with your mind, your feelings, your desires, and all the elements of your inner being, while in the person of another, in most cases, you do it only with your mind. Purely reasoned analysis and understanding in a part is not what we need.
>
> We must take hold of the imagined character with all our being, spiritual and physical. That is the only approach I am willing to accept. (Stanislavsky 1963: 182)

The improvisation is not about the *character's* inner life, but about the *actor's*. It awakens responses in the performer which are primal and personal. Afterwards, they can be analysed and adapted and assimilated into the actor's conception of the role. As they are happening, though, they force the actor to respond directly and imaginatively to the situation, to see her fellow actors as the characters they are portraying and to respond to them within the agreed rules of the 'set' they are jointly constructing. They tighten concentration on the role, since distractions will destroy the edifice the actors are building, and the greatest distractions arise from her own intrusive thoughts. The actor is given no time to think, to stand back and judge and to split herself into simultaneous performer and critic. And it makes the acting company into a genuinely creative ensemble, involved in the 'writing' of their own play, bonding them and tuning them into their own group wavelength.

In approaching this situation, structure and clarity are important. Clive Barker says:

> I rarely use free improvisation, preferring to use some games activity as a structure within which the actors can improvise.
>
> The principal use of improvisation, as far as I am concerned, is to overcome the actors' failure to penetrate the text to the actions which underlie it. The words make sense, but have no real meaning. (Barker 1977: 167)

Improvisation work before textual rehearsal begins bonds the group and establishes a common language and way of working. It may also, in group creative enterprises, begin to evolve any aspect of the piece, whether for Mike Leigh or Improbable or Boal. But working on a pre-existing text at an early stage, and avoiding mere verbalisations, with actors standing, talking and *explaining* at each other, rather than discovering action, it often helps to ask actors to 'translate' the scene into another form: perhaps 'taking away' the text and replacing it with improvised mime or *Grammelot* or 'in-articulate' sounds or singing or dance. The actors have to communicate – perhaps non-verbally at first, through touch and movement or through sounds other than words – rather than simply translate their ideas into words which will only block interaction. If this can be achieved, then the two primary goals of applied improvisation will succeed: the inner actions will be explored, and the inner life will be felt. Scenes in which actors have difficulties with the apparently cloistering implications of the text can also be freed up in this way, perhaps to the accompaniment of music or rhythm, which help to engage the visceral and affective body.

The character to concentrate on is not always one's own. In a solo im-provisation piece the actor feels the burden of having to create everything on his own. This can be overcome by sharing the responsibility for initi-ation (just as in a group piece) with one's own partners – except that, in this case, the 'partners' are the imaginary characters in the scene. Create the other characters in the scene and take *time* to stand back and 'hear' what they have to say. For example, the chosen 'who' might be 'an auctioneer', the 'what' and 'where' conducting an auction in a posh saleroom. Having accepted the 'set' and decided the rhythm and physical shape of the central figure of the auctioneer (the only character the audience will actually see portrayed), the actor needs also to create selectively the other participants in the scene: by imaginatively characterising them, visualising them in the acting space, they can be made to do much of the work.

The little old lady in the grey pullover wonders if she can afford a few pounds more, and the auctioneer has to cajole a bid from her. The red-faced farmer in the pork-pie hat can easily afford it; the auctioneer need only appeal to his greed. Is the housewife continually gesticulating to her friend in the red coat making a bid or not? The **invisible other characters** become a series of *prompts* for the solo actor's imagination. Without these external foci, the scene will quickly lose shape and rhythm; and the actor will probably lose his grip on his own character and descend rapidly into cliché. With them, even a solo performer can develop the simple action (Spolin's 'what') into a consistent and coherent narrative.

Narrative as generative structure

At all points in the process of improvising drama, the actor is involved in creating narrative. This does not mean simply 'telling a story'. That might be the result; but the process is concerned with other activities. All good improvised scenes have content and meaning, though the improviser need not strain to impose them on the work. Handled properly, they arise organically, often created as much by the audience as by the actors.

Keith Johnstone stresses two narrative skills, *free association* and *reincorporation*. These two processes sum up many of the techniques we have already discussed and turn them to account in the creation of a piece to be shared with an audience.

Free association means spontaneous response, 'going with' whatever has been offered, by oneself or by one's collaborators. It means letting one idea generate the next without trying to force it into shape, without trying to *make* it mean something (it undoubtedly *will* mean something). It means accepting, too, that part of the meaning (the true 'content' of the story) will be the performer's revelation of himself. **Free association exercises** (like Johnstone's 'Automatic Writing', 'Lists' and 'Dreams') if used properly can encourage the actor to bypass the 'censor' in himself. It takes a lot of trust. That is why it shouldn't be concerned with interpretation; if the actor realises too soon that the underlying content of the story is sexual, for example, he may not wish to continue it or may try to force the story to change direction.

Johnstone abandons the notion of content and concentrates instead on structure – the key to which is **reincorporation**. When telling a tale, either singly or with others, reincorporation means making use of what has already been introduced. It means coming back to ideas previously established and then using them in ways that both bind the story together and take it forwards. Stand-ups use exactly the same idea: they use the term '**call-back**', referring back to a joke told earlier in the set. The principle underlies the way in which Ross Noble (sometimes with audience prompting) manages always, somehow, to finish the rambling, 'randomist' journeys upon which his audiences have been taken. Free association takes care of invention and development; reincorporation takes care of structure.

> The improviser has to be like a man walking backwards. He sees where he has been, but he pays no attention to the future. His story can take him anywhere, but he must still 'balance' it, and give it shape, by remembering incidents that have been shelved and re-incorporating them. Very often an audience will applaud when earlier material is brought back into the story. They couldn't tell you why they applaud, but the reincorporation does give them pleasure. (Johnstone 1981: 116)

The audience, in fact, is enjoying structuring the story in its mind. They are looking for meaning and making meaning out of what is being offered. Apparent randomness is given sudden illumination by reincorporation. So the applause, laughter or cheering that sometimes greets this reincorporated material is often the audience congratulating *itself* as much as the actor. They are saying 'Got it! Now it makes sense!' – and it's also an affirmation, a way of saying 'Go on! What will happen now?'

The technique of reincorporation is central to the structuring of Chicago long-form improv. Del Close refers to it as 'delayed justification' in that, when an idea mentioned earlier recurs (is reincorporated), it appears to be the justification for the whole scene. 'Nothing is ignored. Nothing is forgotten. And nothing is a mistake.' Whatever is said is heard, picked up, filed away and later brought back into the scene (Halpern *et al.* 1994: 74).

The English comedian Al Murray (whose irascible, politically very incorrect 'Pub Landlord' character won the Edinburgh Fringe's Perrier Award in 1999) exemplifies the *ad hominem* form of reincorporation in his stage act, as many stand-up comics do. At the start of the act Murray talks to the audience and learns the names and occupations of a number of people. After some initial improvised reactions to their jobs (God help any students – the Landlord *hates* students – who of course form the bulk of his audiences) Murray moves into the show proper, only to unexpectedly weave in these names and jobs as part of the performance. Audiences sometimes respond by lying to him, coming up with imaginary, 'funny' jobs. As Close and Halpern argue, in *Truth in Comedy* (Halpern *et al.* 1994: 15, 24), the audiences here are unskilled improvisers, trying to catch Murray out and play for a single laugh – in the suicidal way that hecklers always think they can be funnier than the comedian. Murray usually comically demolishes these lies. And their actual jobs, no matter how mundane, are always funnier and a source of much richer comedy. Sometimes, the real jobs are more gloriously bizarre than anything anyone could invent: he once had a man whose job was to scientifically measure dog dirt for Newham Council (the jingoistic Landlord was incensed that he measured the turds in metric rather than imperial units!).

Mike Alfreds, the founder of Shared Experience, works on **trampoline words** within the known text of the story. These are the transition points from narrative to dialogue. The exercise was developed during rehearsals for Shared Experience's early show, *The First Arabian Night*. In this piece the actor operates both as narrator of learned text and as improviser of action; he has first to find a personal way of narrating (creating his own text so that it bears the performer's personality). A way then has to be found of moving from narration into action.

> Say the actor has text such as: 'When the prince heard this much from his royal sire, he was moved by youthful folly to reply, "Thou art great in age but small in wit"'. (Alfreds 1979–80: 15)

Here the 'trampoline' word is *reply*. At that point he is going to change from narrator to actor. He has to be able to pitch right in to the scene at the correct energy level, that of the prince's youthful indignation,

> so he uses the previous sentence of the narration as a sort of run up, knowing that when he gets to the word 'reply' he has to gather all his forces to take off into the action; he literally has to bounce himself on that word and it gives him the time to change his focus from the audience to his partner in the scene. (1979–80: 15)

Once the transition has been made, improvisation takes over. The partner will respond as the prince's father and a scene will develop (in much the same way as a *commedia* scenario is fleshed out). The sections of learned narrative link the improvised passages together.

The audience's delight in the virtuosity of the actor becomes allied with its pleasure in the developing tale. The third-person narrative 'bounces' into the first-person improvisation, and whenever a scene is complete another narrator will take the thread. Then, as it perceives the complex structure of tale-within-tale, the audience responds with 'this wonderful reaction of "Oh, there it is!!"' (10).

Finally, there are other ways of using improvisation in the creation of a play. Group improvisation has been used by a number of professional play-makers for a long time. It can take the form of collaboration between writers and actors in the generation of an ultimately scripted play. It can lead to a play put together through improvisation in rehearsal – a play created entirely by the acting ensemble. Or it can be totally free, self-generating: the 'play' is entirely created in front of its audience.

We discuss these variants further under the section entitled 'Improvisation and writing' in Chapter 10. We finish this chapter with a couple of examples of the kinds of *journeys* which can be constructed from the work we have been looking at in Part 2.

Sample sequences

Boal's structure for games and exercises appears in Chapter 3; Babbage's sequence for working with Boal's examples is found on page 101.

- Preparing the body
- Games (energy, focus, power)
- Images (dynamisation, transformation)
- Themes

And in practice this may lead to 'desires' – 'Rainbow' work.

Preparation examples are things like mirroring, games like **The Bears are Coming** (Johnston 1998: 249) or the **Slowmo Race** (Boal 1992: 73). A key juncture is the **Complete the Image** exercise (Babbage 2004: 117–18): one partner offers, the other completes, first steps out and returns to complete a second image and so on; it is frequently used to lead to group images, scenarios and issue-oriented work.

Simon Murray gives a sequence of exercises – a kind of 'distillation' compiled with recent Lecoq teacher Thomas Prattki – based around pushing and pulling and leading to the three dramatic modes of melodrama, tragedy

Table 9.1 Exercises and Activities

Preparation		Working together		Towards performance		Applied improvisation	
Activities	*Examples*	*Activities*	*Examples*	*Activities*	*Examples*	*Activities*	*Examples*
Relaxation and balance	Tag	Trust and respect	Trust circle		Blindfold	Who/where/what?	Farmer, field, potatoes
	T'ai chi		Fish dives	Senses	Warm-up		
	Yoga		Blindfold		Massage		
	Feldenkrais		Making contact		Flowing	Objectives and resistances	Intention
	Suzuki	Group games	Relay race		Trust games		Journey
		Making a machine	Machine		Journey		Interrupted routine
			Laughing snake				
Games and body/think	With ball		Body sculptures	Tenses	Presence	Point of concentration	Theme-scene
	Fight in the Dark		Finding by sound		Restoration		
	Grandma's Footsteps			Dramatic modes	Melodrama	Memory	The party
	'What are you doing?'						
	Bears	Showing and telling	Mime-stick	Objects	Naming	'Set'	Magic 'if'

Space and movement	Laban		Entering door	Observation	Telling story	Character	Auctioneer
	Winearls	Entrances and exits			Rhythms		Previous circumstances
	Lecoq				Gestures	Narrative	
Circles of con-centration and attention	Attention	Meetings and greetings	Group walk				Stories
	Listening			Status	Walks		Free association
	Observation				Party Games		Lists
	M. Chekhov				Allocate nos./cards		Dreams
			Use video		Master/servant		Reincorporation
		'Blocking'	Yes/yes but				Trampoline words
Impulses and directions	Starfish		Gibberish	Masks	Neutral		
	Change directions				Expressive/counter mask		
	Éclosion				Counter mask		

(continued)

Table 9.1 Exercises and Activities (*continued*)

OBJECTIVES			
Relax	Interactions	Confront inadequacies	Extend in time/space
Tune-up	Trust/support partners	Extend body awareness	Incorporate/play/want
Balance individual	Encounter as dramatic	Sharpen awareness of inter-action	Develop structures
Feel good	Group structure		Link imagination and organisation
Enjoy	Sensitise to others	Play with possibilities	
			Explore inner action
			Feel inner life
Begin individual 'unblocking'	Recognise mutual dependence	Discover performance dynamics	Develop organisational skills
Explore resistances			
Find mental/physical centredness	Extend sense of 'self'	Extend performance vocabulary	Work with complex structures
Develop 'presence'			
Establish self-confidence	Establish confidence in group	Develop focus and commitment	Generate text
Socialise	Overcome taboos	Liberate imagination	Build sequential performance
ACTIVE MEANINGS			
Psychodynamics (individual)	Psychodynamics (group)	Text as performance	Process of thinking
Play	Meaning as interchange	Signs and meanings	Hierarchies
Readiness/*disponibilité*	Co-creativity	Multiplicity of possibility	Intervention and realignment
Mind-body relationship	Negotiation	Group creativity	Complex imaginative acts
Creativity	Form as process	Organic understanding	New combinations

and *commedia*. They are valuable in emphasising the indispensability of working through basic vectors of bodily movement and of engaging in a committed and sequential manner with the work. Even so they remain somewhat condensed, and it is worth underlining that some of them (for example improvisations on journeys, divorce, reconciliation, etc.) could well both require a very lengthy time-frame to explore all possible nuances and also generate material which could deflect from the goal.

Example: Melodrama:

(*a*) physical preparation: (i) pairs face same way, one close behind holds the other around pelvis, each attempts to move in different direction; (ii) bamboo stick joins partners at palm of hand, they push/pull each other around space;

(*b*) into dramatic territory: pair exercises with imagined link (string or stick) which is used to alter body position, to move around space, and finally to experiment with moving towards or away from each other – subsequently adding single words to this last phase.

Both (*a*) and (*b*) are followed by an improvisation exercise: (*a*) to continue physical exploration by imagining being giants, (*b*) by a 'departure' scenario involving family members, to be played without words. The aim of the sequence is to get students to focus on the space between characters, to see how any movement in that space charges it ('pushes' or 'pulls' it) emotionally. (Based on Murray 2003: 136–40)

Whereas for melodrama the dynamic is 'I push … I pull', for tragedy it is 'I am pushed/pulled' and for *commedia*, 'I push myself … pull myself'; preparation for tragedy moves through aspects of the work on elements (see p. 175) and leads into an exercise producing the sense of being spoken by a choric text, whereas for *commedia* a neutral mask exercise is used to generate the energy to overcome obstacles. No improvisation is given for tragedy, whilst a pair of scenarios ('divorce' and 'reconciliation') is used for *commedia* (Murray 2003: 140–50).

There is in the charting of these exercises no particular confirmation of Lecoq's assertion that 'tragedy is always vertical' and the sentimental – thus melodrama – is diagonal (Lecoq 1997/2000: 83), so they might be a good way to test whether these directions are in fact the most dominant in a spontaneous sense.

The skills and activities we have dealt with in this section promote qualities of focus, consistency and structure in both individual and communal improvised performance, and these qualities allow the performance to present character and narrative. At the same time it becomes clear that these are based on and emerge from the personal and group work outlined earlier and can often profitably return to it. There is no fixed hierarchy in improvisation work, except in the sense that everything has to do with the enriching of *performance*: whether this is seen as individual realisation of action, expression and response; as a communal act of composition; as something shared with an audience; or as a celebration of the full resources of individual being and the ways they can be combined to create new patterns of significance.

PART 3

Why? The Meaning(s) of Improvisation: Towards a Poetics

Introduction

We have looked at *who* improvises and at *what* they do. We need to understand the meaning of these acts for individuals, for performers and for society. Improvisation, like any physical or spoken act, necessarily produces meaning: indeed it may be said to be primarily a way of generating a plurality of meanings through performance. It can tell us a good deal about how we create meaning.

The practice of improvisation works initially to *free* the producer of meanings, both as an individual and in the network of relationships in which he or she operates and to enable him or her to develop a larger 'vocabulary'. There are two main issues here: physical and psychological unblocking, which has both theatrical and paratheatrical implications for the quality of self, creativity, imagination and relational acts between individuals and groups; and the acquisition of an enlarged range of communicative skills, which produce an extension of being, knowing and interacting. These processes impact upon the personal, cultural and political spheres of life.

Both these issues have important psychological, social and aesthetic implications for the nature of performative acts, the creation of form and the concept of 'play'.

Since meaning in improvisation is performative, we also need to consider the kinds of impact improvisation has upon the status of performance, its effects in terms of the relationship between performers, text and audience and the possibility that it represents a tradition in itself, albeit an oblique or contrary one.

The sections which follow therefore examine how meanings are created, shifted, enriched or relocated through improvisation and also reflect on the meaning of this process itself. They both implicitly and explicitly refer back to the examples of practitioners and practices presented in the preceding two parts.

10   Enriching the Communication of Meaning

Communication involves a sender, a receiver and a message. If the message is to be as meaningful as possible, sender and receiver need to be as intelligent, sensitive, skilful and engaged as possible. This is particularly the case with impro and, by extension, performance generally. It isn't simply a static mechanical model in which the sender takes priority and emits 'top-down' and unchangeable data, but an essentially mobile, organic one in which all elements are dynamic and intercommunicative. The basic requirement then is to unblock resistances and develop the responses and skills upon which personal and interpersonal behaviour depend. Many of the practices we have considered work to this effect. Their full implication can, however, be most usefully perceived in the light of paratheatrical and psychodramatic approaches. Developing the sender positively affects the quality of the message and gives him or her more practical resources (verbal and physical imagination) in order to construct it. The vocabulary (sign potential) of the communicative process is thus extended, as is its capacity to generate meaning.

Implications of psychodramatic and paratheatrical approaches

Improvisation activities help to discover, unblock or tune up the psyche and the body, which evidently has implications for performance of any kind. Theatre can be a moral/political thermometer or perhaps a tonic or an emetic: it is related to the health of a society and to the sense society makes of itself as an entity. The improvisatory act focuses on the gathering of energies, the freeing of possibilities of articulation, an alertness of giving and receiving and the establishment of connection. It has to do with developing wholeness through developing the sense of self.

In psychotherapy, the 'protagonist' enacts his life-drama with or without the help of others and may in the course of so doing reveal or give shape to fundamental situations, attitudes, complexes of which he or she may have been only dimly aware or which taboos may have made it impossible to speak about directly. This kind of activity can of course also be valuable in other, not specifically psychotherapeutic, contexts (for example, the use of role-play and simulation exercises in personal and professional development).

'Psychodrama' is related to a whole range of psychotherapeutic techniques which have as their aim the discovery, acknowledging and valuing of 'the whole person', of all aspects of the human being both individually and in all forms of relationship. There are generic similarities between psychodrama, mainly developed by J. L. Moreno and, for instance, Jung's concept of 'integration', Maslow's 'self-actualisation' and Rogers's emphasis on 'client-centred' therapy. Therapy in general has become more eclectic, using techniques from a number of complementary approaches as appropriate, and one finds references to the same kinds of activity under different headings. Many approaches make considerable use of theatre games and impro exercises (for example, trust exercises, role-plays and mirroring) in addition to using active work with scenarios which involve the protagonist, and often the therapist as well, in 'improvising' his or others' roles in life-situations.[1] We discuss aspects of Moreno's 'Psychodrama', Augusto Boal's 'Theatre of the Oppressed' and Jonathan Fox's 'Playback Theatre' elsewhere, but it is worth noting here the example of Boal's recognition of the need to address internal oppressions ('The Cop in the Head') and the structure of desire ('The Rainbow of Desires') as evidence of this spectrum of work; practitioners using theatre process in social contexts – work in prisons, with marginalised or disadvantaged groups, to address particular community issues and so on – have found that a group or community-centred political focus requires means of negotiating the personal, often traumatic, circumstances of participants. Impro and psychodrama are both about transforming what seems closed off, taboo, frightening, inaccessible, impossible, inexpressible, or even just plain boring: disclosing it, not running away from it, releasing its negative or damming energy. The situations through which Grotowski or Johnstone or Lecoq take their 'players' are akin to the psychological or psychosocial situation of not knowing who one is or how to go on. The aim is not necessarily the discovery of a single or stable self in the conventional sense; it may be more the activation of a range of possible roles and modes and the discovery of the ability to play with one's own life. Improvisation, as it extends into the 'paratheatrical', may be a spearhead of methods of changing the environment from within, from the individual outwards.

But as well as the internal, psychological forms, the blockages or resistances have their external and political manifestations, as we shall see.

The censor's nightmare

The chief opponent of the improviser is not the writer of scripted drama; it is the censor. The antonym of 'improvisation' is 'censorship', because while improvisation represents the permission (and self-permission) for artistic expression, and the acceptance of one's own as well as others' creativity, censorship self-evidently stands for denial and refusal. This is true both literally and figuratively; and equally true whether the term refers to an external, political, public manifestation or to an internal, private and psychological process.

Impro has always been the censor's nightmare. The censor functions best when dealing with a precomposed, literary artefact – ideally a manuscript. The censored manuscript of a poem or a novel can be delivered to the printer and the finished artwork disseminated in a controlled manner. Or it can be suppressed utterly, expunged from official culture (though it may appear in unofficial culture as *samizdat*, the underground, secretly circulated, self-published literature of resistance).

But theatre has always been a problem area for censors because of its immediacy and its deployment of 'texts' other than the purely literary. In fact, the 'text' of a play is rightly understood by the censor to include every word *and* every bit of business.[2] The censor's nightmare is that, having licensed a play for performance, and thus given it official sanction, the performers will alter it in performance by improvising. They will make their own substitutions, deletions, insertions and restorations. Or they will introduce non-verbal elements which contradict the censor's intentions.

Joan Littlewood's Theatre Workshop, pioneer of improvisation, was singled out for prosecution in 1958 for the 'very wide divergence' between the text authorised by the Lord Chamberlain and that actually experienced in the theatre. The censor particularly objected to a new scene in which a mock opening ceremony was performed in a public lavatory, by an actor who vocally imitated Sir Winston Churchill while appearing to urinate.

Technically, improvisation has only been possible *on stage* in Britain since 1968 (though, of course, no such restrictions applied to rehearsals). The act of improvisation was seen by many as subversive in itself and allied to subversive politics or, in the British postwar climate, protest.[3] Littlewood's work at Stratford East is exemplary. And the battle against censorship, which reached its climax at the Royal Court in the mid-1960s, was also the battle for the freedom to create appropriate artistic as well as political forms.

Keith Johnstone's Theatre Machine was born in that climate: *Clowning* had to be presented officially as a lecture-demonstration for the Royal Court Studio. Under the censor, improvisation was condemned to remain a rehearsal device: as a performance tool, or even style, it was forced to remain an academic exercise – a lecture-demonstration, not a play. To commit oneself to a vision of a theatre based on improvisation was a remarkable act of faith. (As we signal, Roddy Maude-Roxby is still doing lectures like that, as a kind of ironic comment on his own history!)

At the other extreme, the experiences of Teatr Ósmego Dnia (The Theatre of the Eighth Day) in Poland demonstrate that improvisation may be the best way for a company of artists to function in a repressive situation. Ósmego Dnia began in Poznan in 1964 and at first modelled themselves on Grotowski's Laboratory work before finding their own distinctive style which, although still concerned with the exploration of theatre language, was more consciously political. Tadeusz Janiszewski, one of the actors, explains:

> After 1976 we had more and more trouble from the security services. It was the year of the founding of KOR – the Committee for the Defence of the Workers [punished for the riots in Radom and Warsaw] – and we never tried to hide our sympathies. (Howard 1986: 296)

The theatre group was not allowed to disseminate information about itself, to perform in some cities (especially Warsaw) or to travel abroad. They were actively harassed by the security services and dragged for five years through the courts on trumped-up fraud charges. Two members were imprisoned briefly. Their 1984 production *Absinthe* was based on the farcical but sinister events of that period. Before the upsurge of Solidarity in 1980, most other radical Polish groups had either retreated into naturalism or abstracted themselves from the political situation by doing laboratory research work. Ósmego Dnia's combative relation to the censoring authorities is described by Janiszewski.

> You have a special performance for one person, the censor. A scenario has to be submitted too. ... But it is possible to outmanoeuvre the censor, particularly when there's considerable improvisation. We've been developing our own creative method since 1973, based on improvisation. (Howard 1986: 297)

In the mid-1980s some of the group left Poland, but they returned after 1989 and have continued to work. In recent years they have produced

The Time of the Mothers (2006), focusing on women grieving for their children lost in war, and *Teczki / Files* (2007), in which they traced their own lives through reports and denunciations found in the archives of the communist Ministry of Public Security (http://culture.pl/en/artist/teatr-osmego-dnia).

The condition of working against censorship is not an uncommon occurrence, whether in the form of explicit state oppression or internalised ideological self-repression. Louis Althusser saw ideology as materially operative in society via what he termed 'ideological state apparatuses' (to distinguish them from the more mechanical and punitive forms of oppressive 'state apparatus' such as the government, police, army, prisons, etc.). Among the ideological forms, which operate diffusely in the private realm of life, he lists religious structures, family norms, legal systems, political party and trades' union systems, communications media (press, radio and TV) and culture which includes literature, arts, and even sport (Althusser 1971: 127–86). It is as much against this internalised ideological framework as against formalised state oppression that improvised theatre struggles to liberate itself.

Ideological censorship is reflected in Eugenio Barba's early accounts of working in Poland with Grotowski (Turner 2004: 3–4), no less than in the struggles of Judith Malina and Julian Beck to find a haven for the Living Theatre at the same time in America. It is evident in the responses to the establishment of the politically engaged Indian People's Theatre Association (IPTA) in the 1940s, in the struggle of female Indian artists like Gul Bardhan to emerge from this male-dominated cultural field in the 1950s and, as extreme counterexample, in the tragic 'street-theatre' murder of the playwright and activist Safdar Hashmi by Congressman Mukul Sharma and his followers in 1989 (Yarrow 2001: 178ff., 182–3). It is visible in Augusto Boal's early work in Brazil in the 1960s, his imprisonment and torture, which led to the emergence of his Theatre of and for the Oppressed (Boal 1992: 1–3) and to his resistance to the inner censor, 'the Cop in the Head'. An interface between politics and group therapy is represented by Boal's Image and Forum theatre work which aims directly to empower and give voice to the oppressed, marginalised and silenced, and this empowering is understood as both a therapeutic and developmental process.

Lecoq claims a pivotal status for the rediscovery of the improvisatory at certain moments in history; this could be seen as opening up a space for aesthetic renewal, but at the same time as a psychological and political intervention. For Boal, and later for Ganguly, the two things go explicitly together. The kinds of physical and mental openness and flexibility involved could be seen to produce an (artistic) reconstruction of the 'identity' of the performer and of the form s/he works in and to operate across a dis- and re-articulation of body and language (and of body as language), as a challenge to the closed, the received and the repressive and protective mind-sets which legitimate that repression. If in poststructuralist thought 'performance' mounts a challenge to the hegemony of 'text', then improvised performance represents the epitome of that capacity. In its process, as well as often in its product, it *is* a politics, an operational mode of generating structural and attitudinal change.

In the 2007 edition of this book we wondered how far improvisation has now (in the early twenty-first century) become a norm in itself; previous decades might have appeared to repeat the practice of Lecoq, Grotowski and others. Games and improvisation are now a part of mainstream training, and to a lesser but increasing extent, of public performance: where for instance *Whose Line Is It Anyway* was a fairly rare marker, there have since been many TV shows (and, indeed, some dramas, such as Channel 5's 2014 unscripted crime drama *Suspects*) which draw on the model, and the spectrum of participatory events has been noted above. Improvisation, pragmatically as well as by definition, always needs to unmake and remake *itself*. But as we have shown, it has continued to find many ways of doing that.

La disponibilité

Availability – openness – readiness – acceptance: the precondition of creativity. It implies not resisting, but flowing *with* the world and the self. It implies (to us) nakedness, but not (strangely) defencelessness. The performer is without *armour*, but not without *weapons*: such as wit, agility, mobility and inventiveness. He or she is resource-full. *Disponibilité* is the state of 'armed neutrality' from which all movements are equally possible.

For Lecoq it is a state of calmness, of balance, in which the readiness is all. The performer (most pointedly in improvisation) is always ready, always aware and always able to respond: he or she is 'rendered open to what is happening in a situation, a gesture, a word ... the imagination provoked to the invention of languages' (Lecoq 1987).

By 'open to what is happening' (*'disponible à l'événement'*) we believe Lecoq infers open to all the processes which compose the situation, on all levels. It is a state in which the truth is revealed, not covered up by tricks. By 'the invention of languages' (*'provoquant son imagination à inventer des langages'*) we understand him to mean that the actor is stimulated to create as many types of response to the truth of that situation, gesture or word as are appropriate. The 'languages' may be gestural, verbal or purely tactile, but they give truthful expression to the moment and whatever it holds.

Disponibilité sums up in a single term the condition improvisers aspire to. It offers a way of describing an almost intangible and nearly undefinable state of being: having at (or in) one's fingertips, and any other part of the body, the capacity to do and say what is appropriate and to have the confidence to make the choice. It's a kind of total awareness, a sense of being at one with the context: script, if such there be, actors, audience, theatre space, oneself and one's body.

For Grotowski, technique is not abstract or external: it is how the body accedes to its own resources; how it discovers that it can be, say, do, understand and transmit – with and to anything and anyone. The bodily condition in which that capacity is touched is a tensed and balanced orderliness which – like an act of love, Grotowski says – is not closed off from anything.

Disponibilité suggests not just a theory but an experiential condition – a way of being which can be sought and found. It is a condition of being *centred* (in oneself) and balanced, ready to go in any appropriate direction. We might translate it as *neutrality*, but in English this has unfortunate connotations of asensuality and of being disengaged (like a car idling, without purpose). *Disponibilité* suggests a charged and sensual state: Gide relates it to a process of coming-to-be-aware of the body. In this state the performer is fully inhabiting the world outside and the world within her body. It carries the sense of becoming aware of oneself and one's possibilities and aware of having *choice*. It represents the power to *dispose* of oneself and one's activity. As such, it pre-eminently *embodies* the condition of existentialism.

Disponible suggests, then, that the performer can dispose, can choose and can act. It suggests sensory alertness, even sensual alertness. The whole being is opened to the moment. And the moment of performance includes the audience. Stanislavsky enjoins the actor to keep his intentions 'this side of the footlights', and Grotowski, following Osterwa, warns against 'publicotropism'. But we are not talking of exhibitionism. The improviser accepts (and shares creativity with) the audience. As *art* it may be chancy, less certain of success than other methods, but it is close to the condition sought for by Rilke, a kind of tuning in to organic form. As such, it may be the only way to arrive at genuinely new insights: it is less likely to leave anything out; it doesn't force the pace or the pattern; it has more chance of avoiding the trap of cliché.

It is a condition of relaxed awareness where one does not need to *impose* order on the external world or on the imagination: order is found *in* the world and in the imaginative response to others. One does not need to deny the ordering intelligence, the analytical self. Rather, that self takes its proper place. One does not need to subjugate the mind: the mind knows when not to dominate, and the body knows when to be still as well as when to move. For Lecoq (the body learning to think), *disponibilité* is a natural condition, harmoniously accepted; for Grotowski (the analytical brain learning to move) it is a condition sought through pain and denial. They are moving towards the same point; but they are coming from different worlds. In yet others, it may be called *hana* (the flower of Japanese *Noh* theatre) or *rasa* (the taste of Sanskrit aesthetics). When the flower blooms or the taste is savoured, the full symbolic and aesthetic resonance of the performer's creation is awakened in the audience: it can only ever be as a now-moment in which the sharing is sudden, always new and unexpected, and certain (see George 1999). In neither of these highly technically circumscribed traditions would one initially expect anything called 'improvisation': but in both it is – only – acknowledged as a crowning phase, a sign of mastery, of grasping and being able to deliver the key experience of art, that of being in the moment of the genesis of form.

Disponibilité is a condition of responsiveness, but it implies *giving* as much as receiving. Reciprocal giving between two or more *disponible* creators (like the North American Indian custom of *potlatch* in which individuals and whole communities compete in giving) opens up a truly new form of artistic creativity. We have seen how, for example, the clown gives to his partner on stage, how the improviser passes *élan* to her fellow performer in order to make things possible for both of them or how the failure to do this destroys the possibility of creation. When the blocks are removed, and when the giving is reciprocal, the result is a creativity shared by both the performers and the audience. Murray suggests that '*Disponibilité* is a precondition for play, while *complicité* is an outcome of successful play' (Murray 2002: 70); the latter could also be described as a 'collusion between celebrants' (Complicité programme for *Lucie Cabrol*). Charles suggests that '[i]mprov can be viewed as a comedy of collusion' (2003: 87); Drinko's 'improv consciousness' and Campbell's 'lizard brain' are other formulations.

Transformation and the plural self

Among her 'triggers of transformative experiences', Marilyn Ferguson includes 'improvisational theater, with its requirement of both total attention and spontaneity, [and] Psychodrama, because it forces an awareness of roles and role-playing' (Ferguson 1980: 90). This appears in a list of 'psychotechnologies' which includes mental (meditative) and physical (t'ai chi ch'uan, Alexander) techniques, therapies, self-help and mutual-help networks and programmes, and various 'shamanic and magical techniques'. The function of all these is to shift awareness beyond Watts's 'skin-encapsulated ego' (Watts 1972) to open up new possibilities of being. Many of the methods she mentions figure in drama school activities.

Improvisation frequently has to do with breaking down barriers. Our conscious, rationalising ego operates within boundaries which afford security of behaviour and identity and are useful in many contexts. But boundaries also inhibit, and the kind of lateral thinking which arrives at new insights is precisely an example of the value of bypassing them and discovering a new shape to knowledge and experience. Improvisation in one sense is about 'lateral being', if you like – about allowing and encouraging this productive 'digression' with as much of the organism as possible. One result is to permit subliminal or subconscious material to surface, to make use of the sudden crazy idea and to allow a sequence of action or speech to develop from a sensation or bodily position. This can be both frighteningly insecure (the comfortable limits of 'who/what/why' are left behind) and frighteningly chaotic. But used profitably it is both a discipline in itself and a means of exploring extra possibilities of synthesis. Jung and others suggest that the use and incorporation of subconscious psychic activity (dreams, fantasies and so on) is not irrelevant or narcissistic, but a way of drawing on a different and perhaps more extensive kind of knowing. Improvisation may also frequently work by sudden symbolic associations or make logical leaps; and it often (like some kinds of comedy) appeals to an audience precisely because it stimulates the ability to function likewise. It becomes an exciting game, and in so doing it *makes sense* in another, not merely logico-rational way.

Grotowski, too, sensed that what is occurring in the intense work on the authenticity of self – which in his process has of necessity to be unscripted and non-externally directed – is an encounter with these at first dim, often uncomfortable and confusing forms of knowing and being. But the belief is that pursuing them can result in a more total and organic awareness and a freer capacity for action. Awakening these may require a passage through confusion and unknowing and through a loss of identity as commonly conceived (as with masks). It is no accident that theoretical and textual theatrical visions of recent decades (Artaud, Beckett, and following them Deleuze and Guattari, Badiou) have aimed at a parallel exploration or explosion of the limits of language, self and their accepted configuration. Modernist and postmodernist art of all genres, plus associated theory, has often featured 'difficulty': paradox, lack of conventional plots and characters and frequent digressions. 'Reading' and understanding has become a challenging and perhaps dangerous business, precisely because the act of arriving at a new framework or symbolic nexus is – like reading metaphysical poetry and like the creating of works of art – one which involves a splitting apart and reconstituting of the self in its articulation as word and image. Learning to accept a feeling of loss is an essential part of the process.

This requires a different, and difficult, kind of discipline. Grotowski and his actors have not drawn back from the demands, but the same assumption underlies the work of Chekhov, Copeau, Johnstone, Lecoq and others. That is why Grotowski rejected the label 'improvisation' where it might be thought to equate with a lapse into a vague notion of spontaneity or the imitation of 'primitive' behaviour. He preferred to call his preparatory work 'studies' or 'sketches' and emphasised that they involved intense discipline and a concern for conscious realisation of structure, aiming at a blend, or *conjunctio oppositorum*, of spontaneity and discipline which to him seemed to fuse the best from the Stanislavskian and the Brechtian/Meyerholdian approaches. Similarly, the use of 'neutrality' by Lecoq and others we have discussed has nothing to do with lamenting or attempting to regain some kind of prelapsarian 'innocence' as a form of cultural nostalgia. It identifies a precise psychophysiological condition which is, as with all genuine experiential research, achievable and repeatable by anyone here and now. This condition is 'prior' to language, form and ideas not in an idealist, but in a strictly – though subtly – physical sense. It is not a permanent, or even in most cases a very extended, situation, but a relatively momentary pause, gap or stillness which, like the shaking of a kaleidoscope, allows mental or physical material to begin to form new patterns and impulses. It does not seek any kind of retreat into paradisial vacuity or irresponsibility, but its quest is undertaken with the clear goal of enabling precisely these kinds of re-formation to occur: its focus is towards freer and more extensive action generated by the 'motors' of thought, movement and form.

Improvisation, then, requires a courage which enables you to get *out* of role – although you may then be able to get back *into* it later – and discover other resources which you didn't 'know' you had. That is never an easy option. One of the most difficult improvisatory tasks for any actor is the basis of Lecoq-style red-nose clowning: coming on stage as yourself, with no other resources available, is intensely vulnerable, especially as any 'acting' is immediately 'drummed off'. I Gelati's work with masks similarly transfixes any inauthenticity (masks readily reveal discrepancies between body and gesture or speech) by insisting on maintaining *presence* and input of energy. Maude-Roxby's work, too, is about being fully present, working off whatever is there, being prepared to respond and go with whatever comes up. WildWorks' Sue Hill says, 'We don't know what the destination is, what it's going to look like when it's finished' (Machon 2013: 245). There's nowhere to hide in the face of this scrutiny of presence. Any slip into a familiar – learned or practised – response is a give-away.

Absence of strict form is here only apparent: it is a way of escaping from the fixed, the *a priori*, the already done, the dead and the repetitive. Accepting and *staying with* the state of not knowing 'who' or 'what' is a quite precise step towards activating a degree of present awareness, which is ready to sense and respond to a more coherent and extensive range of sensation, intuition and expression.

This is an authenticity of being which acknowledges that I am what I am in the present moment and is prepared to keep that open for scrutiny rather than cloaked in a role. It acknowledges too that the present includes the full range of the 'past'; both in the historical/genealogical sense and in terms of 'buried' psychic material (for Grotowski this material is overtly that of the levels of collective consciousness of a community, nation or generation). I cannot be fully present unless I own that range of experience as fully as possible in my body.

To be authentic is to be in touch with oneself in this extended sense, which is an opening to one's own life and to levels where it may touch on or merge with the life of others. That is why a great deal of creative energy can be liberated in this kind of work – energy which derives not from 'inspiration' in the clichéd sense of external aid, but from a breathing in, a being in tune with one's own powers as a human being.

The openness of this condition is risky: risky to achieve and risky in that it is always improvising, always performative and never static. Form is dynamic; the self in its articulation is always in the flow of change and needs to adjust to it. Stasis is death and stultification, in self-satisfaction at the 'right' action, word or image; what is crystallised soon becomes brittle. In Tom Stoppard's *Rosencrantz and Guildenstern are Dead* the Player says:

> Why, we grow rusty and you catch us at the very point of decadence. By this time tomorrow night we might have forgotten everything we ever knew. That's a thought, isn't it. We'd be back where we started – improvising. (Stoppard 1967: 16)

Perhaps then, historically and essentially, improvisation is the basis of all theatre and of the creation of a role or a life. 'Forgetting' at that 'point of decadence' may also be the very mechanics by which we gain access to 'everything we ever knew'.[4]

What these perspectives have enabled us to discover is therefore a vital shift in the sense of self and in its function. They start with work which allows a freer sense of (*meaning for*) *self*; offer ways of 'unblocking', both in the personal and psychological sense, and in the social, political sense; move towards an awareness that *self is a capacity for generating a* plurality of *meaning* and establish this as a directable *voluntary* operation through which self ceases to be merely the passive receptacle of deterministic influences and opinions and becomes a *productive agent*. By passing through the condition which Lecoq and Copeau identify as neutrality, Grotowski as disarmament, the self is prised free of its encrustation in habitual role and becomes an active producer of its own meaning.

Under the influence of the improvisatory, self may thus begin to redefine itself: it is liberated both psychologically and semiotically. As it participates more effectively in the making of meaning, it is no longer so limited and closed off in solipsistic regard. It begins to operate as a generator of relationships; that is to say it becomes active in the context (environment), a vital part of processes of exchange. All of this can be seen as important for individual behaviour and for what happens in a theatre between actors and each other and actors and audience. This relocation of the self within the 'community' illustrates an important set of meanings for the 'wholeness' referred to earlier.

Jon Nixon, in an article in *New Theatre Quarterly* (Nixon 1987), suggests that drama in education can be seen as *social interaction* (developing ways of exploring feelings and of imaginative insight into situations), as *discourse* (opening up ways of using language) and as *cognition* (emphasising the *process* of knowing as a move through experiencing towards understanding). Lecoq's teaching results in what Murray terms 'a politics of the imagination' (Murray 2003: 110). Much of what he does acquaints students with the places and forms from which 'languages' arise, and as such it requires the ability to function in between de- and re-construction, to be prepared to accept the condition of not knowing as a prerequisite to creativity. A 'creative pedagogy' (2003: 108) is one which encourages quite the opposite of what passes for knowledge in many subjects and institutions, as Dickens knew very well when he wrote the opening scene of *Hard Times*. You learn only where (and what) you do not know, and you learn most where you have to formulate your knowing as you go.

For Murray, Lecoq represents 'an ethical preoccupation with the power of theatre to break down barriers' (Murray 2003: 109). When you ask people to make the 'theatre to be created', you imply a radicalisation of both form and function: neither the business of teaching nor the business of acquainting students with the processes of deconstruction (as opposed to academic theory about it) is a value-neutral undertaking.

All the functions of improvisation which have emerged from this discussion indicate that it has to do with the extension of being, knowing and communicating. In one sense, you can't train people to improvise. But you can train them to set up the conditions in which improvisation can begin; you can assist them to recognise what inhibits it and to have the courage to face up to those blocks; you can get them to play, to enjoy, to let go and to learn to work with focused but not cramped attentiveness from that state. Such a form of training is most demanding and least coercive, because it leaves the responsibility for how far the process goes and for what emerges from it with the performer.

Site and meaning

In site-specific and immersive performance in particular, the meanings of the location may be evoked and activated; the place itself (a dungeon, a cave, a cowshed, a forest) gets to speak, as it were; and both the performers' and the audience's awareness is tuned up and extended to pick up its resonances. In Brett Bailey's *Orfeus*, created at Spier (Stellenbosch) in 2006 and featured at the Grahamstown Arts Festival (South Africa) in 2007, the setting sun and the calls of birds preparing to roost were not written into the script, but they became strong components of the audience's experience of the link between Orpheus and the world around him, as well as harbingers of his impending journey into darkness to search for Eurydice.

Unexpected 'subtexts' may come alive if space is left for them, just as in participatory performance of many kinds the offer to the audience/co-participants may be taken up (adventurously or banally) and may provoke a range of new moves from the performers. Here, as in much impro work, meaning is being communicated as it is created, on the hoof and as an act of ongoing exchange. We shall pick up some further implications of this in the next chapter.

11   Meaning and Performance

Improvisation promotes the capacity for creating meanings. Those meanings are created in performance, as a process occurring in the present moment. We now turn to some ways in which improvisation illuminates the nature of performative acts: how it amends, revises or interferes with the meanings they appear to offer, how it may interact with texts of various kinds, including the process of writing or constructing them, and how it may suggest alternative models or roles for performance (particularly of theatre) in the context of society.

Meaning as performance (or vice versa): the place of the improvisatory

Improvisation underlies and underlines the fact that meaning is created in performance as the collision or negotiation of different sets of meaning: that, for instance, which appears to reside in the 'text' and that which individual performers perceive and/or mediate; that which the audience expects and that which they receive. Julian Hilton notes that performance involves (*a*) incarnation and transmutation and (*b*) execution and origination (Hilton 1988: 4–5). All of these features are *processes*, that is to say, they are ongoing and open-ended. They involve a change of state and the creation of something new. Improvisation contains all of them but is particularly strong in terms of the second element of each pair. However, that element depends for its realisation upon the first, as for example Lecoq would stress that forms of play must be enacted physically (per-formed). The integrative ('body/think') function of improvisation links the two terms in each pair; it articulates changes of statement through changes of the state of the performer. Since, as we note with reference to the 'message' content of communication, the quality and significance of the communicative act depends on the condition of the actor/communicator (and on that of the responder/receiver), the ability of improvisation work to produce a charged-up condition makes the communicative and performative act much more potentially resonant; it carries an increased capacity for meaning, which means that additional levels or possibilities of significance are opened up.

We would also add to Hilton's categories a third pairing: negotiation and reorganisation, for performers and audiences/participants. The integrative condition sought by impro work is an organic balance, an ease of performance ('free play' in both the mechanical and the aesthetic sense) which may indeed be 'natural' but is not at all 'everyday'. It represents a highly tuned level of activity which invites or stimulates the further integration of performer and audience.

Improvisation also points up another feature of performative acts, namely that each is quite *different* from every other. No two appearances wearing the red nose are the same, nor do they develop the same sequence of events in time and space. Each occurs now, and only now, enacting a new configuration.

Thus all improvised acts can be defined as *integrative*, yet each is also both *specific*, defining itself by its own parameters (for example, its own who/what/why?), innovative and *polysemantic*. This curious and powerful combination may indicate why the experience of performance created in the present can have such wide-ranging effects.

The development of multiple significance is responsible for much of the richness which emerges from performance. One major way in which improvisation can affect this is through *interfering* with what appears to be the established sequence and expectation of meaning: not merely as occasional serendipity or brilliant ad-lib, but as a constant readiness to challenge 'the rules of the game', an alternation of the 'given' and of new invention or realignment. This refraction has political as well as aesthetic implications, as we indicate below in our discussion of improvisation and writing. Improvisation is perhaps supremely the realm of provisional truth, which is an epistemological, historical, philosophical and political statement. And as Peggy Phelan says of performance, it is 'the art form which most fully understands the generative possibilities of disappearance' (Phelan 1993: 27).

This ephemeral quality, much interrogated by writing on performance in recent decades, has always been the core of the improvisatory. Indian and Buddhist aesthetics pre-empt Plato and Shakespeare in recognising that theatre above all arts exemplifies the play (*lila*) of transience (*maya*). It thus manifests both the risk and the revelation of all our assumptions about value, status and significance. Improvisation is a way of living in and out of that moment. It is the ever-renewed filling in the sandwich, the gap which frames the offer. We think that 'theatre', in its fullest sense, has always recognised this. What the improvisatory can highlight is a precise and focused methodology of working towards a particular quality of 'acts' and action. As Parts 1 and 2 have shown, improvisation hones specific skills and mental and physical processes, in marked and identifiable stages, in order to cultivate the ability to reprogramme and regenerate corporeal, linguistic, imaginative, receptive and collaborative abilities. These qualities are essential to makers of theatre and performance alike. It's not surprising that they have surfaced in the range of domains and geographies that we have located.

Writing about Improbable's first piece, *Animo*, Charles says, 'The semiotic potency and complexity of their work is immense, as space, objects and actors are reduced to their most basic constituent elements of form, strength and malleability and are subsequently used as raw resources for the unfolding play' (2003: 58). He also draws on Bakhtin's concept of polyphonic thinking to characterise the mode and operation of improvisation. Performers and things are 'shifted'; performance becomes multi-semantic and dialogic.

Texts, signs and meaning

The changing nature of 'text' is an important issue in the kind of meaning-production implied by the improvisatory style. Many of the theatrical events which give us pleasure and stimulation begin as a written text, the personal creation of an individual mind. On this basis, actors, technicians and directors come together to work. After the completion of a production the published text can, of course, be used to generate new performances. The script of the play does not however always precede the performance. Nor can it convey half the complexity of the finished production: the multiplicity of signs which communicate (though they need the active decoding of alert receivers).[1] These include set, make-up, masks, movement, gesture, spatial relationships, vocal inflexion and so on.

The process of reading theatrical or *performance* text, however, is central to our understanding of how improvisation works. Semiotic analysis reminds us of two things: (1) that the improvising performer is continuously and spontaneously generating information on many levels (much of it unconscious) and (2) that the process does not only involve a 'sender' and a 'receiver' (an 'active' performer and a 'passive' spectator); the spectator is active, too – more than usually so when watching something improvised and/or playing a part in an event which is redrawing its own contours and redesignating the meaning of its own space as it progresses. Decoding information implies the creation of new, often unsuspected or unintended, meanings from the signals received. The audience does not only 'read' the performance, but also, in a very real sense, it 'writes' it, too: performances, as David George says, are 'exercises in restless semiosis' (George 1999: 17).

The shamanic performer's mask, for example, activates what Peirce calls the 'triadic' system of signs. By being *there*, physically present among the audience, and by feeding the audience with simultaneous *iconic*, *indexical* and *symbolic* information, the mask makes the dissolution of the boundary between the actual and the virtual possible.[2] The audience understands or at least operates on all three levels simultaneously. So the shamanic mask enables the spectator to apprehend the intended meaning and also to create that meaning. The performer has to do very little but to be there.[3] The spectator is the active partner, the one generating the meaning and the one 'writing' the play as it happens; and the meaning that is 'read' and 'written' in this way is of vital importance, for it concerns the belief system which underpins the whole community. But all performances put in play belief systems, 'grand narratives', social and cultural assumptions which are thus, ideally (from a deconstructionist viewpoint) revealed as such, as versions or fictions among others, up for grabs and for renegotiation.

The information set supplied (the totality of words, sounds, movements, colours, textures and proxemics) depends for its transmission upon a parallel set within the mind of the spectator. This second set is a matrix of language, associations, memories and images which enables the received information to be simultaneously contextualised and recontextualised. It is the interaction of these two complementary sets – their collision, or fusion perhaps, sometimes called by semioticians 'intertextuality' (Arthur Koestler refers to it as creative 'bisociation' generating '*collision* ending in laughter, or ... *fusion* in a new intellectual synthesis, or ... *confrontation* in an aesthetic experience' (Koestler 1964: 45)) – that creates both purpose and meaning, charging the event with significance.

This indicates the complexity of a 'text' and of the processes by which it is 'read'. In a deconstructive understanding, 'text' principally signifies a network of propositions or provisional narratives, not a definitive statement; playing with meanings, or the play of meaning itself. Thus text itself approaches the *ambiguity* or *hesitation*[4] which is found at the heart of all performance and is the key to improvisation, in the sense that 'anything can happen'.

Improvisation doesn't work entirely without a pre-existent 'text', any more than language or creativity does: but what it does is to operate with the ever present possibility of reorganisation – of shaking the kaleidoscope again – which can keep you on your toes, on the edge of your seat or on the limits of your mental and physical world. It turns text into texturing, into the art of weaving new patterns. We have indicated in Part 1 the range of 'texts' and kinds of retexturing that occur.

In a number of places we have suggested that the methodologies described for performers can be equally useful for writers. Like the other channels of expression theatre and performance employ, writing is part of the spectrum of making meaning. As such it benefits from and has been changed by improvisation methodology. There are now many books which acknowledge this, starting with Keith Johnstone's *Impro for Storytellers*. Some are listed in the Bibliography. Writing for performance is no longer exclusively the solitary business it was taken to be. Its relatively recent history runs parallel to the actor-training and directing developments we have described. Not only the iconic figure of Mike Leigh, who requires actors to research and outline many aspects of a character, but also the work of collectives (Split Breeches and Red Ladder) and collaborative scripting from companies formed by many Lecoq graduates and their successors (Complicité, Frantic Assembly and Improbable) signal this move from the solitary to the shared endeavour. 'Writing' has also in the process shifted ground towards 'devising' and the creation of performance scores including choreography. So in turning our attention here to some further aspects of the relationship between writing and the improvisatory, we are also signalling an historical, theoretical and practical shift of what writing entails and how it is understood.

Improvisation and writing

Michael Chekhov, in *To the Director and Playwright*, makes the point, familiar to anyone who has written a play, that the playwright is as much an improviser as the actor: consciously or unconsciously, the playwright is 'an actor on paper'.

> [T]here is not a single instant of the playwright's creations that is not preceded by improvisation, even though ... maybe all of it, is done mentally. (Leonard 1963: 35)

How much of what has been discussed in this book, therefore, is applicable to the (usually) solitary practice of writing as opposed to the communal activity of playing; how much is transferable from studio to study?

It is easy to accept that 'just as the actor must be his own playwright when he is improvising without a script, so the playwright must be his own actors when he is devising their dialogue' (1963: 35), for, as every writer will admit, the construction of each line, and the inner listening to its imagined responses, is a kind of intellectual improvisation. There are passages in any play which playwrights will say 'wrote themselves', where the writer's critical consciousness dissolves temporarily and they seem to 'channel' the voices and actions of imaginary beings. This inspired, Pirandellian, state is quite common and expresses the organisation at a state just below consciousness of the play's materials. Frequently (generally when there is no one around to think them deluded), writers vocalise lines aloud, as if acting out the parts they have written. They do this to test the *muscularity* of a phrase (its potential for action), as much as its sonority or its ability to catch the imagined rhythm of a character.

So writers naturally improvise (whatever they consciously think of the process). Chekhov suggests that the process is akin to mask-wearing, too, with the 'mask' the playwright wears while creating characters consisting of six elements in simultaneous interplay. These are: (1) surface dialogue (by no means the most important element); (2) the underlying feelings and emotions of the characters; (3) their objectives; (4) their tactics to disguise their wants and feelings; (5) the 'individual, subjective atmosphere' of the character and, finally, (6) the Steinerian 'higher ego' of the playwright, the artistic perception which governs the choices they make. This subjective mental penetration into the diegetic world of the play certainly occurs, whether or not one accepts Chekhov's post-Stanislavskian categories, and differs in kind from the more cerebral processes of research, planning and conscious scripting that are also necessary (Leonard 1963: 165–6).

Improvisation, too, is a tool much used in the *teaching* of creative writing. Keith Johnstone ran the Royal Court Writers' Group under George Devine, from 1958, where playwrights like Wesker, Bond, Jellicoe and Soyinka learned their craft at weekly sessions, and 'anyone suffering from writer's block could bring material into the group where it formed a starting point for improvisation' (Wardle 1978: 199).

Improvisation remains both a personal technique for averting blockages, and an explicitly communal technique for a different kind of writing which resituates the writer as a member of a creative ensemble. The plays of Anthony Neilson, among many other contemporaries, are sometimes deliberately 'unfinished' as they go into rehearsal, because material will be generated in the rehearsal process to complete them. Devising is an increasingly common and acceptable means of play creation in a whole variety of settings and clearly overlaps with improvisation, using many of its techniques to generate and develop a performance text.[5]

In the creative writing classroom, improvisation exercises and games abound, because they serve many of the same needs as in the acting studio. They help young writers overcome the internal censor or 'Cop in the Head';

generate starting points for personal creativity and liberate subconscious ideas; stimulate and stretch the imagination; encourage creative listening and group cooperation; discover alternative possibilities for scenes and characters; suggest lines of plot development; explore subtle shifts in status within scenes; provoke new material for rewrites and actively 'performance test' the written word. Many of the same exercises are easily adapted by more experienced writers, too, as a way of shaking loose stubborn ideas or revitalising a project that is in danger of becoming stale.

Some are useful starters. Del Close's 'Ad Game' (Halpern *et al.* 1994: 52–5) generates energy and teaches writers that everything is usable; everything can be justified and woven into a developing story. Spolin's 'Where–Who– What?' exercise works just as well for a writing improvisation as an acting one. In the writing class, suggestions are solicited from, and elaborated upon by, the whole group. It rapidly becomes clear to them that which- ever factor (character, action and location) is chosen first, the other two are easily generated; if one has two of these factors, the third is always im- plicit in them. A Spolin derivative that works well is to ask for a location, two characters and a random line of dialogue and then tease out the story they contain. Something like 'finding the game' in Del Close's terminology occurs. The pattern-making mind instantly tries to connect the snippets and from them is able to propagate narrative – and ultimately dialogue. The group may come to conclusions about what's going on: individual writers may then write the material up in a personal rather than a collective vein. Keith Johnstone's 'Status' exercises are invaluable, as are his storytelling impros. Writers (like actors) have to learn to see *status* as a verb rather than a noun and to interpret subtle shades and shifts of status, in both language and action. The playing cards liberate the writers from the stress of having to *invent* by simply telling them that the next line (or character, or action) is higher or lower status than the preceding one. Close's 'Three-line Scenes' encourage rapidity and economy but also challenge writers to *listen* closely to lines one and two and to search for the story, scene or 'game' implicit in them, which line three will materialise (Halpern *et al.* 1994: 67–9).[6]

Chris Johnston elaborates on a Keith Johnstone *Newsletter* which lists twelve 'mistakes' to be avoided in impro or impro training, which are emi- nently redeployable in training writers. They include: *Cancelling* (avoiding or negating the project); *Sidetracking* (getting away from the main action and substituting another), or its variant, *Being Original*; *Instant Trouble* (rush- ing straight to the central conflict rather than working up to it); *Gossip* (chat rather than action, conversation rather than dialogue) *Gagging* (playing gags rather than scenes) and *Blocking* (discussed elsewhere: refusing the offer, saying 'no' rather than 'yes, and ...') (Johnston 1998: 190–2). Whatever the terminology, the faults are instantly recognisable to all writers.

Fay Lecoq, in her Afterword to the posthumous, 2002 edition of her husband's book *The Moving Body*, notes an extension rather than a diminution of the École's activities with the addition of an *atelier d'écriture* run by playwright Michel Azama (Lecoq 1997: 186. Azama still teaches at the School [2014]). It seems an important and timely inclusion in the Lecoq curriculum. We have seen many breathtaking performance moments by improvisation-trained graduates yet frequently regretted the lack of a dramaturgical structure to unite them, a coherent narrative to be shared with an audience or a literate verbal text commensurate with the physical lyricism of the actors' bodies. Like Copeau's injunction to Saint-Denis and the Copiaus, at the end of the Burgundian phase of their experiments, to return to working with the playwright André Obey, the establishment of the *atelier d'écriture* signals that improvisation can resume its place as a crucial, but not the only, component in the production of the drama.

Improvisation, which includes the devising of pattern, of movements or words, may also take the form of spatial collective writing or creative participation: a group working on an idea or individuals contributing different (sometimes thoroughly researched) parts to a communal effort. As such it can form part of a working method for groups in education or in creative writing courses.

Incorporating the actors' research – both academic/investigative (going out and taking notes) and physical (finding out what it feels like to walk or talk like that kind of person) – into the performance means on one level involving them in the choices from which the play evolves and on another level making them both discover and generate the 'subtext' or underlying motivation for each character or event. They are involved in an *existential* (how to find the resources in their own experience), *psychological* (how to motivate) and *semiological* (how to present in words and actions) commitment to the development of character and incident. In the case of work in the mode of Forum or Playback, it is their life-experience which forms the core of the play or sketch; and their roles as both contributors and observers – and in the case of Forum as actors as well – give them opportunities to reflect, re-evaluate and reposition their identities and actions, in and through the business of 'scripting the play'.

Emanating largely from the 1980s activist/socialist/feminist spectrum is a considerable body of 'collectivist' work – Caryl Churchill and Joint Stock, John McGrath and 7:84 – and cooperative theatre companies like Red Ladder, Split Breeches and Gay Sweatshop. Similar kinds of input from company members is involved (for example, historical research by cast members for Churchill's *Light Shining in Buckinghamshire*); the process is quite largely collective, though there is usually only one name on the final playtext, in contrast to some well-known anti-apartheid work in South Africa at the same time (Fugard, Kani and Ntshona's *Sizwe Banzi Is Dead* and Simon, Mtwa and Ngema's *Woza Albert*).

The argument that collaborative or collective writing or devising of this kind may be a form of *écriture feminine* also suggests links with Ariane Mnouchkine (see above, pp. 76–7), both in the early cooperative phase of Théâtre du Soleil's work and in her later collaboration with Hélène Cixous. Although not all the companies mentioned have particularly gender-related policies, *écriture feminine* is not only about women writers or solely about a focus on gender issues. It can refer to an increased sensitivity towards the processes of production and a freer, less ratiocentric compositional and structural method. As such it may also be applicable to group devising and creation of all kinds, for example to workshopping with creative writers. The connection with our focus here is in terms of how working like this can:

1. free up inhibition through interactive debate, dialogue and sharing;
2   suspend mainly 'right hemisphere' logocentric process in favour of more spontaneous, imagistic, metaphoric or metonymic activity; and
3. supplement a singular ego-driven dynamic with a more communal, perhaps 'collective' consciousness.

If such a group includes a writer/director, he or she can supply the basic information (or organise its collation); ask the actors to translate it into scenes via improvisation, which they will then take away and write up; or take on the status of a recording mechanism, transcribing the improvised actions and polishing the (probably) clumsy dialogue that emerges.

In the second case, working on an agreed subject, the whole company is the 'writer'. The director is the editor of a fully collaborative process, until, that is, the point is reached at which the work is to be scripted. Here the democratic process may become again, by default, an autocratic one. The editorial voice becomes an authorial voice. It may be that the group wants this to happen. If it doesn't, then the only way to proceed is for the entire company to be involved in assembling the final script – a clumsy way of working sometimes, but often surprisingly fertile. Some writers are afraid of collaboration. It diminishes their sense of their own inviolably unique creativity. But theatre is a collaborative art.

The ultimate form of this is a third case, where the play is the result of a collaboration not just between the members of the acting ensemble before the public is admitted, but between the ensemble and the audience during performance (for examples see Part 1). The audience may be involved in shaping the play that it sees, offering suggestions, even taking roles. Or it may be left implicit, the collaboration of mind and feelings as the actors shape their play in front of the audience, going along one pathway and abandoning others as they sense the mood of the spectators.

Dymphna Callery recalls Zeami's classic principle of *Jo–Ha–Kyu* – and Meyerhold's *otkaz–posil'–tochka* – as ways of rhythmically controlling material and offers the 'circus' or 'variety' show (bound together by spectacle, each act having its own internal rhythm and dynamic) as alternative structuring models which both eschew the causal structure of traditional narrative and avoid involvement in any character's interior journey.

She reminds us that Odin Teatret under Barba's direction have developed 'a distinctive way of using montage to structure improvisation work so that an audience has an active and individual response rather than a collective empathy for a central protagonist' (Callery 2001: 193).

> Barba will suggest a theme to actors; they create improvisations from their personal response to the material, which he then reworks. He does not enter into any dialogue about the actor's motivations, but orchestrates their solo improvisations into 'actions', sequences of action, and scenes, re-ordering and structuring according to his own intuitive sense of tempo and rhythm.   (Callery 2001: 193)

In responding to an Odin production the straightforward pleasure of narrative clarity is frequently denied. Likewise, interpretation is deliberately made difficult. 'Meaning is virtually shunned. It is the experience of the spectators that counts' (2001: 193). There is not always a single visual focus (*Andersen's Dream* is set in a relatively small, specially constructed, encircling and containing theatre 'capsule'; even here, events happen above, around, behind the spectator) or a single character upon whom we can map a developing narrative. There is deliberate discontinuity and discontiguity.

Jane Turner applies Patrice Pavis's narratalogical terminology – the 'condensation' and 'displacement' of narrative readability, via 'accumulators', 'connectors', 'secators' and 'shifters' – to Barba's complex intercultural performance scores (Turner 2004: 86ff.). 'In other words, what we as spectators see and experience, we displace or substitute with a series of our own associations and connections' (2004: 89). Callery summarises:

> This is closer to the idea of circus spectacle than narrative unity, yet
> Barba's work is much more than variety acts. What unifies the work are
> deep philosophical concerns rather than simply entertainment, plus a
> desire to affect the spectator on a primal level.   (Callery 2001: 193).

The process here is prising open the tendency to narrative predictability or
closure, in favour of 'accident' (Fo on the Molière troupe) or 'refraction'.
Performers and/or spectators are offered the space to play (irreverently): as
Philippe Gaulier says, '*Amusez-vous Merde!*' The 'deep philosophical concerns' are enacted as the identification of key moments in which to *intervene in your own story*, not to let it be told only by others.

On a more conscious – though by no means superficial – level, this links
directly with what Frances Babbage notes of Boalian Forum work as a 'space
for dissection and debate', because 'as each intervention takes place ... the
narrative is unmade and remade before our eyes' (Babbage 2004: 45), thus
offering the possibility of imaginative engagement in the production of a
new story of the world. The collision of improvisation and writing opens
up this operation, in which metaphysics and politics are not disjunctive
realms.

Co-creativity

An act of theatre has many sets of meaning. There are those which are
created in the act of performance *jointly* by actors and audience members
and those other kinds of 'performance' which arise *privately* in the mind of
either after the event is concluded or the partners in the original act have
separated.

The meaning of a theatre event (unlike, say, the meaning of a novel) is
not only experienced singly, but communally. This type of meaning derives
not so much from the intention, but from the 'flavour' of the experience.
Obvious examples might be the communal laughter shared during the performance of a successful farce, or the hushed stillness, when the communal
heartbeat of the audience seems to race, during the performance of some
terrifying stunt in the circus.

Meaning is never solipsistic, in spite of the illusion generated by private reading (whose text? whose language?). Where we mean, we bleed:
across our boundaries, out of our skins, into each other. In improvising
meanings, we always depend on others to acknowledge or accept them,
and on 'others' in ourselves sometimes to generate them against the grain
of habit or taboo. On the others we can invoke or conjure or parody or

exorcise too, linguistically or attitudinally or empathetically. I am more than I seem, if I can learn to seem effectively, as Hamlet and others imply. To make music together is a politics, an act and praxis of negotiation, as well as a buzz or a vibe (the South African magazine *Drum* recorded the – illegal – gatherings of artists from many genres, including celebrated jazz musicians, writers and theatre makers, and of many colours, in *apartheid*-era Johannesburg).

Improvisers need proximity. They cannot be isolated from their co-creators. Practically, during improvised performances a lot of *small* things happen. Being spontaneously created, there isn't time for the actor to re-hearse and selectively enlarge them. They happen briefly and are then extinguished. The audience has to be close enough to notice them and to nudge itself in the ribs to call attention to them.

After the claims for decorum laid down by the nineteenth-century thea-tre space, we can observe a kind of Freudian volcanic upsurge of cabaret-type activity at crucial points in the twentieth century – in the 1920s and 1930s in Germany, for instance, or in the 1960s in Britain. Much of this work used the methods of improvisation in its development (especially a direct, creative response to the immediate social and political context) and relied upon acute audience participation. Athol Fugard recalls how, in apartheid South Africa, the audience for *Sizwe Banzi is Dead* – a play con-structed from workshop improvisation with actors John Kani and Winston Ntshona – in a township meeting hall in 1973 not only swamped the audi-torium and spilled over onto the stage, but viewed the event more as a pol-itical meeting than a play, resulting in 'the most amazing and spontaneous debate I have ever heard' *during* the performance (Kruger 1999: 160).

The relationship between theatre – both as institution and as event – and society is a complex and reciprocal one, but it can be argued that forms of social change are at the least reflected, and possibly instigated or sup-ported, in the form and content of much performance. It is not entirely clear what the full range of significances is of the early twenty-first-century appetite for participatory and immersive experience which we have noted. But it goes along with an enormous increase in the spread of 'applied' per-formance activity throughout the world, much of which is Boalian in spirit and operates criteria closely drawn from the menu of improvisatory tactics we have been outlining. How this plays out will at least in part depend not only on socio-political context, but on the inherent resilience of the kinds of processes instigated by improvisatory method. '[H]ow the performative conversation is structured' (Charles 2003: 16) is an important criterion. The varieties of facilitation, leadership, participatory engagement, immersive interaction and so on to be found in the work we have been looking at are moves towards the dialogic, towards 'the event of many voices speaking to one another as *equals*' (2003: 194). Sharing action and construction is also a politics.

Those kinds of questions are being asked in situations where the context is the fundamental rebalancing of many of our essential structures of social, political and ecological organisation; they include but also surpass issues like management of natural resources, government corruption, HIV/AIDS, female foeticide, ethnicity and conflict, land exploitation and the economics of global capitalism.

The improviser marks this possibility and the challenge of operating in these zones too, of defining as it were the extreme limit of play, the edge of the road before it drops over the precipice. If you dare, you can go right up to the edge. And once you know that, it affects the use you subsequently make of the road. We may view our life-scripts in a different way afterwards. The improvisatory mode, as Jacques Lecoq and others have suggested, has frequently posed this challenge to orthodoxy. Its origins seem linked to a cultural matrix which the last few centuries have marginalised and reduced to 'alternative' status: the shamanistic, the clown and the carnival. Though its beginnings may be the beginning of theatre itself (Dionysiac rites, integrating community and environment, and centred on a state of being 'enthused', operating in a kind of psychic overdrive), many social orders have seen the need either to repress or to marginalise (by licensing in a strictly limited way) anything to do with the spirit of creative play. Individual creativity, from the point of view of order, is a dangerous and disruptive thing (as Keith Johnstone and Teatr Ósmego Dnia strikingly record) and even more dangerous if it issues in communal ceremony and performance. The 'double' of society, anything to do with the liberation of instinct and feeling, has frequently been subjected to this kind of treatment. Fo and Rame provide a contemporary example which the figure of the (sometimes 'divine') Fool extends through history in many cultures.

The aesthetics of risk

We are in an era when it has become fashionable to examine the 'aesthetics of risk'. This is largely because academic research itself has increasingly to demonstrate an economic or social implementation potential within civil society, governed by relatively narrow capitalistic interpretations of 'impact' and 'outcomes', and thus needs to identify and evaluate the kinds of risk this might involve. But aesthetics has always been risky, and the improvisatory is the place to get close to it. It is about putting who, what and why you are on the line. It is about daring to intervene in, challenge, reconfigure or remake texts, spaces of being, relationships – in and beyond the confines of a social or geographical norm, sets of behaviour, attitudes and actions. That risk, existential and paradigmatic though it may be in academia and, for the most part, the world of the performing arts in the northern and 'western' world, may in some times and places be more tangible and direct.

Sanjoy Ganguly, who uses Forum Theatre to challenge political agendas without regard to Party in West Bengal, has been at risk of death from apparatchiks on more than one occasion. Augusto Boal was imprisoned and tortured in Brazil. Improvisation was not well received by the Spanish Inquisition or the McCarthy administration, although its record in *apartheid* South Africa suggests that it has some cards up its sleeve.

As our discussion of Indian performers' use of *jugalbandi*, *creación colectiva* in Columbia and *kabigan* in eastern India suggests, improvisatory creativity may have inbuilt tendencies towards the dialogic, the reciprocal, towards tolerance of and engagement with the Other. There are always risks. Stand-ups may die on their feet (or, as they tend to put it, on their arses); Forum practitioners may really die. If we are to reconstruct not merely a level of mutual respect, but a working model of global human democracy, we may need to take some more of those risks, starting right here, right now, within and between each one of us. Because, as Boal knows, aesthetic practice, for all that it is risk, is a supreme procedure for extending humanity in human beings. We need to weigh up how urgent it is to engage with it.

The wager of the Other: an ecology of improvisation?

Meeting the Other isn't always easy or comfortable, since it also involves revision of one's own status and position. So openness to that dimension, which is at the heart of much impro work, does mean accepting risk. Yet there is also risk in refusing to take that step, closing off and remaining within the boundaries of the known. The drive for participatory experience marks a willingness to engage with that risk which is not insignificant. Relationship between individuals, environments and events is being reframed, in an extension of the way improvisation has always, as this book shows, had the potential to do. The improvisatory in a sense *is* risk; it is also the trigger for loss and gain, for less and more, and for letting go of the protected role or image or pattern. 'Nature' is not just a nice view or a manicured park. We do not 'own' it. We are it, and what we are doing as and with it shapes the world we live in and will bequeath to our descendants.

Some way of internalising that bit of border-crossing, of recognition of our co-creativity and co-responsibility, may be vital to what comes next. The bridge which is the improvisatory moment may lead to an abyss; but not crossing it may be more dangerous. Impro, as we have seen, has ways of getting people to listen, to themselves and what is inside and outside them, and to remove the hands from ears and eyes and mouths. If what we see and hear and speak as a result is evil, that is because we have been part of its construction; but it is also something we need to acknowledge and work with. An ecology which accepts the energies of the as-yet-unknown, the unformulated, the possible, is also one which is willing to find that ambivalence in the body and to follow its traces and discover how and what it can become – perhaps to replace the reified protection of the familiar with the possibility of being and doing different and even of hearing 'no' and saying 'yes'.

New combinations; saying Yes, hearing No

The practice of the *via negativa* and *via negationis* ('the negative way' and 'the way of negation') may seem at odds with Keith Johnstone's primary injunction to say 'yes' (or, with Del Close, to say 'yes, and …'), but the contradiction is, really, only apparent. The terms have their origin in Neoplatonic thought – in the Plotinian practice of *apophasis*. Plotinus argued that, since the deity is not an object in creation, no words, no language, can approach its description: all one can say is what God is *not*. The idea is hardly unique to Western theology (the concepts of *neti neti* – god is 'not this, not that'; 'neither this, nor that' – in Hinduism, *ein-sof* in Cabbalistic Judaism and *bila faifa* in Islam address the same impossibility).

Grotowski, along with Barba, Lecoq, Prattki, Gaulier, Pagneux and many others, has a shared understanding that the object of the tuition is, ultimately, indescribable. Hence, they naturally (and no doubt temperamentally) gravitate towards the apophatic in their teaching style. It is frequently only possible to say what is not working, rather than specify what is required (Murray 2003: 143).[7]

A similar apophasis underpins Samuel Beckett's spiritual autobiographies: it is not possible to say what is sought; there is only the constant experience of seeking, and failing, and seeking again. However, this, as with the practitioners referred to above, is not just a question of saying that you can't say it: it is actually about *inhabiting* the area of the unsayable, because that's the only place you haven't been before and therefore the only place worth being now. So to be such a writer, or an actor in such a theatre, means an endless commitment to the search: to saying 'yes' all the time – even as the tutor, director, *metteur en scène*, *auteur*, audience is bound (most of the time) to say 'no' – or, less bluntly but just as frustratingly, 'yes, that's not it either!'

Eugenio Barba's pursuit of 'Disorder' enters the same inexpressible territory of verbal regress. With a lower-case initial, the word signifies 'the absence of logic and rigour characterising nonsensical and chaotic works'. With a capital D, however, it signifies for him 'the logic and rigour which provoke the *experience of bewilderment* in the spectator'. Orthography serves to distinguish what ought to be distinguished in vocabulary, between 'disorder as a loss of energy, [and] Disorder as the irruption of an energy that confronts us with the unknown' (Barba 2005: 50).

As he approached his seventieth birthday, Barba recalled not only forty years of work with Odin Teatret but certain theatrical moments (Brecht's *Die Mutter*, *Kathakali* in Kerala and Grotowski's *The Constant Prince*) indelibly imprinted on his memory which typified for him that strange encounter with the ineffable:

> Similarly, in an unexpected and involuntary way I have experienced and still experience Disorder while working with my actors. From the very beginning, certain designs of their physical or vocal actions, continuously repeated and refined, leap into another reality of being.
>
> I have personally witnessed it: a denser, brighter and more incandescent body than the bodies we possess emerges in the theatrical space from an *elsewhere* which I cannot place. This body-in-life irrupts, regardless of good or bad taste, by a combination of chance and craft or because of an unforeseen event in a highly structured calculation.
>
> Today it is clear to me: theatre has represented a precious tool to make *incursions* into zones of the world that seemed out of my reach. (Barba 2005: 60)
>
> What has the training of my actors been if not a bridge between these two extremes: the incursion into the machine of the body, and an opening for the irruption of an energy that shatters the limits of the body? ... Disorder that rocks my familiar ways of living the space and time around me and, through bewilderment, compels me to discover another part of myself. (2005: 61)

The director Mike Alfreds, who sees the actor as the theatre's only *raison d'être*, concurs:

> Beyond a certain point, theatre cannot be controlled. That is to say, neither should actors be controlled, nor should they be wholly *in* control. Competent actors *make* things happen. Good actors *let*

things happen. That's why theatre always has – or should have – the potential for danger, for the unpredictable. A performance should be a disciplined improvisation. (Alfreds 2007: 344)

Improvisation continually nibbles at meaning and nudges towards meanings. It highlights the way performance can be creative as well as normative, implying a dynamic model for the role of theatre and performance both for individuals and within society. It can assist in shifting the parameters by which we live. In bending the rules it proposes new forms: Lecoq's focus on 'the spirit of play', found in many forms in improvisation work, picks up Schiller's sense that man is fully human only when he plays (Hilton 1988: 45–6): it is the 'will to play' (*Spieltrieb*) which produces new combinations of matter and form.

Notes

Introduction and Preface to Third Edition

1. Bronwyn Preece has compiled a draft chronology in tabular form. It can be accessed by contacting her through her website: http://www.bronwenpreece.com.
2. In first edition: page 4.
3. Here we mean what Durkheim calls the 'taboo sacred'; that which acts as a social or political boundary policed by religious authority. In another sense – closer to the shamanic and the improvisational – the mark of sacred *experience* (as opposed to doctrine) may be said to be precisely that it escapes all such boundaries. See Yarrow *et al.*, *Sacred Theatre* (2007).
4. *'He that schal pleye Belyal loke that he have gunne-powder brennynge In pypys in his handis & in his eris & in his ars whanne he gothe to battel'* (from the fifteenth-century *The Castell of Perseverance* (see Southern 1957: 19). Not recommended for improvisers of a nervous or combustible constitution.
5. The account given by Bakhtin of the grotesque (in particular, the 'grotesque canon of the body') accords not only with ancient representations of the *mimi*, but also with Jacques Lecoq and Philippe Gaulier's modern *bouffonerie* (although Lecoq may be thought to shade out of the true grotesque into the fantastical).
6. Davison cites Michael Billington's observation that Cirque's show, 'for all the skills involved, combined corporate soullessness with spiritual pretension' (2013: 117).

Chapter 1   Improvisation in Training, Rehearsal Practice and Writing (Europe and the UK)

1. See also Martin (2002).
2. 'Improvisation was Vakhtangov's basic experimental technique. Vakhtangov allowed the form of his plays to develop through a series of improvisations by his actors from which he would select the interpretation he considered most appropriate. Then with a more dictatorial attitude, he carried out the final honing. But the discovery through improvisation was a collaborative endeavor' (Hull 1985: 230).
3. Carnicke provides a detailed account of Stanislavsky's ideas, their language, publication and reception. The book, centred on a reinterpretation of Stanislavsky's Russian, includes an excellent glossary (1998: 169–82).
4. 'Doctor Dappertutto' is to be found in E. T. A. Hoffman's *Fantasiestücke in Callot's Manier*, part II.
5. See Doisy (1954: 105); Donahue (2001: 61–72, esp. 69); also Copeau's *Journal, Deuxième partie: 1916–1948*, Vol. 2 (1991: 87) for an account of Bing's work with the Vieux-Colombier actors and children at Morristown. See also Hodge (2000: 69–75); and Kurkinen (2000: *passim*), for a discussion of her mime teaching.

6. See Copeau (1974: 17); images of his original *affiche* appear on the Comédie Française website at http://www.comedie-francaise.fr/aujourdhui/hiervc.php; and, at a more useful scale, can also be seen at http://gallica.bnf.fr/anthologie/notices/ 01549.htm. Copeau's aim was 'to scour the sclerosis of routine from the drama and liberate the expressive spontaneity of the actor' (Doisy 1954: 79; our translation).

7. The second phase of this development was designed by Louis Jouvet, who was stage manager, leading man and part-time architect.

8. Meyerhold's view of the *cabotin* differs from Copeau's; for him 'The cabotin is a strolling player ... a kinsman to the mime, the histrion, and the juggler ... [who] keeps alive the tradition of the true art of acting' (Braun 1969: 122).

9. There is a fascinating reverse parallel here with the puppet alter-egos ('bio-objects') of the Polish director Tadeusz Kantor. These outgrowths, carried on characters' backs in his *Dead Class*, signal the self which has been lost or suppressed by adulthood's subservience to social or political violence. The Copiaus's Masks, on the other hand, embody a celebration or liberation of the inner or 'other' life.

10. Similar difficulties would undermine the Second City troupe in their attempt to find American comic archetypes (see pp. 46–8 and 250, n.6).

11. Since we wrote the first edition of this book, le Théâtre du Vieux-Colombier has been reopened. Purchased by the state in 1986, Copeau's original building was renovated in 1993 by architect Bernard Kohn as a second house for the Comédie Française.

12. It is worth noting that Lecoq, in our interview with him in Paris in April 1987, made a strong distinction between Copeau and the 'Copiaus': for him, it was the work of the latter during this period that laid the foundations of modern impro work. Léon Chancerel's 1935 *Théâtre de l'Oncle Sebastien* specialised in improvised work for children. Dasté and, of course, Saint-Denis expanded performance and training skills.

13. Russian Futurist Velimir Khlebnikov used 'a universally comprehensible speech with deliberate *zaum* (a "trans-sense" language)' (Rudnitsky 1988: 11). The term 'zaum' was coined by another Futurist, Aleksei Kruchenykh in 1913, to mean a 'transrational' language. (Paul Schmidt called it 'beyonsense'). Unlike comic *grammelot* (or *grummelotage*), zaum was a slightly too serious attempt at reconstructing a lost, aboriginal language.

14. One candidate might be the Lyric, Hammersmith, which supported much of the developmental work of Improbable Theatre (see p. 257, n. 11) and staged shows by them which included large elements improvised afresh each performance. The Lyric continues to host similar events by, for example, Secret Theatre – where the audience is not told beforehand what the show will be and it is delivered in a randomly selected order which is different for each performance (Spring 2014). Mainstream theatres have supported plays created through improvisatory means (e.g. Complicité's *Street of Crocodiles* at the National in 1992), but the host's flexibility usually hardens as the technical demands of set design, advance publicity material, etc., get nearer. Michael Boyd, as incoming Director of the RSC in 2003, announced plans for a devised play, *Pontius Pilate*, created via improvisation as part of a project, political rather than necessarily dramaturgical, 'to reinvent the collective theatre-making process at the RSC' which he felt had declined during the previous tenure: it is interesting that group devising emerges again as the expression of dramaturgical democracy. In recent

years (2007–present), The National Theatre, The Old Vic, The Young Vic and The Barbican have been involved as associates, collaborators or co-producers with a range of 'immersive' work by Artangel, Punchdrunk, WildWorks and others; Battersea Arts Centre has hosted 'immersive' work by Punchdrunk, Coney and WildWorks; The Sheffield Crucible has collaborated on work by Wilson + Wilson and the Arcola Theatre has provided actors and support for Punchdrunk. Work of this kind has also been performed at the Royal Opera House, festivals including Chichester and Edinburgh, and toured abroad with support from the British Council.

15. Mike Leigh's works to date fall into four main periods:
   i.   1965–74: mostly stage plays (two out of sixteen were filmed)
   ii.   1975–85: mostly TV (three out of fourteen also staged including *Abigail's Party*)
   iii. 1987–2004: mostly film, including *Secrets and Lies* and *Vera Drake* (three out of thirteen stage only)
   iv.   2005: marks the start of a fourth, mixed period, interspersing plays and films (stage: *Two Thousand Years*, 2005; *Grief*, 2011; the revival of *Ecstasy*, 2011; films like *Happy Go Lucky*, 2008; *Another Year*, 2010; *A Running Jump*, 2012; *Mr Turner*, 2014). For full details of Leigh's early periods see Clements (1983: *passim*); Coveney (1996: 237–43); and Watson (2004: vii). As this edition goes to press in 2015, Leigh has just directed an acclaimed *Pirates of Penzance* for English National Opera (a belated opera debut, perhaps, for the President of the Sullivan Society).

16. Examples of British 'Free Cinema' include Lindsay Anderson, (1923–94), *O Dreamland* (1953), *Every Day Except Christmas* (1957); Karel Reisz (1926–2002), *Momma Don't Allow* (1955, with Tony Richardson (1928–91)); *We Are the Lambeth Boys* (1958); and Lorenza Mazzetti (1928–), *Together* (1956).

Chapter 2   The Improv Scene (US)

1. Throughout this account we notice the importance of the Settlement Houses. The first of these was probably Toynbee Hall, founded by reformers Samuel and Henrietta Barnet in 1884 in London's East End, which many years later saw the first performance directed by Michael Croft of what would become the UK's National Youth Theatre. In America, Neva Boyd worked at Jane Addams and Ellen Starr's Hull-House in Chicago. Margaret Naumburg and Alice and Irene Lewisohn of the Neighbourhood Playhouse worked in association with Lilian Wald's Henry Street. Comedian Eddie Cantor – who was improvising stand-up and dialects at Miner's Bowery Theatre and Hammerstein's Victoria Theatre from as early as 1908 – recorded his gratitude in equal measure to his Grandma Esther Kantrowitz and the Henry Street Settlement for keeping him off the streets of the Lower East Side. Harry Hopkins (who galvanised the Works Progress Administration and the Federal Theatre Project in New Deal America) began his career with unpaid work at Christodora House, founded by Christina MacColl and Sarah Carson on strict Protestant principles in the Lower East Side of Manhattan: he met his first wife there and lost his faith as he discovered so-cial injustice. And the Federal Theatre Project's Hallie Flanagan, a graduate of George Pierce Baker's English 47 Workshop at Harvard, found her inspiration

and her faith in the New Deal at Melville House, Detroit, run by her aunt. The movement improviser Al Wunder, too, first encountered the inspirational choreographer Alwin Nikolais – and improvisation – at the Henry Street Settlement Playhouse in 1962, where he later taught.

2. Main offshoots of the original Compass idea were: Second City, Chicago, founded in 1959 by Sills and still going; The Premise, founded in New York by Theodore J. Flicker, 1960–4; The Committee, founded in San Francisco by Alan Myerson, 1963–73.

3. Lenny Bruce (1925–66): legendary stand-up comic, writer and satirist. Mort Sahl (born 1927 in Montreal): comedian and screenwriter, and at the time of writing still doing stand-up (though perhaps a little less frequently), e.g. Child: 'What did you do in the War, Daddy?' Parent (George W. Bush voice): 'I started it.'

4. See obituary and biography by fellow Harold player Kim 'Howard' Johnson on-line at http://www.geocities.com/SouthBeach/Pointe/2765/KimHowardJohnson/khjdelcl.html (accessed 28 June 2006). Johnson recounts that Del's last joke was to bequeath his own skull to the Goodman Theatre, so he could get acting credits in any future productions of *Hamlet*.

5. The story (Halpern *et al.* 1994: 7) is that Bill Mathieu of The Committee christened the new form facetiously ('What shall we call it?' 'Harold'. 'OK.') and the name stuck: the analogy is made with Beatle George Harrison's moment in the 1964 film *A Hard Day's Night* ('What do you call that haircut?' 'Arthur.'). Close always rather regretted the silly name for a serious invention. For details of other long-form styles, see Lynn (2004: 100ff.) and Kozlowski (2002: *passim*). Matt Fotis's 2014 book, *Long Form Improvisation and American Comedy: The Harold* contains a very detailed account of the emergence of Second City and its offshoots and the Harold. It also usefully extends the discussion beyond the theatre to the Harold's influence on film and television.

6. Compass was founded in Chicago in 1955 by David Shepherd (1924–) and Paul Sills (born Paul Silverberg, 1927–2008). Since Compass, Shepherd founded *ImprovOlympic*, *Responsive Scene Radio Show* (in which listeners create their own stories on-air), *Canadian Improv Games* (with Howard Jerome and Jamie 'Willie' Wyllie), and, since 2011, *Life-Play* – improvised games that can be played on the phone by two or more players. He has worked on improvising video, *MOVIExperience*, with his partner Nancy Fletcher, and written a book called *That Movie in Your Head* (2005). He has received lifetime achievement awards from Second City, Chicago Improv Festival and other organisations and, in 2010, was the subject of a documentary called *David Shepherd: A Lifetime of Improvisational Theater* (directed by Mike Fly, featuring interviews with many of the people referred to in this book – cf. https://www.youtube.com/watch?v=t5wgtkgCH3A).

    i. Compass begat Second City (out of Tonight at 8.30 and Playwrights' Theatre) in 1955. Second City (much of whose teaching was due to Josephine Forsberg) produced Del Close, Charna Halpern, Amy Poehler, Mike Myers, Steve Carell, Tina Fey and Dana Andersen, among a host of others already discussed in the book.

    ii. Alan Myerson (1940–) and Jessica Myerson founded The Committee in San Francisco in 1963, with Del Close. Alan Myerson has since made his name as a film and television director. Bennington-educated Jessica Myerson (originally known as Irene Ryan, then Irene Riordan, then Jessica Myerson, and now known as Latifah Taormina – which suggests a lifetime of improvising new selves) trained with Sills but also with Lee Strasberg, and has had a career in films, television and theatre as an actor and latterly as an arts administrator in Austin, Texas (cf. the documentary film *A Session With the Committee*, 1969, dir. Alan Myerson; and the Austin Chronicle feature article Improvising Every Second, http://www.austinchronicle.com/arts/2006-03-10/346205/). The Committee had a more political edge than many of their contemporaries. Their celebrity status dried up when one of the actors, Gary Goodrow, expressed disapproval of Richard Nixon on TV ('Nixon's a fag' according to Taormina). The company ceased in 1972.

7. LARP theory centres on the Scandinavian countries, and much of it is web-based: see particularly Montola and Stenros (2004); Gade *et al.* (2003); Bøckman and Hutchison (2005) (all contain combative, spiky essays in English); and Geir Tor Brenne's (2005) graduate thesis, 'Making and Maintaining Frames: A Study of Metacommunication in Laiv Play', University of Oslo. The *Amor Fati* website has an extensive electronic library (at http://fate.laiv.org/in_arti.htm) and includes articles on dramaturgy and improvisation in relation to LARPing.

8. The unstoppable rise of the zombie phenomenon is attested not only by the wealth of films and television series emerging in recent years (including the 2015 BBC game show *I Survived a Zombie Apocalyse*, hosted by Greg James), but by the dedication of a whole issue of *Studies in Theatre and Performance* (guest edited by Lee Miller, Roberta Mock and Phil Smith in 2014) to 'Zombies and Performance'. One article – relevant to our discussion of improvising audiences – is 'Our Encore: Running from the Zombie 2.0', by Kris Darby, which describes *Zombies Run!*, an augmented reality audio fitness app for joggers designed by Naomi Alderman, which transforms a 5K run into an escape game 'by aurally layering a zombie apocalypse over the real world' (Darby 2014: 229). (Thanks to Tom Francis for information on LARP and Zombies)

9. Reviews can be seen at http://www.musicalthemusical.com/ reviews.htm.

10. Holmes was hitherto best known for writing *Escape: The Piña Colada Song* and for his compositions for Barbra Streisand, Barry Manilow, Dolly Parton and others. Although a fully trained clarinettist and composer, he was principally a pop song writer and arranger, with no Broadway track record. Britain's Josie Lawrence has a remarkable facility for improvising meaningful lyrics in almost any style, which she has demonstrated on *Whose Line Is It Anyway?* (which has just opened in London's Adelphi Theatre, 27 years after first airing on BBC Radio 4). The playwright, singer, actress and comedienne Victoria Wood also excels at improvised song writing.

11. Richard Christiansen wrote of the Broadway version that it 'catches the customers in an embrace of agreeable partnership' (*The Chicago Tribune*, 17 December 1985). In the Induction scene to Ben Jonson's 1614 *Bartholomew Fair*, the 'covenant' between spectator and playwright and company is ironically drawn up by a Scrivener.

Chapter 3 Improvisation in the Creation of New Modes of Performance

1. 'Impro-Olympics' (and 'Theatre Sports' generally) are booming, one example being the radio and television improvisation game *Whose Line Is It Anyway?* (see Chapter 4). Games (which also make useful exercises) include 'Authors' (impro on an audience-suggested subject in a given literary style), 'Every Other Line' (one partner reads from a classic play, the other improvises an unrelated scene) and 'Improvising a Rap' (improvising rhyme and rhythm).

2. Also, to Grotowski, 'the actor' means 'an individual in action, who aims not at acting, but at acting less than in daily life and who draws others to the simplest, the most human, the most direct actions' (cited in J. Kumiega 1985: 236).

3. Most quotations by Lecoq in this section are derived from brochures published by the École Jacques Lecoq, 57 rue du Faubourg Saint-Denis, Paris (unless otherwise attributed). These are supplemented by information provided by M. and Mme Lecoq themselves during an interview with the authors in Paris in April 1987. All translations are ours.

4. The systematisation of space in Lecoq's analytical work parallels that of Laban, at least in its recognition that 'There's a link, a reverberation between inner and outer space. If I make a physical action – pulling or pushing – it's analogous to internal emotion, love or hate. An oblique gesture can be sentimental, melodramatic. A vertical gesture is tragic. I indicate passions in space' (Hiley 1988).

5. Lecoq's students are often surprised, at least initially, to discover how much time is taken up by the *auto-cours* – and about how much they are expected to teach themselves. But many of the groups stemming from Lecoq first worked together and first discovered common interests in the *auto-cours* sessions.

6. Lecoq calls it 'a state of unknowing, a state of openness and availability for the rediscovery of the elemental' (1972: 41).

7. We are indebted here to Clive Mendus, who has worked with the Mediaeval Players and Théâtre de Complicité, both for his account of training at Lecoq's school and for excellent workshops on improvisation and clowning based on Lecoq's method. Much of Lecoq's clowning work has been developed by some of his early graduates who returned to teach at the school, in particular Philippe Gaulier.

8. There is an English translation of *Mistero buffo* by Ed Emery (1988).

9. 'In my show, because I've worked on it, and especially because I've worked on it with audiences, I get a thousand or so laughs. Here it's a couple of hundred, because they've cut the translation, chucked out what they don't understand, and distorted the overtly political aspects' (Rame 1983: 115).

10. Fo's *Grammelot* is generically related to Saint-Denis's *Grummelotage* (another variant is the 'Cirquish' invented by the Cirque du Soleil). In 'Dario Fo from One Language to Another', Valéria Tasca (1996) defines *grammelot*, a term deriving from Venetian *commedia*, as 'the semantization of free phonemes'. Ron Jenkins describes Fo, at the site of the Oracle at Delphi, translating 'classical Greek poetry into an onomatopoeic simulation of ancient Greek so convincing that classics scholars claim to understand what he is saying' (Jenkins 2001: 13). He even incorporated *grammelot* into his Swedish Nobel acceptance speech.

11. In a conversation on French TV shortly before Lecoq's death, Fo and Lecoq reminisced about their early work together. Lecoq says, 'We just did it; we just made it up, but we had no idea.' And Fo replies, 'We had to throw away everything and construct a world. The world had to be made all over again' (Murray 2003: 14).

12. 'Franca Rame belongs to a family of travelling players which even under fascism performed in the small towns and villages of Italy. It was in this hard school that she learnt the art of improvisation (at which she excels), of working with a minimum of sets and props, and of making a major contribution to a company in which everyone shares in the organisation of a performance' (Hood 1981: iv). She herself says, 'I was born into a family of actors who also were born into a family of actors and puppeteers going back to the seventeenth century, so my

relationship to the commedia dell'arte is in my DNA' (Rame, cited in Jenkins 2001: 79: and see Rame's biography and archive at www.francarame.it).

13. Perhaps related to Lecoq and Gaulier's fascination with the grotesque figure of the *bouffon* (less well known in the UK than in Europe), who is banished to the marshes and comments ironically and satirically on the – supposedly – normal world around him.

14. Fo's attitude towards the unexpected is equally crucial: the 'accident' is the moment at which radical shifts of perspective become available. Fo quotes an exchange between the Italian *commedia* actors and Molière's troupe, in which the *commedia* players asked the French actors how they would react if the roof of their theatre began to fall in. The Parisian actors replied that they would stop the show immediately (no doubt citing seventeenth-century health and safety regulations). Fo then gives the Italian actors' response:

> That's the difference between our theater of improvisation and a theater that relies entirely on a written script ... You drop the curtains and close down in the face of the unexpected ... For you an accident is problematic. For us it is an advantage. We perform the accident. The collapse of the theater frightens you. For us it would be a stimulus to create something new. (Jenkins 2001: 11)

The French reaction is, interestingly, the exact opposite of what Artaud later recommends, but the ability to benefit from the abnormal and 'perform the accident' is a crucial characteristic of the politics and aesthetics of improvisation.

Chapter 4   Improvisation for Change: 'Paratheatre', Participation and Performance Work beyond the Stage

1. One of the most profound influences on Grotowski's work was Polish director Juliusz Osterwa (1887–1949) who founded the Reduta theatre studio in 1919. This was one of the first theatre *communities*: theatre, acting workshop and school, based on the idea of communal sharing. Similar experiments included that of Copeau at Pernand-Vergelesses; Michel Saint-Denis and Charles Dullin's attempts to set up theatrical communities; Stanislavsky's Studio experiments at Eupatoria (on the Black Sea, where each of the actors built his own house and lived in it, sharing all communal tasks); the Group Theatre in the US tried it in the 1930s, and the Becks' Living Theatre and Peter Schumann's Bread and Puppet Theatre in the 1960s. All these are precedents and examples for Grotowski's later work at Brzezinka.

2. Grotowski was not alone here: it was typical Polish practice of the time. Artist, writer and director Tadeusz Kantor 'minced' texts – both his own and Polish classics – and his performers interacted and exchanged continuously on stage with objects and art works; playwrights Witold Gombrowicz and Tadeusz Różewicz ironised, exploded and fragmented conventional theatrical form. The historical context was the political and linguistic oppression of Poland by the Nazis and the USSR, in which the naked and sacrificial (or, for Różewicz, ironically passive) body and the transgression of imposed form became statements of humanitarian and political resistance.

3. In *Faustus* the audience was seated at refectory tables, partaking in Faust's last supper, while the actors used the table tops as their stages; in *Kordian* the spectators sat on the beds of the asylum in which Grotowski set the play; in *The Constant Prince* the audience surrounded the action and looked down on the martyrdom below with the detachment/involvement of observers at a medical operation; and in *Akropolis* they sat on platforms in the midst of the concentration camp – by the end of the play they were hemmed in by metal junk, suggesting oppression and, ultimately, the crematorium.

4. The phases of this work are:
   1969–73: 'paratheatre', working from Polish Laboratory Theatre
   1976–82: Theatre of Sources, working in the Polish forest
   1983–6: 'Objective Drama', based at University of California, Irvine
   1986–99: 'Art as Vehicle', based at the Workcenter of Jerzy Grotowski in Pontedera, Italy

5. The reader is referred to Rene Marineau's excellent attempts to decipher what were probably deliberate obfuscations of Moreno's early life (see Gale 1990).

6. See the Vereinigung Bildender Künstlerinnen Österreichs website http://www.vbk.org/jakob_levy_moreno_elisabeth_bergner.html (accessed on 26 June 2006).

7. This is now disputed: Bergner knew him well, but there's little evidence she acted for him at this time. Lorre, on the other hand, certainly got his start in *Das Stegreiftheater*.

8. See http://www.vbk.org/jakob_levy_moreno_elisabeth_ bergner.html.

9. These concepts and associated exercises are discussed in more detail, for example in Gale 1990: Chapters 2 and 3; many will be familiar to drama students and resemble exercises discussed elsewhere in this book.

10. In Playback Theatre in the US, longer stories have sometimes been given different names. Lucy Smith notes that whereas Jo Salas calls them 'Scenes', she was told of an American facilitator describing this as 'Story Form'. In Ireland and the UK, as otherwise in the US, it is known as 'Long Form' (not the same as Keith Johnstone's one-and-a-half hour longform). Melbourne Playback Theatre also uses the term 'Long Form'. A full story in Playback may be performed in twenty minutes, depending on the actors' and musicians' interpretation (Smith 2015).

11. A central tenet of Paulo Freire's *Pedagogy of the Oppressed* is the empowerment of the learner through recognition of his/her agency. See *Pedagogy of the Oppressed*, translated from the Portuguese by Myra Bergman Ramos (Harmondsworth: Penguin, 1972). Boal and Freire emerged from the same socio-political situation and knew each other; Boal deliberately reflected Freire's title in his own *Theatre of the Oppressed* (first published in 1974).

Chapter 5   Improvisation in Non-Western Performance

1. Zarrilli *et al.* (2006), although claiming to 'relate the histories of performance and theatre throughout the world to the key developments in modes of human communication' (xvii), make only five references to improvisation – and only one to Jacques Lecoq, whose name is misspelt.

2. Literally, 'the place that receives the light' (Watson 2001: 91). See also (Coldiron 2004: 92–9); she indicates that *taksu*, like the Noh *hana*, is a 'performance state' comparable to Csíkszentmihályi's 'flow' – 'merging of action and awareness' (Coldiron 2004: 45).

3. There may be parallels here with the Dutch colonialist character in some *Topeng* performance and the figure of the English *sahib* in Indian folk forms. Both tend to be used as comic relief.

4. In other contexts the term has more profound and theological connotations: the root meaning is 'imitation'. The cognate Turkish term is *taklit*.

5. *Orta* = middle and *oyun* = play: hence 'play in the middle'; *meidan oyunu* means 'play in the open air' or 'play in the round'.

6. In the late nineteenth and twentieth centuries occasional indoor performances were given in large coffee houses or even in Western-style theatres, with audiences segregated by sex. There was a single stage entrance, and (until Kemal Atatürk's social reforms of the 1920s) women in the audience sat opposite it, physically segregated from the men, obscured from the male gaze and from the stage behind a large veil. These women's areas were called *kefes*, or 'cages'.

7. This probably relates to the Anatolian narrative tradition where the *meddah* ('praisegiver', 'panegyrist') or storyteller's solo performance peoples the audience's imaginary stage and to the shadow play, where the *haialdji's* mimicry conjures forth a host of characters from behind the screen. Much African storytelling adopts a similar mode.

8. Usually he is shorter and squatter than Pişekâr, though both of them are typically middle-aged or elderly characters in traditional Turkish dress and form an eternal dyad identical to that of Karagöz and Hadjeivat in the shadow play. Tosun Effendi carries a cudgel as Karagöz sometimes does (both deriving perhaps from an earlier phallophoric comedy) and often lays about him with it.

9. Barber and her collaborators all had the experience of participating in the forms they describe as well as recording them anthropologically. Collins played as a bandsman in the Ghanaian 'Jaguar Jokers' concert party; Ricard made a film about concert party in Lomé; Barber herself acted in small roles with the Oyin Adéjobi Yorùbá popular theatre company.

10. For example, under apartheid, in the work of Athol Fugard with John Kani and Winston Ntshona (*Sizwe Bansi is Dead, The Island*); Barney Simon with Percy Mtwa and Mbongemi Ngema (*Woza Albert*); Workshop 71 and later Junction Avenue (*Sophiatown, Randlords* and *Rotgut* – Malcolm Purkey with the improvisations of the late Ramolao Makhene and others); Handspring Puppet Co. (*Ubu and the Truth Commission, Woyzeck on the Highveld*).

Chapter 6   Preparation

1. Stanislavsky was introduced to *prana yoga* by L. A. Sulerzhitsky (1872–1916). François Delsarte (1811–71) was the first to propound a modern *system of movement* (as opposed to a system of teaching dance). He influenced Émile Jaques-Dalcroze (1865–1950) whose work captivated Copeau and Bing and also powerfully affected Adolphe Appia and Margaret Naumburg. F. Mathias Alexander (1869–1955) remains influential in acting and dance training in Britain and North America especially (thanks initially to Naumburg and John Dewey). The *Méthode naturelle* exercises of Georges Hébert (1875–1957) profoundly affected both Copeau's early work and the young Jacques Lecoq. Continuing to have major influence on dance training throughout Europe, Rudolf Laban (1879–1958) had an impact also on British theatre practitioners like Joan Littlewood and her Theatre Workshop as well as many leading drama schools and university drama departments.

2.   It has been followed by many other books; see Bibliography, and especially Boal
     (1992), Callery (2001), Johnston (1998) and Poulter (1987).

Chapter 8   Moving towards Performance

1.   Proust calls it 'involuntary memory'; believing that it gives us access to the *moi
     permanent* (a sense of self as more than transitory, extending across time, as a
     capacity for cognitive and affective experience), he makes it the core of his life's
     work about the processes of memory, imagination and artistic construction.
2.   See also Grotowski: 'I want to advise you never in the performance to seek for
     spontaneity without a score. In the exercises it is a different thing altogether ...
     Today ... I will create these details and you can try to find their different varia-
     tions and justifications. This will give you an authentic improvisation – other-
     wise you will be building without foundations' (1968: 192).
3.   'All that is on the stage is a sign' was the central tenet of the Prague structur-
     alist Jiri Veltrusky. Everything seen, heard or sensed, including all aspects of
     the actor's present behaviour, has *significance* and becomes available for mean-
     ing-making. In the case of improvisation, major signifiers may be the hesita-
     tions, breathiness, discomfort of the *actor*, rather than the intended signified of
     the character or narrative. Improvisers need to be in control of the signs they
     produce and to draw selectively upon their inner repertoire (see Veltrusky 1940:
     7). We shall make further reference to this idea in Part 3.
4.   Eldredge interviewed or studied with, *inter alia*, Tom Leabhart (the Decroux mime
     specialist), Jacques Lecoq, Bari Rolfe, Carlo Mazzone-Clementi, Peter Schumann
     (of Bread and Puppet Theater), Copeau's daughter Marie-Hélène Dasté and the
     family of W. T. Benda (see below, this chapter, pp. 185–6).
5.   Eldredge regards them as 'wonderful masks, but ... increasingly questionable
     in our multicultural age because their physiognomy immediately signals their
     European heritage ... No one Neutral Mask is appropriate for everyone in our
     diverse culture. The advantage of the simple paper Neutral Mask is that it is
     more abstract. It signals "human face" but has less indication of a particular
     nationality' (1996: 43). We disagree and suggest that the neutral mask signals its
     own *theatricality*. The Sartori-derived neutral mask isn't gendered or suggestive
     of ethnicity: its gaze is not locatable in terms of culture or biology (no one's skin
     is *that* shade of leather). We simply say, 'One mask is slightly bigger than the
     other; choose the one that feels most comfortable on your face.'
6.   Cf. '*Noh* and *Topeng* masks cover either slightly less than the full face or ... the
     upper part of the face only' (Emigh 2004: xvi). Strindberg envisioned the use of
     similar masks by Ensor for *A Dream Play*.
7.   By 'Stanislavsky's psychological model', Eldredge means the 'internal conflict
     between the character's persona and his "real Self"'; by the Brechtian model, a
     'focus on the dialectics of the character', either 'rooted in the external social,
     economic, and political forces' or 'between the psychophysical life of the mask
     (the character) and that of the actor playing the part' (Eldredge 1996: 99–100).
8.   The Tunisian Lassaâd Saïdi (b. 1951), chief exponent of this teaching method,
     was an associate of Lecoq for ten years. His work was taught in Britain by, es-
     pecially, the Lecoq-derived I Gelati group (whose name is a pun on the famous
     commedia troupe, I Gelosi) led by director James MacDonald and Malcolm Tulip
     in the 1980s.

9. Another technique we have found useful is to imagine a scene as a double-act by two cross-talk comedians who have to talk to each other via the audience, standing shoulder to shoulder but looking away from each other so that the focus is always outwards.

10. The idea of Pantalone as a rooster was first suggested by Pierre Duchartre (1924/1929) and eagerly seized upon by Copeau, who played Pantalone and from whom the modern tradition stems. Amusingly, Lecoq – whose name implies a rooster – also specialised in the Mask of Pantalone!

11. Trestle Theatre Company was founded in 1981 by Toby Wilsher and John Wright. Wright is also the co-founder of Told By An Idiot and of the Wright School. His book on comedy (Wright 2006) contains over a hundred games and exercises. Trestle's shows include: *Plastered* (1984); *Top Storey* (1987); *Fool House* (1997); *The Barretts of Wimpole Street* (2000); and *Beyond Midnight* (2005). Improbable Theatre was founded in 1996 by Phelim McDermott, Julian Crouch and Lee Simpson with producer Nick Sweeting; their plays which use masking include *Lifegame* (1996 onwards); *Shockheaded Peter* (1998; actually a Cultural Industry show) and their collaboration with AMICI Dance Theatre Company, *Stars are Out Tonight* (2005) – a piece which simply defies the term 'disability' and demonstrates the psychosocial and political dimensions which increasingly frequently develop from improvisatory work. Geese Theatre (founded in America by John Bergman – who was influenced by Clive Barker – in 1980, and now running in both the US and UK) have always specialised in work in prisons, and make considerable use not only of improvised work but of archetypal masks and Sally Brookes's 'fragment' masks (see Callery 2001: 51).

12. There are other mask teachers who would offer the same thing, for example Simon (2003).

Chapter 9   Improvisation for Scene-Building

1. See also mnemonic games as learning strategies in Buzan (1974).

Chapter 10   Enriching the Communication of Meaning

1. See Blatner (1970, table 4, 131); Jennings (1973, 1988, 1993, 1994); Hodgson (1972); Bentley (1973); Watson (1988); Pörtner (1967); Moreno (1946, 1959); also Yon (1979–80: 42).

2. The (mild, and often mildly absurd – if exasperating) censorship of British drama before 1968 is full of directives to cut stage business as well as the spoken part of the text: 'there must be no scratching of private parts' (*Meals on Wheels*, Charles Wood); 'The statue of President Johnson must not be naked' (*Mrs Wilson's Diary*, Richard Ingrams and John Wells); 'It is understood that, wherever the word "shit" appears, it will be altered, in every case, to "it"' (*Spare*, again by Charles Wood) (Findlater 1967).

3. Protest had a literature, exemplified by writers such as Colin Wilson and Kingsley Amis, and the borrowed writings of Jack Kerouac and Allen Ginsberg. John Osborne gave it a dramatic literature. It found its own proper musical form in affinity with the free, improvised art of jazz.

4. 'Theatre-people must always have found their marginalization puzzling. Non-theatre-people kept accusing them of practising deception, not understanding how one can live with the creation of artefacts that have no continuous material base; theatre-people shrug: we live in a world of elusive temporality; isn't that what the world is actually like? They always knew that their worlds were "unreal", the product of their wills, consciousness, perceptions, sensations, desires, that they had no substance, no "self". Paradoxically, it was theatre-people who never made the cognitive mistake which Buddhists spend their lives refuting. No-one needed to tell them about dependency arising, impermanence, temporality, insubstantiality, no-thing-ness' (George 1999: 35).

Chapter 11   Meaning and Performance

1. Roland Barthes thought of theatre as a paradigm for semiological analysis; so dense and rich are its signs that they offer 'a real informational polyphony' which often daunts the analyst – who retreats into textual study (Barthes 1964, trans. Howard 1972: 262; see also Elam 1980: 19).
2. In Charles Saunders Peirce's triadic semiotic system, an 'icon' is a sign that is similar to what it represents (the masked actor looks like the imagined demon or god – colourful, impressive, larger than life, inhuman; the mask purports to be, and is assumed to be, an image, a likeness of the spirit). An 'index' is a sign that points to other realities (the mask points to the godliness of the performer). A 'symbol' is a sign bearing imputed, learned associations (the colour red stands for the demonic, for example, or green for heroism).
3. In the Indian *Ramlila*, the child actor playing Rama is often described (by outsiders) as passive and immobile. To the Western way of thinking, the signs transmitted are mostly those of the actor's 'inadequacies'. Not so the Indian spectator. To the devotee, the child is holy – Shiva incarnated. As such he does not need to do anything. He has only to be there. His presence provides the necessary visual focus for the act of devotion. It is the spectator who is active and the actor who is passive: the boy player is the blank slate upon which the spectator 'writes' the real drama of the event.
4. The terms figure in Russian Formalism (as does *ostranenie* – recycled by Brecht as *Verfremdung*) and fantasy theory: markers of the cognitive leap from the recognised to the unknown.
5. Devising has its own extensive literature, theory and techniques: see Oddey (1994), Lamden (2000), Bicât and Baldwin (2002) and Heddon and Milling (2006).
6. Close and Halpern's exercises include: 'What makes this day different?' (Halpern *et al.* 1994: 82); 'Start in the middle' (83), 'Finding the scene' and 'Listening for the game' (81ff.): all enjoyable and extremely useful. John Wright's *Why is That So Funny?* (2006) contains many remarkable exercises, including 'Five Steps to Heaven' (172–3), which uses Lecoq's tension cycle to discuss how to 'set-up' comic (and dramatic) scenes.
7. John Wright affectionately characterises Lecoq as 'a confrontational teacher', whose use of the *via negativa* is defined as 'a strategy where the teacher restricts comment to the negative, namely what is *inappropriate* and unacceptable, thus forcing the student to discover what is *appropriate*, whilst avoiding being

prescriptive … (compelling) each individual to find his or her own way in the work through watching, listening and eventually taking a risk in front of the audience. These are invaluable skills for a theatre artist which, in the devising process, have to be found under pressure' (in Chamberlain and Yarrow 2002: 72). Wright and Murray both regard Lecoq's use of the *via negativa* as a way of destabilising and energising his students. Al Wunder deliberately avoids it because, for him, it demoralises the actor while providing no assistance in finding a solution to the perceived problem.

Bibliography

*practical manual, or work containing exercises

Abbott, John, *The Improvisation Book* (London: Nick Hern Books, 2007).*

Abbott, John, *Improvisation in Rehearsal* (London: Nick Hern Books, 2009).*

Ahluwalia, Kiran, quoted in Rockwell, 2005.

Alfreds, Mike, *A Shared Experience: The Actor as Story Teller* [interview by Peter Hulton, London, June 1979], Dartington Theatre Papers, 3rd series, No. 6 (1979–80).

Alfreds, Mike, *Different Every Night: Freeing the Actor* (London: Nick Hearn Books, 2007).*

Allain, Paul, *The Theatre Practice of Tadashi Suzuki: A Critical Study with DVD Examples* (London: Methuen, 2009).*

Althusser, Louis, 'Notes towards an Investigation', in *Lenin and Philosophy and Other Essays*, trans. Ben Brewster (New York: Monthly Review Press, 1971).

Amor Fati website: http://fate.laiv.org/in_arti.htm, an extensive electronic library which includes articles on dramaturgy and improvisation in relation to LARPing, for example, Brian David Philips, 'Interactive Drama: Deconstructing Theatre' (1996), and Susanne Graslünds, 'Building Dramatics' (n.d., *c.*2001), about story-telling in LARP.

And, Metin, *Karagöz: Turkish Shadow Theatre* (Istanbul: Dost, 1975; rev. ed. 1979).

Aristotle, 'The Poetics' [*c.*330 BC], in *Classical Literary Criticism*, trans. T. S. Dorsch (Harmondsworth: Penguin, 1965).

Artaud, Antonin, 'Production and Metaphysics' and 'On the Balinese Theatre', in *Le Théâtre et son Double* (Paris, 1938), trans. Victor Corti as *The Theatre and its Double* (London: Calder & Boyars, 1970).

Atkinson, Jane Monnig and Errington, Shelley (eds), *Power and Difference: Gender in Island Southeast Asia* (Stanford, CA: Stanford University Press, 1990).

Babbage, Frances, *Augusto Boal* (London: Routledge, 2004).*

Baim, Clark, Brookes, Sally and Mountford, Alun, *The Geese Theatre Handbook: Drama with Offenders and People at Risk* (Winchester: Waterside Press, 2002).*

Bakhtin, Mikhail, *Rabelais and His World* (Moscow, 1965), trans. Hélène Iswolsky (Cambridge, MA: MIT Press, 1968).

Bame, Kwabena N., *Come to Laugh: A Study of African Traditional Theatre in Ghana* (New York: Lilian Barber Press, 1985); cited in Etherton (1988); and Barber (2000).

Banham, Martin (ed), *The Cambridge Guide to World Theatre* (Cambridge: Cambridge University Press, 1988).

Banu, Georges, 'Peter Brook's Six Days', trans. Susan Bassnett, *New Theatre Quarterly*, 3/10 (May 1987).

Barba, Eugenio, *The Floating Islands: Reflections with Odin Teatret*, ed. Ferdinando Taviani (Holstebro: Odin Teatret, 1979).

Barba, Eugenio, *Beyond the Floating Islands* (New York: Performing Arts Journal, 1986).

Barba, Eugenio, *The Paper Canoe: A Guide to Theatre Anthropology* (London: Routledge, 1995).

Barba, Eugenio, *Land of Ashes and Diamonds: My Apprenticeship in Poland*, trans. Judy Barba (Aberystwyth: Black Mountain Press, Centre for Performance Research, 1999).

Barba, Eugenio, 'Children of Silence: Reflections on Forty Years of Odin Teatret', trans. from Italian by Judy Barba, in Odin Teatret, Programme booklet for *Andersens Drøm* (Holstebro, 2005), pp. 50–61.

Barba, Eugenio, 'Improvisation: Memory, Repetition, Discontinuity', in The Programme of the 14th ISTA, on Improvisation, Held at Wrocław and Krzyżowa, April 2005.

Barba, Eugenio, Speech of Thanks on the Occasion of the Honorary Degree of Doctor of Letters Bestowed on Eugenio Barba by Queen Margaret University, Edinburgh, 1 July 2014.

Barba, Eugenio and Savarese, Nicola, *A Dictionary of Theatre Anthropology: The Secret Art of the Performer* (London: Routledge, 1991).

Barber, Karin, *The Generation of Plays: Yorùbá Popular Life in Theater* (Bloomington: Indiana University Press, 2000).

Barber, Karin, Collins, John and Ricard, Alain, *West African Popular Theatre* (Bloomington: Indiana University Press; Oxford: James Currey, 1997).

Barker, Clive, *Theatre Games: A New Approach to Drama Training* (London: Eyre Methuen, 1977).*

Barthes, Roland, 'Literature and Signification', in *Essais Critiques* (Paris: Seuil, 1964), trans. Richard Howard as *Critical Essays* (Evanston, IL: Northwestern University Press, 1972), pp. 261–7.

Bauer, Roger and Jürgen, Wertheimer (eds), *Das Ende des Stegreifspiels – die Geburt des Nationaltheaters: ein Wendepunkt in der Geschichte des europäischen Dramas* (Munich: Wilhelm Fink, 1983).

Beare, W., *The Roman Stage* (London: Methuen, 1950; 3rd ed. 1964).

Beckett, Samuel, *'Proust' and 'Three Dialogues with Georges Duthuit'* (originally published in *Transition*, 1949; London: John Calder, 1965).

Beckett, Samuel, *The Beckett Trilogy*, comprising *Molloy, Malone Dies* and *The Unnamable* (first published London: Calder, 1959; London: Picador, 1979).

Beeman, William Orman, 'Middle East', in M. Banham (ed), *The Cambridge Guide to World Theatre* (Cambridge: Cambridge University Press, 1988; rev. ed. 1992), pp. 664–76, esp. pp. 669–70.

Belgrad, Daniel, *The Culture of Spontaneity* (Chicago, IL: University of Chicago Press, 1998); cited in Heddon and Milling (2006), p. 8.

Benda, Władysław Teodor, *Masks* (New York: Watson-Guptill Publications, 1944).

Benda, Władysław Teodor, 'How Benda Revived the Use of Masks', *Boston Transcript* (17 April 1926); cited in Eldredge (1996), p. 171.

Benda, Władysław Teodor, 'Masks On the Stage and Off', *Ladies Home Journal* (1926), reproduced on http://www.americanartsarchives.com/benda.html (accessed 17 April 2014).

Benedetti, Jean, *Stanislavski and the Actor* (London: Methuen, 1998). [An attempt to reconstruct Stanislavsky's actor-training exercises at the Opera-Dramatic Studio.]*

Benedetti, Jean, *The Art of the Actor: The Essential History of Acting from Classical Times to the Present Day* (London: Methuen, 2005).

Bentley, Eric, 'Epilogue: Theatre and Therapy', in Eric Bentley (ed), *Theatre of War: Modern Drama from Ibsen to Brecht* (originally published 1969 in *New American Review*; New York: Viking Press, 1973), pp. 213–29.

Bezā'í, Bahrām, *Namāyesh Dar Irān* ['Performance in Iran'] (Tehran: Roshangaran, 1965, reprinted 2001), p. 55, trans. and cited in Beeman (1992), p. 667.

Bicât, Tina and Baldwin, Chris (eds), *Devised and Collaborative Theatre: A Practical Guide* (Ramsbury: Crowood Press, 2002).*

Blatner, Adam (ed), *Interactive and Improvisational Drama: Varieties of Applied Theatre and Performance* (New York: iUniverse, 2007).

Blatner, Howard, *Psychodrama, Role-Playing and Action Methods: Theory and Practice* (private publication, 1970). See esp. Table 4.

Boal, Augusto, *Games for Actors and Non-Actors*, trans. Adrian Jackson (London: Routledge, 1992a).*

Boal, Augusto, *The Rainbow of Desire*, trans. Adrian Jackson (London: Routledge, 1992b).*

Bøckman, Petter and Hutchison, Ragnhild (eds), *Dissecting Larp* (2005); published to accompany the Knutepunkt (2005), available at http://knutepunkt.laiv.org/ (accessed 2007).

Bogard, Travis, 'American Drama', in *The Revels History of Drama in English* (London: Methuen, 1977), vol. 8.

Boleslavsky, Richard, *Acting: The First Six Lessons* (New York: Theatre Arts Books, 1934).

Bolton, Gavin, *Drama as Education: An Argument for Placing Drama at the Centre of the Curriculum* (Harlow: Longman, 1984).

Boyd, Neva Leona, *Handbook of Recreational Games* (Chicago, IL: Fitzsimmons, 1945; reprinted New York: Dover, 1975).*

Bradby, David, *Modern French Drama, 1940–1980* (Cambridge: Cambridge University Press, 1984).

Bradby, David and Delgado, Maria M. (eds), *The Paris Jigsaw* (London: Routledge, 2002).

Brakel, Clara and Moreh, Shmuel, 'The Term *Bâba* in Traditional Arab and Javanese Masked Theatre', in Clara Brakel (ed), *Performing Arts of Asia: The Performer as (Inter)Cultural Transmitter* (Leiden: International Institute for Asian Studies Working Papers, Series 4, 1996), pp. 35–46.

Braun, Edward, *Meyerhold on Theatre* (New York: Hill & Wang, 1969).

Brenne, Geir Tore, 'Making and Maintaining Frames: A Study of Metacommunication in Laiv Play', MA thesis, University of Oslo (2005), available at http://fate.laiv.org/pub/gtb_opp.htm (accessed 5 June 2015).

Breton, André, *Manifesto of Surrealism* (Paris: Editions du Sagittaire, 1924).

Brook, Peter, *The Empty Space* (London: McGibbon & Kee, 1968).

Brook, Peter, *The Shifting Point: Forty Years of Theatrical Exploration, 1946–1987* (London: Methuen, 1988).

Brown, Frederick, *Theatre and Revolution: The Culture of the French Stage* (New York: Viking Press, 1980).

Browne, Maurice, *Too Late to Lament* (Bloomington: Indiana University Press, 1956).

Browne, Terry, *Playwrights' Theatre* (London: Pitman, 1975).

Brunette, Peter, 'Interview with Mike Leigh', 1991; in Movshovitz (ed) (2000), pp. 31–2.

Buber, Martin, *Ich und Du* (1923; 2nd ed, Jerusalem, 1957), trans. Walter Kaufman as *I and Thou* (Edinburgh: T. & T. Clark, 1970).

Burgess, Thomas de Mallet and Skilbeck, Nicholas, *The Singing and Acting Handbook: Games and Exercises for the Performer* (London: Routledge, 2000).*

Burzyński, Tadeusz, 'Away from Theatre', in T. Burzyński and Z. Osiński (eds), *Grotowski's Laboratory* (Warsaw: Interpress, 1979).

Buzan, Tony, *Use Your Head* (London: BBC Publications, 1974).

Caillois, Roger, *Man, Play and Games* (London: Thames & Hudson, 1962).

Callery, Dymphna, *Through the Body: A Practical Guide to Physical Theatre* (London: Nick Hern Books; New York: Routledge, 2001).*

Campbell, Ken, in Irvine, 2005.

Capra, Fritjof, *The Tao of Physics* (London: Fontana, 1976).

Carlson, Marvin, *Performance: A Critical Introduction* (London: Routledge, 1996).

Carney, Ray, *The Films of John Cassavetes: Pragmatism, Modernism and the Movies* (New York: Cambridge University Press, 1994).

Carney, Ray, *Cassavetes on Cassavetes* (London: Faber & Faber, 2001).

Carnicke, Sharon Marie, *Stanislavsky in Focus* (London: Harwood Academic, 1998).

Carnicke, Sharon Marie, 'Stanislavsky's System', in Alison Hodge (ed), *Twentieth-Century Actor Training* (London: Routledge, 2000), pp. 11–36.

Carnicke, Sharon Marie, 'Stanislavsky: Uncensored and Unabridged', in Schneider and Gabrielle Cody (eds), *Re:Direction: A Theoretical and Practical Guide* (London: Routledge, 2002), pp. 28–39.

Casson, John W., 'Living Newspaper: Theatre and Therapy', *The Drama Review*, 44/2 (Summer 2000), pp. 107–22.

Chamberlain, Franc, 'Michael Chekhov on the Technique of Acting', in Alison Hodge (ed), *Twentieth Century Actor Training* (London: Routledge, 2000a), pp. 79–97.

Chamberlain, Franc, 'Theatre Anthropology: Definitions and Doubts', in Anthony Frost (ed), *Theatre Theories: From Plato to Virtual Reality* (Norwich: Pen & Inc, 2000b), pp. 171–94.

Chamberlain, Franc, *Michael Chekhov* (London: Routledge, 2004).*

Chamberlain, Franc and Yarrow, Ralph (eds), *Jacques Lecoq and the British Theatre* (London: Routledge Harwood, 2002).

Charles, David, *The Novelty of Improvisation: Towards a Genre of Embodied Spontaneity*, PhD dissertation, Louisiana State University and Agricultural and Mechanical College, 2003 (online at etd.lsu.edu).

Charles, David, *A New Paradigm of Popular Play: Playback as Bakhtinian Novelistic Theatre* (New Paltz, NY: Centre for Playback Theatre, online at playbacktheatre.org, 2005).

Chekhov, Michael, *Lessons for the Professional Actor* (New York: PAJ Books, 1985).

Chekhov, Michael, *Lessons for Teachers of his Acting Technique* (Ottawa: Dovehouse, 2000).

Chekhov, Michael, *The Path of the Actor*, ed. Andrei Kirillov and Bella Merlin (London: Routledge, 2005). [Combines Chekhov's 1927 autobiography of this title and extensive extracts from his later *Life and Encounters*.]

Ciantar, Philip, 'From the Bar to the Stage: Socio-Musical Processes in the Maltese *Spirtu Pront*', Peer-Reviewed Electronic Journal (2000), available at http://www.fondazionelevy.it/ma/index/number5/ciantar/cia_1.htm (accessed 3 April 2015).

Clements, Paul, *The Improvised Play: The Work of Mike Leigh* (London: Methuen Theatrefile, 1983).

Clurman, Harold, *The Fervent Years: Group Theatre and the Thirties* (New York: Harcourt Brace Jovanovich, 1975; reprinted New York: Da Capo, 1988).

Coburn, Veronica and Morrison, Sue, *Clown Through Mask: The Pioneering Work of Richard Pochinko as Practised by Sue Morrison* (Bristol: Intellect, 2013).

Coldiron, Margaret, *Trance and Transformation of the Actor in Japanese Noh and Balinese Masked Dance-Drama* (Lewiston, NY: Edwin Mellen, 2004).

Cole, Toby (ed), *Actors on Acting: The Theories, Techniques and Practices of the Great Actors of All Times as Told in their Own Words* (New York: Crown, 1949).

Cole, Toby (ed), *Playwrights on Playwriting: The Meaning and Making of Modern Drama from Ibsen to Ionesco* (New York: Hill & Wang, 1961).

Coleman, Janet, *The Compass: The Improvisational Theatre that Revolutionized American Comedy* (Chicago, IL: University of Chicago Press, 1991).

Copeau, Jacques, 'Notes sur l'education de l'acteur', in *Ecrits sur le Théâtre* (Paris: Michel Brient, 1955).

Copeau, Jacques, *Essai de Rénovation Dramatique* (Paris: Theatre du Vieux-Colombier, 1913), trans. and cited in Roose-Evans (1970).

Copeau, Jacques, *Registres 1. Appels, textes recueillis et établis par Marie-Hélène Dasté et Suzanne Maistre Saint-Denis et al.* (vol. 1, Paris: Gallimard, 1974).

Copeau, Jacques, *Brochure*, [Prospectus] of ideal training school, quoted at length in Rudlin (1986a), pp. 43–4.

Copeau, Jacques, *A Notebook* in the Dasté Collection; cited in Rudlin (1986b).

Copeau, Jacques, *Journal: texte établi*, ed. and annotated Claude Sicard, 2 vols (Paris: Edition Seghers, 1991).

Cossa, Mario, Fleishmann Ember, Sally S., Grover, Lauren and Hazlewood, Jennifer L., *Acting Out: The Workbook* (New York: Brunner-Routledge, 1996).*

Counsell, Colin, *Signs of Performance: An Introduction to Twentieth-Century Theatre* (London: Routledge, 1996).

Courtney, Richard, *Play, Drama and Thought: The Intellectual Background to Drama in Education* (London: Cassell/Collier Macmillan, 1968; 3rd rev. and enlarged ed. 1974).

Coveney, Michael, *The World According to Mike Leigh* (London: Harper Collins, 1996).

Darby, Kris, 'Our Encore: Running from the Zombie 2.0', *Studies in Theatre and Performance* (eds Lee Miller, Roberta Mock and Phil Smith), Vol. 34, No. 3 (2014), pp. 229–35.

Darling Khan, Susannah and Ya'Acov, *Movement Medicine: How to Awaken, Dance and Live Your Dreams* (London: Hay House, 2009).

Davis, Miles, *Kind of Blue* (New York: Columbia Records, 1959). (Number twelve on *Rolling Stone Magazine*'s list of the 500 greatest albums.)

Davison, Jon, *Clown* (Basingstoke: Palgrave Macmillan, 2013).

Derrida, Jacques, *L'Ecriture et la Différence* (Paris: Seuil, 1978), trans. A. Bass as *Writing and Difference* (London: Routledge & Kegan Paul, 1979).

Dewey, John, 'Introduction', in F. M. Alexander (ed), *Constructive Conscious Control of the Individual* (London: E. P. Dutton, 1923; reprinted London: Gollancz, 1987).

Doisy, Marcel, *Jacques Copeau ou l'Absolu dans l'art* (Paris: Le Cercle du livre, 1954).

Donahue, Thomas J., 'Improvisation and the Mask at the École du Vieux-Colombier: The Case of Suzanne Bing', *Maske und Kothurn*, Vol. 44 (2001), pp. 61–72.

Double, Oliver, *Getting the Joke*, 2nd ed. (London: Bloomsbury, 2014) (esp. pp. 351–64 on Improvisation in Stand-up).*

Drewal, Margaret Thompson, *Yoruba Ritual: Performer, Play, Agency* (Bloomington: Indiana University Press, 1992); cited in Karin Barber, *The Generation of Plays: Yorùbá Popular Life in Theater* (Bloomington: Indiana University Press, 2000).

Drinko, Clayton D., *Theatrical Improvisation, Consciousness, and Cognition* (New York: Palgrave Macmillan, 2013).

Duchartre, P. L., *La Comédie italienne* (Paris, 1929), trans. R. T. Weaver as *The Italian Comedy: The Improvisation Scenarios, Lives, Attributes, Portraits and Masks of the Illustrious Characters of the Commedia dell'Arte* (1929; New York: Dover, 1966).

Duffy, Margaret, M., *The Roots of American Improvisation: Play, Process, and Pedagogy*, ProQuest Dissertations, Ann Arbor, MI, 2011.

Elam, Keir, *The Semiotics of Theatre and Drama* (London: Methuen, 1980).

Eldredge, Sears A., *Mask and Improvisation for Actor Training and Performance: The Compelling Image* (Evanston, IL: Northwestern University Press, 1996).*

Eldredge, Sears A. and Huston, Hollis W., 'Actor Training in the Neutral Mask', *The Drama Review*, 22/4 (December 1978), Workshop Issue, 140–7. Also reprinted in Zarrilli (2002).*

Emigh, John, *Masked Performance: The Play of Self and Other in Ritual and Theatre* (Philadelphia: University of Pennsylvania Press, 1996).

Emigh, John, 'Preface', in Margaret Coldiron (ed), *Trance and Transformation of the Actor in Japanese Noh and Balinese Masked Dance-Drama* (Lewiston, NY: Edwin Mellen, 2004).

Etherton, Michael, 'Ghana', in M. Banham (ed), *The Cambridge Guide to World Theatre* (Cambridge: Cambridge University Press, 1988; rev. ed. 1992), pp. 392–4.

Evans, Mark, *Jacques Copeau* (London: Routledge, 2006).*

Farrell, Joseph, *Dario Fo and Franca Rame: Harlequins of the Revolution* (London: Methuen, 2001).

Fava, Antonio, *The Comic Mask in the Commedia dell'Arte: Actor Training, Improvisation and the Poetics of Survival* (Chicago, IL: Northwestern University Press, 2006).

Feldenkrais, Moshé, 'Image, Movement, and Actor: Restoration of Potentiality' [interview with Richard Schechner], *Tulane Drama Review*, 10/3 (1966), 117ff.

Feldenkrais, Moshé, *Awareness through Movement: Health Exercises for Personal Growth* (New York: Harper & Row, 1972; London: Arkana, Penguin Books, 1990).*

Felner, Mira, *Apostles of Silence* (Toronto: Associated University Presses, 1985).

Féral, Josette, 'Building up the Muscle: An Interview with Ariane Mnouchkine', in Schneider and Cody (eds) (2002), pp. 258–65.

Ferguson, Marilyn, *The Aquarian Conspiracy* (Los Angeles, CA: J. P. Tarcher, 1980).

Findlater, Richard, *Banned! A Review of Theatrical Censorship in Britain* (London: MacGibbon & Kee, 1967).

Flaszen, Ludwik, *Cyrograf* ('The Bond') (2nd ed., Kraców: Wydawnictwo Literackie, 1974); cited in Kumiega (1985).

Fleishman, Mark, interview with Ralph Yarrow (22 July 2005).

Fo, Dario, *Mistero buffo; Giullarata popolare nuova edizione aggiornata nei testi e nelle note* [1969] (Verona: Bertoni, 1977).

Fo, Dario, interview, *Playboy*, Italian issue (December 1974); cited in Mitchell (1984).

Fo, Dario, *Accidental Death of an Anarchist* programme, Washington Arena Stage production (1984); cited in Mitchell (1984).

Fo, Dario, *Manuale minimo dell'attore* (Milan: Einaudi, 1987), trans. J. Farrell as *The Tricks of the Trade* (London: Methuen, 1991).*

Fo, Dario, *Mistero buffo – Comic Mysteries*, trans. Ed Emery (London: Methuen, 1988).

Fo, Dario and Rame, Franca, *Theatre Workshops at Riverside Studios, London* (London: Red Notes, 1983).*

Forsberg, Linnea and Josephine, *Improvisation for Speech and Theater* (Dubuque: Kendall Hunt, 2010; 2nd rev. ed. 2012 by Linnea Forsberg).

Foster, Hal, *The Return of the Real: The Avant-Garde at the End of the Century* (Cambridge: MIT Press, 1996).

Fotis, Matt, *Long Form Improvisation and American Comedy: The Harold* (Basingstoke: Palgrave Macmillan, 2014).

Fowler, Richard, 'The Four Theatres of Jerzy Grotowski: An Introductory Assessment', *New Theatre Quarterly*, 1/2 (May 1985), 173–8.

Fox, Jonathan, *Acts of Service: Spontaneity, Commitment, Tradition in the Nonscripted Drama* (New Paltz, NY: Tusitala Publishing, 1994; reprinted 2003).

Frank, Waldo, *The Art of the Vieux-Colombier* (New York: Nouvelle Revue Française, 1918).

Fritz, Birgit, *InExActArt: The Autopoietic Theatre of Augusto Boal*, trans. Lana Sendzimir and Ralph Yarrow (Stuttgart: Ibidem, 2012).*

Fritz, Birgit, 'Auf den Spuren des revolutionären Theaters von Augusto Boal zur autopoietischen Theaterarbeit ins 21. Jahrhundert', PhD Dissertation, University of Vienna, 2013.

Frost, Anthony, '*Timor Mortis Conturbuit Nos*: Improvising Tragedy and Epic', in C. McCullough (ed), *Theatre Praxis* (Basingstoke: Macmillan, 1998), pp. 151–73.

Frost, Anthony, 'The Taking of Faces: Aristotle among the Arabs', in A. Frost (ed), *Theatre Theories: From Plato to Virtual Reality* (Norwich: Pen & Inc, 2000), pp. 45–68.

Gade, Morton, Thorup, Line and Sander, Mikkel (eds), *As Larp Grows Up*, electronic publication to accompany the Knudepunkt LARP festival in Denmark (2003), available at http://www.laivforum.dk/kp03_book/ (accessed 2005).

Gale, Derek, *What is Psychodrama? A Personal and Practical Guide* (Loughton: Gale Centre, 1990).*

Ganguly, Sanjoy, 'Theatre – A Space for Empowerment: Celebrating Jana Sanskriti's Experience in India', in Richard Boon and Jane Plastow (eds), *Theatre and Empowerment: Community Drama on the World Stage* (Cambridge: Cambridge University Press, 2004), pp. 220–57.

Ganguly, Sanjoy, *Jana Sanskriti, Forum Theatre and Democracy in India* (London: Routledge, 2010).

Ganguly, Sanjoy and Ganguly, Sima, *Notes of Workshop* (Lille: TOP Théâtre, 2013); recorded by Ralph Yarrow.

Gardner, Lyn, 'Join in the Murder Game at Battersea Arts Centre', *The Guardian* (19 October 2009).

Garzia, Joxerra, 'A History of Improvised *Bertsolaritza*: A Proposal', *Oral Tradition*, 22/2 (2007), pp. 77–115. [We are greatly indebted to our colleague, the playwright Timberlake Wertenbaker, who grew up in the Basque country, for introducing us to *bertso* and the *bertsolaris*.]

Gaulier, Philippe, *Le Gégèneur* (*The Tormentor*) (Paris: Éditions Filmiko, 2006).

Geertz, Clifford, *Religion of Java* (Glencoe: Free Press, 1960).

Gelb, Michael, *Body Learning: An Introduction to the Alexander Technique* (London: Aurum Press, 1981).*

George, D. E. R., *Buddhism as/in Performance: Analysis of Meditation and Theatrical Practice* (New Delhi: D. K. Printworld, 1999).

Gide, André, *Les Nourritures Terrestres* (Paris: Gallimard, 1917–36).

Gillison, Gillian, 'Living Theater in New Guinea's Highlands', in *National Geographic*, 164/2 (August 1983). See also the Editorial, 'On Assignment'.

Gillison, Gillian, *Between Culture and Fantasy: A New Guinea Highlands Mythology* (Chicago, IL: University of Chicago Press, 1993).

Goldberg, RoseLee, *Performance Art: From Futurism to the Present* (London: Thames & Hudson, 1979; rev. ed. 1988).

Gontard, Denis (ed), *Le Journal de bord des Copiaus, 1924–1929*, ed. with commentary by Denis Gontard (Paris: Seghers, 1974).

Gooch, Steve, *Writing a Play* (3rd ed., London: A. & C. Black, 2001).*

Gordon, Mel, '*Lazzi*: The Comic Routines of the *Commedia dell'Arte*', in Ginnine Cocuzza and Barbara Naomi Cohen Stratyner (eds), *Performing Arts Resources* (New York: Theatre Library Association, 1981), vol. 7.*

Gordon, Mel, *The Stanislavsky Technique: Russia: A Workbook for Actors* (New York: Applause, 1987).*

Gray, Paul, 'Stanislavsky and America: A Critical Chronology', *Tulane Drama Review*, 9/2 (Winter 1964).

Green, Alissa (ed), *World's Worst: Improv Magazine* (published online at web.mit. edu) (2005).

Gregory, R. G., *The World of Instant Theatre: Its Origins, Practice and Implications* (Wimborne: Word and Action Wanda Publications, 1990).

Grimes, Ron, 'The Theatre of Sources', *The Drama Review*, 25/3 (T-91) (Fall 1981), Actor/Director Issue, 67–74.

Grotowski, Jerzy, 'Aktor ogolocony' ('The Actor Bared'), *Teatr*, Vol. 17 (1965), pp. 8–10; cited in Burzyński and Osiński (1979).

Grotowski, Jerzy, 'I Said Yes to the Past' [interview by Margaret Croyden], *Village Voice* (23 January 1969a), pp. 41–2.

Grotowski, Jerzy, 'The Theatre's New Testament' [interview with Eugenio Barba], trans. Jörgen Andersen and Judy Barba, in Grotowski *et al.* (eds), (1969b).

Grotowski, Jerzy, 'Holiday', *The Drama Review*, 17/2 (T58) (June 1973), Visual Performance Issue.

Grotowski, Jerzy *et al.*, *Towards a Poor Theatre*, ed. Eugenio Barba (Copenhagen: Odin Teatrets Forlag, 1968; English translation, London: Eyre Methuen, 1969).

Gwinn, Peter & Halpern, Charna, *Group Improvisation: The Manual of Ensemble Improv* (Colorado Springs, CO: Meriwether, 2004).*

Halpern, Charna, Close, Del and Johnson, Kim 'Howard', *Truth in Comedy: The Manual of Improvisation* (Colorado Springs, CO: Meriwether, 1994).*

Hatley, Barbara, 'Theatrical Imagery and Gender Ideology in Java', in Atkinson & Errington (eds), (1990), pp. 177–207.

Hauck, Ben, *Long-Form Improv: The Complete Guide to Creating Characters, Sustaining Scenes and Performing Extraordinary Harolds* (New York: Allworth Press, 2012).*

Hayes, Jill, 'Dance Therapy: Process and Performance?' *Studies in Theatre Production*, Vol. 13, No. 1 (1996), pp. 29–38.

Heddon, Deirdre and Milling, Jane, *Devising Performance: A Critical History* (London: Palgrave Macmillan, 2006).

Heritage, Paul, 'Augusto Boal and the Journey to the Centre of the Theatre of the Oppressed (Paris)', in David Bradby and Maria Delgado (eds), *The Paris Jigsaw* (London: Routledge, 2002), pp. 146–52.

Hethmon, Robert and Strasberg, Lee, *Strasberg at the Actor's Studio* (New York: Viking Press, 1965).*

Hiley, Jim, 'Moving Heaven and Earth' [interview with Jacques Lecoq], *Observer* (20 March 1988), p. 40.

Hilton, Julian, *Performance* (London: Macmillan, 1988).

Hilton, Julian (ed), *New Directions in Theatre* (Basingstoke: Macmillan, 1993a).

Hilton, Julian, 'Theatricality and Technology: Pygmalion and the Myth of the Intelligent Machine', in J. Hilton (ed), *New Directions in Theatre* (Basingstoke: Macmillan, 1993b).

Hippe, Eva and Hippe, Lorenz, *Theater Direkt – das Theater der Zuschauer: Ein Beitrag zur Kollektiven Kreativität* [A German Account of R. G. Gregory's Word and Action] (Weinheim: Deutsche Theaterverlag, 2011).

Hirst, David L., *Dario Fo and Franca Rame* (London: Macmillan, 1989).

Hoban, Russell, *The Moment Under the Moment* (London: Jonathan Cape, 1992).

Hodge, Alison (ed), *Twentieth-Century Actor Training* (London: Routledge, 2000).

Hodgson, John (ed), *The Uses of Drama: Sources Giving a Background to Acting as a Social and Educational Force* (London: Eyre Methuen, 1972).

Hodgson, John, *Mastering Movement: The Life and Work of Rudolf Laban* [1997] (London: Methuen, 2001).

Hodgson, John and Richards, Ernest, *Improvisation* (London: Methuen, 1966; 2nd ed. 1974).*

Holmes, Rupert, Essay for the Toronto Shaw festival production of *The Mystery of Edwin Drood* (2001), available at http://www.rupertholmes.com/theatre/essdrood.html (accessed 2 March 2015).

Homann, Greg (ed), *At This Stage* (Johannesburg: Wits University Press, 2009).

Hood, Stuart, 'Introduction', in Dario Fo and Franca Rame (eds), *Female Parts*, trans. Margaret Kunzle, adapted Olwen Wymark (London: Pluto Press, 1981).

Hood, Stuart, 'Introduction', in Dario Fo (ed), *Mistero buffo*, trans. Ed Emery (London: Methuen, 1988).

Hooker, Lucy, 'The Secrets Behind Hungary's Escape Games Craze', *BBC News* (online business report, Budapest, 19 December 2014).

Howard, Tony, '"A Piece of Our Life": The Theatre of the Eighth Day', *New Theatre Quarterly*, 2/8 (November 1986).

Huizinga, Johan, *Homo Ludens* (Leiden, trans. by the author; London: Paladin, 1970).

Hull, S. Loraine, *Strasberg's Method: As Taught by Lorrie Hull* (Woodbridge, CT: Ox Bow, 1985).*

Hunt, Albert, *Hopes for Great Happenings: Alternatives in Education and Theatre* (London: Eyre Methuen, 1976).

Hurst, Deirdre, 'The Training Sessions of Michael Chekhov' [interview by Peter Hulton, July 1978], *Dartington Theatre Papers*, 3rd series, No. 9 (1979–80).

Hyde, George, 'Poland: Dead Souls under Western Eyes', in Ralph Yarrow (ed), *European Theatre, 1960–1990* (London: Routledge, 1992), pp. 182–219.

Irvine, Lindesay, 'Say Yes to Improv', *The Guardian*, 22 November 2005.

Iser, Wolfgang, *The Implied Reader: Patterns of Communication in Prose Fiction from Bunyan to Beckett* (Baltimore, MD: The Johns Hopkins University Press, 1974).

Iser, Wolfgang, *The Act of Reading: A Theory of Aesthetic Response* (Baltimore, MD: The Johns Hopkins University Press, 1978).

Jeffries, Stuart, 'I told them I wanted to set it on a spaceship in the 29th century', interview with Mike Leigh about his (actually rather more traditional) production of *Pirates of Penzance* for ENO, *Guardian*, 20 April, 2015, pp. 16–17.

Jenkins, Ron, *Dario Fo and Franca Rame: Artful Laughter* (New York: Aperture, 2001).

Jenkins, Ron and I Nyoman Catra, 'Invisible Training in Balinese Performance', in Ian Watson (ed), *Performer Training: Developments across Cultures* (Amsterdam: Harwood Academic, 2001), pp. 85–91.

Jennings, Sue, *Remedial Drama: A Handbook for Teachers and Therapists* (London: Pitman; New York: Theatre Arts, 1973).

Jennings, Sue (ed), *Dramatherapy: Theory and Practice for Teachers and Clinicians* (London: Routledge, 1988).

Jennings, Sue, *The Handbook of Dramatherapy* (London: Routledge, 1993).

Jennings, Sue, *Dramatherapy with Children and Adolescents* (London: Routledge, 1994).

Johnston, Chris, *House of Games: Making Theatre from Everyday Life* (London: Nick Hern Books, 1998).*

Johnston, Chris, *The Improvisation Game* (London: Nick Hern Books, 2006).

Johnstone, Keith, *Impro: Improvisation and the Theatre* (London: Methuen, 1981).*

Johnstone, Keith, *Theatresports and Lifegame Newsletter*, Issue 1 (Calgary: University of Calgary, 1987); cited in Chris Johnston (1998), pp. 190–2.*

Johnstone, Keith, *Impro for Storytellers: Theatresports and the Art of Making Things Happen* (London: Faber, 1999).*

Kearns, John, Interview with Ralph Yarrow (Norwich, July 2013).

Kennedy, Emma, 'The Zombie Shopping Mall, Reading', *Saturday Guardian*, Travel Section (20 October 2012), p. 10.

Kennedy, Scott, *In Search of African Theatre* (New York: Charles Scribner, 1973).

Kiernander, Adrian, 'The Théâtre du Soleil, Part One: A Brief History of the Company', *New Theatre Quarterly*, 2/7 (August 1986).

King, Eleanor, 'Reflections on Korean Dance', in *Korean Dance, Theater and Cinema*, ed. The Korean National Commission for UNESCO (Seoul: Si-sa-yong-o-sa Publishers, 1983).

Kirby, Ernest T., *Ur-Drama: The Origins of Theatre* (New York: New York University Press, 1975).

Kirkland, Christopher D., 'The Golden Age, First Draft', *The Drama Review*, Vol. 19, No. 2 (1975), pp. 97–103.

Koestler, Arthur, *The Act of Creation* (London: Hutchinson, 1964; rev. Danube ed., London: Pan, 1970).

Kozlowski, Ron, *The Art of Chicago Improv: Shortcuts to Long-Form Improvisation* (Portsmouth, NJ: Heinemann, 2002).*

Krips, Henry, *Fetish: An Erotics of Culture* (Ithaca, NY: Cornell University Press, 1999).

Kruger, Loren, *The Drama of South Africa* (London: Routledge, 1999).

Kruskall, Megan, Interview with Ralph Yarrow (Cape Town, July 2012).

Kumiega, Jennifer, *The Theatre of Grotowski* (London: Methuen, 1985).

Kurkinen, Marjaana, 'The Spectre of the Orient: Modern French Mime and Traditional Japanese Theatre in the 1930s', Unpublished dissertation, University of Helsinki, Finland, December 2000. A PDF version is available at http://ethesis. helsinki.fi/julkaisut/hum/taite/vk/kurkinen/ (ISBN 952-91-2963-7) (accessed 15 April 2015).

Laban, Rudolf, *Choreographie, Erste Heft, vol. 1: Choreography* (Jena: Eugene Deiderichs, 1926); discussed in Hodgson (2001), pp. 127–9.

Laban, Rudolf, *Des Kindes Gymnastik und Tanz* (Gymnastics and Dance for the Child) (Oldenburg: Gerhard Stalling, 1926); discussed in Hodgson (2001), pp. 125–7.

Laban, Rudolf, *Choreutics*, ed. Lisa Ullmann [1939] (London: MacDonald & Evans, 1966); discussed in Hodgson (2001), vol. 1, pp. 135–41.

Laban, Rudolf, *The Mastery of Movement* (rev. Lisa Ullmann, 4th ed., Plymouth: MacDonald & Evans, 1980).

Lamden, Gill, *Devising* (London: Hodder & Stoughton, 2000).*

Lan Fang, Mei, 'My Life on the Stage', orig. *Chinese Literature Monthly*, 11 (1961). [Originally published just after Mei's death, and before the throes of the Cultural Revolution and Madame Mao's reforms of the Chinese Opera.] Republished together with Sergei M. Eisenstein's *The Enchanter from the Pear Garden* (1935) (English translators not credited) (Holstebro: ISTA Publications, 1986).

Langer, Susanne, *Feeling and Form* (London: Routledge & Kegan Paul, 1959).

Lavery, Carl and Williams, David (eds), *Good Luck Everybody: Lone Twin: Journeys, Performances, Conversations* (Aberystwyth: Performance Research Books, 2011).

Lavy, Jennifer, 'Theoretical Foundations of Grotowski's *Total Act, Via Negativa,* and *Conjunctio Oppositorum', Journal of Religion and Theatre*, Vol. 4, No. 2 (Fall 2005), available at http://www.rtjournal.org/vol_4/no_2/lavy.html (accessed 16 June 2006).

Leabhart, Thomas, *Modern and Postmodern Mime* (Basingstoke: Macmillan, 1989).

Leabhart, Thomas (ed), *Theatre and Sport*, edition of *Mime Journal* (Claremont, CA: Pomona College Theatre Department, 1996).

Lecoq, Jacques, *Le role de l'improvisation dans l'enseignement de l'art dramatique*, transcript of a lecture-demonstration by Lecoq at the Institut International du Théâtre, Bucharest (1964), p. 136; cited in Felner (1985).

Lecoq, Jacques, 'Le mouvement et le théâtre', *ATAC Informations*, 13 (December 1967).

Lecoq, Jacques, *Stage d'été* (Paris: Brochure, 1971); cited in Felner (1985).

Lecoq, Jacques, 'L'Ecole Jacques Lecoq au Théâtre de la Ville', *Journal du Théâtre de la Ville*, Vol. 15 (January 1972).

Lecoq, Jacques, 'Mime – Movement – Theater', *Yale Theatre*, 4/1 (Winter 1973); cited in Towsen (1976).

Lecoq, Jacques (ed), *Le Théâtre du Geste* (Paris: Bordas, 1987).*

Lecoq, Jacques, 'Moving Heaven and Earth' [interview with Jim Hiley], *Observer* (20 March 1988), p. 40.

Lecoq, Jacques, 'Theatre of Gesture and Image', in Patrice Pavis (ed), *The Intercultural Performance Reader* (London: Routledge, 1996), pp. 140–7.

Lecoq, Jacques, Carasso, Jean-Gabriel and Lallias, Jean-Claude, *Le Corps poétique* (Paris: Actes Sud-Papiers, 1997), trans. David Bradby as *The Moving Body* (London: Methuen, 2000, rev. ed. 2000).*

Lecoq, Jacques, n.d., *Brochure* of L'Ecole Jacques Lecoq, 57 rue du Faubourg Saint-Denis, Paris. [All translations by R. Yarrow (1987).]

Lee, Stewart, *How I Escaped My Certain Fate: The Life and Deaths of a Stand-Up Comedian* (London: Faber & Faber, 2010).

Lee, Stewart, *Stewart Lee!: The 'If You Want a Milder Comedian, Please Ask For One' EP* (London: Faber & Faber, 2012).

Leep, Jeanne, *Theatrical Improvisation: Short Form, Long Form and Sketch-Based Improv* (Basingstoke: Palgrave Macmillan 2008).*

Leigh, Mike, *Abigail's Party* and *Goose Pimples* [plays devised from scratch through improvisation] (Harmondsworth: Penguin, 1983a).

Leigh, Mike, 'An Account of the Development of my Improvised Plays 1965–69: An Application for the George Devine Award, 1969'; cited in Clements (1983b).

Leigh, Mike, *All or Nothing* (London: Faber & Faber, 2002).

Leigh, Mike, *Two Thousand Years* (London: Faber & Faber, 2006).

Leigh, Mike, *The BBC Collection*, including *Abigail's Party* and *Nuts in May* (DVD, London: BBC Video Releases, 2009).

Leonard, Charles, *Michael Chekhov's 'To the Director and Playwright'*, compiled and written by Charles Leonard (New York: Harper & Row, 1963; New York: Limelight Editions, 1984).

Littlewood, Joan, *Joan's Book: Joan Littlewood's Peculiar History as She Tells It* (London: Minerva, 1995).

Loven, Klarijn, *Watching Si Doel: Television, Language and Culture Identity in Contemporary Indonesia* (Leiden: KITLV Press, 2008).

Lugering, Michael, *The Expressive Actor* (London: Routledge, 2013).*

Lust, Annette Bercut, *From the Greek Mimes to Marcel Marceau and Beyond: Mimes Actors, Pierrots and Clowns: A Chronicle of the Many Visages of Mime in the Theatre* (Lanham, MD: Scarecrow Press, 2000). [See esp. chapter on Lecoq, pp. 99–108.]

Lynn, Bill, *Improvisation for Actors and Writers: A Guidebook for Improv Lessons in Comedy* (Colorado Springs, CO: Meriwether, 2004).*

Machon, Josephine, *Immersive Theatres: Intimacy and Immediacy in Contemporary Performance* (Basingstoke: Palgrave Macmillan, 2013).

Mamet, David, *True and False: Heresy and Common Sense for the Actor* (New York: Random House, 1997).

Marineau, Rene F., *Jacob Levy Moreno, 1889–1974: Father of Psychodrama, Sociometry and Group Psychotherapy* (London: Routledge, 1989); cited in Gale (1990).

Martin, John, 'The Theatre Which Does Not Exist: Neutrality to Interculturalism', in Chamberlain and Yarrow (eds) (2002), pp. 57–70.

Martin, John, *The Intercultural Performance Handbook* (London: Routledge, 2004).*

Martinovich, Nicholas N., *The Turkish Theatre* (1933; New York: Benjamin Blom, 1968).

Maslow, Abraham, *Toward a Psychology of Being* (New York: Van Nostrand Reinhold, 1968).

McCullough, Christopher (ed), *Theatre Praxis* (Basingstoke: Macmillan, 1998).

McGinley, Paige, 'A New Generation of Ensemble Performance', *The Drama Review*, Vol. 54, No. 4 (2010), pp. 11–38.

Merlin, Bella, *Beyond Stanislavsky: The Psycho-Physical Approach to Acting* (London: Nick Hern Books, 2001).*

Merlin, Bella, *Konstantin Stanislavsky* (London: Routledge, 2003).*

Meyer-Dinkgräfe, Daniel, *Theatre and Consciousness: Explanatory Scope and Future Potential* (London: Intellect Books, 2005).

Meyerhold, Vsevolod, 'The Fairground Booth', in Braun (ed), (1969), pp. 119–28.

Middleton, Deborah K., 'At Play in the Cosmos: The Theatre and Ritual of Nicolás Núñez', *TDR: The Drama Review*, Vol. 45, No. 4 (2001), pp. 42–63.

Millar, Mervyn, *Journey of the Tall Horse: A Story of African Theatre* (London: Oberon, 2005).

Miller, Lee, Mock, Roberta and Smith, Phil (eds), *Studies in Theatre and Performance*, Special Issue, 'Zombies and Performance', Vol. 34, No. 3 (November 2014).

Milling, Jane and Ley, Graham, *Modern Theories of Performance* (Basingstoke: Palgrave Macmillan, 2001).

Mitchell, Tony, *Dario Fo: People's Court Jester* (London: Methuen, 1984; 2nd rev. ed. 1986).

Montola, Markus and Stenros, Jaakko (eds), *Beyond Role and Play: Tools, Toys and Theory for Harnessing the Imagination* (Helsinki: Ropecon, 2004); published for Solmukohta 2004, the Nordic role-playing convention: now only available electronically at http://www.ropecon.fi/brap/ (accessed 7 March 2015).

Moore, Sonia, *The Stanislavski System: The Professional Training of an Actor* (New York: Viking Penguin, 1960 as *The Stanislavski Method*; 2nd rev. ed. 1984).*

Moreh, Shmuel, *Live Theatre and Dramatic Literature in the Medieval Arabic World* (Edinburgh: Edinburgh University Press, 1992).

Moreno, Jacob Levy, *Psychodrama, I* (New York: Beacon House, 1946).

Moreno, Jacob Levy, *Psychodrama, II* (New York: Beacon House, 1959).

Moreno, Jacob L., *Théâtre de la spontanéité*, trans. Jean-François de Raymond, intro. by Anne Ancelin Schützenberger, Preface by Guy Dumur (Paris: ÉPI, 1984; originally pub. as *The Theatre of Spontaneity*, New York: Beacon House Inc., 1947 – this is a translation of the 2nd expanded edition, 1972).

Moreno, Zerka T., *The Quintessential Zerka: Writings by Zerka Toeman Moreno on Psychodrama, Sociometry and Group Psychotherapy*, ed. Toni Horvatin and Edward Schreiber (London: Routledge, 2006).

Moreno, Zerka T., Rützel, Thomas and Blomkvist, Leif Dag, *Psychodrama, Surplus Reality and the Art of Healing* (Hove: Routledge, 2000).

Morley, Sheridan, 'Mike Leigh: Anything but Anarchy' [interview], *The Times* (15 July 1977); reprinted in Movshovitz (2000), pp. 3–5.

Morton, Timothy, *Ecology without Nature* (Cambridge, MA: Harvard University Press, 2007).

Moseley, Nick, *Acting and Reacting: Tools for the Modern Actor* (London: Routledge/ Nick Hern Books, 2005).*

Movshovitz, Howie (ed), *Mike Leigh: Interviews*, Conversations with Filmmakers (Jackson: University Press of Mississippi, 2000).

Mudge, Saxon, *The Money, A Kaleider Production – Review*, available at http://exeter northcottyoungcritics.wordpress.com/page/6 (accessed 20 November 2013).

Murray, Simon, 'Tout Bouge: Jacques Lecoq, Modern Mime and the Zero Body: A Pedagogy for the Creative Actor', in Chamberlain and Yarrow (eds), (2002), pp. 17–44.

Murray, Simon, *Jacques Lecoq* (London: Routledge, 2003).*

Nagler, A. M. (ed), *Source Book in Theatrical History* (New York: Dover, 1952).

Natadze, R., 'On the Psychological Nature of Stage Impersonation', *British Journal of Psychology*, Vol. 53, No. 4 (November 1962), p. 421.

Naumburg, Margaret, *Child and the World: Dialogues in Modern Education* (New York: Harcourt Brace, 1928).

Newlove, Jean, *Laban for Actors and Dancers: Putting Laban's Movement Theory into Practice: A Step-by-Step Guide* (London: Nick Hern Books, 1993).*

Nicoll, Allardyce, *Masks, Mimes and Miracles: Studies in the Popular Theatre* (London, 1931; New York: Cooper Square, 1963).

Nicoll, Allardyce, *The World of Harlequin: A Critical Study of the Commedia dell'Arte* (Cambridge: Cambridge University Press, 1963).

Nixon, Jon, 'The Dimensions of Drama: The Case for Cross-Curricular Planning', *New Theatre Quarterly*, Vol. 3, No. 9 (February 1987), pp. 71–81.

Nooshin, L. and Widdess, R, 'Improvisation in Iranian and Indian Music', *Mumbai: Journal of the Indian Musicological Society*, Vol. 36, No. 37 (2006), pp. 104–19, available at https://eprints.soas.ac.uk/5430/1/NooshinWiddess, p. 107.

Novack, Cynthia J., *Sharing the Dance: Contact Improvisation and American Culture* (Madison: University of Wisconsin Press, 1990).

Núñez, Nicolás, *Anthropocosmic Theatre*, trans. Ronan J. Fitzsimons (Amsterdam: Harwood OPA, 1996).

Oddey, Alison, *Devising Theatre: A Practical and Theoretical Handbook* (London: Routledge, 1994).*

Odin Teatret, *Andersens Drøm* [programme of production *of Andersen's Dream ('dedicated to Torzov and Doctor Dappertutto')*]. Contributions from, *inter alia*, Eugenio Barba, Judy Barba (translator), Kai Bredholt, Fabio Butera, Roberta Carreri, Jan Ferslev, Tage Larsen, Augusto Omolú, Iben Nagel Rasmussen, Luca Ruzza, Nando Taviani, Julia Varley, Torgeir Wethal, etc. (Holstebro, Denmark: Nordisk Teaterlaboratorium, 2005).

Osiński, Zbigniew, 'In the Theatre', in T. Burzyński and Z. Osiński (eds), *Grotowski's Laboratory* (Warsaw: Interpress, 1979).

Otto, Beatrice K., *Fools Are Everywhere: The Court Jester around the World* (Chicago, IL: University of Chicago Press, 2001).

Papadopoulo, Alexandre, *Islam and Muslim Art*, trans. Robert Erich Wolf (Paris: Mezenod, 1976; New York: Harry N. Abrams, 1979). (See esp. 'The Making of a Muslim Aesthetic', pp. 48ff.)

Papaioannou, Spyros, 'Immersion, "smooth" spaces and critical voyeurism in the work of Punchdrunk'. *Studies in Theatre and Performance*, Vol. 34, No. 2 (2014), pp. 0: 16–74.

Paterson, Douglas L., 'Theatre of the Oppressed Workshops', available at http://www.wwcd.org/action/Boal.html (originally 1997, accessed 17 July 2006).

Peacock, Louise, *Serious Play: Modern Clown Performance* (Bristol: Intellect, 2011).

Perrucci, Andrea, *Dell'arte rappresentativa: premeditata e dall'improvviso* (Naples, 1699), trans. S. J. Castiglione; cited in Nagler, *Source Book in Theatrical History* (New York: Dover, 1952).

Phelan, Peggy, *Unmarked: The Politics of Performance* (London: Routledge, 1993).

Pitches, Jonathan, *Vsevolod Meyerhold* (London: Routledge, 2004).*

Pitches, Jonathan, *Science and the Stanislavsky Tradition of Acting* (London: Routledge, 2006).

Pörtner, Paul, 'Psychodrama: Theater der Spontaneität: Morenos Weg von Wien nach den USA', *Theater Heute* (Vienna: Bohlau, September 1967), pp. 10–15.

Poulter, Christine, *Playing the Game* (Basingstoke: Macmillan, 1987).*

Preston-Dunlop, Valerie, *Rudolf Laban: An Extraordinary Life* (London: Dance Books, 1998).

Rame, Franca, [interview], *Sipario* [Italian theatre magazine] (September 1983); cited in Mitchell (1984).

Rame, Franca and Fo, Dario, *Female Parts*, trans. Margaret Kunzle, adapted Olwen Wymark (London: Pluto Press, 1981).

Rame, Franca and Fo, Dario, *Theatre Workshops at Riverside Studios, London* (London: Red Notes, 1983).*

Rancière, Jacques, *The Emancipated Spectator* (London: Verso, 2009).

Rath, Eric C., *The Ethos of Noh: Actors on their Art* (Cambridge, MA: Harvard University Asia Center, 2004).

Richards, Thomas, *At Work with Grotowski on Physical Actions* (London: Routledge, 1995).

Riley, Jo, *Chinese Theatre and the Actor in Performance* (Cambridge: Cambridge University Press, 1997).

Risum, Janne, 'The Sporting Acrobat: Meyerhold's Biomechanics', in Thomas Leabhart (ed), *Theatre and Sport*, edition of *Mime Journal* (Claremont, CA: Pomona College Theatre Department, 1996), pp. 67–111.

Risum, Janne, 'A Study in Motley: The Odin Actors', in Watson (ed), (2001), pp. 93–115.

Roberts, Philip, *The Royal Court Theatre, 1965–72* (London: Routledge, 1986).

Robbins Dudeck, Theresa, *Keith Johnstone: A Critical Biography* (London: Bloomsbury, 2013).

Rockwell, Teed, 'The Many Faces of Ghazal' [interview with Kiran Ahluwalia], in Jaya Padmanabhan (ed), *India Currents: The Complete Indian American Magazine*, (2005), availabe at https://www.indiacurrents.com/articles/2005/11/10/the-many-faces-of-ghazal (accessed 8 March 2015).

Rolfe, Bari, *Behind the Mask* (Oakland, CA: Persona, 1976).

Roose-Evans, James, *Experimental Theatre: From Stanislavsky to Today* (New York: Avon Books, 1970).

Rowe, Nick, *Playing the Other: Dramatizing Personal Narratives in Playback Theatre* (London: Jessica Kingsley Publishers, 2007).

Rudlin, John, *Jacques Copeau* (Cambridge: Cambridge University Press, 1986).

Rudlin, John, 'Play's the Thing', in Leabhart (ed), (1996), pp. 17–29.

Rudlin, John and Crick, Ollie, *Commedia dell'Arte: A Handbook for Troupes* (London: Routledge, 2001).*

Rudlin, John and Paul, Norman H. (eds and trans), *Jacques Copeau, Texts on Theatre* (London: Routledge, 1990).

Rudnitsky, Konstantin, trans. Roxane Permar, ed. Lesley Milne, *Russian and Soviet Theatre: Tradition and the Avant-Garde* (London: Thames and Hudson, 1988).

Ryan, Paul Ryder, 'A Ru-howzi Evening', *The Drama Review, Indigenous Theatre edition*, 18/4 (T64) (December 1974), pp. 114–15.

Saint-Denis, Michel, *Training for the Theatre: Premises and Promises*, ed. Suria Saint-Denis (New York: Theatre Arts Books, 1982).

Salas, Jo, *Improvising Real Life: Personal Story in Playback Theatre* (New Paltz, NY: Tusitala Publishing, 1993).

Sandercoe, Helen Vivien, *The Work of Monika Pagneux*, MEd thesis, University of Melbourne, 2001.

Sargeant, Jack, *Naked Lens: Beat Cinema* (Berkeley, CA: Soft Skull Press, 2008; orig., London, Creation Books, 1997 and 2001).

Sawyer, R. Keith, *Improvised Dialogues* (Westport, CT: Ablex, 2003).

Sbait, Ḍirghām Ḥ, 'Debate in the Improvised-Sung Poetry of the Palestinians', *Asian Folklore Studies* Vol. 52, No. 1 (1993), pp. 93–117, available at http://www.jstor.org/stable/1178452 (accessed 14 April 2014).

Schechner, Richard, *Between Theater and Anthropology* (Philadelphia: University of Pennsylvania Press, 1985).

Schechner, Richard, *Performance Studies: An Introduction* (London: Routledge, 2002).

Schiller, Friedrich, *On the Aesthetic Education of Man, in a Series of Letters*, trans. Elizabeth M. Wilkinson and L. A. Willoughby (Oxford: Clarendon Press, 1967).

Schneider, Rebecca and Cody, Gabrielle, *Re:Direction: A Theoretical and Practical Guide* (London: Routledge, 2002).

Seham, Amy E., *Whose Improv Is It Anyway? Beyond Second City* (Jackson: University Press of Mississippi, 2001).

Sells, Michael A., *Mystical Languages of Unsaying* (Chicago, IL: University of Chicago Press, 1994).

Shrubsall, Anthony, 'Jos Houben: Understanding the Neutral Mask', in Chamberlain and Yarrow (eds), (2002), pp. 99–110.

Sicard, Claude, Copeau's editor, on website, http://www.culture.fr/culture/actualites/celebrations/copeau.htm.

Sills, Paul, 'The Celebratory Occasion' [interview with Charles Mee Jr], *Tulane Drama Review*, 9/2 (Winter 1964).

Simon, Eli, *Masking Unmasked: Four Approaches to Basic Acting* (New York: Palgrave Macmillan, 2003).*

Smith, A. C. H., *Orghast at Persepolis* (London: Methuen, 1972).

Smith, Lucy, email communication to Ralph Yarrow, 29 May 2014.

Snow, Jackie, *Movement Training for Actors* (London: Methuen, 2012).*

Southern, Richard, *The Medieval Theatre in the Round* (London: Faber, 1957).

Spolin, Viola, *Improvisation for the Theater* (Evanston, IL: Northwestern University Press, 1963; London: Pitman, 1973).*

Stafford-Clark, Max, *Workpack*, compiled by Maeve McKeown, with additional research by Ian Redford, published by Out of Joint Theatre Company, available at http://www.outofjoint.co.uk/wp-content/uploads/2010/09/Max-Stafford-Clark-Workpack.pdf.*

Stanislavsky, C., *An Actor Prepares*, trans. Elizabeth Reynolds Hapgood (London: Geoffrey Bles, 1937).*

Stanislavsky, C., *Building a Character*, trans. Elizabeth Reynolds Hapgood (London: Reinhardt & Evans, 1950).

Stanislavsky, C., *Creating a Role*, trans. Elizabeth Reynolds Hapgood (London: Geoffrey Bles, 1963).*

Stoppard, Tom, *Rosencrantz and Guildenstern are Dead* (London: Faber & Faber, 1967).

Strasberg, Lee, *A Dream of Passion*, ed. Evangeline Morphos (London: Bloomsbury, 1988).

Sutherland, Efua T., 'Theatre in Ghana', in Janice Nesbitt (ed), *Ghana Welcomes You* (Accra: Orientation to Ghana Committee, 1969); cited in Kennedy (1973).

Sutherland, Efua T., *The Original Bob: The Story of Bob Johnson, Ghana's Ace Comedian* (Accra: Anowa Educational, 1970); cited in Barber *et al.* (1997) and Etherton (1992).

Suzuki, Tadashi, *The Way of Acting: The Theatre Writings of Tadashi Suzuki*, trans. J. Thomas Rimer (New York: Theatre Communications Group, 1986).

Svich, Caridad, 'Dreaming Out Loud: Interview with Phelim McDermott about Improbable Theatre', in Svich, Caridad (ed), *Trans-Global Readings: Crossing Theatrical Boundaries* (Manchester: Manchester University Press, 2003).

Sweet, Jeffrey, *Something Wonderful Right Away* (New York: Avon Book, 1987).

Tasca, Valéria, 'Dario Fo from One Language to Another', in Patrice Pavis (ed), *The Intercultural Performance Reader* (London: Routledge, 1996), pp. 114–19.

Tan, Yifan, 'Real-Life Takagism Games Bring Thrills to Escapers', *Shenzhen Daily*, available at http://www.szdaily.com (accessed 12 July 2013).

Taubin, Amy, 'Heir to the Anger' [interview with David Thewlis on Mike Leigh's *Naked*], *Village Voice* (14 December 1993), p. 70; and cit. Watson (2004), p. 29.

Taylor, Rogan, *The Death and Resurrection Show: From Shaman to Superstar* (London: Antony Blond, 1985).

Temkine, Raymonde, *Grotowski* (New York: Avon Book, 1972).

'The Theatre of Dario Fo', *Arena*, BBC TV documentary, Dennis Marks, 28 February 1984.

Towsen, John H., *Clowns* (New York: Hawthorne Books, 1976).

Turner, Jane, *Eugenio Barba* (London: Routledge, 2004).*

Vatsyayan, Kapila, *Traditional Indian Theatre: Multiple Streams* (New Delhi: National Book Trust, 1980).

Veltrusky, Jiri, 'Man and Object in the Theatre', in Paul L. Garvin (ed and trans), *A Prague School Reader on Esthetics, Literary Structure, and Style* (Washington, DC: Georgetown UP, 1964), p. 84; also cited in Elam (1980).

Ventura, Michael, *Cassavetes Directs: On the Set of Love Streams* (Harpenden: Kamera Books, 2007).

Wardle, Irving, *The Theatres of George Devine* (London: Jonathan Cape, 1978).

Wardle, Irving, 'Introduction', in Johnstone, (1981).

Watson, Garry, *The Cinema of Mike Leigh: A Sense of the Real* (London: Wallflower Press, 2004).

Watson, Ian, 'Catharsis and the Actor: The Aristotelian Concept in the Context of Contemporary Performance', *New Theatre Quarterly*, Vol. 4, No. 16 (November 1988), pp. 306–14.

Watson, Ian (ed), *Performer Training: Developments across Cultures* (Amsterdam: Harwood Academic, 2001).

Watts, Alan, *The Book: On the Taboo against Knowing Who You Are* (New York: Random House, 1972).

Whelan, Jeremy, *Instant Acting* (Cincinnati, OH: Betterway Books, 1994); cited by Phelim McDermott, in Caridad Svich (ed), *Trans-Global Readings* (Manchester: Manchester University Press, 2003), and also discussed by him available at http://www.nationaltheatre.org.uk/?lid=13041, April during rehearsals for *Theatre of Blood* (April 2005). See http://www.on-cue.org.uk/acting14.html, which summarises the 'Whelan Tape Technique' approach.*

White, Gareth, *Audience Participation in Theatre* (Basingstoke: Palgrave Macmillan, 2013).

Williams, David (ed), *Collaborative Theory: The Théâtre du Soleil Sourcebook* (London: Routledge, 1999).

Willis, Ronald A., 'The American Lab Theater', *Tulane Drama Review*, 9/1 (Fall 1964).

Winearls, Jane, *Modern Dance: The Jooss-Leeder Method* (London: Adam & Charles Black, 1958; 2nd ed. 1968).

Wolford, Lisa, 'Ambivalent Positionings: Grotowski's Art as Vehicle and the Paradox of Categorization' in Watson (ed), (2001), pp. 117–32.

Wunder, Al, *The Wonder of Improvisation* (Ascot Victoria: Wunder Publishers, 2006).

Wright, John, 'The Masks of Jacques Lecoq', in Chamberlain and Yarrow (eds), (2002), pp. 71–84.

Wright, John, *Why is that Funny? A Practical Exploration of Physical Comedy* (London: Nick Hern Books, 2006).*

Yarrow, Ralph, *Indian Theatre: Theatre of Origin, Theatre of Freedom* (London: Curzon, 2001).

Yarrow, Ralph, 'Theatre as Development', *Seagull Theatre Quarterly*, 39, special edition on the AHRC Vidya Project, pp. 60–8 (Kolkata: 2007).

Yarrow, Ralph, Haney, William S. II, Malekin, Peter, Chamberlain, Franc and Lavery, Carl, *Sacred Theatre* (London: Intellect Books, 2007).

Yon, Keith, 'Communication Therapy with Mentally Handicapped Adults', *Dartington Theatre Papers*, 3rd series, No. 4 (1979–80).

Zaporah, Ruth, *Action Theatre: The Improvisation of Presence* (Berkeley, CA: North Atlantic Books, 1995).*

Zarrilli, Phillip B., *Acting (Re)Considered: A Theoretical and Practical Guide* (London: Routledge, 1995; 2nd ed. 2002).

Zarrilli, Phillip B., McConachie, Bruce, Williams, Gary Jay and Sorgenfrei, Carol Fisher, *Theatre Histories: An Introduction* (London: Routledge, 2006).

Zeami, Motokiyo, *Fushikaden (The Transmission of Style and the Flower)*, composed c.1400–1418: trans. as *The Spirit of Noh*, by William Scott Wilson (Boston & London, Shambhala, 2013; originally published as *The Flowering Spirit: Classic Teachings on the Art of Noh*, Tokyo, Kodansha, 2006).

Index of Games and Exercises

General Index